C0-ASI-892

DEVELOPMENT OF INFORMATION SYSTEMS FOR EDUCATION

KHATEEB M. HUSSAIN
New Mexico State University

Prentice-Hall, Inc. Englewood Cliffs, New Jersey

Library of Congress Cataloging in Publication Data

Hussain, Khateeb M.
Development of information systems for education.

(Educational administration series)
Includes bibliographies.
1. School management and organization. 2. Universities and colleges—Administration.
3. System analysis. I. Title.
LB2806.H8 371.2'0028'5 72-8769
ISBN 0-13-207407-9

10 9 8 7 6 5 4 3 2 1

Printed in the United States of America

Educational Administration Series
William Ammentorp, Editor

Prentice-Hall International, Inc., *London*
Prentice-Hall of Australia, Pty. Ltd., *Sydney*
Prentice-Hall of Canada, Ltd., *Toronto*
Prentice-Hall of India Private Limited, *New Delhi*
Prentice-Hall of Japan, Inc., *Tokyo*

To Akhtarunnissa Begum

Contents

Preface

This book is addressed primarily to the administrator and would-be administrator in educational administration. The examples cited in the book are largely from higher education, but the methodology discussed is applicable to all levels of education (elementary and high school) as well as to public administration and industry.

The purpose of this book is to explain the logic and methodology of information system development as well as to provide the administrator with knowledge of the analytical tools and basic concepts necessary to participate in developing an information system. Such participation will ensure that the administrator gets the information system he needs and knows how to use it effectively when he does.

This book does not discuss all aspects of an information system. The selections are based primarily on relevancy to the administrator as the ultimate user of the information systems. In the topics discussed, no attempt is made to present all sides of the issue but merely to identify and explain those relevant to the administrator.

The draft versions of this book were used as a textbook in two introductory courses in information systems for students majoring in business administration, computer science, and educational administration. It is most appropriate as a one semester text for students at the senior or graduate level in educational administration and public administration. The book could also be used for in-service training for both administrators and systems analysts in educational institutions.

Many people contributed to the preparation of this book. Dr. Tom Mason read Chapter 18 and made valuable comments. J. H. Brill and F. R. Hoose helped with the bibliographies. Dr. Pettibone and Burt Cohn read the manuscript and made suggestions for improvement. Barbara Rabkin did most of the typing. To all of them I am very grateful.

K. M. Hussain

part one

INTRODUCTION AND TOOLS OF ANALYSIS

1

Introduction

In the past decade there has been an increasing demand for the services provided by information systems. The world of microcircuitry and transmission of data at speeds approaching that of light is generating information at an explosive rate. Administrators of organizations in this environment expect information that is precise, accurate, and timely. This information is used for record-keeping as well as for decision-making, using techniques such as operations research, econometrics, systems analysis, and PPBS (Program, Planning, and Budgeting Systems). Information has been used successfully in business and industry for these purposes in situations similar to those arising in educational institutions. Consequently, it is postulated that the performances of educational institutions could be upgraded by the use of properly designed and implemented information systems.

In industry there is evidence that information systems contribute to higher profits (resulting from efficiency) and greater effectiveness.[1] Thus, there is a demand from legislatures that such systems also be used in education, where the growth rate is high and is continuing to increase. Since the founding of the Boston Latin School in 1635, the education industry has haphazardly evolved to become the nation's largest, with an annual budget of 70 billion dollars in 1970. Projections made by the U.S. Department of Health, Education, and Welfare[2] show that in the 10 years between 1967–77, the fall enrollment at all levels of education will increase from 56.2 to 61.6 million, an increase of less than 10%. During this period expenditures are to be increased from 54.8 to 76.3 billion dollars (in 1967–68 dollars), an increase of about 40%. With other demands for public funds, it appears that the increase in the supply of resources will be relatively less than the demand for them in education. This situation will, therefore, require more effective methods of running educational institutions, thereby increasing the need for efficient information systems such as those that have proved so successful in government and industry.

There are also non-economic forces that increase the demand for information systems in education; for instance, the demands for more information on educational operations from state,[3] regional,[4] and national[5] agencies. In addition to external demands, there are internal pressures. Students are demanding a faster and more effective system for handling their records. Since they can inquire about the availability of an airplane seat and make instant reservations on the phone, they expect equally fast and effective responses at the time of their registration for classes. Faculty members are making similar demands for more and faster information, which is necessary for their work to be effective. All these pressures increase the need for information systems in education.

[1]J. T. Garrity, "Top Management and Computer Profits," *Havard Business Review,* XLI, No. 4 (July–August 1963) 6–13, 172–74.

[2]K. A. Simon and M. G. Fullam, *Projections of Educational Statistics to 1977–78,* U.S. Department of Health, Education, and Welfare (Washington, D.C.: Government Printing Office, 1968), inside cover.

[3]L. H. Woolfatt, "An Automated Statewide Information System," in *Automated Educational Systems,* ed. E. Haga (Elmhurst, Ill.: The Business Press, 1967), pp. 66–79.

[4]B. Lawrence, "The Western Interstate Commission for Higher Education Management Information Systems Program," in *Management Information Systems in Higher Education: The State of the Art,* eds. C. B. Johnson and W. G. Katzenmeyer (Durham, N.C.: Duke University Press, 1969), pp. 109–22.

[5]T. Drews and S. Drews, "HEGIS: A Report on Status and Plans," in *Management Information Systems in Higher Education: The State of the Art,* eds. C. B. Johnson and W. G. Katzenmeyer (Durham, N.C.: Duke University Press, 1969), pp. 79–99.

ADMINISTRATION AND MANAGEMENT

The use of operations research and related techniques of decision-making, mentioned earlier, aims at maximizing or near maximizing an objective. This objective can be economic, in which case the result is that of achieving economic rationality. This has been done extensively in business and industry where such decision-making is considered part of the function of a manager. In educational institutions, decisions are not all maximizing decisions but what Simon calls "satisficing" decisions, i.e., decisions that are "satisfactory" or "good enough."[6] Simon categorizes the "satisficing" decision-maker as an "administrative" man and contrasts him to the "economic" man who maximizes. In educational institutions, many decisions are made by the administrative man and are satisficing decisions.

There is another aspect of decision-making in education. It is what Baughman calls political rationality. It "is never based on the merits of the proposal but rather on who makes it. Compromise is the essence of political rationality, and therefore proposals are debated, objected to, redefined, and so forth, until major opposition disappears." Baughman argues for a balance "between political rationality and economic rationality." This can be achieved through the use of an information system which influences "the amount of economic rationality used in the university decision structure." But it "cannot, and should not, replace political rationality as a basis for university action for it is this rationality that has preserved the university as a highly conservative, secure, and protective institution that permits the inventive individual to thrive."[7]

Some decisions in educational institutions are economic; they are made by managers of the Business Offices, Purchasing Offices, Data Processing Centers, Bookstores, and Food Services. Other officials in education, though not referred to as managers, make management-type decisions, such as the presidents and deans who plan, organize, and direct people, and control their activities.[8] But, as Cook points out, the term management "in educational circles has not had wide acceptance" even though the activities that "educa-

[6]H. A. Simon *Administrative Behavior* (2nd ed.), (New York: The Macmillan Company, 1958), pp. xxiv–xxv.

[7]G. W. Baughman, "Evaluating the Performance and Effectiveness of University Management Information Systems," in *Management Information Systems: Their Development and Use in Administration of Higher Education,* eds. John Minter and Ben Lawrence (Boulder, Colo.: Western Interstate Commission for Higher Education, 1969), p. 3.

[8]T. L. Hungate, *Management in Higher Education* (New York: Bureau of Publications, Columbia University, 1964), pp. 1, 91.

tional personnel often perform are more appropriately managerial than administrative."[9]

To conform to current practice, the terms "administrator" and "administration" will be used in this book but with the understanding that the corresponding terms "manager" and "management" are in many cases applicable to educational institutions and will become increasingly so in the future.[10]

ADMINISTRATORS AND INFORMATION SYSTEMS

Administrators need an information system for many purposes: to maintain records, to plan, evaluate, control, and also to provide a basis for receiving operating funds. This is especially the case in state-supported institutions, where legislators demand justifications for all requests for funds.

The information systems technology, as discussed in this book, enables the administrator to achieve many objectives more effectively and efficiently than formerly possible, and to achieve other objectives never before possible. But it also places a burden on the administrator who wishes to use the system. The administrator must learn about, and participate in, the development of the system. He must learn to ask new questions and to ask old questions differently. Otherwise, though he may get what he asks for, he may not get what he wants or what he should have asked for.

The new systems technology places another burden on the administrator. He must define his problem, his objectives, and his constraints clearly, specifically, and in operational terms. Otherwise, he will be the victim of the "Monkey's Paw." This refers to the story told originally by W. W. Jacob of England and retold by Norbert Wiener.[11] In this story, the owner of the monkey's paw could ask for any three wishes and have them granted. Part of the story goes that one owner of the monkey's paw made his first wish by asking for $200. He received the $200, but it was to compensate for his son being killed by the machinery which he was operating. The second wish was for his son to be returned. The son did reappear but in the form of a mutilated ghost knocking at the door. The third wish was for the ghost to disappear.

[9]D. L. Cook, *Program Evaluation and Review Technique, Applications in Education,* U.S. Office of Education, OE–12024, Cooperative Research Monograph, No. 17 (Washington, D.C.: Government Printing Office, 1966), p. 3.

[10]For an interesting discussion of this subject, see F. E. Rourke and G. E. Brooks, *The Managerial Revolution in Higher Education* (Baltimore, Md.: The Johns Hopkins Press, 1966), pp. 1–17, 101–29.

[11]N. Wiener, "The Monkey's Paw," in *The New Technology and Human Values,* ed. J. G. Burke (Belmont, Ca.: Wadsworth Publishing Company, Inc., 1968), pp. 130–34.

The story has relevance to systems development in that the user must state not only his needs, but also all the constraints within which his needs must be accomplished. This is the part of the process of systems development in which the administrator must participate actively.

The determination of what information is to be generated by the information system is one of the first steps in the development process and is the responsibility of the administrator. Furthermore, he must specify when and where the information must be delivered. How this is done is basically the function of the systems analyst. He contributes the technical knowledge necessary for transforming the specifications of the user into the desired finished product. Collectively, the administrator and the systems analyst must specify and implement the organizational changes necessary. This may require taking down old fences and constructing new boundaries. Together, the administrator and the systems analyst must develop the system if it is to be both effective and efficient.

Traditionally, a distinction has been made between the user and the developer. Typically, the user is the administrator and the developer is the systems analyst. I take the position that both the administrator and the systems analyst are developers. The development of an information system is a highly interactive one. Seldom can either party justifiably claim neutrality for an inefficient or ineffective system. Both must cooperate, understand each other's capabilities and limitations, and support each other throughout the development process. A successful information system is largely dependent on such mutual understanding and interaction as well as on the active participation of the administrator.

A lack of interest in information systems on the part of the administrator can lead to serious undesirable consequences. Ackoff, in discussing the development process, states that "Managers who are not willing to invest some of their time in this process are not likely to use a management control system well, and their system, in turn, is likely to abuse them."[12] The danger of neglecting information system development has also been observed by Schoderbek, who comments: "Too often in the past top management has relinquished its responsibility by allowing the EDP (electronic data processing) group to determine its own objectives, set up its own standards, and measure its own performance. This is management by default."[13]

Contemporary information systems are mostly computer systems, with their inherent danger of dehumanizing the organization and the individual by machine. It is the administrator's duty as a developer to prevent the machine

[12]R. L. Ackoff, "Management Misinformation Systems," *Management Science: Application* (Series B), XIV, No. 4 (December 1967), B-156.

[13]P. P. Schoderbek, ed., *Management Systems* (New York: John Wiley & Sons, Inc., 1968), p. 291. The parenthesis is provided by the author for the purpose of clarity.

from mechanizing man and, instead, see that the new system, if necessary, humanizes the machine.

For the administrator to effectively discharge his role in the development of an information system, he must have the following qualities: the ability to use basic tools of analysis; the knowledge of the fundamentals of the structure of information systems and data organization; and, finally, an understanding of the process of the development of information systems. These are the topics discussed in this book. Their understanding will enable the administrator to communicate with the systems analyst and contribute effectively to the development process. It will enable the administrator to ask for the right system, help design and implement such a system, and then be able to use it effectively.

SCOPE OF THE BOOK

The remaining two chapters in Part One introduce two tools of analysis. They are important to the process of development of an information system, and are used as media of communication in this book. Hence they are introduced early.

Part Two is a discussion of systems, information, and information systems. This is followed by a discussion of data and its organization in Part Three, and the development of an information system in Part Four. The final part, Part Five, is concerned with the use of information systems and conclusions concerning future information systems for educational administration.

Material Not Included

A great deal of material relevant to the subject discussed in this book has been excluded. This material includes the theoretical and mathematical formulations of information systems,[14] Information Theory,[15] Communication Theory,[16] Cybernetics,[17] the organization of a Systems Department and its location in the organization chart.[18] Also, information systems needed for

[14]B. Langefors, *Theoretical Analysis of Information Systems* (Kobenhavn: Akademisk Forlag, 1966), I & II, 400 pp.

[15]F. M. Reza, *An Introduction to Information Theory* (New York: McGraw-Hill Book Company, 1961), 496 pp.

[16]C. E. Shannon and W. Weaver, eds. *The Mathematical Theory of Communication* (Urbana, Ill.: University of Illinois Press, 1949), 117 pp.

[17]Stafford Beer, *Cybernetics and Management* (New York: John Wiley & Sons, Inc., 1959), 214 pp.

[18]D. F. Heany, *Development of Information Systems: What Management Needs to Know* (New York: The Ronald Press, 1968), xiv, pp. 344–68.

retrieval of textual data, such as bibliographical abstracts, or factual data retrieved in libraries are also considered beyond the scope of this book and, therefore, are not discussed.

The exclusions are made not because the material is unimportant but because of constraints of space. However, many references are provided for the interested reader in the footnotes as well as in an annotated bibliography at the end of this chapter. This bibliography also contains some references on the general topic of Information Systems and, more specifically, on Systems Approaches to Educational Administration.

Another related area that is excluded concerns computers. Many information systems, especially medium-sized and large information systems, use computers. A knowledge of computers, their operations, the storage and retrieval of data, and programming is required for the development of information systems. But in most cases this knowledge is provided by the professional information scientist. The typical reader, the educational administrator, does not necessarily require this knowledge. However, he must know about the capabilities and limitations of information systems and its process of development so that he can participate actively and meaningfully in the development of his system. This knowledge will be offered in Parts Three through Five of this book.

ORGANIZATION OF BOOK

The five parts of the book are each introduced by a summary which, when read in sequence, is designed to provide a summary of the entire book.

In each chapter, the text is followed by a summary section, which in a few cases includes some conclusions. This section is followed by a list of key terms introduced in the chapter and is followed by a set of review questions. In some chapters, there is also a set of exercises along with their solutions. Advanced material and reference material appear in the appendices.

Each chapter has an annotated bibliography selected for further study.

Glossaries

There are two glossaries. A conventional one for reference appears at the end of the book and another one in prose is presented as an introduction to Part Four. The latter glossary reviews many of the terms and concepts discussed in the previous chapters and introduces some new ones used in Part Four. This glossary attempts to describe the process and environment of an information system. It has no prerequisites and can be read at any time before Part Four, but at least should be read just before it.

Prerequisites

There are no specific mathematical or statistical prerequisites for the study of this book. The traditional preparation of educational administrators will suffice. Some of the tools of analysis needed will be discussed in Chapters 2 and 3 and others will be introduced in other chapters whenever they are needed.

KEY TERMS

Efficiency
Effectiveness
Satisficing
Economic Man
Administrative Man
Economic Rationality
Political Rationality
Administrator
Manager
User
Developer

REVIEW QUESTIONS

1. Distinguish between
   Efficiency and Effectiveness
   Economic Man and Administrative Man
   Economic Rationality and Political Rationality
   Administrator and Manager
   User and Developer
2. Why has the demand for information systems increased?
3. For what purposes do administrators require information?
4. What part does the administrator play in the development of an information system?
5. What abilities must an administrator have in order to effectively participate in the development of an information system?

CHAPTER 1: SELECTED ANNOTATED BIBLIOGRAPHY ON COMPUTERS AND INFORMATION SYSTEMS

AARON, J. D., "Information Systems in Perspective," *Computing Surveys,* I, No. 4 (December 1969), 213–36. An excellent survey of the field with special emphasis on MIS (Management Information Systems). It covers communications and graphics. It is addressed to the computer scientist but is not too technical.

BLUMENTHAL, S. C., *Management Information Systems: A Framework for Planning & Development.* Englewood Cliffs, N.J.: Prentice-Hall, Inc., 1969, 219 pp. Presents a formal framework for information systems and is recommended to the serious reader.

DAVIDSON, C. H., and E. C. KOENIG, *Computers: Introduction to Computers & Applied Computing Concepts.* New York: John Wiley & Sons, Inc., 1967, 596 pp. An introduction to computers and computer programming (FORTRAN). Discusses many applications also.

DESMONDE, W. H., *Computers and Their Uses.* Englewood Cliffs, N.J.: Prentice-Hall, Inc., 1964, 296 pp. This is a good overview of computers and their implications. It includes a discussion of punched-card machines, machine logic, concepts of programming, applications, and social considerations of computers.

HEANY, D. F., *Development of Information Systems: What Management Needs to Know.* New York: The Ronald Press Co., 1968, 421 pp. An excellent text on information systems and is written in nontechnical terms.

KANTER, J., *The Computer and the Executive.* Englewood Cliffs, N.J.: Prentice-Hall, Inc., 1967, 134 pp. It is successful in its claim of exploring the computer world from the management viewpoint "in terms familiar to the executive or the aspiring executive."

MC DONOUGH, A. M., and L. J. GARRETT, *Management Systems Working Concepts and Practices.* Homewood, Ill.: Richard D. Irwin, Inc., 1965, 325 pp. A good text for an information system in the business and industrial environment.

MEADOW, C. T., *The Analysis of Information Systems: A Programmers Introduction to Information Retrieval.* New York: John Wiley & Sons, Inc., 1967, 301 pp. This is a technical book but is excellent on the design of an information retrieval system and an introduction to data structures.

PRINCE, T. R., *Information Systems for Management Planning and Control.* Homewood, Ill.: Richard D. Irwin, Inc., 1966. The text is applications-oriented and has many case studies from industry.

SISSON, R. L. and R. G. CANNING, *A Manager's Guide to Computer Processing.* New York: John Wiley & Sons, Inc., 1967, 124 pp. These authors have written a series of books for managers. This one is a "management-oriented" explanation of information systems and computers and their role in managing a company.

CHAPTER 1: SELECTED ANNOTATED BIBLIOGRAPHY ON RELATED MATERIAL SYSTEMS APPROACHES IN EDUCATIONAL ADMINISTRATION

BANGHART, FRANK W., *Educational Systems Analysis.* London: Macmillan and Co. Ltd., 1969, 330 pp. The best book in the field because it is the only one. It has a collection of Operational Research techniques that can be found in many other textbooks. It has two chapters on information systems design but these are brief and mostly outdated. But the book is a good attempt at integrating systems techniques to education and has an interesting chapter on Scientific Administration. The 1969 edition has numerous printing errors including the omission of node numbers which makes ten pages on the Planning and Control chapter totally worthless.

BUSHNELL, DON D., and DWIGHT W. ALLEN, eds., *The Computer in American Education.* New York: John Wiley & Sons, Inc., 1967, 300 pp. This book is a set of readings by educators and computer scientists. The topics discussed include: individualized instruction and social goals, computers in instruction and research, teaching the computer sciences, information processing for education systems. It discusses the potentialities and limitations of computer technology in education.

GERARD, RALPH W., ed., *Computers and Education.* New York: McGraw-Hill Book Company, Inc., 1967, 307 pp. This book is a collection of papers and discussions of a workshop that took place in the fall of 1963. As such, it is outdated. But it does have good discussions on library automation, CAI (Computer Aided Information), administrative applications, as well as regional and national networks.

GOODLAD, JOHN I., JOHN F. O'TOOLE, JR., and LOUISE L. TYLER, *Computers and Information Systems in Education.* New York: Harcourt, Brace & World, Inc., 1966, 152 pp. The book gives an overview of Education and Computer Technology; EDP in Education, present developments and technical aspects; the state of the art; applications of computers and information systems in education; and discusses problems, issues, and recommendations pertaining to electronic data systems.

GROSSMAN, ALVIN, and ROBERT L. HOWE, *Data Processing for Educators.* Chicago: Educational Methods, Inc., 1965, 362 pp. Covers history of automated information systems; developing an educational data processing system; equipment, personnel, and design requirements; typical educational applications; impact of EDP on schools; and the potential for education. It has many samples of output and is largely school oriented.

GRUMAN, ALLEN J., *Workbook: Data Processing for Educators.* Chicago: Educational Methods, Inc., 1965, 138 pp. This workbook is designed to be used with Grossman and Howe, *Data Processing for Educators,* provides exercises covering costs of equipment; pay scales; machines and their functions; systems study; systems design; punch card design; scanner forms design; paper forms design; test scoring; attendance records and accounting; student scheduling; and cumulative records.

HAGA, ENOCH, ed., *Automated Educational Systems* Elmhurst, Ill.: The Business Press, 1967, 343 pp. This book is a series of readings on school data processing. It is in two parts. The first part discusses "concepts and patterns" with a heavy emphasis on regional and national educational information systems. The second part discusses applications and techniques including the CARDPAC and Plato Systems.

HARTLEY, HARRY J., *Educational Planning-Programming-Budgeting: A Systems Approach.* Englewood Cliffs, N.J.: Prentice-Hall, Inc., 1968, 290 pp. Topics discussed are educational planning and economic rationality; overview of systems analysis procedures; systems analysis in education; PPBS; need for budgetary reform; program structures and economic issues in schools; administrative issues and implications of PPBS.

JOHNSON, C. B., and W. G. KATZENMEYER, eds., *Management Information Systems in Higher Education: The State of the Art.* Durham, N.C.: Duke University Press, 1969, 191 pp. A set of readings including discussions of a "Theory of University Management": national (HEGIS) and regional (WICHE) systems; and modeling in management of information systems.

KAIMANN, RICHARD A., and ROBERT W. MARKER, *Educational Data Processing: New Dimensions and Prospects.* Boston: Houghton Mifflin Co., 1967, 326 pp. Perhaps the best overall book in educational data processing. Contains fifty different articles covering the field of computers in education. Discusses computer concepts specifications; personnel required; who should control; centralization *vs.* decentralization; applications; starting an EDP program; determining need for data processing; simulation; and data banks.

KERSHAW, J. A., and R. N. MCKEAN, *Systems Analysis and Education.* Santa Monica, Cal.: RAND Corporation, 1959, 64 pp. This old book in its field is a research memorandum-working paper, and contains formal quantitative comparisons of specific education systems with variants of them in which changes and innovations are incorporated. This memorandum is concerned with elementary and secondary schools only.

LOUGHARY, JOHN W., *Man-Machine Systems in Education.* New York: Harper and Row, 1966, 242 pp. This book covers such topics as: computers and instruction; instructional MIS (Management Information Systems); computers in school management; applications to state departments of education; district applications; educational policy development; computers for pupil personnel services; and implementing man-machine systems.

PFEIFFER, JOHN, *New Look at Education.* New York: The Odyssey Press, 1968, 162 pp. A paperback written in nontechnical terms. It emphasizes the roles of models in educational decision-making and gives numerous samples from schools and colleges.

STOLLER, D. S., *Abstracts of Technical Notes of the Division of Operations Analysis,* Technical Note No. 44. Washington, D.C.: U.S. Office of Education, the Division of Operations Analysis, revised 1968. This document has titles and abstracts of 48 Technical Notes of the Division of Operational Analysis of the U.S. Office of Education.

Systems Analysis for Educational Planning. Paris, France: Organization for Economic Cooperation & Development, 1969, 219 pp. An excellent annotated bibliography of the literature from the U.S. and abroad. Has 306 entries subdivided into nine sections including selected techniques applied to education, data processing and information systems for education, and studies in selected topics of systems analysis.

UNESCO, *IIEP, Educational Planning,* A Bibliography. Paris, France: UNESCO, 1964, 131 pp. Somewhat outdated yet a good collection of 540 entries. The entries are annotated and cover the literature from around the world. The material reviewed includes cases and educational planning, as well as organization and administration.

WHITLOCK, JAMES W., *Automatic Data Processing in Education.* New York: The Macmillan Co., 1964, 144 pp. Application to local school districts, state departments of education and institutions of higher learning; student personnel accounting; school business and personnel functions; and installation planning. This book is largely EAM equipment oriented and is, therefore, largely outdated.

2

Tools of Analysis

INTRODUCTION

In this chapter, two important tools used in analysis of systems will be discussed: flowcharts[1] and network diagrams. Other charting tools will be mentioned. Some of the concepts and terms used in systems analysis will be introduced and defined.

THE BLACK-BOX APPROACH

An organization can be thought of as a "black-box" with an input and an output as shown in Figure 2–1.

[1]This word is sometimes written as two words: flow chart.

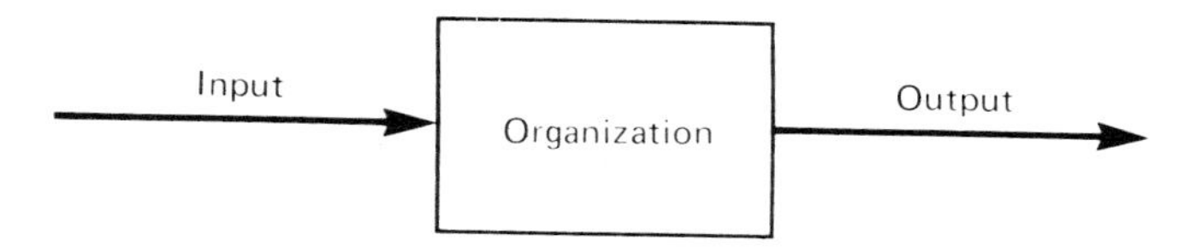

Figure 2–1. The Black-Box Approach to an Organization

There is input going into the organization and output coming out of it. Neither the mechanics nor the logic of the transformation from input into output are explained. The organization performing the transformation is unexplained and is treated as a black-box. We are not necessarily able to see into the box and understand its working but merely know the relationship of its input to its output.

The black-box concept comes from the electrical engineer. He gets equipment in the form of a "box" which he may not open or examine; yet he needs to use it and hence to know how it behaves. He applies inputs in the form of voltages and currents, and measures the output on instruments. By experimentation with different inputs, he is able to draw conclusions about the contents and behavior of the box. The color black of the box comes from the fact that it was once a popular color for electrical equipment.

We use the black-box approach many times in our everyday lives. For example, we treat a plant as a black-box. We feed it water, sun, and fertilizer in order to produce growth but we do not necessarily know how the transformation takes place. We do not care to know, do not have the ability to understand the technicalities, or do not find it feasible to know. It is not feasible to learn about the transformation relationship of a particular plant without digging it up and examining its root structure, but this may destroy the plant. We, therefore, are content with knowing the inputs (water, sun, and fertilizer) required for a desired output (growth) and treat the plant itself as a black-box.[2]

An information processor or a computer can also be looked upon as a black-box, as is shown in Figure 2–2.

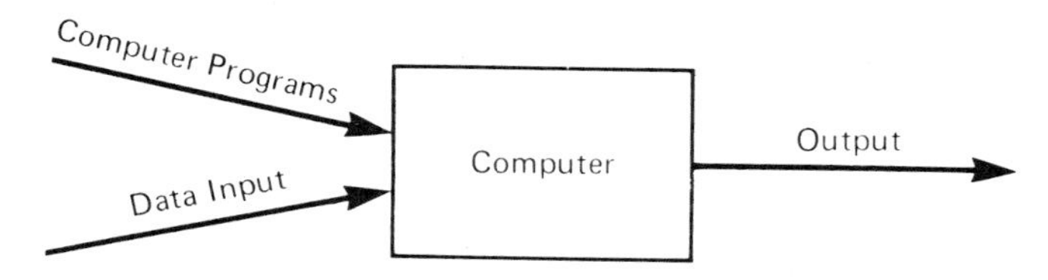

Figure 2–2. A Black-Box Approach to a Computer

[2]For other examples of the "black-box" approach, see Van Court Hare, Jr., *Systems Analysis: A Diagnostic Approach* (New York: Harcourt, Brace & World, Inc., 1967), pp. 29–37. For a more mathematical discussion, see W. R. Ashby, *An Introduction to Cybernetics* (London: Chapman & Hall, Ltd., 1961), pp. 86–117. For a management approach, see M. Anshen, "The Manager and the Black-Box," *Harvard Business Review,* XXXVIII, No. 6 (November-December 1960), 85–92.

The computer is a special type of equipment that will accept input to produce a desired output. The input to the computer includes data as well as programs. The programs are instructions necessary to communicate with the computer in order to get the desired results.

Many administrators treat the computer as a black-box, much as they treat the engines under the hoods of their automobiles. To know the workings of internal combustion engines could help in the case of breakdowns and could otherwise contribute to more efficient operations and longer lives for the automobiles. But such knowledge of an automobile or a computer is not essential and they can be treated as black-boxes. What is necessary, however, is to understand the relationships of the inputs and outputs, their capabilities and limitations. Without this knowledge, the computer cannot be used effectively and, in fact, it may even be dangerous, just as an automobile can be dangerous if the driver does not know the relationship of the speed response to pressure on the accelerator. The administrator must know the relationship between inputs and outputs to a computer as well as to other man-machine combinations so that he may help design a system to meet his needs. A system in this context is a grouping of men and machines to perform specific tasks. This concept will be defined and discussed in detail in a later chapter.

To design a system for his needs, the administrator must work closely with systems personnel. This group of people includes systems analysts, those who analyze and design systems; computer programmers, those who write computer programs; operations researchers, those who have knowledge of specialized mathematical and statistical methods and techniques used in systems; and other related professionals. The number of people in each profession working on a system development will vary with the nature and complexity of the system.

An important element in a systems operation is the "control" function: the correction of undesirable deviations of the actual performance from the desired performance. Information on this deviation is fed back to alter the input so that the undesirable deviations are eliminated. This feeding back of information is called feedback and is shown diagramatically[3] in Figure 2–3.

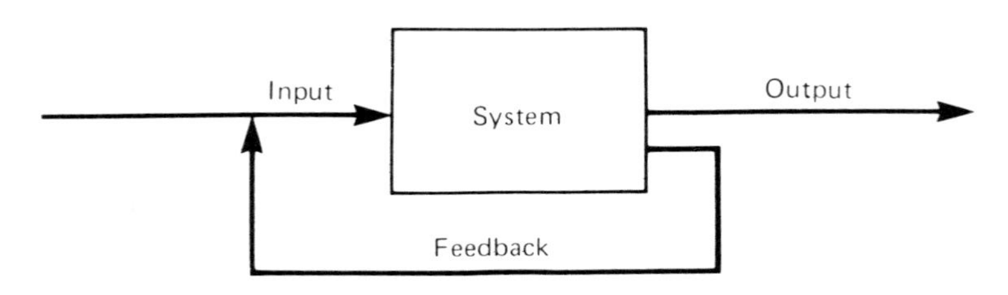

Figure 2–3. Diagram Showing Feedback

[3]For other representation of the feedback concept, see M. Alexis and C. Z. Wilson, *Organizational Decision Making* (Englewood Cliffs, N.J.: Prentice-Hall, Inc., 1967), p. 324.

This conventional representation does not identify the condition that results in a feedback. Feedback need not necessarily occur continuously but only when actual performance does not match desired performance. The condition that triggers the feedback is not clearly identified. It can be identified by using another tool called a **flowchart.** This tool is not only used extensively in the development of a system but is also an important means of communication. As such, it is used extensively as a medium of presentation in this book. Hence the need for introducing it so early in the book and discussing it in detail.

THE FLOWCHART

This discussion will start with a definition, followed by a discussion of symbols, types of flowcharts, and, finally, by a discussion of their advantages and disadvantages.

A flowchart can be defined as a diagrammatic representation of a sequence of operations and the logic (when relevant) that determines the sequence.[4] Flowcharts express complex phenomena in terms of their simplest components in the graphics of diagrams. It is a language of representation for the systems analyst, much as the number system is for the mathematician. This flowchart language enables us to analyze, synthesize, and communicate about the complexities and workings of a system.

Use of Symbols

Flowchart representations consist of geometric figures and symbols. The earliest were designed by Dr. Gilbreth and were used in analyzing production problems. These were followed by conventions adopted by the American Society of Mechanical Engineers. In the field of data processing systems, large computer manufacturers found these symbols insufficient for their field and designed their own symbols. This led to confusion. An important function of the flowchart, that of communication, was lost because of the lack of standardized symbols. In 1963, a committee of the American Standards Association (currently renamed ANSI, the American National Standards Institute) published a set of standard symbols for information processing, then known as the American Standard.[5] These were revised in 1965, 1966, and 1968. In 1970,

[4]Another definition given by Pomeroy: "A flow chart can be defined as a pictorial representation, using geometric shapes to which conventional meanings have been assigned, of a systematic sequence of activities performed by individuals for the accomplishment of a business (or business-like) purpose." R. W. Pomeroy, "Flow Charting," *Ideas for Management, 20th International Systems Meeting* (Cleveland, Ohio: Systems and Procedures Association, 1967), p. 20.

[5]"Proposed American Standard Flowchart Symbols for Information Processing," *Communications of the ACM,* VI, No. 10 (October 1963), 601–4.

these standards were again revised to match closely the International Standards. These important steps in the standardization and acceptance of flowchart symbols have greatly increased the value of the flowchart as a means of communication.

In this chapter, only a few symbols will be discussed. These are the ones that will be used extensively in the rest of the book, and are the symbols that administrators would encounter in their work with systems personnel.

There are three types of symbols: basic, specialized, and additional miscellaneous. The basic symbols are shown in Figure 2–4.

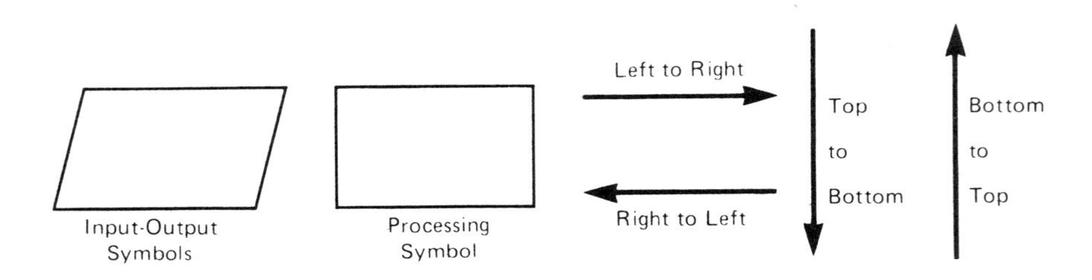

Figure 2–4. Basic Symbols of Information Processing

The directional arrows are not necessary if the directional flow is "normal," that is left to right and top to bottom. The arrows are necessary if the flow is abnormal. Also, they are used for purposes of emphasis and clarity.

The size of the symbols may vary but the dimensional ratios and the rotational position of the symbols must be maintained as specified in the ANSI standards.

An example of the generic use of these symbols is shown in a system's flowchart in Figure 2–5.

This diagram is referred to as a **system's flowchart** because it represents the system's overview. It identifies the input, processing, and output. The system's flowchart identifies the "process" by one symbol. It says nothing about the nature of the process and its logic. This is done in yet another type of flowchart: the **program flowchart.** The program flowchart breaks down the details of processing into simple arithmetic and logic operations, which are represented by numerous processing symbols.

The program flowchart evolves from the system's flowchart. It is sometimes used by the system's personnel to identify the logic of a problem before it is programmed.

The program flowchart is also called a **logic diagram** or a **block diagram.** The latter terminology is confusing since diagrams other than flowcharts, such

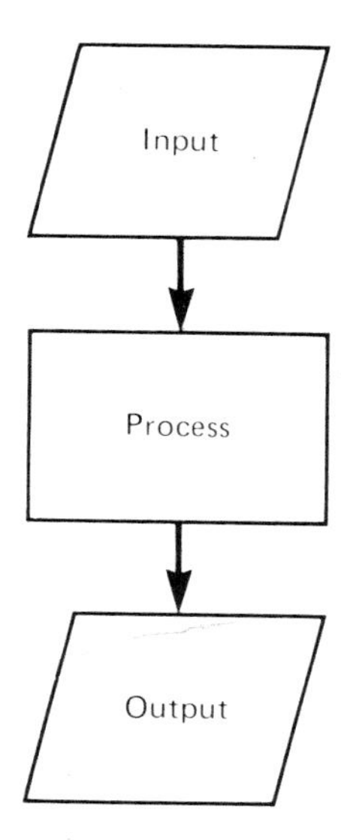

Figure 2–5. A System's Flowchart

as in Figures 2–1, 2–2, 2–3, are also called **block diagrams.** To avoid confusion, **program flowcharts** in this book will not be referred to as **block diagrams.**

In order to express the logic of the processing and also to express in greater detail the type of input or output media used, specialized symbols are required. Some of these are shown in Figure 2–6.

Specialized Symbols for Input and Output

The symbol for a card is used mostly for input. A card could also be an output, but most frequently it is used again as input after it has been resequenced and rearranged with other cards.

The magnetic tape is a medium for storing data. As such, it could be used both as output to store data and then as input when the data is needed for processing. For its size and weight, it can hold many times the information that can be stored on cards. One tape can hold the card equivalent to what is held in a normal file cabinet. But unlike cards and documents, it is not readable by the human eye. It is, therefore, used almost exclusively by systems personnel and is seldom handled by administrators.

The document symbol is used both for input, such as forms ready to be processed in an optical scanner, and for output, such as paper reports from a printer.

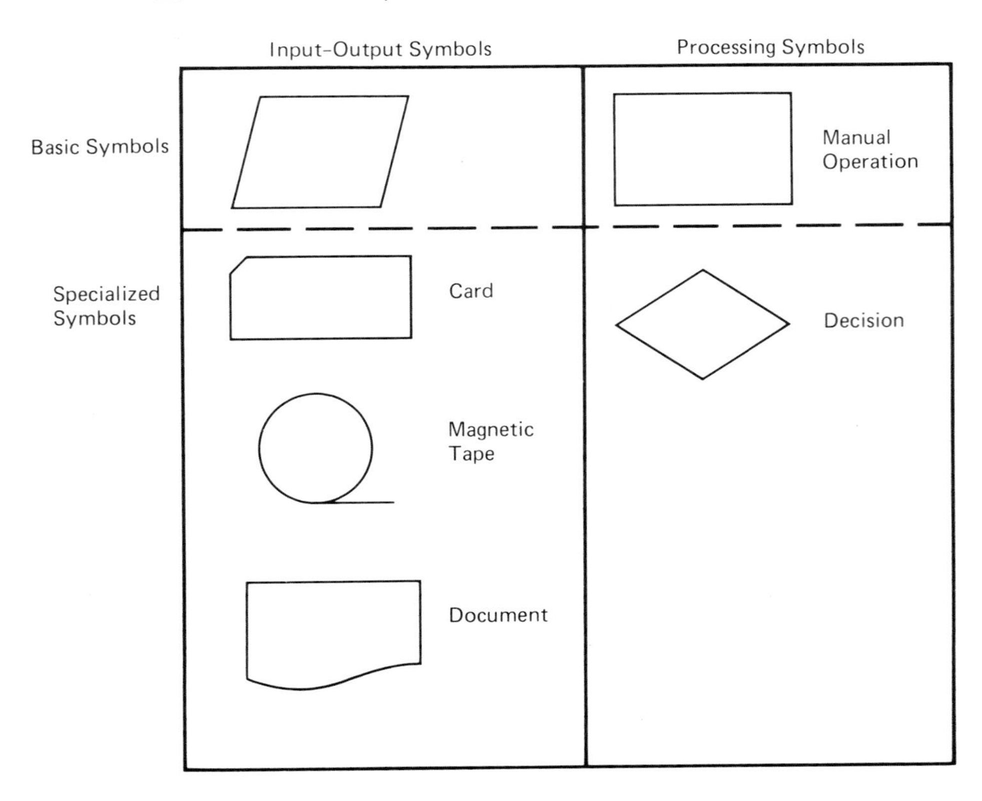

Figure 2–6. Some Basic and Specialized Symbols

Specialized Symbols for Processing.

The symbol for manual operations would be used for situations such as the manual rearrangement of cards mentioned earlier. Other examples of manual operations could be coding, checking details, filling in missing information, checking data.

The diamond-shaped symbol represents a decision point. The decision may be a two-way binary decision, (such as yes or no); a three-way decision (such as a gradepoint average equal to 2.0, greater than 2.0, or less than 2.0); or a multiple decision (such as choice between the many types of levels of students).

The most common decision symbol used by administrators is the two-way choice. The use of this symbol and some of the other specialized symbols are illustrated for the feedback problem examined earlier. The diagram in Figure 2–3 will now be represented in flowchart form, shown in Figure 2–7.

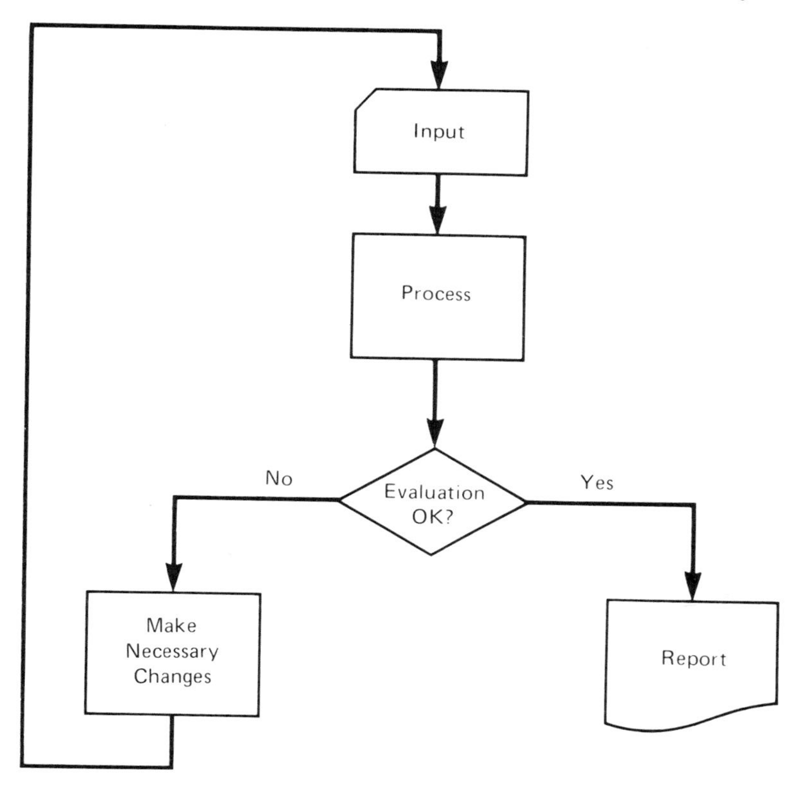

Figure 2–7. The Feedback Concept Illustrated in a Flowchart

The process in Figure 2–7 is checked and if the evaluation is unsatisfactory, then the input is adjusted accordingly. Only when the test is satisfactory, is a report printed as output.

Miscellaneous Symbols

There are a few additional symbols and conventions required to complete a flowchart. These are shown in Figure 2–8.

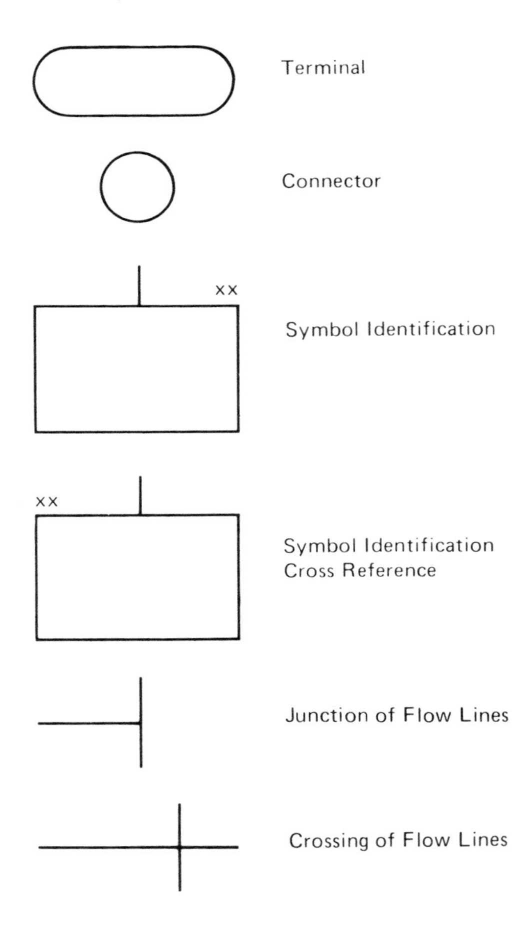

Figure 2–8. Miscellaneous Additional Symbols

The terminal symbol represents a terminal point in a system such as the start or an end. The connector symbol is used to connect one part of the flow to another when it is interrupted. The interruption could be caused by an overflow to another page of the flowchart, or it could be created in order to avoid criss-crossing of flow lines in a complex diagram. Each of two or more connectors for a flow has an identifying reference marked within it. This number can be arbitrarily chosen but should be unique. It should identify the page number in cases of more than one-page flowcharts.

A flowchart symbol can be identified for reference by a number on the top right-hand corner. A number on the top left-hand corner identifies docu-

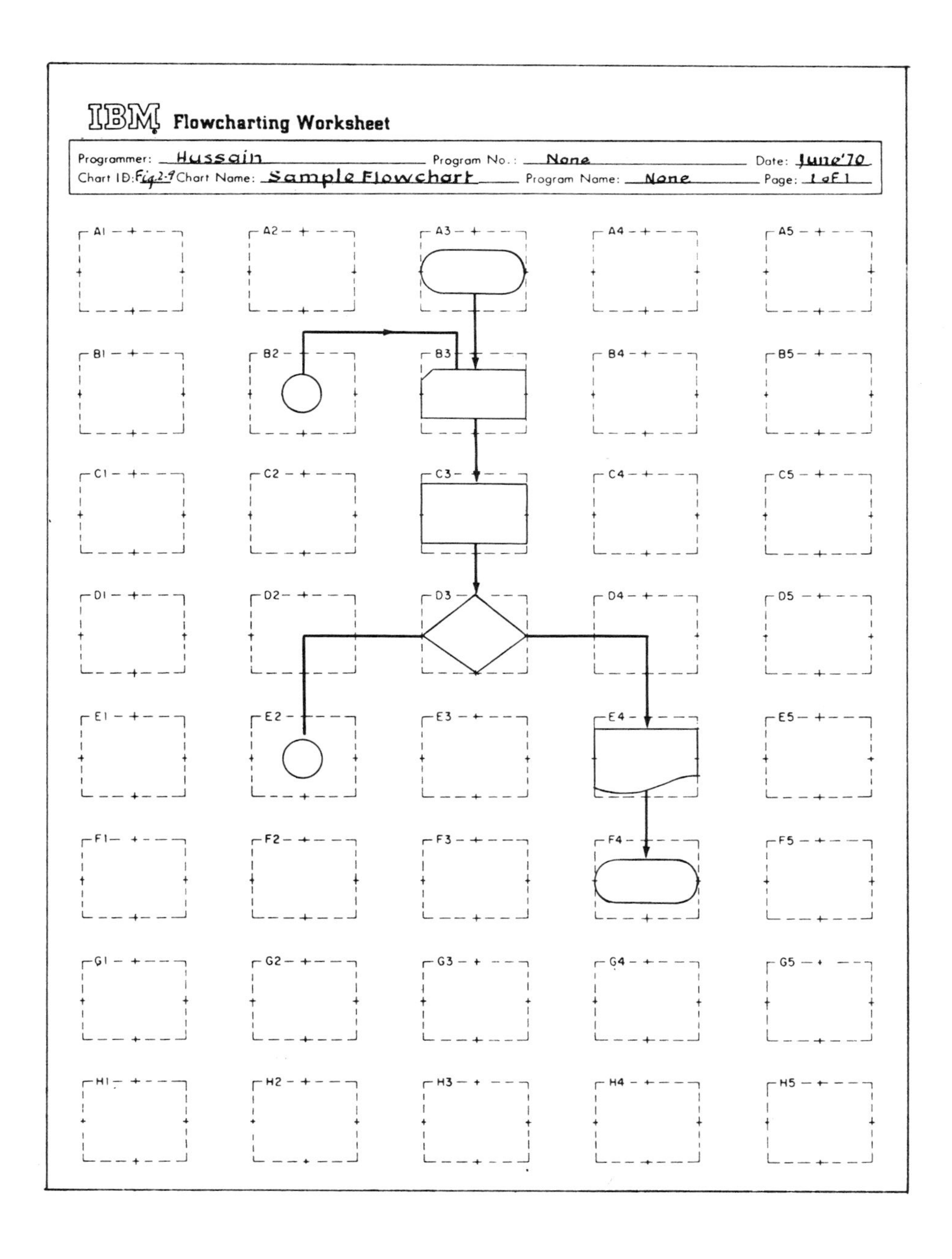
IBM Flowcharting Worksheet
Programmer: Hussain
Program No.: None
Date: June'70
Chart ID: Fig.2-9
Chart Name: Sample Flowchart
Program Name: None
Page: 1 of 1
A1
A2
A3
A4
A5
B1
B2
B3
B4
B5
C1
C2
C3
C4
C5
D1
D2
D3
D4
D5
E1
E2
E3
E4
E5
F1
F2
F3
F4
F5
G1
G2
G3
G4
G5
H1
H2
H3
H4
H5

Figure 2–9

mentation relating to the symbol. This number may be the page number and is used in flowcharts with complex processes expressed by one symbol.

The conventions for symbol identification and crossing of flow lines under the ANSI standards conflict with those of the International Standards Organization. The symbol identification shown in Figure 2–8 is according to the ANSI standards. The International Standards Organization uses some conventions that are exactly the opposite (i.e., the symbol identification is on the top left-hand side of the symbol and the symbol identification cross-reference is on the top right-hand side of the symbol). The ANSI standard uses connectors as shown in Figure 2–8, while the International Standards Organization allows the crossing of flow lines.

The use of the additional miscellaneous symbols is demonstrated in Figure 2–9. The problem is exactly the same as in Figure 2–7. The connectors used in Figure 2–9 are not necessary but have been used for demonstration purposes. The "no" exit of the logical box 4 enters the input symbol 2 through connectors.

This flowchart has been drawn on special flowcharting paper. Some systems personnel find it easier to use, while others find it confusing. It has been used here only to acquaint the reader with its appearance.

The reader will find some differences between Figure 2–7 and Figure 2–9 other than those already discussed, such as the titles used within the symbols and the absence and positions of arrows. These variations are allowed by the ANSI standards. In spite of the symbol standardization, there are so many legal variations allowed that seldom do two people draw the same flowchart.

Template

It may seem that it is difficult to draw the different symbols as presented and yet maintain the restrictions on dimension ratios and rotation. This problem is solved by using a **template**—a plastic plate with most of the required symbols cut out of it. Tracing the desired symbol in the template greatly facilitates the drawing of a flowchart. One template[6] is shown in Figure 2–10.

Advantages of Flowcharts

There are three important advantages of flowcharts: they are useful for analysis, synthesis, and documentation. Flowcharts are useful for analysis

[6]All the symbols on this template do not correspond to the ANSI conventions and yet it is one of the most common templates available.

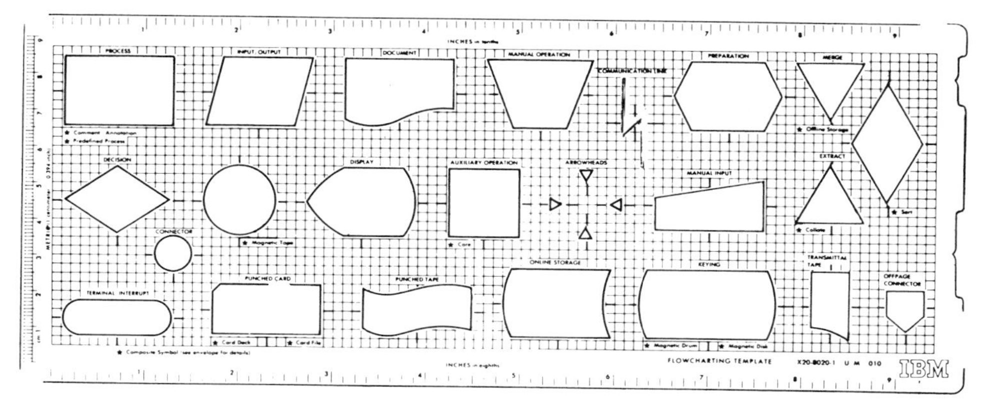

Figure 2–10. A Template for Flowcharting

because they facilitate the understanding of complex problems. They are a shorthand to express quickly and graphically the logic involved in a problem, which can easily be analyzed by following each logic step. Flowcharts enable the synthesis of a solution by combining detailed elements into a whole. This detailed chart can then be used for programming a solution. Flowcharts are also an effective means of documentation and of communication among systems personnel and also between systems personnel and administrators. They can be used effectively in instruction as visual and graphic reinforcement of a narrative.

Because of the above advantages, flowcharts are used extensively in many stages of the development of a system. This will be demonstrated in Part IV of this book.

Disadvantages of Flowcharts

The flowchart, like the narrative, mixes a set of logical conditions with its respective sets of actions. In some problems, it is only with difficulty that the conditions associated with each action can be traced. The flowchart is also somewhat difficult to change, though easier than the narrative. It shows each condition and action in a sequential order, but it is not always clear whether the sequence is essential, desirable, or immaterial. For complex problems with many decision rules, the flowchart can be complicated and cumbersome.

The disadvantages of flowcharts can be overcome by another tool of systems analysis: the **decision table.** This is the topic of Chapter 3.

Flowchart for Reading Rest of Part I

The flowchart will now be put to practical use. It will be drawn to represent the author's recommendations for reading the remainder of Part I of this book. This is done in Figure 2–11.

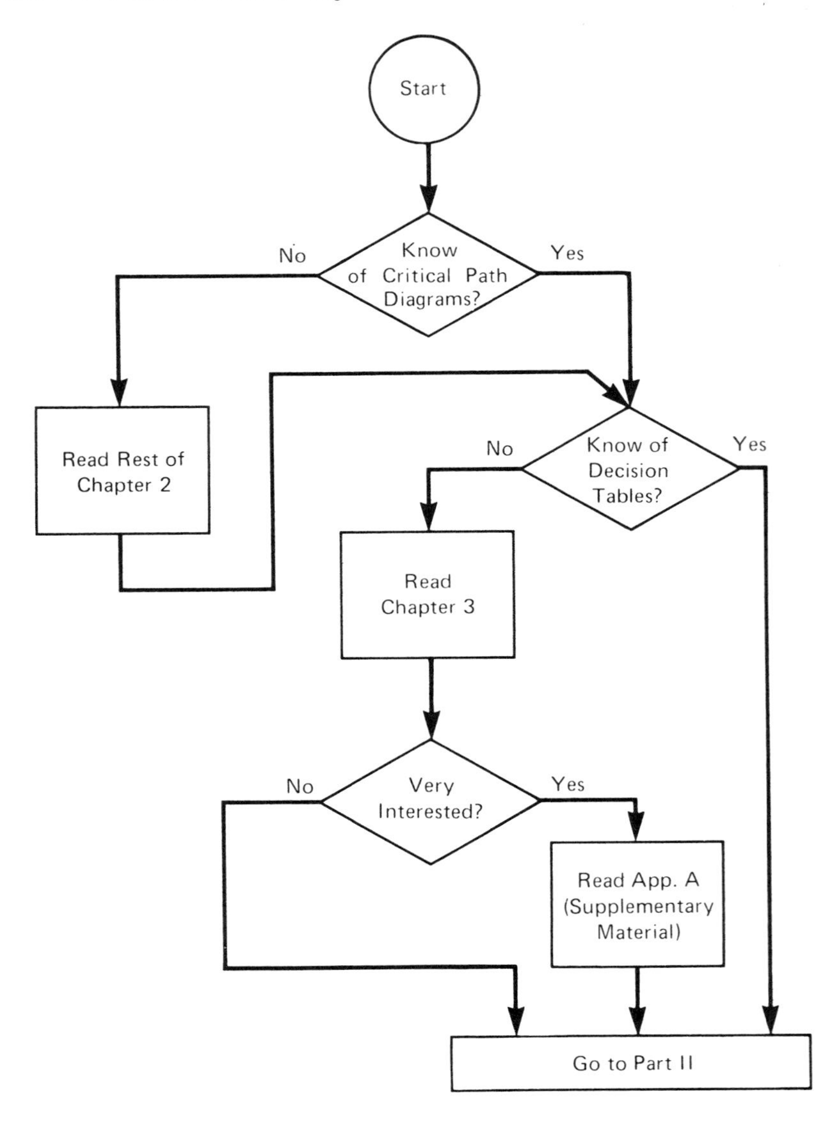

Figure 2–11. Flowchart for Reading Rest of Part I of Book

OTHER TOOLS OF SYSTEMS ANALYSIS

In addition to the flowchart and the decision table, there are other charting methods that are useful in systems work. Some are listed below:

- Flowcharts
  - System's Flowcharts
  - Program Flowcharts
- Decision Tables
  - Limited Entry
  - Extended Entry
  - Mixed Entry
- Tools of Organizational Analysis
  - Organization Chart
  - Work Distribution Chart
  - Linear Responsibility Chart
- Tools for Designing Input and Output
  - Statistical Charts
  - Input-Output Grids
- Charts for Analysis
  - Operational Sequence Diagrams
  - Process Charts
  - Schematic Flowcharts
  - Forms Flowcharts
  - Forms Distribution Chart
  - Plant Layout Chart
- Project Management Techniques
  - GANNT Chart
  - Critical Path Diagrams
    - Critical Path Method (CPM)
    - Program Evaluation Review Technique (PERT)

The tools of Logical Analysis have already been discussed or mentioned. The tools of Organizational Analysis as well as tools for designing input and output will not be discussed in this book, since many administrators are already aware of these tools from experience or through their study in other disciplines. However, charts for analysis will be discussed later in the context of systems development because it is easier for the author to explain and for the reader to understand these charts in the context of a problem rather than in the abstract.

CRITICAL PATH DIAGRAMS

Critical Path Diagrams will be used extensively in Part Four of this book. The subject includes the concepts of an **activity**, an **event**, and a **critical path.**

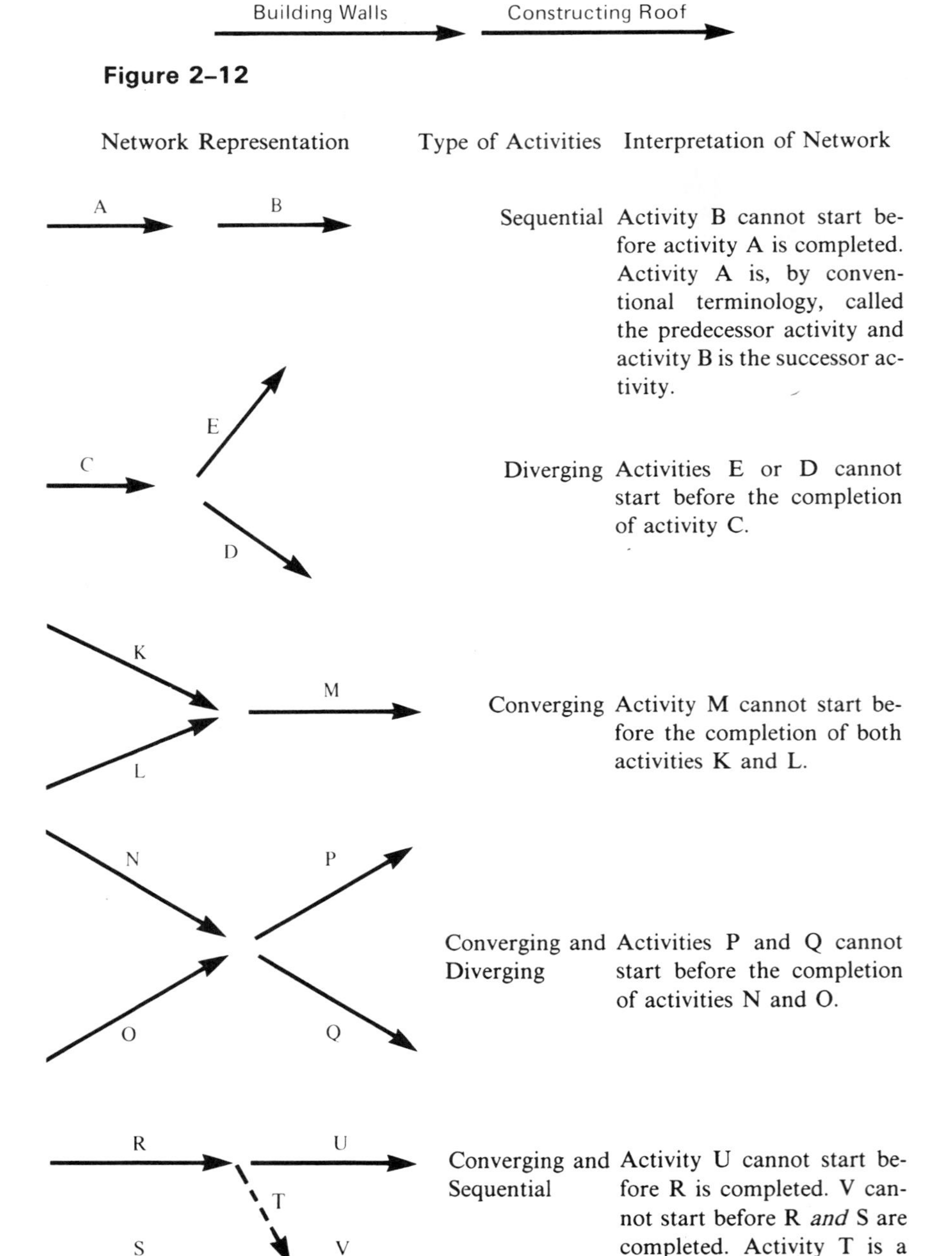

Building Walls
Constructing Roof
Network Representation
Type of Activities
Interpretation of Network
A
B
Sequential
Activity B cannot start before activity A is completed. Activity A is, by conventional terminology, called the predecessor activity and activity B is the successor activity.
C
E
D
Diverging
Activities E or D cannot start before the completion of activity C.
K
L
M
Converging
Activity M cannot start before the completion of both activities K and L.
N
O
P
Q
Converging and Diverging
Activities P and Q cannot start before the completion of activities N and O.
R
S
T
U
V
Converging and Sequential
Activity U cannot start before R is completed. V cannot start before R *and* S are completed. Activity T is a dummy activity.

Figure 2–12

Figure 2–13

These concepts will be used throughout the book, hence, they are discussed now. A definition will be followed by a discussion of their graphic representation.

Activities

An activity can be defined as a task or a job that consumes resources. The resources may be time, labor, or equipment, or a combination.

An activity can be represented by an arrow. The size of the arrow or the angle at which it is drawn is immaterial. However, what precedes or succeeds the arrow is crucial.

For example, consider the activities of building the walls of a house and constructing the roof. These activities can be represented as in Figure 2–12.

The arrow representing the building of the walls must precede the arrow representing the construction of the roof, since the roof cannot be constructed without the walls. The relationship of the arrows (activities) represents this sequential condition.

There are many combinations of activity relationships. These are summarized in Figure 2–13.

To indicate that R and S precede V (but only R precedes U) a dummy activity T is used to connect R and V. The dummy activity indicates the dependence of V on R but separates S from U. To indicate that the dummy activity T only signifies dependence of sequence, the dummy activity is represented by a dashed arrow.

Perhaps an illustration of a dummy activity is required. Consider, as an example, the course requirements in a high school as shown in Figure 2–14 below.

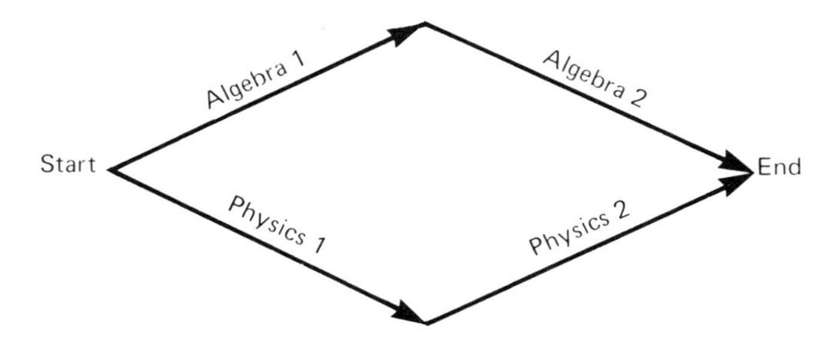

Figure 2–14

What sequence of courses can a student take? There are many possible permutations including Physics 1, Physics 2, Algebra 1, and Algebra 2. Now consider a change in curriculum that requires Algebra 1 as a pre-requisite for Physics 2. This makes the sequence above impossible. But how can this be shown in the network diagram? By using a dummy activity W between Algebra 1 and Physics 2 as shown in Figure 2–15.

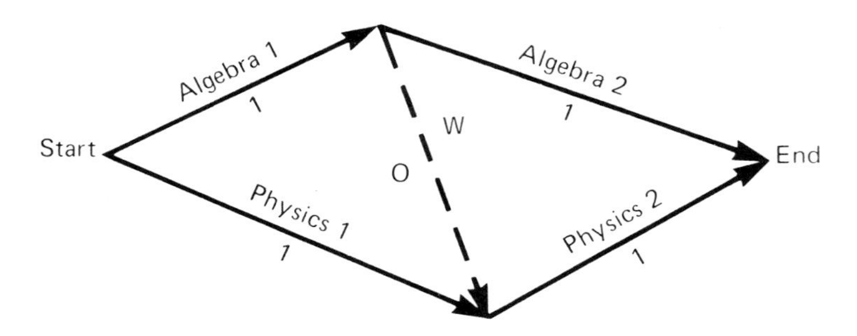

Figure 2–15

Note that the dummy activity requires no additional resources but merely imposes a restriction on the sequence of another activity. Hence, the additional activity is a dummy in terms of resource utilization and this is indicated by resource 0 under its arrow. The 1's below the other activities represent the time required for these activities, which is one semester.

Drawing Arrows

In drawing arrows to represent activities, certain rules must be followed. These are:

Rule A–1. A solid arrow represents an activity that utilizes resources.

Rule A–2. The arrow identifies the logical conditions of dependency. The angle at which an arrow is drawn is not significant. The length of the arrow, unless drawn on a time scale, is also not significant. These are determined by convenience and need of clarity.

Rule A–3. Each activity must be represented by a unique arrow. However, if part of one activity is dependent on another activity, it should be shown as two activities and two arrows. For example, consider the construction of a wall. The wooden framework must be constructed before the electrical wiring is done. In such a case, wall construction should be shown as two activities: the construction of the framework of the wall and the remaining construction of the wall. The wiring must be done between these two wall construction activities. The resulting network should appear as follows in Fig. 2–16.

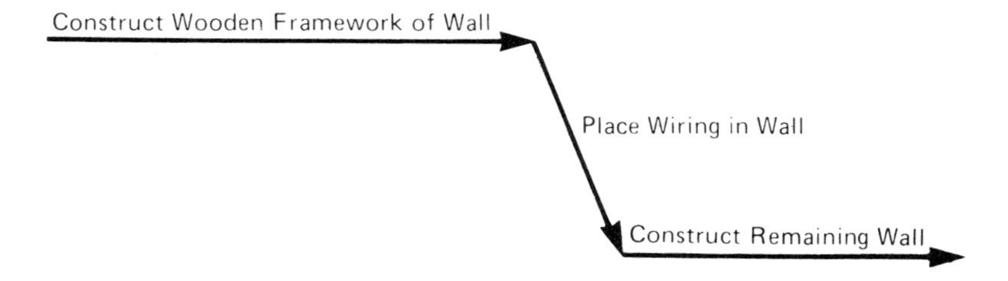

Figure 2–16. Network Diagram Example

Rule A–4. Dummy activities must be shown to complete the logic of the network, and are conventionally indicated by dashed arrows.

Rule A–5. No set of activities can form a circular loop. For example, consider Figure 2–17.

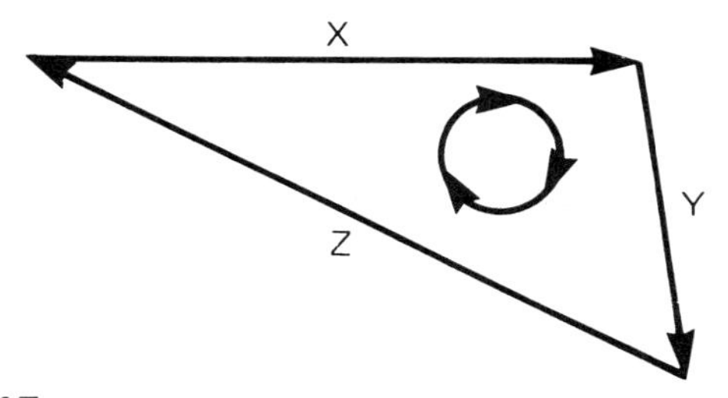

Figure 2–17

X is required for Y which, in turn, is required for Z. Therefore, X must be performed before Z starts. However, from the left hand part of Figure 2–17, Z must be completed before X starts. These conditions cannot all be met simultaneously. Hence, such a loop is not allowed.[7]

Events

So far we have represented activities by arrows referred to by symbols. They can, however, be referred to by the extremities of the arrows provided that the extremities can be referenced.

[7]This is not only a common type of error but is often time consuming in detection. Some computer programs have diagnostics for such loops. However, the programming is complicated and expensive.

To illustrate this, let us reconsider activities in Figure 2–15. Let us now number the points of interaction between activities and enclose them by circles[8] as shown in Figure 2–18.

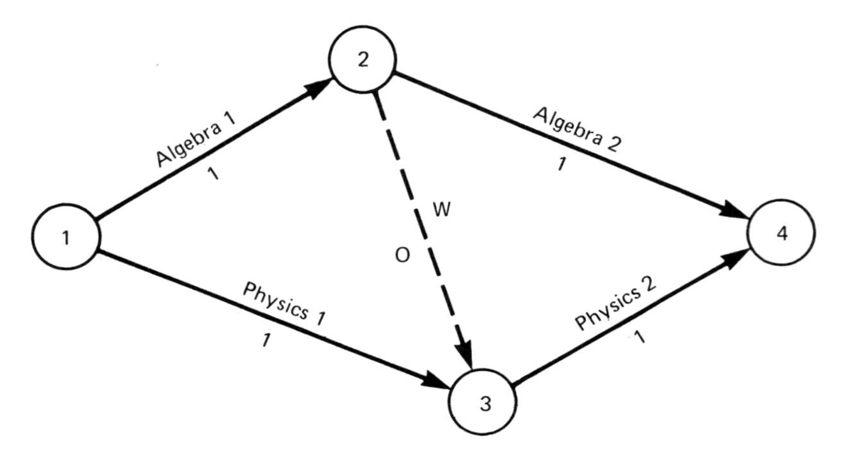

Figure 2–18

The equivalence between Figure 2–15 and Figure 2–18 is shown in Table 2–1.

Table 2–1

Figure 2–15	Figure 2–18
Algebra 1	1–2
Algebra 2	2-4
Physics 1	1–3
Physics 2	3-4
W	2–3

The activity, Algebra 1, is now represented by the extremities of Algebra 1 which are points 1 and 2. These points are the starting and ending of this activity, and are referred to as **events.** An event can be defined as representing a state of accomplishment, it may be the completion of a job or a project or it may be the start of a job or project. An event is also called a node. A

[8]There are other conventions, besides circles for drawing geometric patterns. For identification of types of activities and responsibilities for the activities, see R. L. Levin and Charles Kirkpatrick, *Planning and Control with PERT/CPM* (New York: McGraw-Hill Book Company, Inc., 1966), p. 49; J. J. Moder and C. R. Phillips, *Project Management with CPM and PERT* (New York: Reinhold Publishing Corp., 1964), p. 57; and R. D. Archibald and R. L. Villoria, *Network-Based Management Systems (PERT/CPM)* (New York: John Wiley & Sons, Inc., 1967), p. 59.

representation of the relationship of activity and event appears in Figure 2–19.

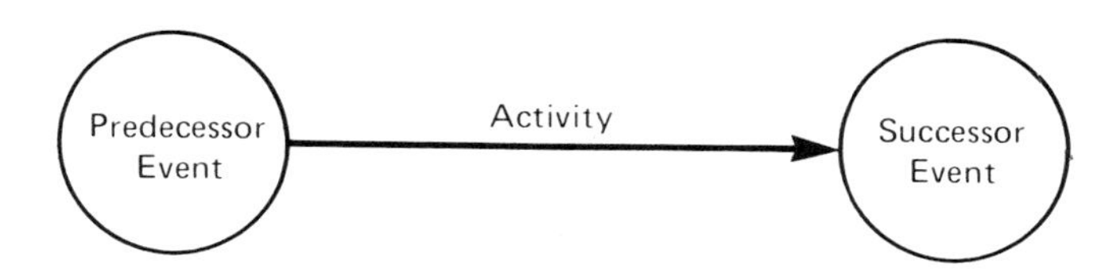

Figure 2–19

Either the activity or the event can serve the purpose of referencing. The activity orientation is also referred to as activity-on-the-arrow and was originally used in the Critical Path Method (CPM) technique. The event orientation referred to as activity-on-the node was originally used in the Program Evaluation Review Technique (PERT).

Numbering of Events

There are many rules that must be observed in the numbering of events. These are as follows:

Rule E–1. All events must be numbered.

Rule E–2. The same number cannot be used for more than one event. This is necessary so that each activity can be uniquely identified.

Rule E–3. No two events can be the extremities of more than one activity. For example, consider the two parallel activities shown in Figure 2–20.

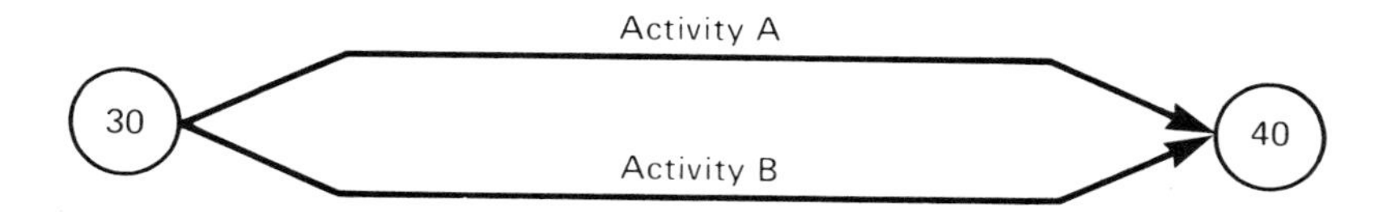

Figure 2–20

The representation in Figure 2–20 does not enable the unique identification of activities by using the event numbers (both are 30–40). To avoid this problem, an additional activity, called a dummy activity is added. It does not use any resources, as do other activities, but provides an extra event for purposes of identification. This is illustrated in Figure 2–21 where a dummy activity 30–35 is added to Figure 2–20.

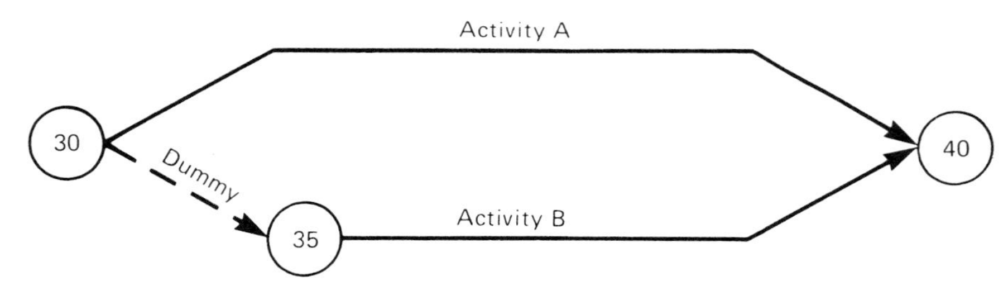

Figure 2–21

Now activity A can be identified as 30–40 and activity B as 35–40 while activity 30–35 is a dummy.

Rule E–4. Theoretically, events can be numbered in any order (increasing, decreasing, or both; such as 13, 12, 15, etc.). It is best to number them in increasing order though, because a network diagram is often programmed for a computer, and some computer programs require that each event number be larger than any predecessor event.[9] This rule is also recommended for manual work, since a manually prepared diagram may some day require a computer program.

If the above rule is followed, it is then desirable to number the events in multiples of 5 or 10. For example, an order could be 10, 20, 30, 40. This enables additional events to be added to the network (such as 11, 21, 35, etc.) and still maintain an ascending order without having to renumber the events.

Rule E–5. The start of the project and the end of the project should be identified by events and these should be numbered. This rule is required for some computer computations and enables unique identification.

Critical Path

The final concept to be introduced in this introduction of critical path diagrams, also referred to as network analysis, is that of the critical path. It

[9]For a discussion of this requirement, see A. B. Kahn, "Skeletal Structure of PERT and CPA Computer Programs," *Communications of the ACM*, VI, No. 8 (August 1963), 475–76.

can be discussed in the context of Figure 2–22 below. In it, each activity has its time duration specified below its arrow representation, and its value is in weeks.

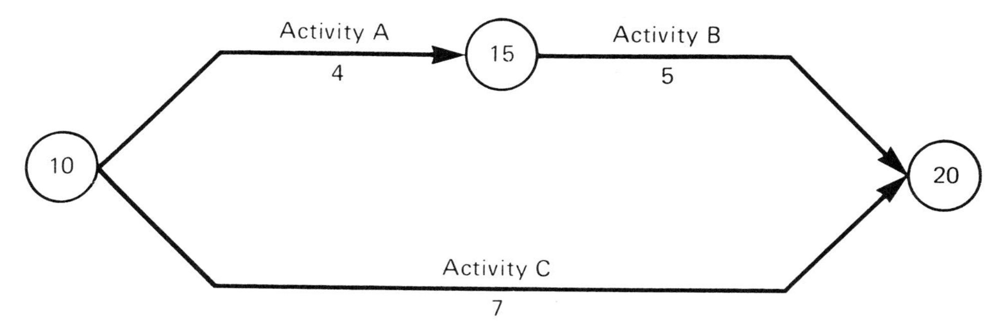

Figure 2–22

The project in Figure 2–22 has two parallel paths: 10–15–20 (activities A and B), and 10–20 (activity C). They take nine and seven weeks respectively. The project is completed in nine weeks because that is the duration of the longest path. This path is referred to as the **critical path.** Any delay in the completion of the activities on the critical path will delay the entire project.

The path 10–20 is not critical. It has time to spare. This spare time is referred to as **slack** or **float.** Its value for activity 10–20 is two (i.e. the duration required for critical path less the duration required for the path in question). If this activity is delayed two or more weeks, it will then become "critical," assuming the duration of the other path remains constant.

The critical path concept is very important in scheduling activities, and is used in two important techniques of scheduling. One is the Critical Path Method, referred to as CPM. The other is the Program Evaluation Review Technique, referred to as PERT. They differ mainly in their estimation of the time required for completing an activity. The CPM method uses one time estimate, while the PERT uses three time estimates for each activity.

SUMMARY

The first tool of analysis to be examined in this chapter is the flowchart. It represents graphically the flow and logic of a systems problem and is needed extensively for analysis, synthesis, documentation, and communication. Its use in communication was demonstrated by using it for representing the author's recommendations for reading the remainder of Part One. The flowchart will be used often throughout the book as a means of communication between the author and the reader.

A flowchart, however, has some disadvantages. It is cumbersome for complex problems; it is not easy to modify; and it does not clearly associate sets of actions with their corresponding sets of conditions. These difficulties can be overcome by another tool of analysis called the decision table, a topic to be discussed in Chapter 3.

Other tools of analysis are listed, among them project management techniques that are used extensively in the latter part of the book. The basic concepts of project management techniques are introduced and illustrated.

KEY TERMS

"Black-Box"
System
System Analyst
Computer Programmer
Control
Feedback
Regulated System
Flowchart
Network Analysis
Activity
Event
Dummy Activity

REVIEW QUESTIONS

1. Distinguish between
   a. System's Flowchart and Program Flowchart
   b. Activity and Dummy Activity
   c. Activity and Event
   d. CPM and PERT
2. What are the advantages and disadvantages of flowcharts?
3. In flowcharting, what is represented by the following symbols?
   a. Diamond
   b. Circle
   c. Rectangle
4. What is a dummy activity? List the occasions when it is used.
5. What makes a network path critical? What is the significance of a path being critical?

EXERCISES ON FLOWCHARTS

Three exercises are discussed below. Each is stated in narrative form (Cases A). These are followed by their solutions, i.e. representations, stated in flowchart form (Cases B).

Exercise 1. Assigning of Grades
Case A. Decision Rules in Narrative Form

All scores below 30% should be assigned an F grade. All scores between 35–45% should be assigned a D grade. All scores between 50–60% should be assigned a C grade. All scores between 65–75% should be assigned a B grade. All scores above 79% should be assigned an A grade.

All other scores should be identified with a special message as being "borderline" cases. These scores will be reexamined before a grade is assigned to them.

Assume that all grades are in whole numbers and not in fractions.

Exercise 2. Hiring a Secretary
Case A. Exercise in Narrative Form

Consider the decision rules for hiring a secretary, as follows:

If the candidate has a typing speed of 50 words/minute or better, a shorthand speed of 100 words/minute or better, a good reference, and a degree, she will be hired. If she is attractive, degree and reference requirements are not necessary, and even a 10% reduction of the typing and shorthand speeds is acceptable.

If, however, her typing and shorthand speeds are equal to or greater than 10% less than the hiring standards and she is not attractive but has a good reference, she is recommended to the campus personnel officer for hiring elsewhere on campus. If she does not qualify for hiring or recommendation to the Personnel Officer, she is told so and is advised to seek a job elsewhere, and the search for a secretary continues.

Exercise 3. Doctoral Degree Requirements
Case A. Exercise in Narrative Form

A secretary in the Office of the Dean of the Graduate School has to follow and control the progress of each student in a doctoral program for an Ed.D. according to the following rules:

The student must apply and be approved by the department head in order to be accepted in the program. Once he is approved, he must file a topic for his dissertation. After this filing he is allowed to take his three comprehensives in the following areas:

1. Foundations
2. Major
3. Minor

If the student fails to pass any one of his comprehensives more than once he is dropped from the program and his file is closed.

If he fails one comprehensive he can retake it, but only after a delay of one semester. After he has passed all three comprehensives he is scheduled for an oral. If he fails the oral but did not fail any comprehensives on the first try he can wait one semester and retake the oral. If he fails the oral twice, or the oral in addition to having failed one or more than one comprehensive on the first try he is dropped from the program. If he passes the oral he is awarded the degree and his file is closed.

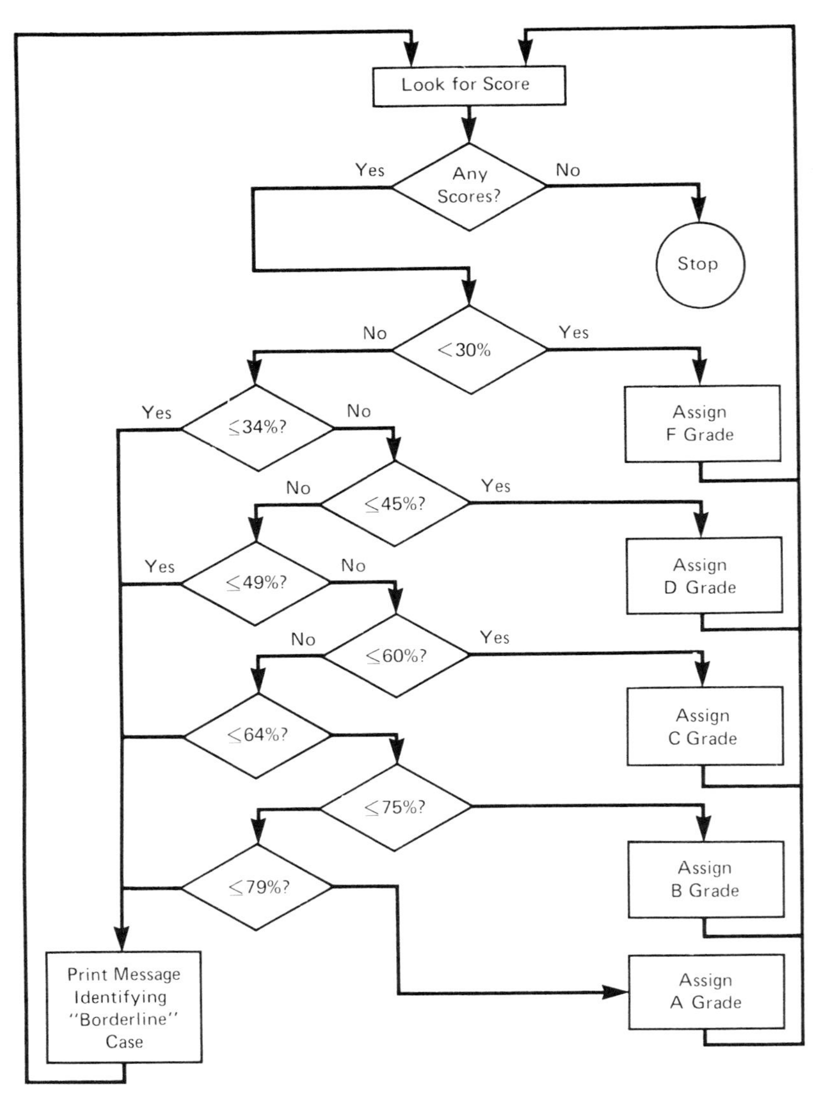

Solution to Exercise 1. Case B. Decision Rules in Flowchart Form

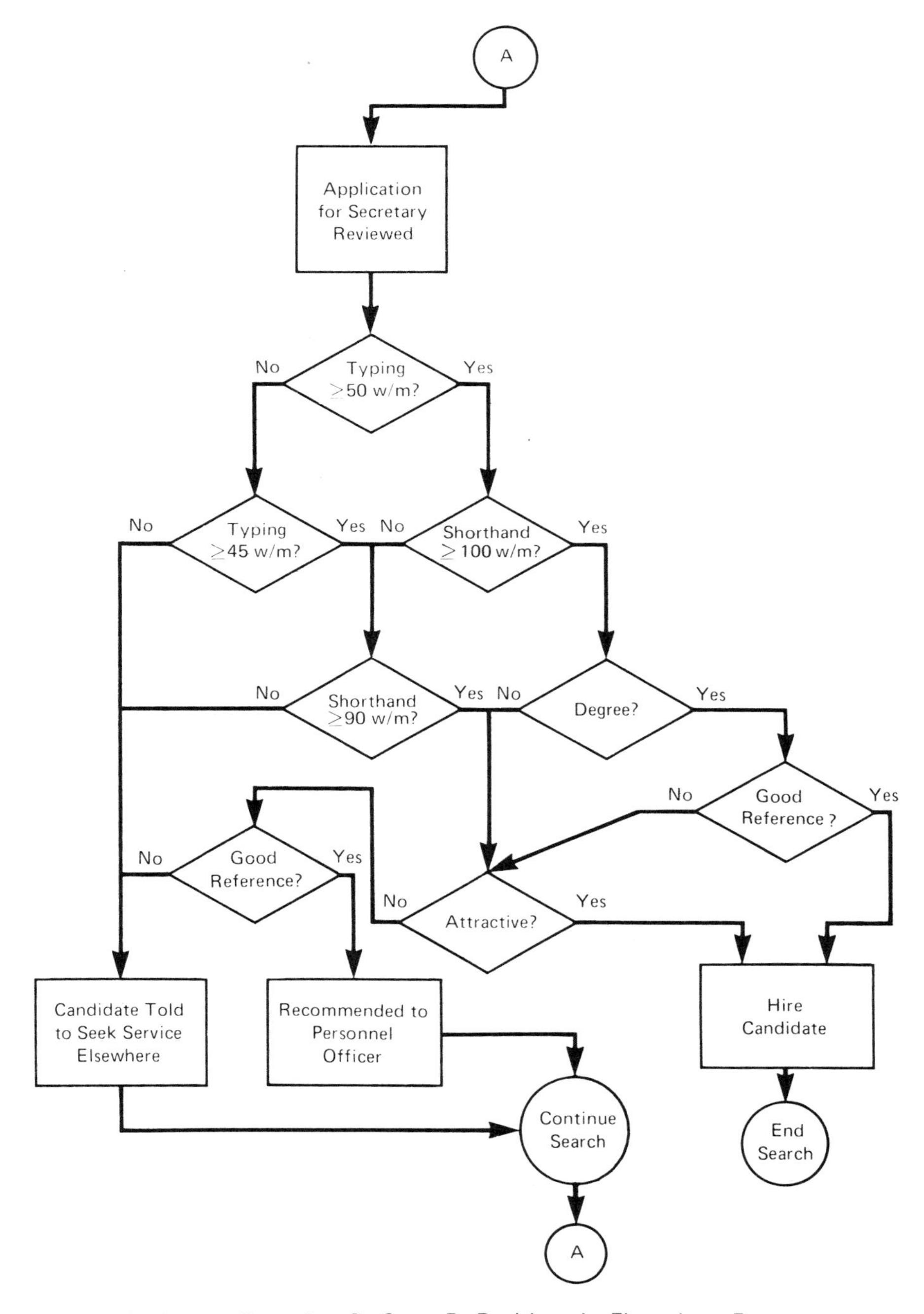

Solution to Exercise 2. Case B. Problem in Flowchart Form

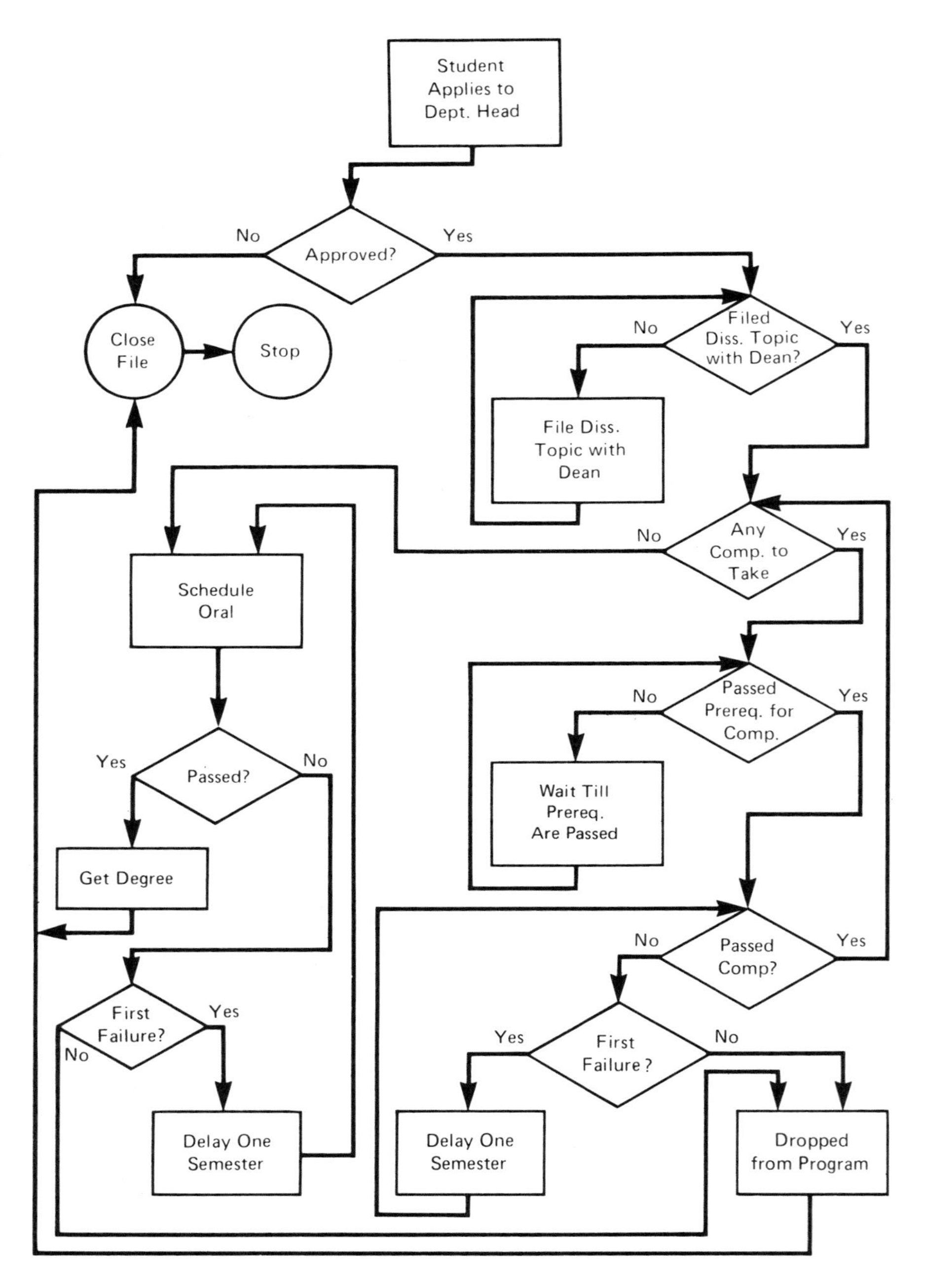

Solution to Exercise 3. Case B. Flowchart (From Viewpoint of Secretary in Graduate Dean's Office)

NOTES ON SOLUTIONS

1. In Exercise 1, it was assumed that the given values were "inclusive." For example, "scores between 35% and 45% should be assigned a D grade" was interpreted as meaning that scores of 35% and 45% should also be assigned a D grade. There are, of course, other interpretations, and this emphasizes the danger of a prose text being misinterpreted.
2. The logical decisions in the flowchart followed the order of the decision rules in the problem as stated in prose. Consequently, the resulting flowchart is not necessarily the most economical to follow from the viewpoint of a programmer.

CHAPTER 2: SELECTED ANNOTATED BIBLIOGRAPHY

Flowcharting

CHAPIN, N. "Flowcharting with the ANSI Standards: A Tutorial," *Computing Surveys,* II, No. 2 (June 1970), 119–46. The emphasis in this article is on the use of standard procedures in flowcharting. Chapin discusses standard conventions, distinguishes between system charts and flow diagrams, and presents excellent guidelines for flowcharting. The emphasis is on using flowcharts as a tool of communication between people.

IBM Flowcharting Techniques (No. C20–8152–0). White Plains, N.Y.: International Business Machines Corporation, 34. Systems flowcharts are differentiated from program flowcharts. Basic symbols and special symbols are discussed for each. Also, techniques and conventions such as cross-referencing, stripping, and decision techniques are discussed.

POMEROY, RICHARD W., "Systems Charting," in *Systems & Procedures* (2nd ed.), ed. V. Lazzaro. Englewood Cliffs, N.J.: Prentice-Hall, Inc., 1968, pp. 59–89. This article is an elementary discussion of the types of charts (including flowcharts) that can be used in systems planning. Included are comments on the economics of charting costs and a brief introduction to PERT.

Network Analysis

EVARTS, HARRY F., *Introduction to PERT.* Boston: Allyn & Bacon, Inc., 1964, pp. 17–23. An excellent introduction to network analysis. Very elementary.

HANDY, H. W., and K. M. HUSSAIN, *Network Analysis for Educational Management.* Engelwood Cliffs, N.J.: Prentice-Hall, Inc., 1969. This book has illustrations of the use of network analysis in education administration and has a good bibliography.

3

Tools of Analysis: Decision Tables

INTRODUCTION

A decision table is an alternative to a flowchart for representing the logic of a problem. In it, each set of possible alternatives is explicitly identified, with its set of desired actions. Furthermore, the logical representation is done according to specific conventions.

Decision tables will be discussed in the context of an example: the determination of scholastic action in a university. The decision rules of this problem as it may appear in the university catalog are as follows:

Scholastic action is determined at the end of each full semester. For scholastic purposes, a full semester is a regular semester (Fall or Spring) or *both* summer sessions combined. If a student has a Cumulative-Gradepoint-Average of less than 2.0 and a last semester Gradepoint-Average of less than 2.0, he is put on probation. If he has a Cumulative-Gradepoint Average of less than 1.8, irrespective of his last semester Gradepoint-Average, he is put on suspension.

The decision logic listed above can be stated in the form of a flowchart, as in Figure 3–1. There is yet another way of expressing the decision logic: the use of a table, such as shown in Table 3–1. It states the rules of decision-making in tabular form and has the *basic* format of a **decision table.** It has the advantage of being more compact and less ambiguous than either the narrative or the flowchart. It provides a clear explanation of the logic, is easier to expand or revise, and has other advantages that will be discussed later. Before that is done, however, the structure of a decision table will be briefly examined.

Table 3–1. The Scholastic Decision Problem in Table Form

	Rule 1	Rule 2
End of full semester?	Yes	Yes
Cumulative GPA < 2.0?	Yes	—
Cumulative GPA < 1.8?	No	Yes
Last semester GPA < 2.0?	Yes	—
Student put on probation	Yes	—
Student put on suspension	—	Yes

STRUCTURE OF DECISION TABLES

Reconsider Table 3–1. Looking at it vertically, we find the **condition statements** are the top rows while the **action statements** are the bottom rows. The separation is accomplished by a horizontal double line as shown in Table 3–2(a). Similarly, looking at Table 3–1 horizontally, we can divide or separate all the statements on the left, called **stubs,** from the **entries** concerning those statements on the right. This separation is accomplished by a vertical double line, as shown in Table 3–2(b).

Table 3–2. Components of a Decision Table

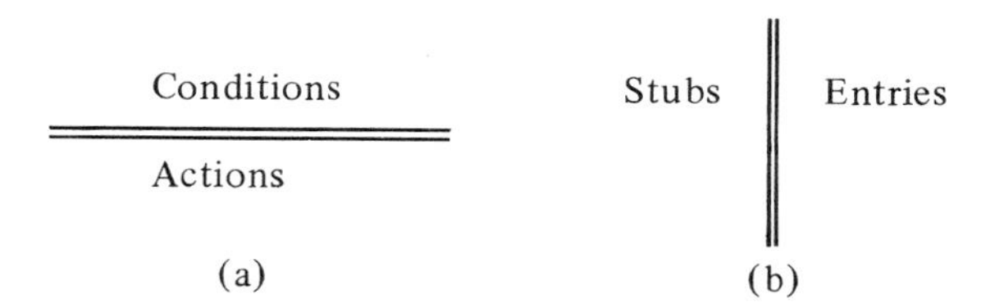

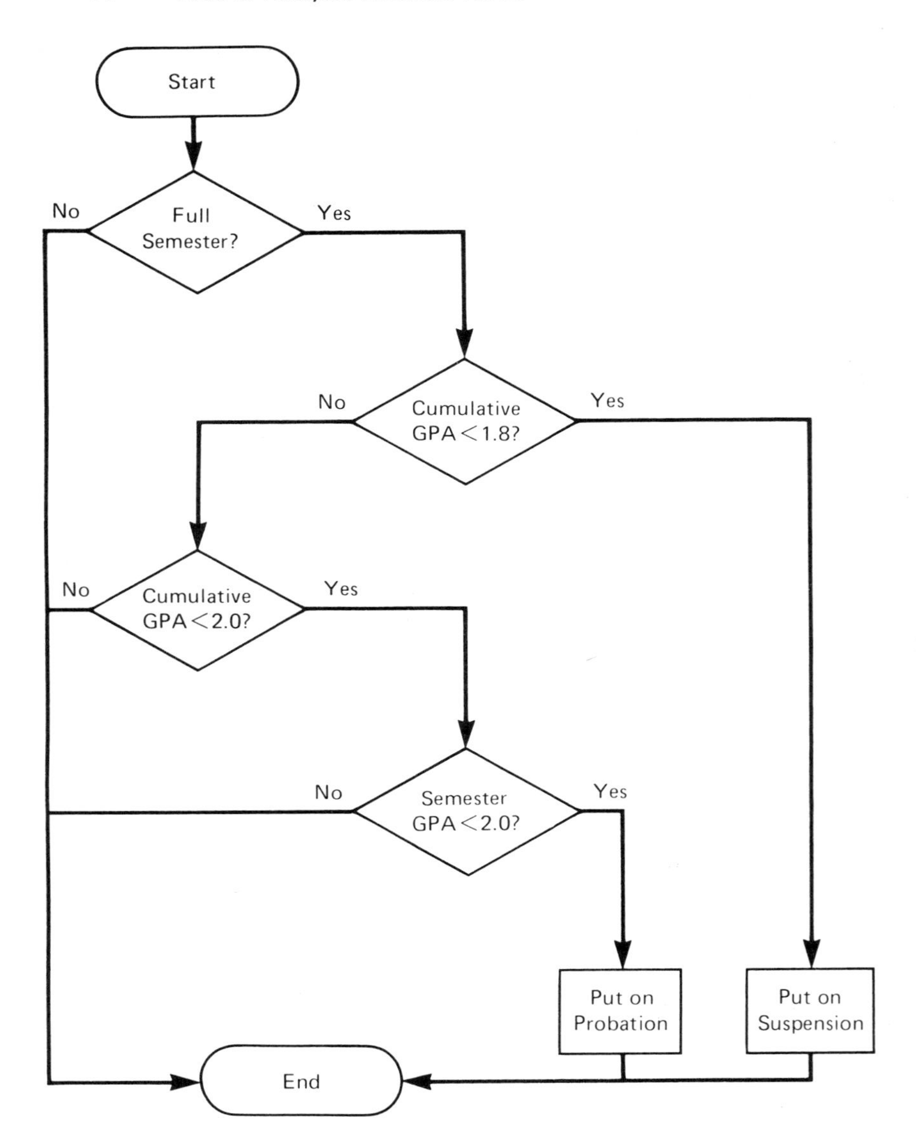

Figure 3–1. Flowchart of Scholastic Standing Problem[1]

[1]The symbol "<" represents the condition "less than"—i.e., "< 2.0" means "less than 2.0." The symbol Cum. GPA stands for cumulative gradepoint average.

The two sets of double lines in Table 3–2 are superimposed to clearly separate the components of a decision table in Table 3–3.

Table 3–3. Components of a Decision Table

Condition Stubs	Condition Entries
Action Stubs	Action Entries

The data in Table 3–1 is now superimposed on the framework of Table 3–3 giving Table 3–4. The entries "yes" and "no" are now replaced by symbols "Y" and "N" respectively. The action entry "Yes" is replaced by an "X." These are merely conventions that are commonly used.

Table 3–4. Decision Table for the Scholastic Action Rule

	Rule 1	Rule 2
End of full semester?	Y	Y
Cumulative GPA < 2.0?	Y	–
Cumulative GPA < 1.8?	N	Y
Last semester GPA < 2.0?	Y	–
Student put on probation	X	–
Student put on suspension	–	X

Table 3–5 can be looked at as a set of columns, each column representing a set of conditions associated with a specific action or set of actions. Each column is called a **rule.** Thus, Rule 1 states that *if* it is the end of a full semester, and *if* the cumulative GPA is less than 2.0, and *if* it is not less than 1.8, and *if* the last semester GPA is less than 2.0, *then* the student must be put on probation. In general terms, a **rule** states, that *if* condition 1 *and* condition 2 . . . *and* condition n are satisfied, *then* action 1 *and* action 2 . . . *and* action m must be executed. There may be any number of these rules. This is shown in Table 3–5 (with k rules).

Table 3–5 also illustrates the flexibility of the decision table for revision and expansion. Revision of existing conditions and actions can be made by changing the respective entry cells. Expansion of the rules can be made by adding columns to the table. Expansion of conditions and/or actions can be made by adding rows to the table. If the table gets too large, it can be segmented with the segmented tables linked together.[2]

Table 3–5. General Form of Rules in a Decision Table

	Rule 1	Rule 2	.....	Rule K	Rule:
Condition 1? . . . Condition n?					If all of these conditions apply
Action 1 . . . Action m					*THEN* All these actions must apply

In Table 3–5 note that a rule is composed of condition entries representing a logical **and** relationship. If one of these rules is not applicable, it is implied that the next rule should be tried, and so on, until one rule is applicable. In a decision table, only one rule should apply for any given set of conditions.

The Else Rule

What happens if all the rules do not apply? In the case of the scholastic action problem, if the rules on probation and suspension do not apply, then the student is in "good standing" and he is considered for registration without conditions arising from scholastic action. This could be specified as a separate rule called the Else Rule and is shown in Table 3–6.

The Else Rule by definition completes a table by ensuring that all possible sets of combinations are accounted for. If no Else Rule is used, there is a formal theorem that determines whether or not the table is complete. This is discussed in the Appendix.

Also discussed in the Appendix are theorems for checking for contradictions among rules and for combining some rules, thereby reducing redundancies and improving efficiency.

[2]For a discussion of linking tables, see N. Chapin, "Parsing of Decision Tables," *Communication of the ACM,* X, No. 8 (August 1967), 407–10, 512.

Table 3–6. Table Illustrating the Else Rule

	Rule 1	Rule 2	Else Rule
End of full semester?	Y	Y	
Cumulative GPA < 2.0?	Y	–	
Cumulative GPA < 1.8?	N	Y	
Last semester GPA < 2.0?	Y	–	
Student put on probation	X	–	–
Student put on suspension	–	X	–
Student with good standing	–	–	X

Limited Entry Table

In all the above tables, the entry is limited to a simple symbol "Y" or "N" or "X" or a dash "–." The dash condition entry indicates that the testing of this particular condition (for that rule) is immaterial, and a dash action entry indicates that the action in question is not to be executed.

Because all entries are "limited" to one character in this table, it is called the **limited entry table.**

Extended Entry Table

In some cases, the condition, or action, variable may have many alternatives. Each alternative could, of course, be represented by a horizontal row, but this would make for a cumbersome table. This problem is overcome by stating the condition in the stub in its general form and "extending" its *value* into the entry position of the table. Such an entry is termed an **extended entry.**

As an example, consider the condition relating to the cumulative GPA shown as limited entries in all the tables above. This could be stated as an extended entry, as done in Table 3–7.

Table 3–7. Table with Extended and Limited Entries

	Rule 1	Rule 2	Else Rule
End of full semester?	Y	Y	
Cumulative GPA	2.0	1.8	
Last semester GPA <2.0?	Y	–	
Student put on probation	X		
Student put on suspension		X	
Student with good standing			X

Mixed Entry Table

In Table 3–7, the condition variable of cumulative GPA is stated in the condition stub while the value of the variable is extended into the entry part of the table. Similarly, an action could be extended into the entry part of the table. A table with all such entries (for the condition or action) is called an **extended entry decision table.** Table 3–7, however, has both types of entries (limited and extended) and, hence, is called a **mixed entry table.**

For a given condition in the mixed entry table, a set of entries could be either "limited" *or* "extended." This is so because in extended entry, the stub identifies only the variable and not the value of the variable. Hence, for such a stub a limited entry would be meaningless. Similarly, the stub for a limited entry specifies the value of the variable and, hence, an entry other than a limited one of Y or N would be meaningless.

Reviewing the discussion on the types of decision tables, it can be said that a limited entry table is used when all the decision variables have a response of "yes" or "no," such as male or female, married or unmarried, and personnel available or not available. When the variables have numerous values the extended entry is used. Examples of such variables are: value of GPA, age, and marital status where it is necessary to know not only whether a person is married or unmarried, but also whether the person is a divorcé, a divorcée, a widow, or a widower. However, many decision problems have variables that are neither entirely of the limited nor the extended type, but are mixed entries. Examples in education would be problems in updating files—hiring of personnel, determination of a student's scholastic standing—and inventory control —determination of tax deduction and computation of insurance premiums.

The example chosen in this chapter of the scholastic action case is a realistic one, but the problem as stated is a simplified one. In many actual situations, the conditions for scholastic action are many and may include variables such as the level of the student, the college in which he is registered, the number of semester units taken, and even his potential as a football player. In such complex cases, the comparative advantage of the decision table over the flowchart and the narrative is much greater.

ADVANTAGES OF DECISION TABLES

In the above discussion, some advantages of decision tables were explicitly stated, others were implied. For purposes of emphasis and reference, these are all formally stated below:

1. A decision table has a standard format for problem definition in which each set of conditions and its set of actions are clearly and unambiguously identified.
2. The decision table is concerned with the logic of the decision rules. In contrast, the flowchart indicates the logic (though less clearly) as well as the sequence of steps necessary for computer programming. Thus, the flowchart is programming-oriented while the decision table is problem-oriented. The decision table can be converted to flowcharts before programming, and, in some programming languages, the decision table is directly incorporated in the computer program, thereby, reducing programming costs.
3. The structure of a decision table enables a logically complete and consistent definition of the problem, thereby eliminating the danger of incomplete and inconsistent program logic.
4. Decision tables can be easily checked for redundancies, thereby leading to possible economies in implementing decision tables.
5. The format of decision tables facilitates easy expansion, contraction, or revision of the logic.
6. Decision tables are a useful tool for systems analysts, not only in stating the logic of the problem and in documentation,[3] but also in analysing decision rules which arise during the development of an information system (this will be discussed further in Chapter 11).
7. Decision tables are an effective means of communication, not only between programmers and analysts, but also between systems personnel and administrators.
8. Decision tables aid an administrator in checking the decision rules, resulting in greater accuracy and completeness of the solution.

SUMMARY

A decision table is a set of decision rules in which each rule identifies a set of conditions with its set of actions.

Decision tables are of three types:

1. Limited Entry
2. Extended Entry
3. Mixed Entry

The limited entry table specifies both the variable and the value in the condition stub, but the extended entry specifies the variable in the condition

[3]For a further discussion of this subject, see D. L. Fisher, "Data, Documentation and Decision Tables," *Communications of the ACM,* IX, No. 1 (January 1966), 26–31.

stub and the possible values in the condition entry portion of the table. The mixed entry table has both "limited" and "extended" entries.

Each type of decision table has a prescribed standard format with the following component sets:

1. Condition Stubs
2. Action Stubs
3. Condition Entries
4. Action Entries
5. Rules

The relationship of the above components is shown in Table 3–8 below.

Table 3–8. Components of a Decision Table

	Rule 1	. . . .	Rule n
Condition Stubs	Condition Entries		
Action Stubs	Action Entries		

The sets of conditions resulting in sets of actions are all identified by symbols in a column of entries. These constitute a decision rule. A set of such decision rules constitutes a decision table representing all the possible logical sets of conditions with their corresponding sets of actions.

The decision table relates its conditions to its corresponding actions, thereby graphically and clearly identifying the logic of the decision rules. It is easy to construct and read. It enables an easy modification of the logic.

It is important for the administrator to know how to use decision tables because often it is he alone who can check the decision-making logic.

Decision tables can be tested for redundancy, contradiction, and completeness, which contributes greatly to their effectiveness. The rules for such testing are somewhat mathematical and are hence discussed separately in Appendix A.

KEY TERMS

Decision Table
Decision Rule
Stubs
Entries

Else Rule
Conditions
Actions
Limited Entry
Extended Entry
Mixed Entry

REVIEW QUESTIONS[4]

1. What are some main advantages of decision tables over flowcharts?
2. Distinguish between:
   a. Limited Entry and Extended Entry Table
   b. Limited Entry and Mixed Entry Table
   c. Simple Decision Rule and Complex Decision Rule
   d. Condition Stub and Action Stub
   e. Condition Entry and Action Entry
3. List some of the advantages and limitations of a decision table.
4. What are the four main components of a decision table and their relationship to each other?
5. What are some applications in your functional field in which decision tables offer a comparative advantage?
6. Make a complete decision table for one of the applications listed in Question 5.
7. What is meant by the term "parsing" and some techniques for using it? (Hint: Refer to bibliography for applicable article.)

EXERCISES ON DECISION TABLES

Prepare decision tables for each of the exercises in Chapter 2; either from the narrative (Cases A) or from the flowchart (Cases B). The reader can then compare his results with solutions that appear below (Cases C).

From the point of view of preparing decision tables, the three exercises are of increasing complexity. The first exercise requires a limited decision table; the second lends itself to the use of an extended decision table; and the third requires reference to a table within a table.

In solving the third exercise, the following information may be helpful: a "perform" action can be used to execute another table. After one of the rules in the performed table is satisfied, control is returned to the next action in the original table with the perform action.

Exercise 1
Case C: Decision Rules in Decision Table Form

	Rule 1	Rule 2	Rule 3	Rule 4	Rule 5	Else Rule
Grade less than 30%	Y	N	N	N	N	
Grade between 35-45%*	N	Y	N	N	N	
Grade between 50-60%*	N	N	Y	N	N	
Grade between 65-75%*	N	N	N	Y	N	
Grade above 79%	N	N	N	N	Y	
Assign F grade	X					
Assign D grade		X				
Assign C grade			X			
Assign B grade				X		
Assign A grade					X	
Give message of "border-line" case						X

*Inclusive values are assumed.

Exercise 2
Case C: Exercise 2 in Decision Table Form

	Rule 1	Rule 2	Rule 3	Rule 4	Rule 5	Else Rule
Typing speed	$\geq$ 50 w/m	$\geq$ 50 w/m	$\geq$ 45 w/m	$\geq$ 45 w/m	$\geq$ 50 w/m	
Shorthand speed	$\geq$ 100 w/m	$\geq$ 100 w/m	$\geq$ 90 w/m	$\geq$ 90 w/m	$\geq$ 100 w/m	
Has degree?	Y	N	—	—	N	
Reference is good?	Y	—	—	Y	Y	
Is attractive?	—	Y	Y	N	N	
Hire	X	X	X			
Recommend to Personnel Officer				X	X	
Ask candidate to seek job elsewhere						X

Can these two simple rules be combined into one?

Exercise 3
Case C: Decision Tables

Table 1

	Rule 1	Rule 2	Rule 3	Rule 4	Rule 5
C1: Approval of dept. head	N	Y	Y	Y	Y
C2: Filed diss. subject to dean	–	Y	Y	N	N
C3: Passed prerequisite courses for a comprehensive	–	Y	N	N	Y
Satisfy C2				X	X
Satisfy C3			X	X	
Perform Table 2		X	X	X	X
Close file for student	X	X	X	X	X

Table 2

	Rule 1	Rule 2	Rule 3	Rule 4	Else Rule
Passed first comp. on 1st try?	Y	Y	Y	N	
Passed second comp. on 1st try?	Y	Y	N	Y	
Passed third comp. on 1st try?	Y	N	Y	Y	
Wait for one semester		X	X	X	
Perform Table 3		X	X	X	
Schedule for oral	X				
Perform Table 4	X				
Drop from program					X
Exit	X	X	X	X	X

Exercise 3
Case C: Decision Tables, continued

Table 3

	Rule 1	Rule 2
Passed comprehensive on 2nd try?	Y	N
Schedule for oral	X	
Perform Table 4	X	
Drop from program		X
Exit	X	X

Table 4

	Rule 1	Rule 2	Rule 3	Rule 4
Failed one comprehensive?	N	Y	N	Y
Passed oral on 1st try?	Y	Y	N	N
Confer degree	X	X		
Wait one semester			X	
Perform Table 5			X	
Drop from program				X
Exit	X	X	X	X

Table 5

	Rule 1	Rule 2
Passed oral on 2nd try?	Y	N
Confer degree	X	
Drop from program		X
Exit	X	X

NOTES ON SOLUTIONS

1. In Exercise 1, it was assumed that the given values were **inclusive** values. This is the same assumption made for the solutions to exercises given at the end of Chapter 2.

2. The typical decision rules in some cases follow the order of the decision rules stated in prose (Case A). Consequently, the resulting decision rules in some instances are simple decision rules and can be combined for greater efficiency.

CHAPTER 3: SELECTED ANNOTATED BIBLIOGRAPHY

ANSHEN, MELVIN, "The Manager and the Black Box," *Harvard Business Review,* XXXVIII, No. 6 (November-December 1960), 85–92. This is a general discussion of how computers and mathematical decision-making techniques will affect management. In this book there is a classification of management decisions by function including structured versus unstructured.

CHAPIN, N., "Parsing of Decision Tables," *Communications of the ACM,* X, No. 8 (August 1967), 507–10. An excellent presentation of the parsing technique for reducing large decision tables to smaller and more manageable tables. Clear examples aid the reader in following and visualizing the linkage between parsed decision tables and factors which affect decision-table parsing.

CHESEBROUGH, W. C., "Decision Tables as a Systems Technique," *Computers and Automation,* 19, No. 4 (April 1970), 30–33. This is a clear introduction to decision-table symbology, construction, and compression. Decision tables are presented as a method of business problem analysis.

DIXON, PAUL, "Decision Tables and Their Application," *Computers and Automation,* XIII, No. 4 (April 1964), 14–19. Here is an excellent treatise on the fundamentals of decision tables and their applications. Included are 11 advantages of decision tables, and an extensive bibliography.

FISHER, D. L., "Data Documentation and Decision Tables," *Communications of the ACM,* IX, No. 1 (January 1966), 26–31. A technical description is provided of several tabular approaches to documentation, and how these techniques can aid in systems management. Recommended reading for those familiar with the use of decision tables.

POLLACK, S. L., "Conversion of Limited-Entry Decision Tables to Computer Programs," *Communications of the ACM,* VIII, No. 11 (November 1965), 667–82. Two algorithms intended to aid in the efficient conversion of decision tables into computer programs are presented. One is a method for converting a decision table into a flowchart, and the other is a method for conversion of a decision table into a computer program.

SANDERS, D. H., *Computers in Business: An Introduction.* New York: McGraw-Hill Book Company, Inc., 1968, Chap. IX, pp. 187–206. Both flowcharts and decision tables are discussed along with the advantages and limitations of each. Recommended reading for gaining an initial insight into these tools of analysis.

SHOBER, J. A., "Decision Tables for Better Management Systems," *Systems & Procedures Journal,* XVII, No. 2 (March-April 1966), 28–33. The author gives a general presentation on the advantages of decision tables and their worth as logic-following aids. Included is a brief comparison between decision tables and flowcharts.

part two

INTRODUCTION TO INFORMATION SYSTEMS

Before discussing the development of an information system, it is necessary to know some basic concepts and terms associated with information systems. These will be defined and examined in the next three chapters.

Chapter 4 defines the concept of a system and identifies its components. The concept of system environment and boundary are explained, along with some rules for determining the boundary. Objectives and constraints of a system are discussed, along with control and feedback. Finally, the concepts of an "integrated" and "total" system are examined and critiqued.

Chapter 5 begins with a comparison of two basic elements of an information system: data and information. The concept of an information system is then defined and its uses are discussed. Desirable attributes of information are developed. This is followed by a discussion of the types of information systems and the various modes of processing.

The American Airlines information system is discussed in detail in the last section of this chapter. This example provides a framework for important aspects of design and development which will be discussed later in this book.

Chapter 6 discusses the functions of an information system. These are identified as record-keeping, control, institutional research, planning, and top decision-making. Each of these functions and their demands on an information system are discussed with special reference to the context of educational administration.

The discussion of information systems in Part Two is largely functional. There are theoretical[1] and mathematical[2] formulations of information systems, but these are beyond the scope of this book.

[1]B. Langefors, *Theoretical Analysis of Information Systems* (Kobenhavn: Acadamisk Forlag, 1966), I and II, 400 pp. and 400 pp.

[2]R. B. Briggs, *A Mathematical Model for the Design of Information Systems* (Master's thesis, University of Pittsburg, 1966), p. 88.

4

Systems: Some Basic Concepts

INTRODUCTION

The term **system** is used in many contexts. In the natural sciences we speak of the solar system, molecular systems, and ecological systems. Discussing the human body, we can identify the circulatory system and the central nervous system. In daily life we encounter political systems, communications systems, highway systems, and many others. In all contexts, the word system denotes an assemblage of components or an order. One group of authors defines a system as "an organized or complex whole, an assemblage or combination of things or parts forming a complex or unitary whole, . . . it will be helpful to define systems more precisely as *an array of components designed to accomplish a particular objective according to plan.*"[1]

[1]R. A. Johnson, F. E. Kast, and J. E. Rosenzweig, *The Theory and Management of Systems* (2nd ed.) (New York: McGraw-Hill Book Company, Inc., 1967), p. 113

This definition identifies the important concepts that characterize systems of the type to be discussed in this book: an assemblage of components forming a whole, designed for an objective and organized according to a plan.

In this chapter, the components of systems will be discussed, and system boundaries and subsystems defined. Various classifications of systems will be examined. The concepts of integrated systems and the total system are discussed. The examples used for illustration will be mostly those that will contribute to an understanding of systems using computers for processing information in an educational institution.

COMPONENTS OF A SYSTEM

The basic components of a system are: inputs, processor, feedback, control, and outputs. The three components to be discussed first are: input, processor, and output. These are illustrated in the block diagram in Figure 4–1.

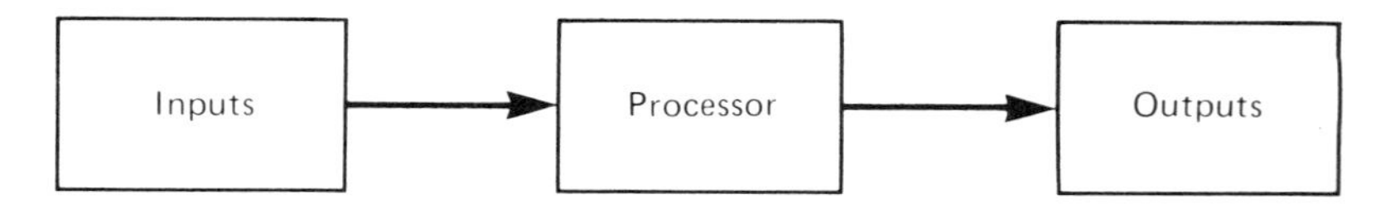

Figure 4–1

Using an educational institution as an example of a system, the inputs would include students, materials, equipment, and informational input such as policies, objectives, and teaching methods. The processor would be the faculty and administrators who execute the transformation rules (teaching, research) required for the conversion of the input into desired outputs (graduates, products of research, and public service).

System components will be illustrated by examining a computer system. Its input component consists of data and instructions telling the computer how to process the data. The processor is called the Central Processing Unit (CPU). The CPU has three parts: (1) the arithmetic and logic unit, (2) the memory or storage unit, and (3) the control unit. This is illustrated in Figure 4–2. The arithmetic and logic unit performs the arithmetic operations (such as addition and multiplication) and logical operations (such as comparison). These operations are performed on data input which is stored in the memory or storage unit until it is ready to be processed. Also stored are the instructions concerning the computations to be performed, intermediate calculations, and other information related to the transformation of input. Once all the necessary computations are performed the output is generated.

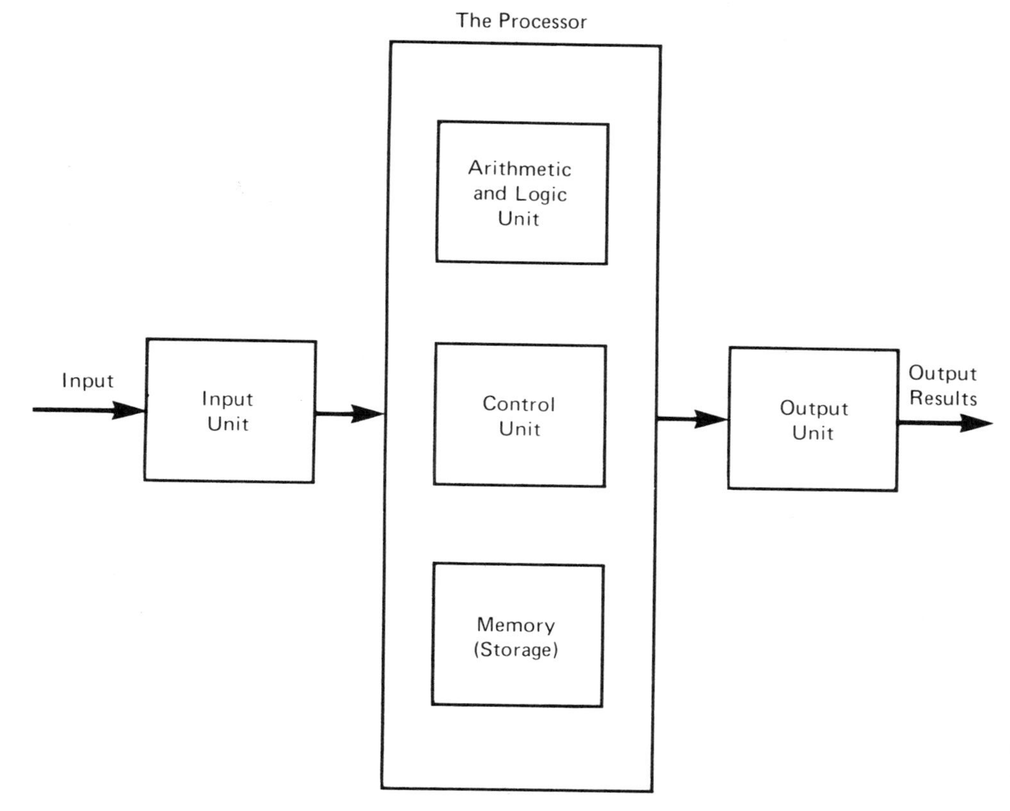

Figure 4–2. The Organization of a Computer System

The control unit in the processor performs the coordinating and monitoring of all other units, including the input and output units. It performs "control" in the sense that it compares the actual state with the desired state (the state which was specified in the instructions) and takes appropriate action to meet the desired state.

The functions performed by a computer are very similar to those performed by a human. Consider a human being calculating the gradepoint average (GPA) for a student at the time of admission. The components in this manual computation system are illustrated in Figure 4–3.

The human (usually a clerk) receives the input in the form of a transcript. She identifies and selects the data elements required for the computation (function of the control unit in a computer) and records these on a scratch pad (corresponding to a memory unit in a computer) if they are lengthy. The selected data elements are operated upon according to a set of decision rules

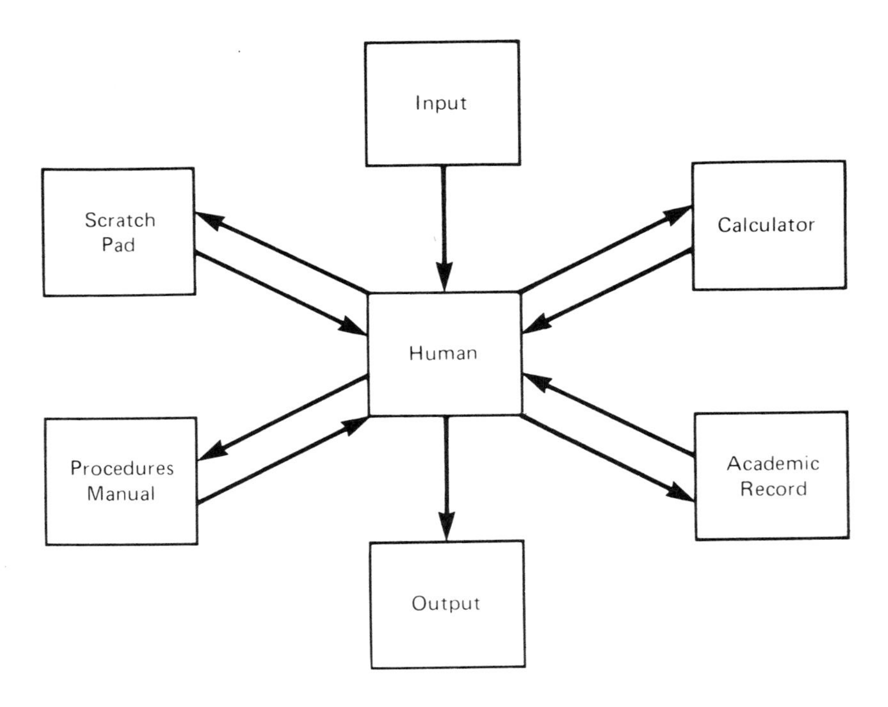

Figure 4–3. Organization of Human Computation

stated in a procedures manual (stored in a computer as instructions). The computations can be done on a desk calculator (corresponding to the arithmetic and logic unit in a computer). The intermediate calculations may be stored on a scratch pad until needed. The human mind then selects the appropriate arithmetic or logical operations to perform. (For example, in one institution, the human operator may find that a student has taken more than five units in physical education and, following procedures at that institution, the additional units will not be added to the units taken for GPA purposes. This corresponds to a logical operation in the computer.) After all computations are done, the GPA is recorded on his academic record (on a memory device) and the results listed as output needed for further action in the admissions process.

The human operator and the computer have equivalent functions and components but each has its relative advantages. In the case of the GPA computation, a clerk can spot special cases and make adjustments accordingly. Many of these rules and adjustments can be programmed into a computer, but some cannot. Humans have the advantage over computers in unstructured jobs where all the variables cannot be measured and where decision rules are not quantifiable. But this inability of a computer is more than compensated for by its many advantages. It is faster, more accurate, and more reliable for jobs that are clearly specified in terms of logic. Thus both "heuristic man" and the "algorithmic machine" have their respective advantages. Each must be assigned tasks that it accomplishes best. As Norbert Wiener put it:

> Render unto man the things which are man's and unto the computer the things which are the computer's. This would seem the intelligent policy to adopt when we employ men and computers together in a common undertaking.[2]

The problem is that of identifying the respective roles of man and the computer, a subject that will be discussed repeatedly in future chapters, especially in Chapter 11.

Objectives and Constraints

For the design of any effective and efficient system, the input must include information on objectives as well as the expected constraints.

There is an important distinction between an objective and a constraint. An objective is a variable value that can be either underfulfilled or overfulfilled, with benefits usually accruing if overfulfilled. For example, an objective of an institution may be that of having 200 graduates next year. If the actual result is more, the objective is overfulfilled and the system benefits. In contrast, a constraint has a limiting value that cannot be violated. If the constraint is overfulfilled, there is usually no resulting benefit. For example, a building may have only six classrooms, which constitutes a constraint that no more than six classes can be scheduled at any one time in that building. If the constraint is overfulfilled, that is less than six classes are held simultaneously, there is no resulting benefit. (The less wear and tear on an unused room has a benefit of negligible value.)

There are many examples of objectives in an educational institution: graduates, research, and service to the community. One difficulty with these objectives is that many of them cannot be measured. For example, how can one measure a university's contribution to the knowledge of its graduates? Or the contribution of a research report? Another problem is getting agreement on the weights assigned to each objective. For instance, how much more important is it to have a Ph.D. student than an undergraduate student? Or a graduate in Chemistry compared to one in Fine Arts? These problems will be discussed further in Chapter 12.

Constraints are mainly financial such as the availability of funds, or physical such as the availability of buildings or equipment. Sometimes policies constitute constraints, where policies can be defined as rules made by top administration. For example, a policy may state that no more than one person

[2] N. Wiener, *God & Golem, Inc.* (Cambridge, Mass.: The M.I.T. Press, 1964), p. 73.

from a family may be employed in the same department or institution. This then becomes a constraint on employment.

Information on objectives, policies, and constraints must be provided by the administrators who are the users of the system. These are represented in Figure 4–4 as inputs to the system, along with other inputs that are self-explanatory. These are labor, materials, data, and processing instructions.

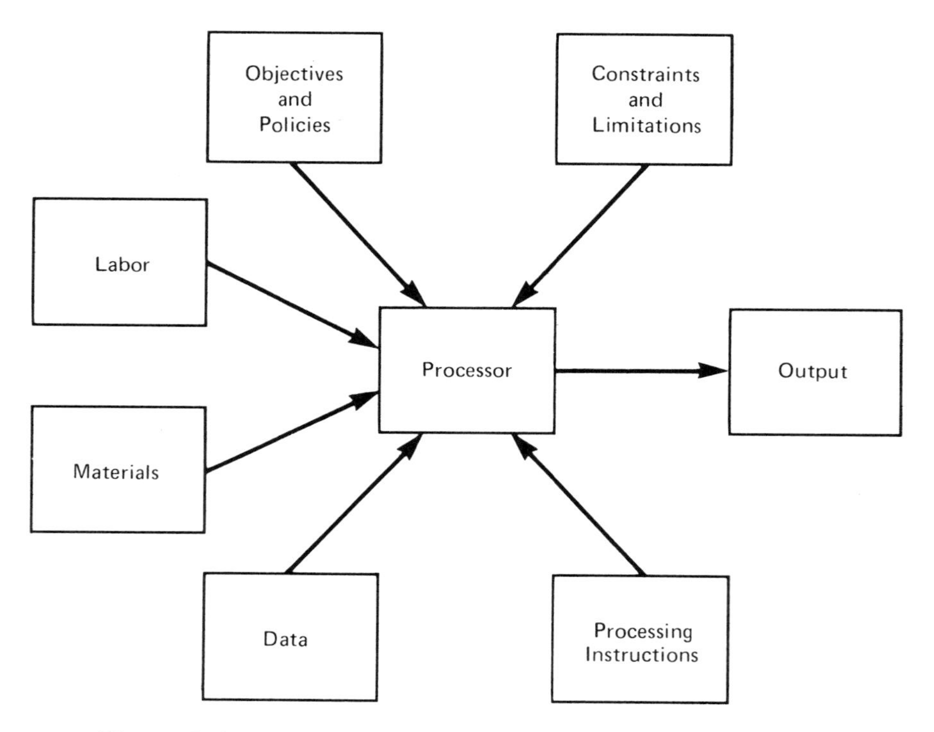

Figure 4–4. A System Showing Input and Output Components

Control and Feedback

The achievement of a single output at a point in time is not sufficient for a continuing system. The system must continue to perform according to the objectives and planned performance levels. Deviations beyond allowable tolerances must be detected (sensed) and corrected quickly and effectively. This can be done by a feedback mechanism, which is an essential part of the control function—the comparison of actual with desired performance and the initiation of appropriate corrective action. The feedback mechanism, when properly designed and used, will often anticipate undesirable deviations, triggering corrective actions that will eliminate the causes of such deviations prior to their occurrence.

A simplified control system is illustrated in Figure 4–5. The initial actions are shown by the set of continuous lines from goal-setter to output. The output is checked by a **sensor** which compares its deviations from the desired output against allowable deviations set by the controller. Deviations greater than those allowed are reported to the controller, which then takes appropriate action modifying the input which in turn modifies the output. These modified actions are shown by the dashed lines. This cycle should be continuous during the life of the system. It enables the output to stay within specified limits decided upon by the controller, who in turn operates within the objectives and constraints specified by the top administrator (shown by continuous lines from goal-setter to controller and sensor).

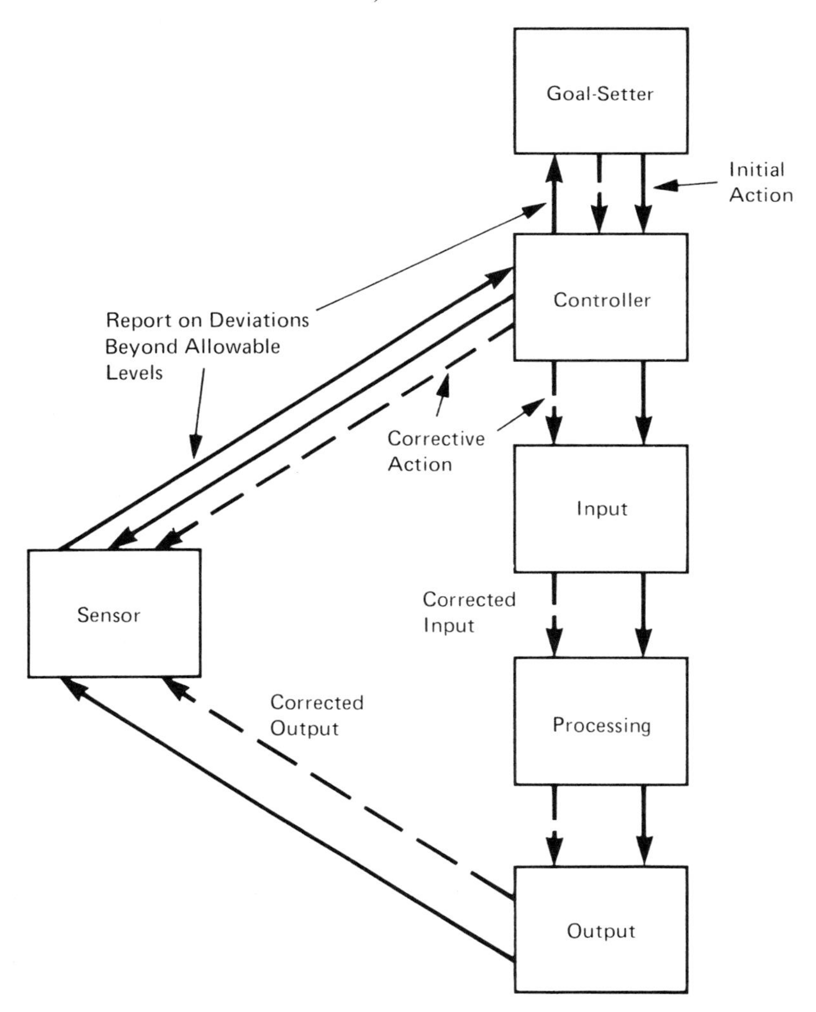

Figure 4–5. A Simplified Feedback System

In Figure 4–5 the administrator is the goal-setter. In an educational institution this may be a university president, high-school principal, or a board of trustees. The controller could be a vice-president, a dean, or director of services. (In a small organization or system, the goal-setter and controller may be the same person.) His corrective action may be to make changes in the quantity or quality of inputs, such as different sets of labor, equipment, and informational inputs. If the changed resource configuration is insufficient to achieve desired performance levels, then the performance levels or resource availabilities must be adjusted by the goal-setter. This information must be conveyed to the sensor through the controller as shown by the dashed lines from goal-setter to controller and controller to sensor. The sensor could be a staff or line person responsible for monitoring system performance, such as a supervisor or clerk making observations. These observations must be planned and scheduled or else an uncontrolled system may go undetected and do considerable harm.

The goal-setter and controller may receive information from sources outside the system to supplement information received from within the system. For the sake of simplicity these are not shown in Figure 4–5.

THE BOUNDARY CONCEPT

A system has been defined as an assemblage of components forming a complex or unitary whole. The extent of a system is confined by a **boundary.** Robert Chin discusses the boundary as follows:

> The boundary of a system may exist physically: a tightly corked vacuum bottle, the skin of a person, the number of people in a group, etc. But, in addition, we may delimit the system in a less tangible way, by placing our boundary according to what variables are being focused upon. We can construct a system consisting of the multiple roles of a person, or a system composed of varied roles among members in a small work group, or a system interrelating roles in a family. The components or variables used are roles, acts, expectations, communications, influence and power relationships, and so forth, and not necessarily persons. . . . In small groups we tend to draw the same boundary line for the multiple systems of power, communications, leadership, and so on, a major advantage for purposes of study.
>
> In diagnosing we tentatively assign a boundary, examine what is happening inside the system and then readjust the boundary, if necessary. We examine explicitly whether or not the "relevant" factors are accounted for within the system, an immensely practical way of deciding upon relevance. Also, we are free to limit ruthlessly, and neglect some factors temporarily, thus reducing the number of considerations necessary to be kept in mind at one time. The variables left outside the system, in the "environment" of the system, can be introduced

one or more at a time to see the effects, if any, on the interrelationship of the variables within the system.[3]

Drawing System Boundaries

There are many approaches to drawing system boundaries. One is to draw a boundary that incorporates all the basic elements and components of the known system. Usually, the first of the components that is known is the output. The rest may be unknown at first, as illustrated in the block diagram in Figure 4–6. The unknown components are shown with question marks. These must be specified to complete the system.

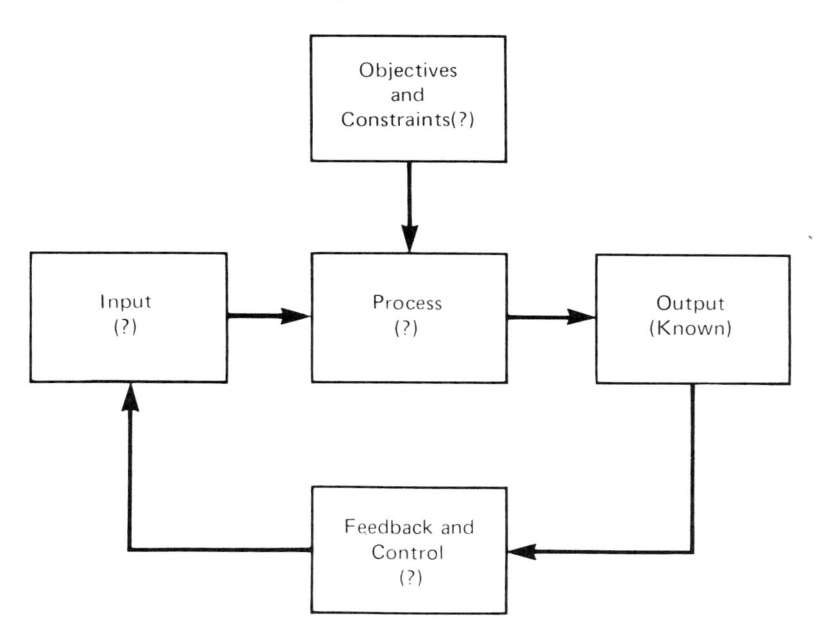

Figure 4–6. Known and Unknown Components of a System

In specifying the components of the system, there is the danger of including too much, resulting in a system that is too large to be handled effectively. Reconsider the problem of computing gradepoint averages. If the processor chosen was a computer system, it may well be determined that the incremental cost for other related computations is negligible and should also be processed.

[3]R. Chin, "The Utility of Systems Models and Developmental Models for Practitioners," in W. G. Bennis, K. D. Benne, and R. Chin, *The Planning of Change* (New York: Holt, Rinehart, and Winston, Inc., 1961), pp. 203–4.

Soon the stated objectives may be restated as being the determination of students on probation and suspension. Extending this further, it may be logical for the information system to register and schedule the student. And so the system expands. Unless this expansion is carefully planned, the system becomes overextended and uncontrollable.

When specifying the input component, it may be considered necessary to include in the system the sources of income, which for many institutions are state funds. The input component then includes the state legislature. For some institutions, income sources include federal funds, in which case the input component includes the House and Senate in Washington, D. C. In certain years even that is not sufficient. For example, the war in Vietnam has affected not only the federal source of income but also the flow of students to higher education. Thus, the foreign commitments of the country must also be considered. Such an extension is, of course, impractical from the viewpoint both of the institution's resources and of technology. The system must then be reduced to a manageable size and scope. All inputs and all outputs cannot always be included in the system. The selection of which variables to include is difficult but is sometimes made easier by using a network diagram. The guiding rule here is that of minimizing the intersections of the boundary with inputs and outputs, but still including most relevant activities.

As an illustration, consider the network of activities shown in Figure 4–7.

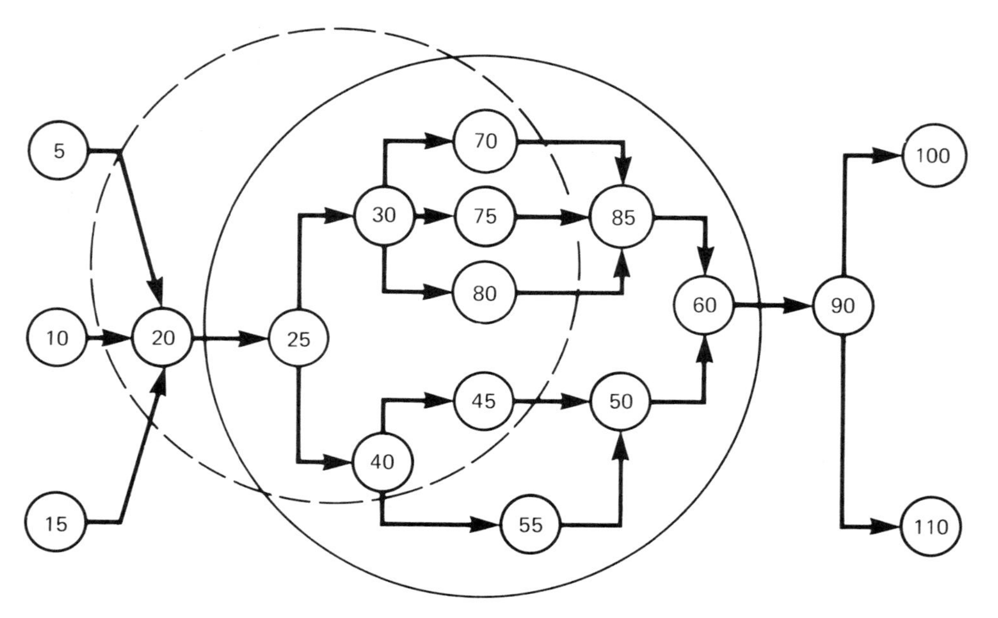

Figure 4–7. Boundaries of a System

For illustration purposes two boundaries have been drawn. Many others are, of course, possible. The dashed boundary has three inputs (three activities coming into the system encircled by the boundary) and five outputs (the activities going out). The boundary drawn with the continuous line has only one input (activity 20–25) and one output (activity 60–90). This reduces the system's relations with its environment to one input and one output and still includes all other interrelated activities. Therefore, it is a better boundary than the one shown by the dashed line.

The analyst drawing boundaries is not always so fortunate in finding such obvious solutions as the one in Figure 4–7. Fortunately for him, there are many occasions where he has no choice. The boundary is dictated by constraints of time and physical resources. On other occasions, the boundaries of the system are defined by the administrator, and the analyst is asked to investigate and solve the problems in that system. As Hoag states it, this course

> is the natural one for an administrator to take, for he is charged with looking after an organization whose boundaries will usually have been defined. But it is only accidentally a natural course for an analyst. And for him it is often a dangerous course, because administratively determined systems will be too narrow for some problems, leading to bad analyses through unduly restrictive criteria, and too broad for others, leading to unnecessarily complicated analyses. Administrative and analytical definitions of systems each have their rewarding but usually separate places. They will, I suspect, only occasionally coincide.[4]

The drawing of a boundary is often a compromise between the desire to include all the relevant variables and relationships, and the constraints imposed by the organization. It should be done jointly by the administrator and the analyst.

SUBSYSTEMS

Subsets of systems with certain properties are called **subsystems.** They too have components similar to systems, but their objectives are restricted to functions and subgoals. For an example of subsystems, consider the computer system discussed earlier. It has four subsystems: the memory unit, the control unit, the arithmetic and logic unit, and the input and output unit. The input and output could be separate subsystems, but since they are similar in their operations and in the equipment they use, they are often treated as one subsystem.

Subsystems are part of a hierarchy, or are possibly systems themselves. Thus, in an automobile system an engine is a subsystem, but to an engine mechanic, an engine can also be considered a system with its own subsystems

[4]M. W. Hoag, "What is a System?," *Operations Research,* V, No. 3 (June 1957), 445.

such as the cooling subsystem, the electrical subsystem, and the internal-combustion engine subsystem. Whether an entity is considered a system or subsystem depends on its location in the hierarchy and on which part of the hierarchy is being examined. For example, in an educational setting, if a specific educational institution was being studied, it would be a system, but if its state's educational system was being studied, that institution would be a subsystem.

Drawing Subsystem Boundaries

The problems and approaches to drawing boundaries for a subsystem are similar to those for systems, except for the problem of scale. This can be illustrated by reconsidering Figure 4–7 as it appears in Figure 4–8. Dashed boundaries are drawn within a system boundary. Each dashed boundary identifies a group of interrelated activities with one input and one output each. They are interconnected at events 25 and 60 which are part of the system. Within the dashed boundaries, however, they are independent of each other and constitute subsystems. Thus, in drawing subsystem boundaries, one should look for groups of interrelated activities and draw the boundary around the groups, while minimizing the intersections of the subsystem with inputs and outputs.

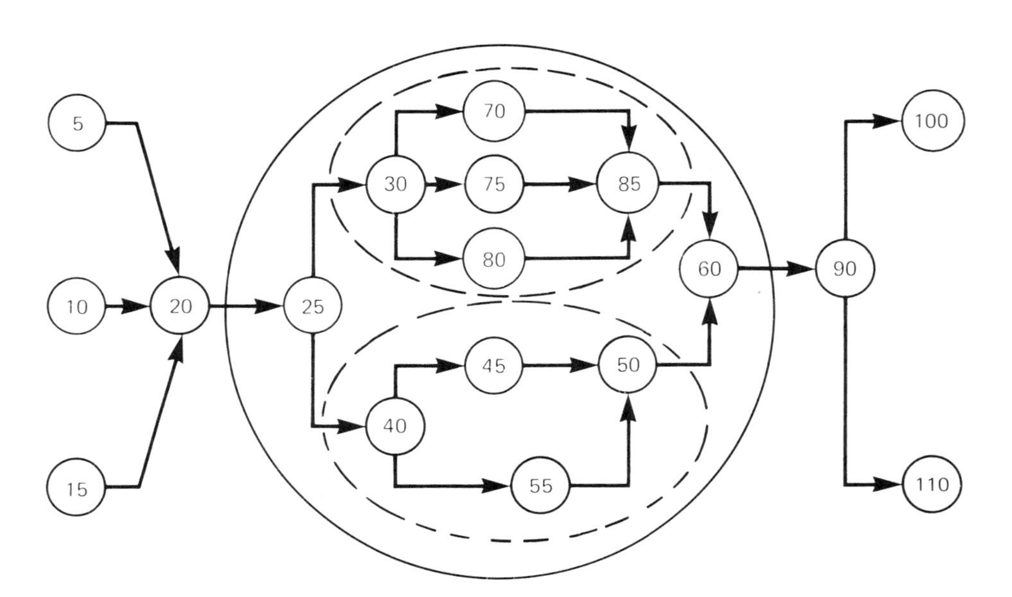

Figure 4–8. Boundaries of Subsystems

INTEGRATED SYSTEMS

With systems divided into subsystems, problems of coordination and compatability between subsystems arise. They should be united and coordinated in order to achieve system effectiveness. The unification of subsystems within a system is referred to as **integration.**

The nature and advantages of integration can be explained by the illustration in Figure 4–9.

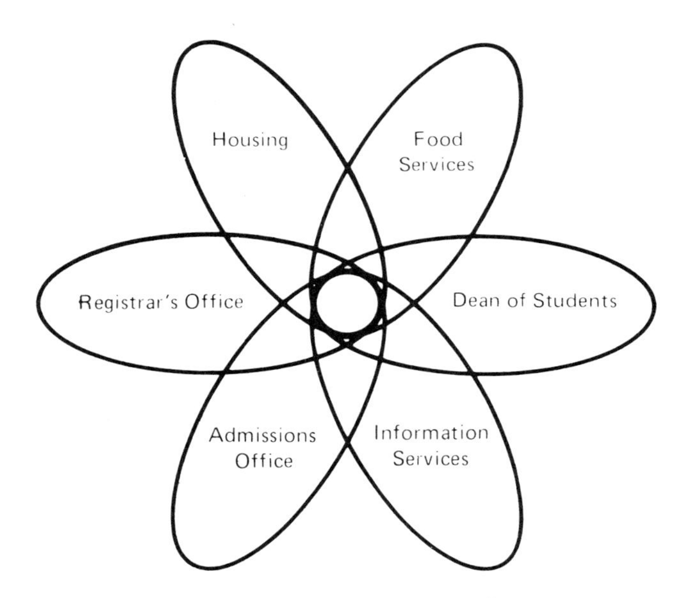

Figure 4–9. An Unintegrated Information System

It identifies the many subsystems that handle student information in a university. Each subsystem needs information unique to itself but there is some information common to all the subsystems. The common information is represented by the area where subsystems overlap in Figure 4–9. The figure is not to scale and is simplified in that it doesn't identify all subsystems, such as the Police Department wanting information on students' cars, or the Business Office, the Testing and Counseling Center, etc. It does, however, illustrate the existence of an overlapping part which enables integration.

Horizontal Integration

All of the subsystems in Figure 4–9 require some common basic elements, such as name, address, sex, college, and major of student. In addition, they need elements unique to their functional needs. To provide this, many institutions require that the students fill out a packet of separate sheets or cards, in some cases up to 20 different documents, which are distributed to each of the subsystems that maintain their own processing systems. These documents are not only processed separately but updated and maintained separately. This duplication results in a great waste of effort for the institution. It also means a great waste of effort for each student, who must enter the overlapping part of the documents repeatedly. The university treats the student as a "free good." His time does not cost the university anything but the extra effort does represent a social resource. If that extra effort were priced at even the minimum federal wage, the bill would stagger many an administrator. He can reduce and eliminate this wastage by integrating the system. Such a design is illustrated in Figure 4–10.

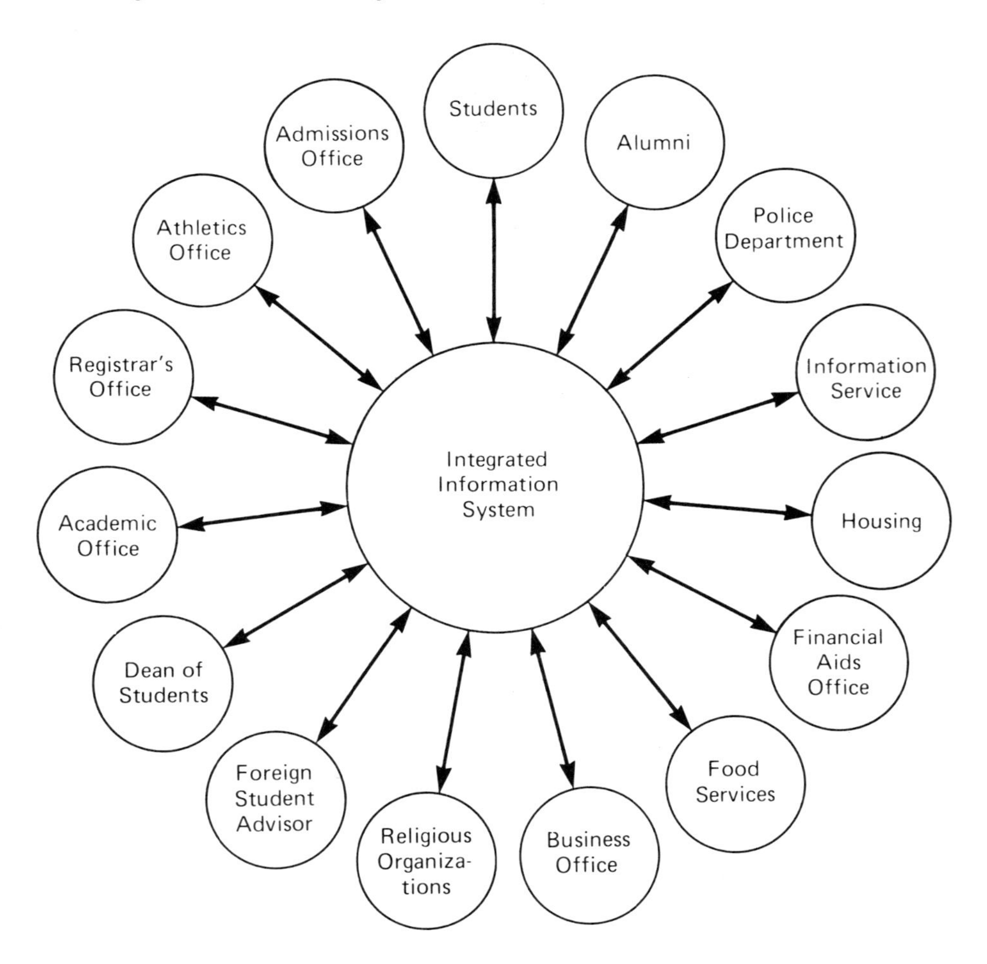

Figure 4–10. An Integrated Information System

The student in this system provides the required information only once. Other subsystems may also contribute some information. In Figure 4–10 the Registrar's Office provides information on the courses offered. All of this information is processed once and the different subsystems then get the information they need and are authorized to receive. The effort spent in collecting and processing the information is greatly reduced. Another advantage is that the raw data is processed according to standardized definitions and procedures, which leads to consistency of information.

The system integration could also be applied to subsystems external to the system. This is shown in Figure 4–11.

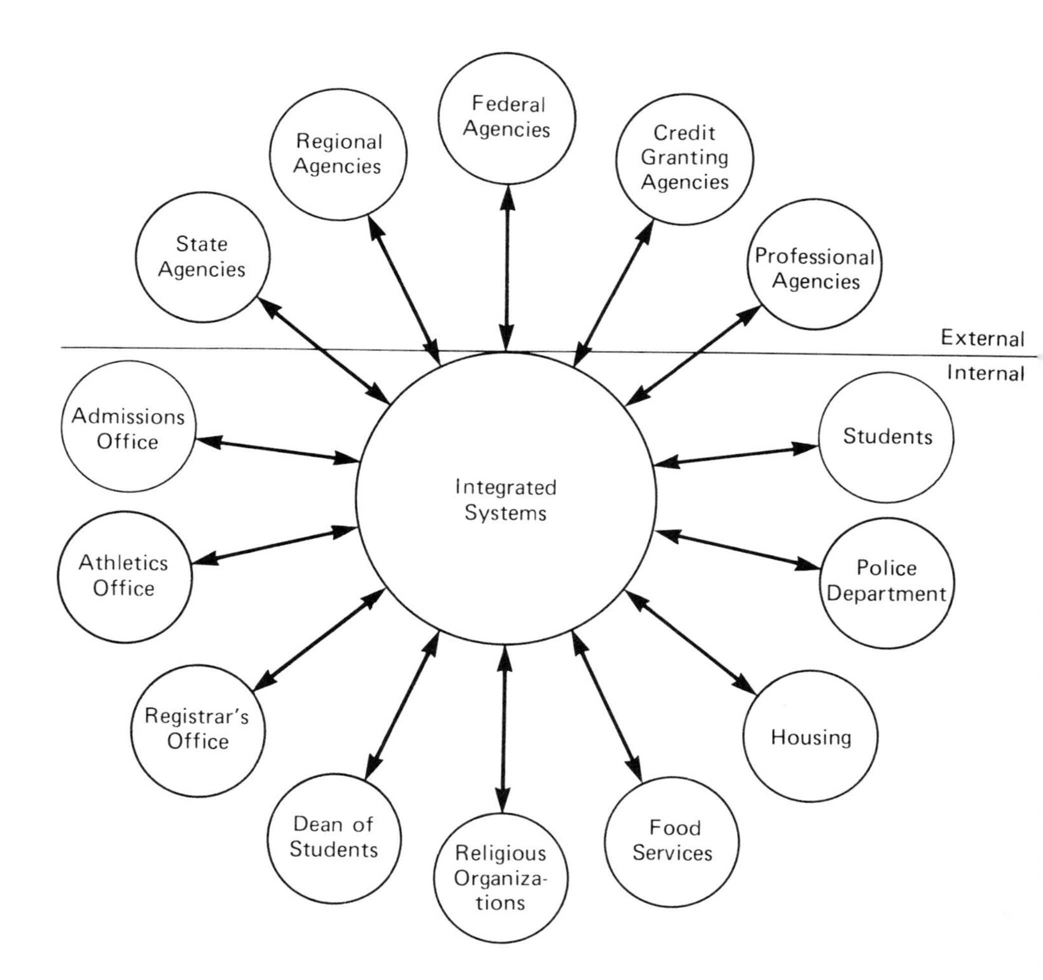

Figure 4–11. Integration of Internal and External Subsystems

The type of integration illustrated in the above example has all been at the same level, that of processing. This is known as **horizontal integration.**

Vertical Integration

Another type of integration is vertical integration, where an earlier point of production (input) and a later point of production (output) are integrated.

The concept of vertical integration is well known to industry. For example, a steel firm integrated its different plants horizontally so that their production was complementary. But it soon learned that to control quality and insure continued production it needed a good supply of iron ore, so it bought iron-ore mines. It then bought coal mines to make certain of its other raw material. This ensured the quality of its steel but did not guarantee a market for it, so it started its own retail outlets and so on. This is known as **vertical integration.**

In a university system concerned with information, there are similar needs for vertical integration. An information processing center receiving machine-readable input prepared elsewhere (for example, punched cards that can be directly read by a computer) may find that its input is prone to error. The only way to ensure error free input may be for the information processing center to generate its own input. Hence, it takes over the work of preparing data in machine-readable form and integrates the source of its data. In terms of output, vertical integration would require that the administrator know how to use and utilize the output for purposes of planning and decision-making. However, before he can use the output, he must receive it promptly, which means that the output distribution system may have to be integrated, which is another example of vertical integration.

Longitudinal Integration

Another dimension of integration is the time dimension. We are interested not only in system performance as of today, but as of yesterday, and even five or ten years ago. This information is needed for record purposes and for predicting future values of variables such as student enrollment, staffing patterns, and curricula programs. Such integration is known as **longitudinal integration.**

Total Systems

A system can be integrated horizontally, vertically, and longitudinally. An example is the American Airlines reservation system. It is longitudinally integrated because it carries information on its reservations from the time of reservation to the time the seat is used. It is horizontally integrated by including the entire process of reservation for all of its reservation agents. It is somewhat vertically integrated because the system includes subsystems related to reservations, such as the subsystem that reports on the availability of planes. The problem is that in spite of such integration, all its needs are not satisfied. The reservation agent now requires information on the reservation status of other airlines in the U.S. which send passengers to and are sent passengers by American Airlines. Soon the demand will increase further to include foreign airlines, and so the system keeps growing.

The demand for integration has escalated to the point where there is now a demand for one system integrating all other related systems and subsystems. This integration is of all types (horizontal, vertical, and longitudinal) and includes all types of information (record-keeping and decision-making) and is at all levels (operational, control, and top administrative). Such a system is often referred to as a "total system."

Some writers in the field feel that there are few if any total systems[5] and that they are not feasible because the necessary effort and technology is not available.[6] Crowley is more emphatic.

> In the past ten years, there have been many dreams of attaining the goal of *total integration,* but up to this date it is still a dream. . . . I do visualize *total integrated* systems that will collect, digest and deliver decision-inspiring data to management, but only that which can be generated from the flow of activities carried on by the firm's own employees, that is data relating to inventory, availability and price; manpower availability and cost; sales and deliveries, and so on.
>
> I do not visualize total integrated systems that will synthesize for management decision purposes all the facts relating to ambient political, economic, and other factors that the management would like to have at its fingertips in order to remove all hazards from business projections and decisions.[7]

The impracticalities of achieving a total system in the design of systems, however, doesn't preclude the desirability for planning in that direction. Schoderbek argues for planning for "a total system approach even though such a procedure appears to be a highly ambitious project and to approximate utopian proportions. Unless this approach is pursued there will be much duplication of inputs at diverse hierarchial levels and in functional areas as well."[8]

[5]R. L. Ackoff, "Management Misinformation Systems," *Management Science: Applications* (Series B), XIV, No. 4 (December 1967), B–147.

[6]W. M. A. Brooker, "The Total Systems Myth," *Systems and Procedures Journal,* XVI, No. 4 (July-August 1965), 28–32 for a critical view on "total systems."

[7]W. J. Crowley, "Can We Integrate Systems Without Integrating Management," in *The Computer Sampler: Management Perspectives on the Computer,* eds. W. F. Boore and Jerry R. Murphy (New York: McGraw-Hill Book Company, Inc., 1968), pp. 269–81.

[8]P. P. Schoderbek, ed., *Management Systems: A Book of Readings* (New York: John Wiley & Sons, Inc., 1967), p. 109.

OTHER SYSTEMS TERMS

One final set of concepts associated with the term system is **systems analysis** and **systems design.** These concepts will now be defined.

Systems analysis is a technique of analyzing and evaluating systems alternatives facing decision-makers. Borko has defined systems analysis as being "a formal procedure for examining a complex process or organization, reducing it to its component parts, and relating these parts to each other and to the unit as a whole in accordance with an agreed-upon performance criterion. *Systems design* is a synthesizing procedure for combining resources into a new pattern."[9]

The technique of systems analysis was used extensively in the Department of Defense under Secretary McNamara. The term is often used synonomously with cost-effectiveness, cost-benefit analysis, and even operations research.[10] The confusion can be reduced by identifying the characteristics of systems analysis, as done by Fisher.

1. A fundamental characteristic is the systematic examination and comparison of alternative courses of action that might be taken to achieve specified objectives for some future time. Not only is it important to systematically examine all of the relevant alternatives that can be identified initially, but also to *design additional ones* if those examined are found wanting.[11] Finally, the analysis, particularly if thoroughly and imaginatively done, may frequently result in modifications of the initially specified objectives.
2. Critical examination of alternatives typically involves numerous considerations; the two main ones are assessment of the cost (in the sense of economic resource cost) and the utility (the benefits or gains) of each of the alternatives being compared to attain the stipulated objectives.
3. The time context is the future—often the distant future (five, ten, or more years).
4. Because of the extended time horizon, the environment is one of uncertainty —often great uncertainty. Since uncertainty is an important facet of the problem, it should be faced up to and treated explicitly in the analysis. This means, among other things, that wherever possible the analyst should avoid the exclusive use of simple, expected value models.
5. Usually the context in which the analysis takes place is fairly broad (often very

[9]H. Borko, "Design of Information Systems and Services," in *Annual Review of Information Science and Technology,* ed. C. A. Cuadra (New York: Interscience Publishers, 1967), II, p. 37.

[10]A book on "Systems Analysis" by Gonzalez and McMillan is actually not a book in Systems Analysis, as the term was used originally in the Defense Department, but really a book on Operations Research using simulation.

[11]E. S. Quade, Military Systems Analysis (The RAND Corporation, January, 1963), RM–3452–PR, p. 1.

broad) and the environment complex, with numerous interactions among the key variables in the problem. This means that simple, straightforward solutions are the exception rather than the rule.

6. While quantitative methods of analysis should be utilized as much as possible, because of items (4) and (5),[12] purely quantitative work must often be heavily supplemented by qualitative analysis. In fact, I stress the importance of *good* qualitative work and of using an appropriate combination of quantitative and qualitative methods.
7. Usually the focus is on research and development and/or investment type decision problems, although operational decisions are sometimes encountered. This does not mean, of course, that operational considerations are ignored in dealing with R&D and investment type problems.[13]

SUMMARY AND CONCLUSIONS

In this chapter a system was defined and its components discussed. The components include the physical components (input, processor, and output); the goals and objectives to be achieved (provided as input); the feedback and control necessary to make performance conform to the objectives; and the human components, which include administrators who set the goals, controllers, sensors, and workers who operate the system. These components are designed as a "whole" to make a system work according to a development plan.

The term, system, connotes order and organization. It represents a frame of mind and framework of the interrelated whole for solving problems. This theme will be developed and demonstrated in later chapters of this book.

Also discussed were system boundaries, which define the limits of a system. Boundaries can be selected aribtrarily, but one choice of a boundary is made by identifying the one which intersects the least amount of inputs and outputs, but still includes enough activities for system effectiveness.

Subsystems, which are parts of systems, were defined. A subsystem consists of related activities and is a subset of the system. There is a hierarchy of systems and subsystems; some subsystems are also systems with their own subsystems. Whether a system is considered a system or a subsystem depends on which part of the hierarchy is being studied.

A very important concept discussed was integration of systems. Three types of integration were explained: horizontal, vertical, and longitudinal.

[12]And also because of inadequate data and information sources.

[13]G. H. Fisher, *The Analytical Bases of Systems Analysis,* P–3363 (Santa Monica, Ca.: RAND Corporation, May 1966). Also printed in D. I. Cleland and W. R. King, *Systems, Organizations, Analysis, Management: A Book of Readings* (New York: McGraw-Hill Book Company, Inc., 1969), p. 207.

Integration is the coordination of subsystems to prevent overlapping and duplication. In horizontal integration, the system is integrated at one level, such as processing. All subsystems which perform processing are coordinated so that no subsystem does the same processing as another. In vertical integration, a system is integrated from an earlier point of production (input) to a later point of production (output). Longitudinal integration brings in the time dimension. The system is integrated with what has occurred in the past because this is necessary for record-keeping and making predictions for the future.

The total system was defined. A total system is integrated horizontally, vertically, and longitudinally and includes the totality of related variables. Other concepts defined were systems analysis and systems design.

The discussion of systems in general provides the conceptual background for a discussion of a special type of system; an information system. This is the topic of the next chapter.

KEY TERMS

System
Input
Output
Processor
Objective
Policy
Constraint
Feedback
Subsystem
System Boundary
Integrated System
Horizontal Integration
Vertical Integration
Longitudinal Integration
Total System

REVIEW QUESTIONS

1. Distinguish between
   System and Subsystem
   Objective and Constraint
   Objective and Policy
   Policy and Constraint
   Horizontal Integration and Vertical Integration
2. What is the need for control? How is it performed?
3. What is the role of the human component in a system?
4. What principles should be followed in defining a system boundary?
5. What are the advantages and problems of system integration?
6. Is it desirable and practical to strive for a total system? Why?

CHAPTER 4: SELECTED ANNOTATED BIBLIOGRAPHY

BEYNON, R., "The Total Systems Concept: Research Implications," *Data Processing for Education,* V, No. 11 (December 1966), 1–6. This article was presented at the 1966 National Conference on State Educational Information Systems and consists of four very readable parts: (1) systems definition, (2) systems theory, (3) systems principles, and (4) research implication. Ten system principles are discussed which, if carefully followed, the author believes should result in a system design that should produce expected results.

CHURCHMAN, C. W., *The Systems Approach.* New York: Dell Publishing Co. Inc., 1968, 243 pp. This extremely readable text contains excellent discussions on "systems" thinking, efficiency, and some basic considerations for systems. Included is an example of how management scientists incorporate models and simulation techniques to aid in decision-making. Further, the discussion of management information systems gives broad guidelines for feasibility, reliability of data, security, and validity of user's requirements. An annotated bibliography is included.

CROWLEY, W. J., "Can We Integrate Systems Without Integrating Management," *Journal of Data Management,* IV, (August 1966), 4–18, 23–24. Mr. Crowley believes that it doesn't make much difference how we answer the question "Can we integrate systems without integrating management?" We are going to progress toward integrated systems, i.e., systems which will: (1) supply historical data and analysis of that data; (2) supply "on-line" data, that is, factual material picked right out of the system as fast as it is generated, and (3) supply data in "real time" fast enough so that management can exercise necessary management control instantly. This well-written and informative article also covers the place of the EDP specialist in top management, three kinds of management decisions (operational, tactical and strategical), and what the author terms as unanswerable questions beyond the total integrated system.

HARVEY, A., "Systems Can Too Be Practical," *Business Horizons* VII, No. 2 (Summer 1964), 59–69. The author presents and explains the following practical shortcuts that make the application profitable in many common business situations: (1) a realistic systems approach does not have to take into account every contingency, (2) both short and long-term variables can be identified, (3) the system can live with "real-life" limitations, and (4) practically applied, the systems approach can be implemented step-by-step. Management attitude is, in the opinion of the author, the largest factor in system failure or success.

HOCKMAN, J., "Specifications for our Integrated Management Information Systems," *Systems and Procedures Journal,* XVIII, No. 5 (February 1963), 40–41. Systems designers desiring general statements concerning the objective, scope, and content of an integrated management information system will find this article rewarding reading. The main points are that the system should provide only relevant information in the required amount, and the system should be capable of evaluating and redefining objectives.

JOHNSON, R. A., F. E. KAST, and J. E. ROSENZWEIG, *The Theory and Management of Systems* (2nd ed.). New York: McGraw-Hill Book Company, 1967, Chap. IV, pp. 71–91. The authors have blended their academic experience gained as members of a respected graduate school of business administration with actual operational situations to present a very informative and very readable treatment of the systems concept. Chapter 4 provides readers with a clear and nontechnical explanation of the control and systems concept. Control functions include the measurement of output, the comparison of output with some predetermined standard, and the adjustment of inputs to restore the system to its planned norm. Included is a section on the applications of control systems in an educational system.

KELLER, J., "Higher Education Objectives: Measures of Performance and Effectiveness," in *Management Information Systems: Their Development and Use in the Administration of Higher Education* (2nd ed.), eds. J. Minter and B. Lawrence. Boulder, Colo.: Western Interstate Commission for Higher Education, 1969, pp. 79–84. The author exhibits four parameters which can be used to study the causes of poor performance at the university level. Keller states that a better understanding for university outputs, the relationships between them, and the costs involved could be achieved through a formal analysis of the chosen parameters.

WILKINSON, BRYAN, "A Systems Approach to Marketing Information," *Journal of Systems Management,* XX, No. 10 (October 1969), 7–10. Although a short article, it should be used as a standard reading assignment for the subject of components of an information system. It provides eleven characteristics of good output, six good input characteristics, and eight good processing characteristics. It is a straightforward narrative presentation for which no programming or mathematical expertise is required.

5

Introduction to Information Systems

INTRODUCTION

This chapter will define two basic elements of information systems; data and information. It will then define an information system, identify its users, and discuss some important attributes of information. Different modes of information-system operation will be discussed, followed by one case study.

CONCEPTS OF DATA AND INFORMATION

Data consist of a set of characters or signals to which a significance can be assigned. Information, on the other hand, is selected data that have been processed to make them meaningful.

Consider a set of characters, 585281928F, stored in a space reserved for a student's social security number and sex code. These are data because the nine digits identify a person by his social security number, and the "F" is a code that identifies a person's sex. If the number is associated with a name, say Cheryl Glass, and the F code identifies this person's sex, which when decoded means female, then we know that Cheryl Glass is a female student. This is meaningful and is information. Thus the data, 585281928F, are information when processed (decoded and related to other data).

The importance of the "selection" of data can be illustrated by considering this problem further. If Cheryl Glass were to register in a freshman course, the data on sex would not constitute information to the registrar because sex is irrelevant when enrolling in a class and hence would not be "selected" for use. However, the data on sex would be selected by the Head Resident who has to assign Cheryl Glass to a dormitory room on a coed campus. To the Head Resident, characters 585281928F (when decoded and related to other data) do constitute information. This selection aspect of information is emphasized by Schoderbek, ". . . information concerns *selected data*—data selected with respect to problem, user, time, place, and function."[1]

Schoderbek also emphasizes the role of information as reducing uncertainty.[2] Other authors have emphasized other characteristics of information. To Wilson and Wilson, information is the "*capacity* for increasing knowledge"[3] and to Boutell it is a "significance derived from the data."[4] McDonough defines information as a label for

> *evaluated data* in a specific situation. When the individual singles out one of his problems and finds among his data materials that help him solve the problem, he is converting or isolating information from data. . . . (It is a) change from data to information when it is put to use in making a decision. The distinction between data and information gives opportunity to create classifications that can be used for further analysis.[5]

McDonough and his co-author Garrett discuss the transformation of information as the transmission of "data to 'relevant' people in the organization, informing them and thereby becoming 'information.' Until it reaches this last stage in a system, data is only potential information."[6]

[1] P. P. Schoderbek, ed., *Management Systems: A Book of Readings* (New York: John Wiley & Sons, Inc., 1968), p. 44.

[2] *Ibid.,* p. 43.

[3] I. G. Wilson and M. E. Wilson, *Information, Computers and System Design* (New York: John Wiley & Sons, Inc., 1965), p. 22.

[4] W. S. Boutell, *Computer-Oriented Business Systems* (Englewood Cliffs, N.J.: Prentice-Hall, Inc., 1968), p. 115.

[5] A. M. McDonough, *Information Economics and Management Systems* (New York: McGraw-Hill Book Company, Inc., 1963), pp. 71–72.

[6] A. M. McDonough and L. J. Garrett, *Management Systems Working Concepts and Practices* (Homewood, Ill.: Richard Irwin, Inc., 1967), p. 4.

The definition of information as a transfer of data through processing is illustrated in Figure 5–1.

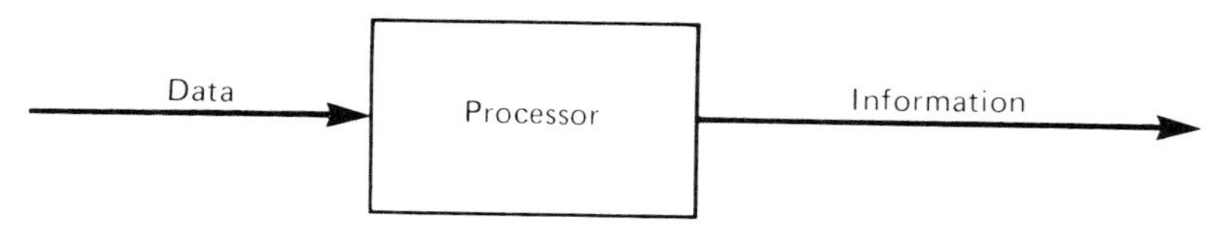

Figure 5–1. Transformation of Data Into Information

In the example cited earlier, processing involved the relating of a number to a name and the decoding of a sex code into a sex condition. In other cases, the processing may require arithmetic or mathematical operations, data reorganization, and other processing of data.

The production of information implicitly requires a user, the one who identifies the information needed and uses it. After the information is used, it may again become data which, along with other data, is reprocessed and the cycle of information production continues. This cycle is depicted in the block diagram of Figure 5–2.

One could consider the start of the cycle the original data (box 1) that is checked and edited (box 2). If necessary, the data is modified to ensure that it is complete and has no apparent errors and inconsistencies. The data is then processed (box 3) and information is generated (box 4). The information is then sent to the user (box 5). The satisfaction or dissatisfaction concerning this information is then fed back, which may modify the needs for information (box 6). The modified needs for information then determine the new data (box 7), which is used for the next cycle of reprocessing, again with the checking and editing (box 2). The modified needs for information (box 6) also affect the instructions for processing (box 8), which in turn determine future processing.

The information once generated (box 4), in addition to being sent to the user (box 5), also becomes part of the historic data (box 9). An example would be the payroll for the month. Social Security and other deductions will be carried over as historic data for the following month. The nature of the historic data needed will be determined by the modified needs for information as shown by the arrow between box 6 and box 9. This data is used for processing (box 3) and need not be edited or checked for validity (box 2) since it has already once gone through that stage.

AN INFORMATION SYSTEM

Also shown in Figure 5–2 are most of the basic components of a system. It has input (boxes 1, 7, 9), processing (box 3; box 2 could also be considered

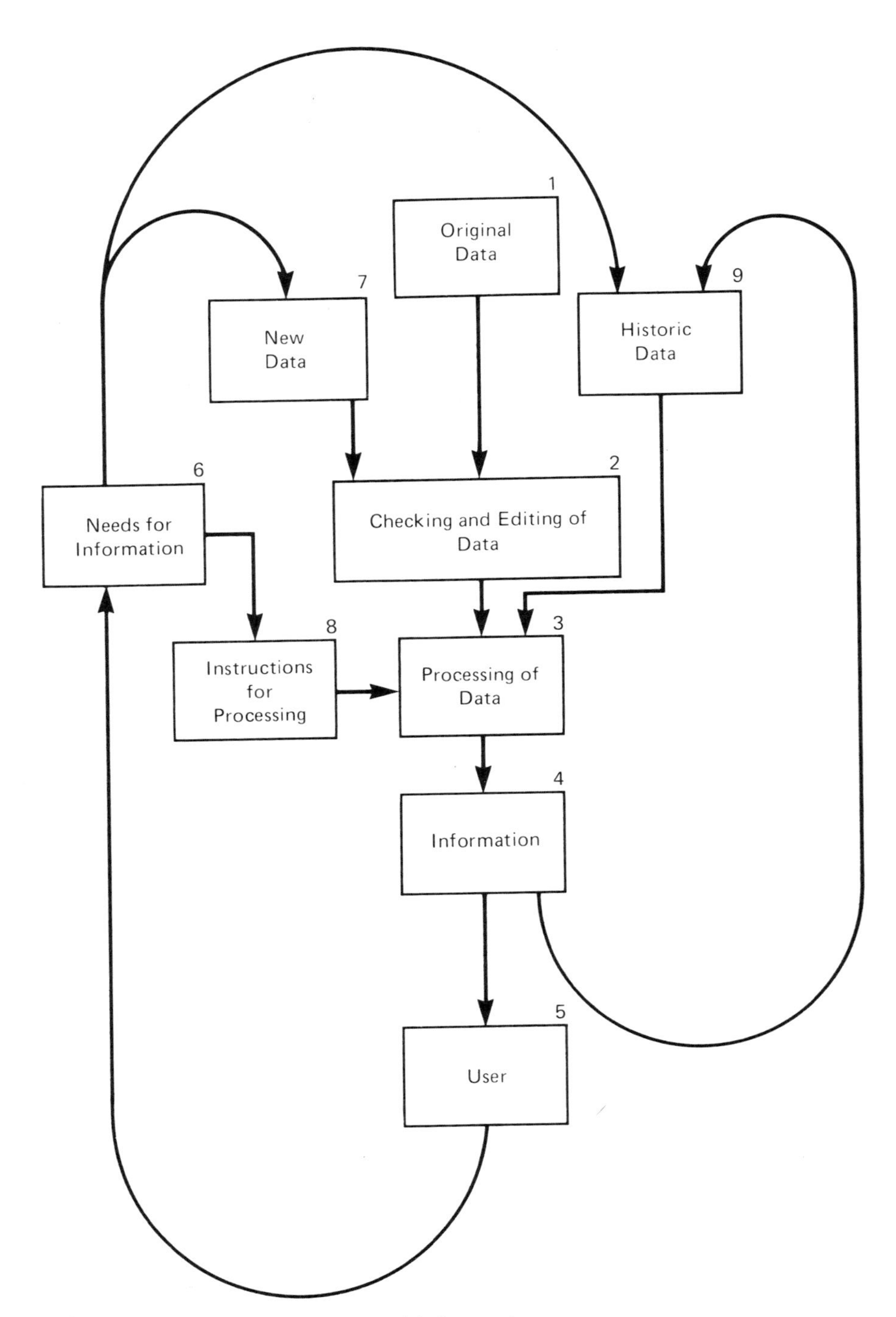

Figure 5–2. Production of Information

as processing and will be discussed later), control and feedback (boxes 5, 6, and 8), and output (box 4). If the system has a "wholeness" because it has a common plan and objective, then Figure 5–2 represents a system, or more specifically, an information system—a system that produces information.

More specifically, one can define an information system as being an assemblage or combination of things or parts forming a complex or unitary whole to produce information according to a plan.

There is more than one type of information system. Aron makes the following distinction: "An information system is intended to provide information needed by the user in the conduct of his business. . . . In particular, the management information system (MIS) . . . is defined as 'an information system which provides the manager with the information he needs to make decisions.' "[7]

The existence of an MIS is questioned by the *EDP Analyzer,* "The term 'Management Information System' is so ambiguous that one could draw almost any conclusion one wants about such systems. Defined in one way, they do in fact exist today; defined in another way, their realization is not even close."[8]

The need of an MIS is questioned by Ackoff who lists and then challenges the five assumptions of an MIS:

> (1) the critical deficiency under which most managers operate is the lack of relevant information, (2) the manager needs the information he wants, (3) if a manager has the information he needs his decision-making will improve, (4) better communication between managers improves organizational performance, and (5) a manager does not have to understand how his information system works, only how to use it.[9]

The issues raised by Ackoff are important ones, though he has overstated his case in some instances.[10] The case on MIS can best be understood in the context of the types and hierarchy of information generated and the nature of the users of an information system. The former subject is the topic of Chapter 6; the latter subject, the users of information, will be discussed below.

[7]J. D. Aron, "Information Systems in Perspective," *Computing Surveys,* I, No. 4 (December 1969), 213. For other definitions, see B. A. Colbert, "The Management Information System: Pathway to Profit," *Price Waterhouse Review,* Spring 1967, p. 4; and G. W. Dickson, "Management Information-Decision Systems," *Business Horizons,* XI, No. 6 (December 1968), 18. For a survey of five other definitions of an MIS, see "What's the Status of MIS?" *EDP Analyzer,* VII, No. 10 (October 1969), p. 5.

[8]"What's the Status of MIS?" p. 1.

[9]R. L. Ackoff, "Management Misinformation Systems," *Management Science: Application* (Series B), XIV, No. 4 (December 1967), B–147.

[10]For a critique of Ackoff's case, see A. Rappaport's Letter to the Editor, "Management Misinformation Systems—Another Perspective," *Management Science: Application* (Series B), XV, No. 4 (December 1968), B-133–36.

Users of an Information System

The main users of an information system in educational institutions are the administrators, the students, and the faculty. There are also indirect users. For example, through the administrators, the indirect users of an information system are the Board of Trustees (the School Board), the alumni, and the legislators. They need information concerning the institution before they make policies and allocate funds. Some users of information are also suppliers of data and information. For example, a clerk in the office of admissions receives processed information concerning the admission status of students. In addition, the clerk supplies data related to the student's application. Similarly, a policeman making his campus rounds uses information, such as lists of students and their addresses and generates data on parking and other violations.

The faculty is another important user of information and supplier of data. It uses information on students for purposes of advising them, and supplies data on students' grades. The student is still another user of information and supplier of data. He or she provides data such as social and academic background, and uses information on the curriculum and his or her academic status (including grades).

The student is often given a low priority as a user and hence his needs are not always considered explicitly in determining the needs for information. This may result in a waste of his time (like waiting to be registered or waiting to make a change in a course), and hence a great waste of social resources. Unfortunately, the student does not command the same recognition for services as does a customer of a business. In business, other than monopolies, if the customer is dissatisfied with the service he receives, he selects another business firm. However, the student has less choice and mobility. Because of location, choice of subject material, or because of academic standards, the student is restricted to a few educational institutions. Also, the student currently does not demand informational services. Hence, there is relatively less pressure in educational institutions to provide efficient and effective informational services for the student, but this may change. Students, seeing that the government and businesses do provide information efficiently and effectively, will demand such similar services from educational institutions. If students can in a few seconds reserve a seat on a plane leaving from New York, why shouldn't they be able to register for a course they desire with equal speed? The demonstration of such services elsewhere will have a "demonstration effect" on education, because students will demand that educational institutions also become efficient and effective in their handling of information.

There is another indirect user of information, the parents of the students. They are often involved in the selection of classes the student takes and are interested in the grades the student gets. The parents, too, will demand that such information be made available effectively. If dissatisfied, the parents may exert pressure through the community, trustees, or legislators. For an institution dependent on public funds, the public image is important. The indirect public user, therefore, cannot be entirely ignored.

ATTRIBUTES OF INFORMATION

The attributes of information to be discussed in this chapter are: timeliness, accuracy, relevancy and completeness.

Timeliness

The knowledge of having a crack in a tire after it has caused a fatal accident is of statistical value, but negligible as compared to its value had it been known in time to prevent the accident.

Timeliness of information may not be of such life and death significance in educational administration but is nonetheless of great importance. In the example cited earlier concerning grade reports, timeliness is very important. In some institutions grades of a semester are not known until after the next semester starts. This results in many students having to withdraw from classes that require the prerequisite courses in which they failed. By this time it may be too late to register in other desirable courses and so the student's entire program is disrupted. Emotional strain is added to dislocation when students are told they are suspended after they have started classes. The resulting withdrawal from classes, the school band, the dorm, a school job, and other activities can be emotionally hard on the student. It also results in much extra work for administrative offices. All this could be avoided if information on student grades and scholastic standings was made available promptly and before the start of the next semester.

Another example of the need for timely information concerns the staff and faculty directory that lists names, addresses, and phone numbers. In one university where I worked, this information was not available until six to eight weeks after a semester had started. By that time, most people had prepared their own lists, and by the time the information system had distributed its directory it had lost most of its value and usefulness. The same problem exists concerning information on students such as their campus address, the courses they are taking, their major, and other basic information. This is often available weeks after registration, but it is needed most immediately after registration, when advisors and administrators need to trace students for their anxious parents who call inquiring about them. Such information is unlike wine. It does not improve with age.

Another example of timely information concerns advising. Many a student has approached graduation date to be informed that he has not completed a required set of courses. If this information had been available earlier, perhaps the student could have completed the required courses and graduated. In general terms, it is necessary to control and monitor the process and identify deviations (such as the noncompletion of a required course) early enough so that corrective action can be taken. In some cases, behavior and performance can be predicted and the undesirable ones can be prevented by timely information leading to timely action. Therefore, timeliness is a very desirable attribute of information.

The need for timeliness of information may sometimes not be unanimous. Different users may have different and conflicting needs. For example, consider the information on final grades assigned at the end of the semester. The student wants the information as soon as possible even if it is incomplete and subject to some change. The timeliness of information to him is very important. To the records clerk, the timing is not so important. In fact, her preference is that the grading information be available after it is completely stabilized (after all grade changes have been made) so that she has fewer changes to make in her records. Such a conflict of interest must be resolved by the administrator or administrators involved.

Timely information is often desirable, but it has a cost in resources. In fact, as the time required to produce information approaches zero, the cost approaches infinity. Thus the administrator must consider the costs involved and then compare its benefits. Costs fortunately can be measured, but benefits cannot always be measured. What is the benefit of relieving the tension of students waiting for their grades? This is impossible to measure. Such problems of benefit measurement arise repeatedly in the design of information systems. One solution is not to measure benefits in absolute terms, such as in dollars, but to compare them with costs in an ordinal sense. Thus the cost of a 24 hour turn-around on grades may be computed to be X dollars and the administrator must then be asked: is it worth X dollars? It is easier for the administrator to answer such a question than to assign a dollar value to benefits. The administrator must weigh all the benefit considerations, including the effects on parents and the institutional image, and then make his choice.

Accuracy

Accuracy is the absence of error. The smaller the error, the greater the accuracy. Gregory and Van Horn have defined accuracy in terms of correct answers and have related it to "reliability." To them accuracy is "the long-run ratio of correct answers to total answers that comprise information—in short, its reliability."[11] Thus, by the above definition, if an event occurs on each of

[11]R. H. Gregory and R. L. Van Horn, *Automatic Data-Processing Systems, Principles and Procedures* (2nd ed.) (Belmont, Ca.: Wadsworth Publishing Company, Inc., 1963), p. 516.

ten days but the information system records it as occurring on only nine days, the system has an accuracy of 0.9.

Different activities require different levels of accuracy (or accuracy ratios). In the preparation of our paychecks, we demand that our checks be accurate to the last penny, and we normally get such accuracy. This performance is partly the result of our demands for such services. Our demand for accuracy leads to a greater effort and as a result we achieve higher accuracy. Our expectations for accuracy then rise and our demands for accuracy increase. Thus there is a spiraling cycle resulting in higher and higher accuracy ratios.

Many institutions do not have the same standards of accuracy in keeping students' records and in making grade and scholastic computations, although these should be considered equally vital since they are of importance to the student and are also values we cannot always completely check. If these records are wrong and adversely affect the student, the error will most likely be identified by him. But if there is an error in favor of the student, there is a possibility it will go undetected. Unlike the payment of funds, we do not have totals that are compared in order to identify discrepancies. Errors made in calculating grade performances can and often do go undetected. It is, therefore, very important that errors in such cases be reduced and accuracy be improved.

To reduce errors, one must look at the sources of errors. There are four main sources of errors: input errors; poorly designed or improperly followed procedures; incorrect processing rules; and, finally, equipment or processing breakdowns. Methods of detecting and reducing such errors are discussed later. However, errors resulting from faulty equipment or mental processes are not mentioned elsewhere in this book and will therefore be discussed briefly at this point.

The human brain has the ability to think and learn, but it does forget, is relatively slow in processing, and is not consistently accurate. The computer, in comparison, has a memory that does not forget, it processes very rapidly, and is very accurate. Among machines, computers are relatively more reliable. Gruenberger compares the computer's accuracy with that of a household appliance—the TV set.

> A home television receiver is also a bit-manipulating device. Bit patterns are created at the TV studios, at the rate of about 10,000,000 bits per second. These patterns are transformed into radiofrequency signals, which are propagated through the air to your receiving antenna. Your TV receiver operates on the signals, to recreate bit patterns which activate electron guns in the picture tube to produce pictures similar to those seen by the video camera. In the entire process, perhaps 1 or 2% of the 10,000,000 bits per second become altered. Some are lost, and new (spurious) bits are gained, due to noise, attenuation, and other factors. If 98% of the bits originally created reach your screen intact, you would

probably comment on the clarity of the picture. When the error rate gets about 2%, you may become annoyed at the bad reception. Thus, you can tolerate a gain or loss of up to 200,000 bits per second and still enjoy your program.

The bit-manipulation rate in small computers is quite comparable to that of the TV set, but the tolerance to errors is less. The error level for a computer is precisely one bit. In the computer, a gain or loss of *one* bit is too much. In nearly all computers, error-checking circuits will detect most one-bit errors and cause the machine to halt.

A modern machine, using solid state circuitry (that is, electronic circuits having no hot cathodes) and integrated circuits, would be expected to have a mean free time between errors of at least 100 hours. That does not mean that you can count on uninterrupted 100-hour runs; the next error could occur within one second. It does mean that you will experience many periods of 100 hours or more without a single bit failure. In fact, it is not uncommon to experience periods of six months of heavy duty operation with no detected electronic bobbles. Devices with moving parts, such as card readers, disk drives, and typewriters, will have many breakdowns in the same period of time.

In other words, a computer is expected to fail no more than once in every 4 trillion bit transfers, or in every 35 billion executed instructions. No other device available to the public comes even close to this standard of reliability.[12]

There is one type of error that arises both in hardware processing as well as in programming. This concerns rounding of numbers which, when reused in calculations, result in compounded errors. This problem is overcome in some computer equipment by what is known as "double precision." It involves the use of a number double the size that is required. Thus, instead of using a five significant digit number, the computer uses ten significant digit numbers in its computations and rounds the results after all computations. Rounding errors are thus eliminated. If the equipment does not have this capability, it can be programmed for greater precision and accuracy.

Perhaps there is a need to distinguish between precision and accuracy. As an example, we can say that the housewife keeps track of her checkbook accounts to the cent. But this does not ensure that her balance matches her bank statement. Her accounts are then precise but not necessarily accurate. Many a housewife will ignore an error (inaccuracy) of a few cents but not more than a dollar. As for an administrator, how much inaccuracy can he afford? At what accuracy level should he operate? Why not operate at an accuracy ratio of 1.0? The answer is often no; because the cost of such accuracy is often more than its benefits. One must achieve at least an accuracy level where the benefits of the results outweigh the costs of achieving the results. The optimum level would be a situation in which the positive difference between benefits and costs of accuracy is maximized.

[12]F. Gruenberger, *Computing: An Introduction* (New York: Harcourt, Brace and World, Inc., 1969), pp. 5–6.

The problem can best be discussed by referring to the benefit-cost curves in Figure 5–3.

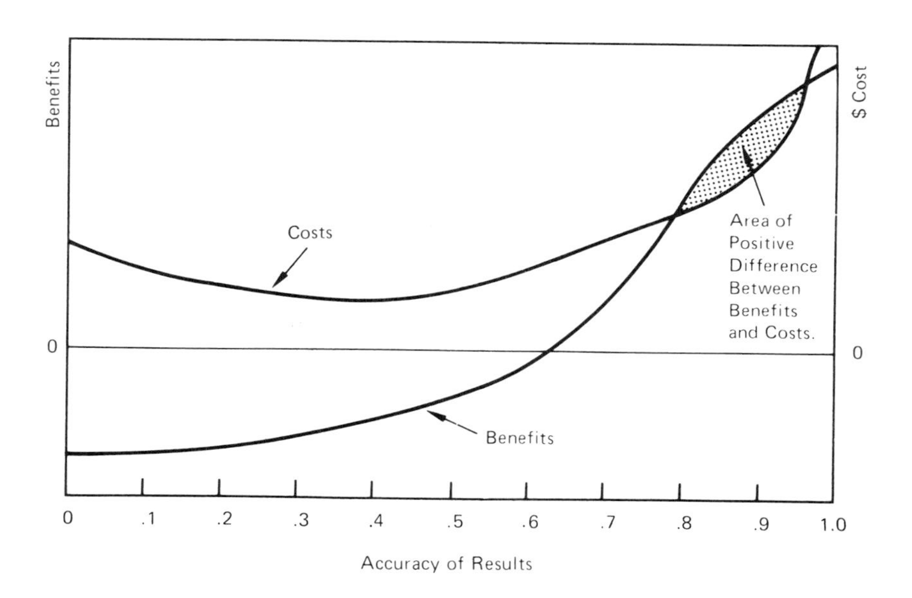

Figure 5–3. The Benefits and Costs Relative to Accuracy of Results[13]

The above curves are generalizations and do not apply to all situations concerning accuracy. But they do identify some basic relationships between costs and benefits. One is that costs are always positive but benefits are negative at lower levels of accuracy. In this area, no information is better than inaccurate information, because there is a loss when information is so inaccurate that the inaccuracies cause disruption and confusion. For example, consider again the case of calculating scholastic standings of students. If an inaccurate computation suspends a student when he should not be suspended, the cost of this inaccuracy could be high. He could lose a semester in the process but even if he did not, the inaccuracy may cause the student (and his parents) considerable psychic harm. If the story gets to a sympathetic press, the image of the institution could suffer. Thus in such cases of doubts of accuracy, it may be better not to take any action than take a wrong action.

As accuracy increases, benefits also increase until they equal the costs.

[13]R. H. Gregory and R. L. Van Horn, *Automatic Data-Processing Systems, Principles and Procedures* (2nd ed.) (Wadsworth Publishing Co., 1963), p. 518. Adapted by permission of the publisher.

Thereafter, benefits increase until they level off when the accuracy ratio approaches the value 1.0, while the cost curve increases sharply. This indicates that the benefits of eliminating the final inaccuracies are very small. The costs then are much greater than the benefits. This indentifies the regions where higher accuracy does not pay because of the relatively higher increases in costs.

Sometimes perfect accuracy can be achieved by duplication (such as writing another computer program to check the first one) but this almost doubles the cost. Such an additional cost would be justified in the case of computations that determine the allocation of capital funds among campuses. In other situations, the benefits are less than the costs in which case it would be best not to have perfect accuracy. An example would be the case of calculating scholastic standings where the probability of an inaccurate calculation may be 1 in a 1000. To eliminate this error may cost the institution $15,000. In such a case, the administrator may choose to allow the error and not pay the extra costs.

Such choices are not uncommon in industry. In determining optimal inventory levels, the manager knowingly takes a chance that he will be short of inventory and may lose customers. But the loss of revenue is less than the cost of avoiding any shortages. He, therefore, knowingly takes the loss.

The above analysis is only possible if one can draw a benefit-accuracy relationship. But this is not always possible. An administrator may not be able to assign values to accuracy, such as the benefit of accurately calculating the scholastic standings of students, or preparing correct paychecks. In that event the administrator must try and minimize the costs involved. The cost components to be considered are as follows: the cost of trying to reduce errors in input (organization, transcription, communications, procedures, and processing); the cost of detecting errors; the cost of making the corrections; and the costs resulting from errors. The sum of these costs components must be minimized and in many cases this will lead to less than perfect accuracy.

Relevancy and Completeness

Relevant information is that which is related and applicable to the problem being considered. When all the relevant information is included, then information is "complete."

The problem with relevancy and completeness is not only conceptional but also practical. Consider the problem of designing a "complete" information system for advising. All of us will agree in principle that an advisor should have complete information on his advisee before he advises. The problem lies in listing what constitutes a "complete" set of information. Should it include all the student's academic records, including his performance in high school? Should it include all his testing outside school, such as ACT, SCAT, and other professional and graduate-school tests, when applicable? Is it necessary that the course record at the current institution include the names of the instructors that taught the courses? Should the grades that were repeated and attempted but not earned also be identified? Do we need the record on all scholastic actions, such as probation and honors, listed? Don't we also need information on the student's socioeconomic background to help explain his past performance? Would the knowledge of his hobbies and his extra-curricular interests contribute to predicting his future performance? If these questions were asked of a group of ten persons representing a cross-section of administrators and faculty, more than one person would most likely answer "yes" for each question. This makes the complete set of information economically infeasible for many an institution. The resources (time and labor resources) required would exceed those available. One then has to compromise. Part of information design is the art of compromise in balancing conflicting needs and in producing information with resource constraints. This subject will be discussed further in Part Four of this book.

In many cases there is the danger in collecting or maintaining information that is irrelevant. Information that was once needed but is now obsolete and irrelevant must therefore be purged. Information that is "nice-to-have" but not necessary should be avoided. Information that is unrefined, and hence not usable, as well as obsolete information can be a liability, for it obscures important information. Too much information is as bad as too little information. Only information that is relevant should be included.

There are no mathematical rules for determining relevancy. The final choice must be a judgment in terms of balancing the cost of processing, the danger of its obscuring good usable information, and the perception of the need for information.

MODES OF PROCESSING

The attributes required of information will largely determine the type of processing that is required. If the information set is complete or nearly complete, if it is required for a large number of persons, and if it has to be timely and accurate, then computers become indispensible. Other information systems, such as manual systems and noncomputer machine systems have a comparative advantage in many situations and are often important complements to computerized information systems.[14] The principles of design and development to be discussed later in this book are generic ones and applicable to all types of information systems. The emphasis, however, is on computerized information systems. Such systems can be operated in many different

[14]For an excellent discussion of the different information systems, see C. Heyel, *Computers, Office Machines, and the New Information Technology* (New York: The MacMillan Company, 1969), pp. 235–50. Heyel's discussion includes the manual system, the Electro Mechanical System, the Service Bureau System, and the Electric Accounting System.

modes. The three main modes are batch processing, on-line processing, and real-time processing.

Batch processing requires that jobs to be processed are batched into groups to facilitate and expedite processing. This reduces the time and cost for setting up the job. Most information-processing currently operates in this mode. The response time will vary with the demand for processing and the procedures instituted at each processing center.

When data is an input directly to the computer (central processor) or information is received directly from the computer, then the processing mode is referred to as "on-line" processing.

Off-line processing is processing done without direct contact or communication with the computer. An example is a keypunch, which is not in communication with the computer. In contrast, a card reader or a printer which is under the control of the computer processor is on-line equipment. A terminal connected to a computer system that receives input and later provides direct output is on-line equipment. Thus on-line equipment eliminates the intermediary stages of keypunching the input and sometimes also the off-line printing of the output.

Real-time processing receives input and delivers output on-line. In addition it processes rapidly and keeps the information updated. Martin defines a real-time system as one "which controls an environment by receiving data, processing them, and taking action or returning results sufficiently quickly to affect the functioning of the environment at that time."[15]

There are many real-time systems currently operating in both business and educational institutions. One of the earliest advanced systems outside the Defense Department[16] is the SABRE system, used for passenger reservations by American Airlines. This system will be discussed in great detail because of its usefulness in illustrating aspects of design and development, which are to be discussed later in the book. Even though this is not a case from educational institutions, it is useful to study it because many of its features are applicable to education. Also, all readers may have some acquaintance with the system. If not, the next time they travel by a commercial airline, they will most likely benefit from a system very similar to the SABRE system.

The SABRE System

The need for an information system such as the SABRE arose from the fact that American Airlines found it increasingly difficult to maintain accurate

[15]J. Martin, *Design of Real-Time Computer Systems* (Englewood Cliffs, N.J.: Prentice-Hall, Inc., 1967), p. 5.

[16]A more advanced information system in the Department of Defense is known as the SAGE System. For a discussion see H. Sackman, *Computers, System Science and Evolving Society* (New York: John Wiley & Sons, Inc., 1967), pp. 259–72.

and timely records of all its passengers. There was the need for keeping records effectively and, hopefully, more efficiently. There was another reason, the need to control reservations. Under the conventional system the airline agents were assigned quotas of seats. If the demands were larger than the quotas assigned to agents of an airline, the passengers making additional demands were lost to that airline, even though other quotas across the country were unfulfilled. Thus the airline lost revenues. What was needed was a centralized reservation system that would assign all the seats available, including seats just canceled, anywhere around the country. An on-line, real-time system was required.

Such a system was operational in 1964. The system has since been under continual modification. It currently works as follows: a potential passenger inquires about a flight from one of the airline agents. The agent has a terminal, similar to an electric typewriter. He (or she) types the coded numbers of the flight and the date of prospective travel in order to inquire about space availability. In an average of 2.3 seconds, the typewriter starts typing a reply. It indicates the number of available spaces in each class on each desired flight. Other relevant information is also made available.

The potential passenger then makes his choice. The agent enters the necessary information about the passenger such as his name, the number of seats desired, the flight number, date of travel, and other special information such as the need of a wheel chair, a special diet, or a rental car. Other information such as the passenger's phone number is also recorded. The agent identifies himself or herself by a code and then presses a specific key on the terminal. The space, if still available, is reserved and a message with all the necessary information is typed out for the agent to check visually. If the passenger has not changed his mind, he has his reservation, and the transaction is completed in a matter of a few minutes.

The system, in addition to keeping records and making reservations, also performs many checking functions. It will not accept an incorrect code such as one for a non-existent flight. It will not make a reservation order unless the agent provides all the essential information about the passenger. It also checks the number of names entered with the number of seats desired and if inconsistent, it notifies the agent of the discrepancy. The system automatically follows up each case. If for example, a flight is canceled by the airline, the agent is informed of the passengers to be notified. If the passenger cancels out, his seat is returned to inventory for use by other potential customers. If the passenger has connecting flights, the system relays this message and makes connecting reservations. This in itself is a big task since more than a third of the passengers use more than one airline. (It is somewhat analogous to a large school providing information on all its transferring graduates to the educational institutions involved.) The system as described by Boutell also processes

> all advance and decision flight information received from the dispatch centers in the system, notifies affected cities of any overbookings that occur, and adjusts

> basic schedule information such as flights, stops, and authorizations. In short, central reservations control performs those sales control and local control functions previously handled by individual offices throughout the system not now handled internally within Sabre.[17]

The information system not only serves the passenger, helps the agent, and increases the usage of seats, but also performs a large number of internal functions. It estimates the meal requirements for the airlines caterer; provides the passengers information as to arrival and departure gates; provides passenger loading and weight information to flight control, which in turn uses the information for assigning aircraft, crew personnel, and maintenance workers. The system keeps accounts of funds receivable for each day, week, month, flight, and route. This information and other statistical information is available to management for control and planning purposes. The system is designed around reservations, incorporating other related subsystems into an integrated system that achieves a high level of efficiency and effectiveness.

The processing for the SABRE system is done by a centralized processing system which has two computers in Westchester County, New York. One computer is sufficient for a normal load. The other is on "standby" and takes over in cases of hardware breakdown or maintenance. Between them, the two computers provide continuous service. They are connected by 12,000 miles of high-speed telephone lines to more than a thousand sale agents all across the country. A graphic representation of the one exchange is shown in Figure 5–4.

As of 1964, there were 43 such interchanges. Each one services the main air terminal and local airports in the neighborhood. The system as a whole services an average of 40,000 reservation transactions per day, each one requiring around ten separate inputs and generating 80 different actions. The system has a capacity of 600,000 reservation records.

The cost of the system as of 1964 is stated as 30 million dollars. It was developed jointly by IBM and American Airlines. It took ten years to develop. The chronology as given by Parker was as follows:[18]

Preliminary Study	1954–1958
Precontractual analysis	1958–1959
Contract	1959
Functional requirements	1960–1962
Program specifications	1960–1962
Program coding	1961–1964
Single path testing	1961 on
Equipment arrival	January 1962
Package testing	1961–1962
Final checkout	Oct.–Dec. 1962
Test city parallel operation	Dec. 1962–Mar. 1963

[17]Boutell, *Computer-Oriented Business Systems,* p. 193.

[18]R. W. Parker, "The SABRE System," *Datamation,* XI, No. 9 (September 1965), 52.

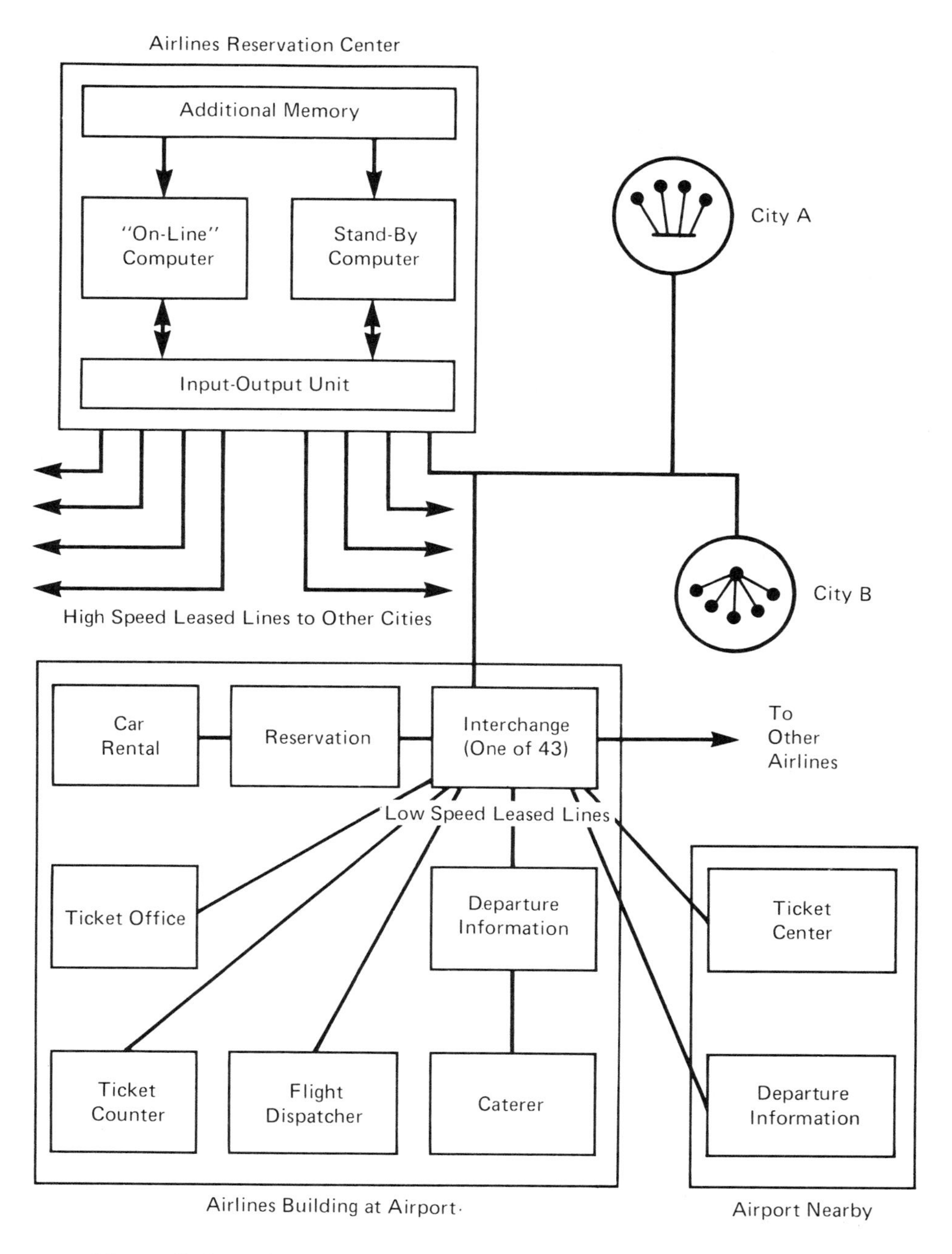

Figure 5–4. A Graphic Representation of Part of an Airline Reservation System

First firm cutover	April 1963
Several more cities cutover	May 1963
Further cutover delayed pending addition of memory to 7090	June–Nov. 1963
Remainder of American cities added to system	Nov. 1963–Dec. 1964

With the above background it is now meaningful to examine the intentions and expectations of the original designers of the system. The project was originally spelled as SABER, an acronym for Semi-Automatic Business Environment Research. The terms in this name are all significant. The "Research" part of the name reflects the uncertainty of success in achieving the stated goals. The "Business Environment" specification stresses the designers' concern with the business environment in addition to the internal operations of the system. The "Semi-Automatic" term emphasizes the recognition of the human factors in the system which will never be fully automated.

The degree of automation is continuing not only at American Airlines but also in the entire airlines industry, where reservation systems like the SABRE system are now a standard service. Eastern Airlines already has a system more advanced than the original SABRE system. It has over 1700 sets for agents that produce entire page images on equipment similar to small TV screens, and handles over 60,000 passengers per day. (Imagine handling over 60,000 student registrations per day!) The needs of these passengers are fulfilled by the following capabilities as listed by Jenkins:

> *Schedule Information.* Depressing a special key plus a simple input of date, city pair (from-to) and time, will obtain 10 current flight schedules, displaying flight number, city pair departure and arrival, type of equipment, meal service and number of stops.
>
> *Availability.* Depression of another key and the same input will display schedules of four available flights. The computer spans a 34-hour period in its search for seats available nearest the time requested.

A seat may be sold on one of the displayed flights by entering only the line number, class of service, and number of seats, followed by all mandatory elements required in the PNR. If the agent fails to enter an element, the computer politely reminds the agent what has been omitted. Mandatory items are:

> Passenger name(s) which must correspond to seats sold
> Telephone contact
> Ticketing information
> Who booked the reservation[19]

Other plans as listed by Buchanan include the performance of the following functions:

[19]W. E. Jenkins, "Airline Reservation Systems," *Datamation,* XV, No. 3 (March 1969), 31.

1. Construct and display fares for all worldwide itineraries.
2. Confirm a passenger's reservation and issue the ticket by extracting information from the airlines' central reservations computer in a remote location. The ticket number, rather than being preprinted as today, will be assigned by the computer and printed accordingly.
3. Provide quick, self-service ticketing for credit card holders with or without an advance telephone reservation. Within this concept, the passenger could insert his credit card into a ticketing device which checks the validity of the card, verifies or creates the reservations record, and issues the ticket.
4. Permit a passenger with an automated ticket to make a rapid exchange of a flight coupon for a machine-readable boarding pass at his first contact with the airport on day of flight.

In addition, other refinements will be possible. The system will have the capability to:

1. Reject used or invalid tickets and boarding passes.
2. Process instantaneously no-show information and keep track of standby passengers according to priority.
3. Direct passengers to an airline employee for asistance when necessary.
4. Provide continuous information to the airline on the number of passengers boarding an aircraft according to destination, class of service and by type of fare.
5. Provide automatically alternative routings for passengers in the event of flight cancellation, equipment change or other similar circumstances.[20]

The system under future plans (next ten years) will extend from the terminal right into the airplanes. Each plane will have its own computer that will monitor its parts and issue instructions and schedules for the repair and replacement of airplane components. These computers will also enable the airlines to pinpoint the location of each aircraft at all times and to keep their traffic officers aware of all variables that affect resource allocation.[21]

Many professionals in the systems business have little doubt that the plans listed above will materialize. It is just a matter of time. The plan is now less in the research phase and more in the implementation phase.

Advanced Information Systems

There are many advanced information systems other than those in the airline industry. There are information systems in the petroleum industry that automatically control the production process and output mix. In some facto-

[20]G. A. Buchanan, "The Outlook for Improved Passenger Systems," *Datamation,* XV, No. 3 (March 1969), 25.

[21]See S. G. Tipton, "Airline Challenges for the Future," *Datamation,* XV, No. 3 (March 1969), 23, for a discussion of this topic.

ries, information systems help in product design, keep track of every job on the floor, and identify each effort contributed to that job by means of worker badges that input information on-line to a central information system. Other information systems integrate all the actions activated by a salesman receiving an order, to the point of delivery to the customer. This includes optimal warehouse selection, calculation of inventory levels with optimal reorder quantity, generation of bills of lading, and the creation of all accounting documents.[22]

There are also many advanced information systems in the defense industry. One such system enabled the coordination and control of the Apollo 11; it required over 15 million parts, involving 20,000 industrial firms and over 400,000 persons.[23]

Other advanced systems now in the research and development stages envisage the input, processing, and output of pictures;[24] bibliographic search in a dialogue mode;[25] voice, handwriting, and fingerprint recognition; the production of films; text composition by computer; and even machines that perform "intelligent" tasks.

Some of the research efforts listed above may not materialize but there is little doubt that our capacity for information-processing will increase greatly in the next decade. Diebold, a reliable commentator in information-processing, predicts, "We anticipate a seven-to-one improvement between now (1965) and 1973; taking into account technical developments in speed, accuracy, flexibility, and capacity."[26]

Even if the actual factor of improvement is half as much as Diebold has predicted, there still lies a great opportunity for the use and exploration of such capability, especially in the field of education which is way behind business and industry in its use of information technology. The exploration of this technology requires developing a system, a subject to be discussed in Part Four of this book. Meanwhile, we need to understand the nature of the functions of an information system, the subject of the next chapter.

[22]For actual case studies of the above, see G. Burck and the Editors of Fortune, *The Computer Age* (New York: Harper & Row, 1965), Chap. II–III, pp. 26–72.

[23]"To Another World and Back," *IBM Computing Report,* V, No. 4 (August-September 1969), 13.

[24]A. Rosenfeld, "Picture Processing by Computer," *Computing Surveys,* I, No. 3, (September 1969), 147–76, and A. Van Dam, "Computer Driven Displays and Their Use in Man/Machine Interaction," *Advances in Computers,* VII (New York: Academic Press, 1966), pp. 239–90.

[25]"A Search 1967 Style," *SDC Magazine,* X, No. 9 (September 1967), 15–18.

[26]J. Diebold, "What's Ahead in Information Technology," *Harvard Business Review,* XLIII, No. 5 (September-October 1965), 77. The parentheses are provided by the author of this book to facilitate a comparison of time.

SUMMARY AND CONCLUSIONS

This chapter defined the terms, data, information, and information systems. Data consist of a set of characters to which a meaning can be assigned; "information" is selected data that are processed, and an "information system" is a system that generates or produces information.

The main users of information systems in educational administration have been identified as administrators, faculty, and students. The main indirect users may be the Trustees (School Board members), legislators, and parents.

The students are the group among the users not adequately considered in the design and development of information systems. This results in much social waste.

Attributes of information were examined. These were timeliness, accuracy, relevancy and completeness. A system developed primarily to produce timely information (the SABRE system) was examined.

This chapter discussed many concepts and illustrated possible applications of an information system. It perhaps raised more questions than it answered. Hopefully, some of these answers will be discussed in the part on Systems Development, Part Four. Meanwhile, we need to discuss another aspect of an information system: the functions of an information system.

KEY TERMS

Data
Information
Information System
Attributes of Information
Types of Information Systems
Modes of Processing
Demonstration Effect
Double Precision

REVIEW QUESTIONS

1. Distinguish between
   Data and Information
   Relevant and Complete Information
   Precise and Accurate Information
   Batch Mode and On-line Mode of Operation
   Real-time and On-line Information System
2. What are some factors in determining how accurate an information system should be?
3. Is the SABRE system a total system? Discuss.

4. How does the SABRE system use operational data to provide managerial information?
5. What are the main sources of error in an information system, and how can they be minimized?
6. What two factors should be compared in determining the degree of system accuracy?

CHAPTER 5: SELECTED ANNOTATED BIBLIOGRAPHY

BOUTELL, W., *Computer-Oriented Business Systems.* Englewood Cliffs, N.J.: Prentice-Hall, Inc., 1968, pp. 192–98. An excellent diagrammative description of the SABRE system is presented which illustrates the complexity of such complete systems. Although the SABRE system was specifically designed as an airline-reservation system, the author points out that all of the functions normally associated with a business firm can be encompassed within its framework. SABRE is a good example of a sales-oriented approach that business firms might use to design and implement an integrated EDP system. Also discussed are two other possible approaches—a production-oriented approach and a management information system approach.

FURTH, S. E., "Automated Retrieval of Legal Information: State of the Art," *Computers and Automation,* XVII, No. 12 (December 1968), 25–28. This discussion is aimed at potential users of automated retrieval systems who desire to understand, in general terms, the operating principles of such a system. System organization and types of data bases involved are discussed.

GREGORY, R. H., and R. L. VAN HORN, *Automatic Data-Processing Systems* (2nd ed.). Belmont, Ca.: Wadsworth Publishing Co., 1963, Chap. XIV, pp. 516–51. This is a nontechnical discussion of accuracy, control, and auditing as they pertain to a data system. Accuracy may be increased by providing extra system capacity through means such as: (1) check-digits and verification for originating data, (2) message numbering, (3) proof-and-hash-totals, and (4) duplicate processor circuitry or programmed checks. One method for improving control and audit is suggested—the incorporation of control methods into processing programs. The author also presents good distinctions among errors, mistakes, and malfunctions.

PARKER, R. W., "The SABRE System," *Datamation,* XI, No. 9 (September 1965), 49–52. A detailed discussion of the SABRE system components and a description of how the number of terminal interchanges, agents, and file size requirements were determined. Also discussed is the software development process.

6

Functions and Hierarchy of Information

INTRODUCTION

This chapter identifies the different administrative activities and the characteristics of information required for each type of activity. The correspondence of these types of activities with hierarchial levels of information are then examined. Other related topics discussed are the threshold of information, the exchange of information between levels of administration, and the relationship between information systems and other systems.

ACTIVITIES FOR WHICH INFORMATION IS NEEDED

Information is needed for five main sets of administrative activities: planning, organization, direction, operation, and control. Two related activities that often need information-processing are institutional research and record-keeping. Each of these activities will be discussed, their interrelationships identified, and their correspondence to different levels of administration examined.

Planning

Planning has been defined extensively and in different ways in the literature of organization theory,[1] business,[2] and operations research.[3] For the purposes of this book, planning will be considered to consist of the following activities:

1. Setting of overall goals and objectives.
2. Developing substantive plans for pursuing the overall goals and objectives.
3. Stating overall plans and objectives in terms of subparts and sub-objectives (or subgoals).
4. Assigning weights and priorities to objectives, plans, and subplans.
5. Stating constraints for the organization, apart from physical constraints and others to be defined later.
6. Setting standards and levels of performance. These may be objectives or constraints.
7. Reviewing the above in the context of changing internally generated information about the organization, or of information received from external sources concerning the environment, and then making necessary changes.[4]

Once the planning is done, it is necessary to organize.

Organization

The organizing function is the marshaling of resources necessary to accomplish the goals, subgoals, plans, and subplans of the institution. The resources to be marshaled and organized include men, materials, and equipment. These have to be organized in terms of the activities to be performed, and grouped into units and subunits with the responsibilities for the performance of these activities assigned to line or staff personnel.

The organizing function consists of the following set of activities:

[1]J. March and H. A. Simon, *Organizations* (New York: John Wiley & Sons, Inc., 1963), p. 140 and Chap. VII.

[2]R. N. Anthony, *Planning and Control Systems: A Framework for Analysis* (Boston: Harvard University, 1965).

[3]R. L. Ackoff and M. W. Sasieni, *Fundamentals of Operations Research* (New York: John Wiley & Sons, Inc., 1968), pp. 428–29.

[4]This list and the four others that follow are an adaption of lists given by Z. S. Zannetos, "Towards Intelligent Management Information Systems," *Industrial Management Review*, IX, No. 3 (Spring 1968), 22.

1. Acquiring resources—both physical and human. The acquisition of human resources includes the hiring and firing of top and middle personnel.
2. Allocating physical resources necessary for the achievement of the plans and subplans.
3. Assigning responsibility and authority for the achievement of the stated plans and subplans.
4. Determining variables that need to be controlled and specifying signals necessary for control.
5. Instituting and monitoring the mechanism for controlling operations, i.e., control the controlling of operations.
6. Motivating personnel to further institutional goals.

Direction

The direction of activities (sometimes called **execution**) consists of the following activities on a day-to-day basis:

1. The stating of goals and subgoals in terms of operations functions and procedures.
2. The assigning of resources to perform these functions.

Operation

This is the actual carrying out of the functions and procedures on a day-to-day basis.

Control

The control function can be considered to consist of the following activities:

1. Sensing and measuring variables to be controlled.
2. Comparing performance values with allowable values to determine deviations.
3. Evaluating deviations.
4. Informing top management of deviations when they go beyond specified levels, i.e., feedback information needed to make necessary adjustments.
5. Designing and implementing procedures for correcting undesirable deviations after they occur.
6. Coordinating and facilitating activities that will reduce undesirable deviations and discourage those that will increase deviations after they occur.

7. Motivating and implementing of activities that promote efficiency and effectiveness.

The Cycle

The functions discussed above are related in a cyclic pattern. This is illustrated in the activity oriented diagram shown in Figure 6–1.

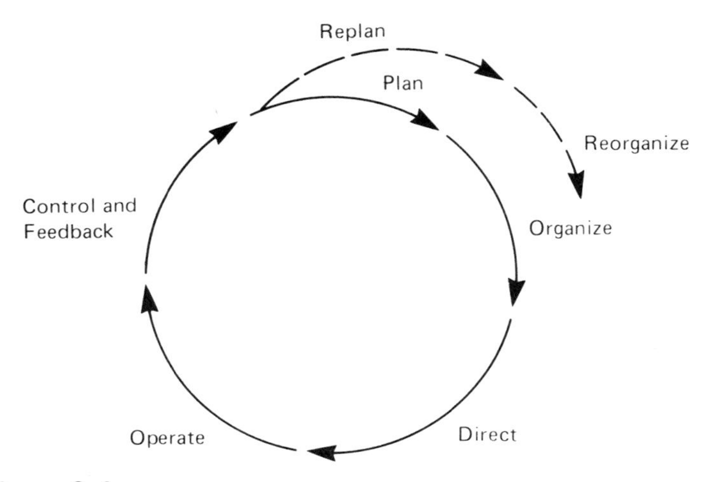

Figure 6–1

The cycle starts with the planning activity which determines *what* must be done. The organizing and directing activities state *how* it is done. After the activity operates, the control and feedback evaluates what was done. If the evaluation is satisfactory, the system continues its operation undisturbed. If, however, the feedback, the external information available, or a change in top administrative personnel require a change in plans, then replanning occurs and the cycle continues as shown partly by the dashed lines in Figure 6–1.

HIERARCHY OF FUNCTIONS AND ADMINISTRATION

The functions discussed above can be considered as belonging to a hierarchy, as shown in Figure 6–2, and still maintain the cycle of functions discussed above.

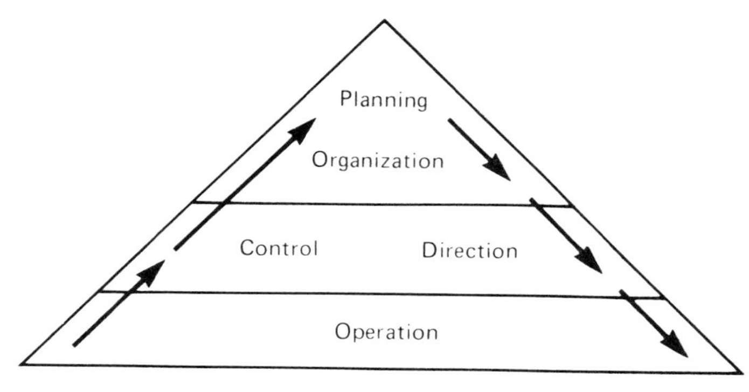

Figure 6–2

The functions of planning and organizing are done by top administrators. Direction and control are performed by middle-level administrators, while operations are performed by the operations personnel. This correspondence between levels of administration and the functions performed is shown in Figure 6–3.

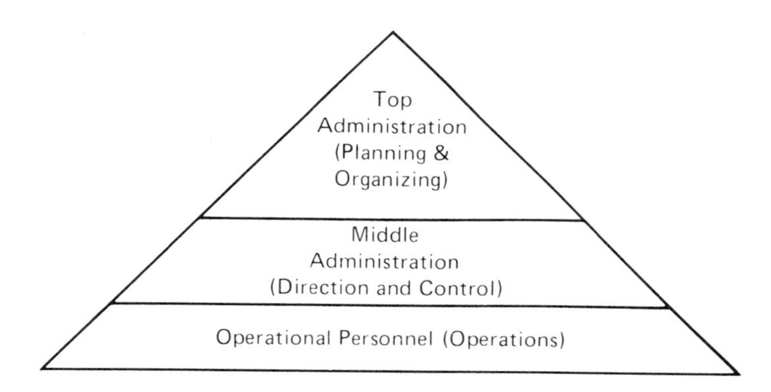

Figure 6–3

In educational institutions, especially those of higher education, there are two types of personnel organized in parallel: the academic and the non-academic. Each has its own level of administrators and its own operational personnel. Among the academic personnel, the operational personnel are the instructional faculty. They are directed and controlled by their department chairmen and academic deans (middle-level administrators) and their top administrators are the academic vice-president and his associate vice-president. Among the non-academic personnel, the secretaries, semiskilled, and unskilled workers constitute the operational personnel and are directed and controlled by their supervisors, directors, and non-academic deans (middle level administrators). They, in turn, are supervised by top administrators, who are the non-academic vice-presidents or equivalent ranking personnel. Both the academic and the non-academic top administrators report to the topmost administrator of the entire institution.

HIERARCHY OF INFORMATION

In performing the different functions at the different levels of hierarchy in administration, there is a need for information relevant to each function, with a correspondence between each level of administration and each level of information. This is shown in Figure 6–4.

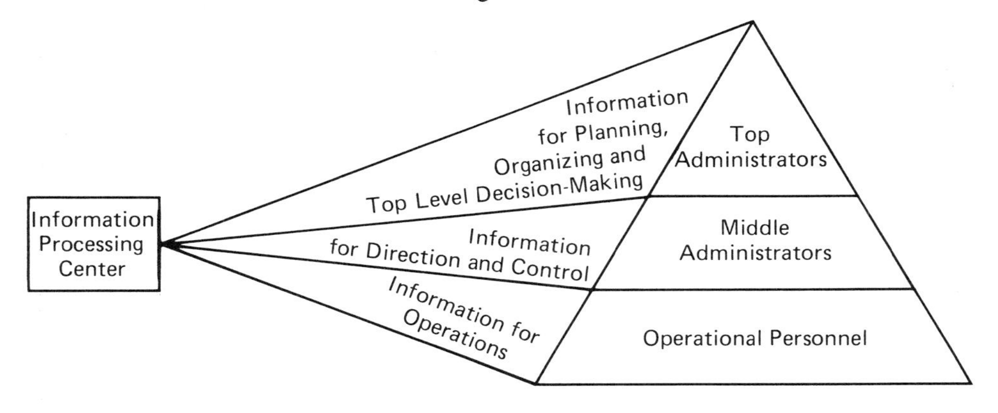

Figure 6–4. Hierarchy of Levels of Information

The content and characteristics of information are different at each level. These are discussed below with examples of such information needed in educational institutions. The diagram in Figure 6–4 shows only the information generated by the information-processing center. Data received by the information-processing center as input is discussed in the next chapter.

Operational Information

Operational information is the factual reporting of the daily operations. In education, most of this information is seasonal, with peaking at times of registration and grading. Examples of such operational information are listings of classes offered, class listings of students registered, grade reports, listings of students admitted and their ACT scores, faculty listings, and so on. During the remaining part of the semester, examples of operational information needed are reports on rooms and faculty available for purposes of scheduling; lists of faculty with their teaching loads; lists of students with their addresses, courses being taken, along with other basic data for each student; and accounting data on transactions related to salaries and departmental expenditures.

Numerous lists are needed at the operational level for purposes of checking. The design of the system should be such that these listings can be easily cross-referenced by a keyword, such as a unique identification number. Cross-reference reports should also be available, such as lists of names showing each identification number, and lists by identification numbers showing names. Furthermore, these reports should be listed by the administrative units using these lists. Thus, student lists should be listed by department and division to meet departmental and divisional needs, and should be listed by institution for registration needs. Sometimes, the registrar has most of the control over the information system and hence there is only one unsorted institutional list. Such a method is a poor one. With computers, the sorting process involved in such listings has a trivial development cost and very low running costs. This capability should be exploited with both the institutional and sorted lists. Such an alternative requires an understanding of information systems on the part of the users, the type of understanding that will come from the study of the remaining part of this book.

Operational information has a special characteristic: it is cyclic, which means it is needed repeatedly and corresponds to an administrative cycle, such as the academic term or the calendar month. Furthermore, operational information must be timely or it loses all or most of its value. The importance of timeliness places a great burden on data-gathering and information processing in educational institutions, especially during periods when the work load is peaked. This is especially true of institutions that have a policy of registering during the week and starting classes the very next day. Providing all the information when needed may become impossible without large expenditures in overtime and equipment. These consequences should be weighed against the advantages of the policy of end-of-work-week-registration. This is a good example of how institutional policies have an important affect on the effectiveness and efficiency of information processing and why it is necessary that policy makers be involved in developing information systems.

Record-Keeping

Records are kept for one or more reasons. These are explained and illustrated below:

1. *Operations:* Records are used often for operational purposes. An example could arise if a student returned for study after an extended absence. His

academic records would be retrieved and used for operations during his stay. Another example would be the need of a transcript.

2. *Audit:* Records must be kept for purposes of auditing. Examples would be financial records such as ledgers.
3. *Historical:* Historical records are kept for many reasons: to trace the history of the institution; for use in prediction of variables such as student enrollment; or for institutional research.
4. *Back-up:* All **vital** records should be kept for use in the event that operational data is destroyed. Records can be defined as being **vital** when they are essential for the resumption of activities after a catastrophe, such as the burning of a processing center. Vital data required would be the financial bookkeeping records, as well as records on student enrollment in courses they are currently taking.

The control of records involves many considerations. These are summarized in the following list and will be discussed further in Parts Four and Five of this book.

- Costs consideration
  - Space
  - Equipment
  - Material
  - Manpower
- Media
  - Selection
    - Costs
    - Retrieval capability
    - Ease of operation
  - Maintenance and operation
- State of records
  - Protection from hazards
  - Completeness
  - Documentation
  - Compatability
  - Labeled and indexed
- Purging and updating
  - Rules
  - Schedule

Information for Control

By definition, control is the comparison of desired performance with actual performance and action taken to eliminate undesirable deviations. To facilitate control, information is needed on current performance in a form that will quickly facilitate its comparison with desired performance.

The difficulty with control information is that of defining performance levels and measuring them. This is very difficult in education because the products are instruction, research, and service, and there is no generally accepted criterion for measuring these products.[5]

Often, however, the educator uses this as an excuse to make no attempt to control performance and practices. Take for example, grading practices. There may be no absolute standard for measuring a faculty member's grading practices, but these could be compared with the grading practices of his peers in his department, college, or institution. Using longitudinal data, one could identify grading practices that are outside specified deviations (typically stated in terms of standard deviations) and then these could be examined for special circumstances. Such control could identify practices that should not be allowed. For example, in one institution an instructor was found to consistently assign more grades than students registered in his class (he gave grades to students who had dropped his course). Such a practice could be easily identified and brought to the attention of the relevant administrators.

An important consideration relating to control information concerns the timing of the information. When should a report be generated for it to be timely and useful? This varies with the nature of the information concerned. Some control information (such as an expenditure twice the value allowed in the budget) must be acted upon immediately. Other information can be "batched" or provided regularly (such as payroll information), or provided when available (such as control information on grading practices). The timing must be determined by the administrator, and must then be enforced.

Information for Direction

To be able to direct operations, one must have information on performance as well as related information on deviations (control information), in order to eliminate deviations. Thus, there is an overlap of operational and control information with information required for direction. In addition, information for direction includes information required by formal techniques of decision-making, such as those used in Management Science and Operations Research. Such a decision-making function of information is not a traditional one but will become increasingly important in the future.

Information needed at the level of direction should consist of operational information, but aggregated for administrative units. In a university, the ad-

[5]For excellent reference material, see Lawrence, *et.al.*, eds., *Outputs of Higher Education: Their Identification, Measurement and Evaluation* (Boulder, Colo.: Western Interstate Commission for Higher Education, 1970), 130 pp. For an excellent bibliography, see pp. 117–24, and for articles on measurement of output in higher education see pp. 19–23, 27–38, and 51–58.

ministrative unit aggregation should be at both the departmental and the divisional (college) level. Thus a department chairman and dean should have reports on their department and division respectively, which include individual teaching loads and load analysis, faculty grading records, budgetary and ledger information, building utilization reports, curricula offering analysis, and student profile analysis. For reference, available operational information should include records on each faculty member and each student majoring in the department, inventory listings of plant and equipment, class lists, grade lists, room utilization reports, and detailed statements of accounts.

In some institutions, administrators have on-line equipment on which they can make random inquiries such as: What is the status of my out-of-state travel account? What is the academic record of John Doe? What has been the teaching load of A. B. Smith for the last four semesters? In each case the query may be coded and the keyword (such as the account number or social security number) may have to be typed in. The information system then informs the user of the level of aggregation and the types of reports available and asks him to make a selection. For example, where the travel account status is queried, the system may give the following choices for analysis:

1. Faculty member using account
2. Expenditures by each day to date
3. Expenditures by each week to date
4. Total expenditures to date

The user, having made the choice, will then receive the reports he desires.

Information systems using the dialogue mode are currently in use in some educational institutions. The main problems are their high cost, and considerations of security of information. Undoubtedly, these problems will be resolved and such query capabilities will become more common in the next decade.

Information for Top Decision-Making

Information for goal-setting seldom comes from an information system. It is a product of the personality and background of the top decision-makers, and the environment and constraints on the institutions. Information system, however, can help in better assessing the institutional and environmental constraints, and they can be helpful in the "organizing" and "directing" function, especially in allocating resources, where simulation and other operations research techniques are being used with increasing success. These techniques require basic data which must be generated by the information system.

Top administrators are, of course, interested in all levels of institutional operations, but because of human limitations they cannot control all levels of the organization. They should, however, be informed, and receive **selected** information concerning "exceptions."

Selectivity of information is necessary in this age of computerized information systems where even a moderate-sized computer prints out reports at over one thousand lines a minute. Such fast production can soon swamp the administrator with information he cannot read, let alone absorb. He, therefore, needs selected information that only concerns exceptions. Examples of exceptions may be the following:

1. Operations that are above or below the acceptable levels.
2. Problems that cannot be corrected at the operational or control level.
3. Variables that have a major effect on institutional goals and plans.
4. Undesirable trends (including those inside prescribed control limits).

The variables that must be reported, and their "exceptional" levels, vary with institutions and with administrative personnel. These must be defined by the top administrators. In some cases, of course, the variables may be qualitative and cannot be measured, in which case their variations cannot be reported.

In addition to exceptional information, top administrators must be given summarized operational information as well as statistical aggregate information. This information must be both current and longitudinal.

Often it is necessary to analyze information in order to establish trends and to make predictions. In cases of "exceptional" information on deviations it is necessary to identify the causes for the exceptional behavior. Such an analysis is often done by Offices of Institutional Research working in a staff capacity with top administrators.

Institutional Research

The relationship of institutional research to an information system and top administration is shown in Figure 6–5 (this is actually an extension of Figure 6–4). In it the top administrators receive information on the environment and advice from Institutional Research, in addition to information on planning and organizing generated by the processing center. In some situations, institutional research offices may advise the administrators performing the functions of direction and control. This is the "prescriptive" and "normative" role of institutional research. In addition, institutional research has a "descriptive" and "positive" role. It describes how the institution operates and performs. In many cases, this descriptive role is a prerequisite to the prescriptive role, for it is necessary to know what the institution currently does before any prescriptions for the future are made. But the descriptive role of institutional research is also important as self-defense to support the institution's

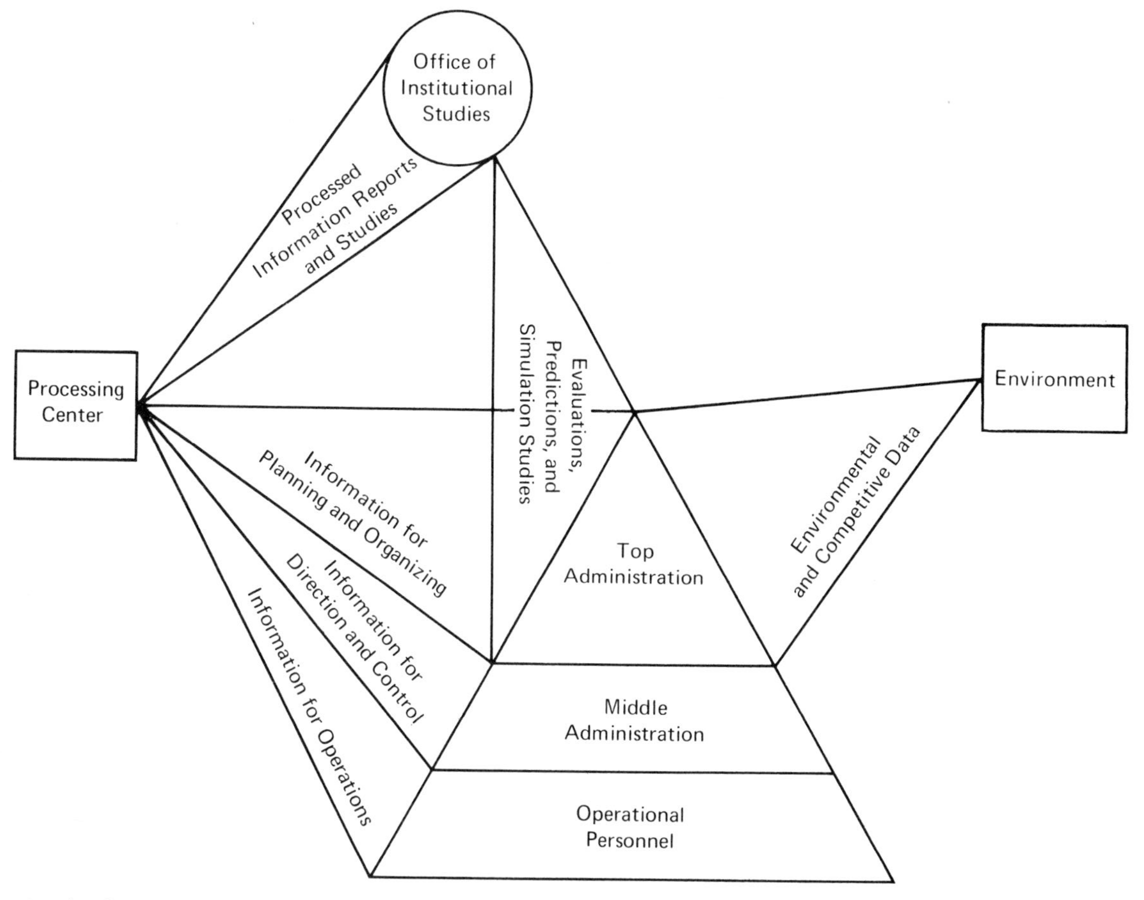

Figure 6–5. Institutional Studies and Hierarchy of Information

demands for appropriations. Otherwise, fund appropriations may be made based on false information or no information.

The functions of institutional research in higher education as seen by directors of institutional research are reported in the study done by Rourke and Brooks in 1966.[6] They conducted 209 interviews at 33 colleges and universities and central governing boards in 16 states. Their results are shown in Table 6–1.

Table 6–1. Institutional Research as Seen by Directors

Major Role of Institutional Research Agency	Number of Schools	Percentage
A basic data-gathering agency	55	43
A participant in major university decision-making	24	20
Both	33	26
No opinion	16	11
Totals	128	100

Rourke and Brooks found that 64 per cent of all institutional research agencies report directly to the presidents of the institutions and occupy a staff position on most campuses.[7] The study also found one institutional research director complaining of the low priority his office gets in the use of computers. This should change if institutional research is to perform the function of describing, analyzing, and prescribing. Also, operational information must be analyzed for anticipating problems and controlling them. These are very important complementary functions to the generation of information by information systems.

INFORMATION THRESHOLD

Thus far, the information levels have been shown to correspond to levels of administration. But there is a mobility between levels of information depending on what one commentator of information processing calls the information threshold.[8] This is illustrated in Figure 6–6 (a) and (b).

[6]F. E. Rourke and G. E. Brooks, *The Managerial Revolution In Higher Education* (Baltimore, Md.: The Johns Hopkins Press, 1966), p. 62.

[7]Rourke and Brooks, *The Managerial Revolution in Higher Education,* p. 52.

[8]R. V. Head, "Management Information Systems: A Critical Appraisal," *Datamation,* XIII, No. 5 (May 1967), 23–25. The diagrams on information thresholds and some other diagrams in this chapter are adaptions from the article by R. V. Head.

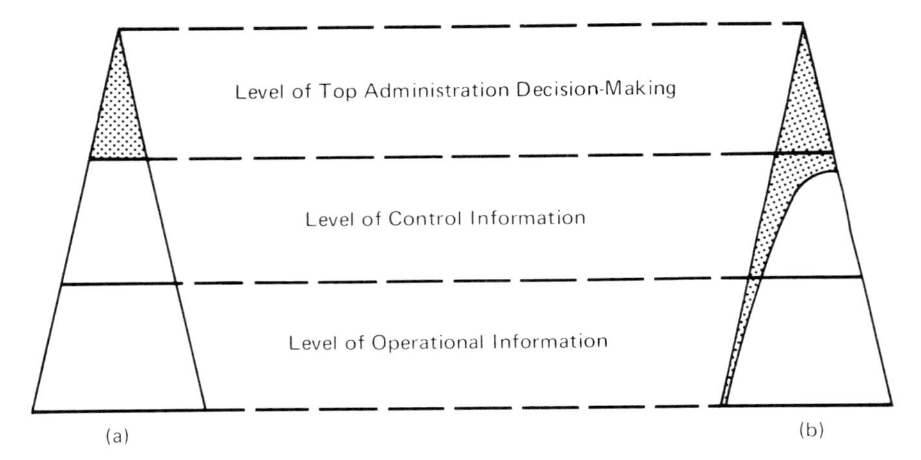

Figure 6–6. Different Information Thresholds

Figure 6–6 (a) illustrates the information threshold of one type of top administrator, who uses information designed especially for his administrative level, such as exceptional information, staff reports, and summary presentations; he is not interested in details of operational and control information. In contrast there is another top administrator, who uses not only information designed for top level administration but also some detailed information on control and operations. Such an administrator's information threshold is illustrated in Figure 6–6 (b). There are many other variations not shown in Figure 6–6.

Dean Acheson in his memoirs[9] describes President Truman as an administrator with an information threshold similar to that shown in Figure 6–6 (b). In contrast, President Eisenhower had a reputation for relying almost exclusively on staff papers, exceptional reports, and summarized briefings, which corresponds to the information threshold shown in Figure 6–6 (a).

Like top administrators, administrators at the middle level have varying information thresholds which extend into the operational level of information. The extent of these informational thresholds (for the top and middle-level administrators) is a function of the administrator's personality, his "style" of administration, the complexity of the institution, his span of control, his professional background, and the abilities of personnel reporting to him.

The variation of the information threshold poses an important and difficult problem to the designer of information systems: he must design a system that can easily adapt to different thresholds, since these will vary with changes

[9]Dean Acheson, *Present at the Creation: My Years at the State Department* (New York: W. W. Norton and Co., 1969).

in administration. A good system should not have to be redeveloped every time there is a change in administrators and a resulting change in the administrator's information threshold. This subject will be discussed further in Part Four.

EXCHANGE OF INFORMATION BETWEEN LEVELS OF ADMINISTRATION

In addition to the movement of information resulting from different information thresholds, there is also a movement of information between levels of administration. Such information may be functional and follow organizational lines. This is illustrated in Figure 6–7.

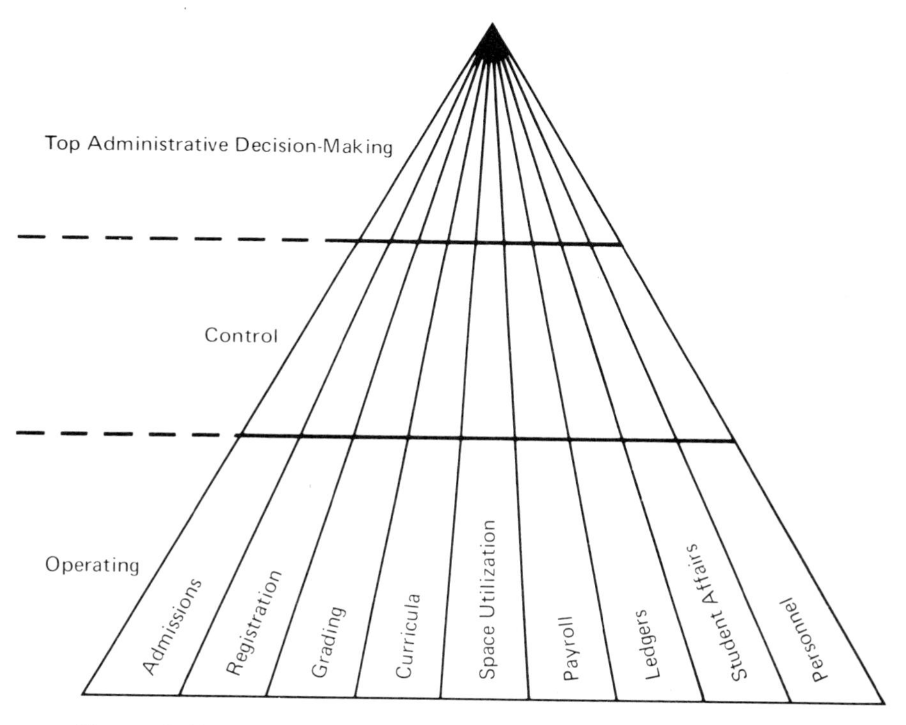

Figure 6–7. Information along Organizational Lines

Another approach to information exchange between administrative levels is to integrate information designed to facilitate the performance of administrative functions. This is illustrated in Figure 6–8, where information needed for control is sent from the operational level through middle management to the top administrators in the form of analytical and exceptional information.

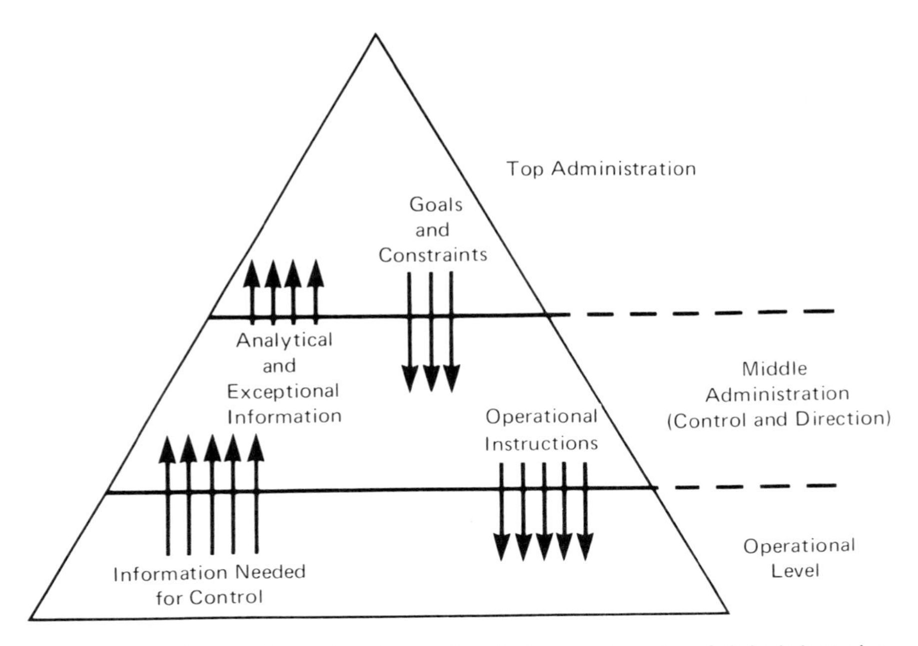

Figure 6–8. Flow of Information between Levels of Administration

The flow of information in the opposite direction and down the hierarchy of administration is sent in the form of revised objectives, sub-objectives, plans, subplans, and constraints from top to middle-level administrators. These are transformed into operational instructions and are sent as directives by the middle-level administrators to operational personnel. This completes the "loop" of feedback and control as discussed in Chapter 4 and is consistent with the administrative cycle shown in Figure 6–2.

In the situations depicted in Figures 6–7 and 6–8, an important problem arises in selecting the information that reaches each level of administration. The content and extent of this information will greatly influence decisions made by administrators; hence the decision on content is crucial. It must be determined by the administrator receiving the information or else, by default, it will be made by the systems analysts or operations personnel.

RELATION OF INFORMATION SYSTEM WITH OTHER SYSTEMS

The generation of information outside an information system was referred to earlier (e.g. in Figure 6–5). This is emphasized in Figure 6–9 where the formal information system for an organization is depicted as a collection of subsets of other systems.

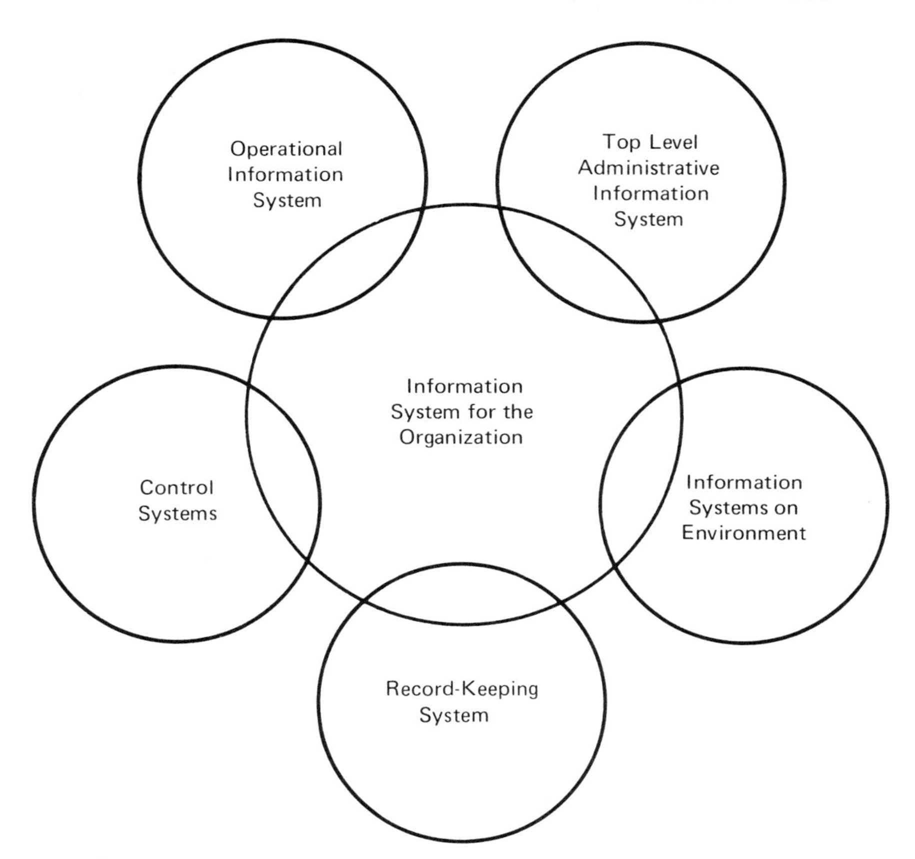

Figure 6–9. Relations of an Information System for an Organization with Other Systems

The excluded parts are and may remain outside the jurisdiction of a formal automated information system for some time to come. To illustrate the problem, consider a record-keeping system of a university. Part of its records are often part of a computer information system. But other records, such as letters of correspondence, letters of reference, documents recording the action on the student, and past transcripts are not in computer memory. Some day technology may make this economically feasible, but for a long time to come such information must remain outside the information system. Similarly, some information for control, operation, and top decision-making must remain outside the formal information system. The crucial question that arises concerns the decision as to what information stays inside and what stays outside a formal automated information system. Some rules have been mentioned previously in the discussion on the comparative advantages of man and machine processing. In the final analysis, though, the extent of information automation depends on the resources available, both human and equipment. The specification of these will be discussed in Part Four. Before that, however, we need to discuss the organization of data, the subject of the next part of the book, Part Three.

SUMMARY AND CONCLUSIONS

In this chapter the different types of information that should come from a formal information system were discussed. The information needed at the various levels of administration, operations, and institutional research were explained. These were discussed in the context of educational institutions. The concept of information threshold was also explained.

The mobility between levels of information depends on the information threshold of administrators. One type of administrator uses only the information designed especially for his administrative level. Another administrator uses that information and also information designed for administrative levels below him. An information system, therefore, should allow for changes in information threshold.

The types of information necessary are those for the activities of planning, organization, direction, operation, and control. These activities can be considered as belonging to a hierarchy. The functions of planning and organization are performed by top administrators. Direction and control are performed by middle-level administrators, while operations are performed by operations personnel. In performing these functions there is a need for relevant information for each function. Thus, there is a hierarchy of information corresponding to the hierarchy of administration. At each level, the content and characteristics of information are different.

The types of information flowing into and from the levels are summarized in Figure 6–10. It is self-explanatory and will not be discussed further.

KEY TERMS

Exceptional Information
Institutional Research
Record-Keeping
Information Threshold
Mobility of Information
Administrative Activities
Hierarchy of Functions and Administration
Hierarchy of Information

REVIEW QUESTIONS

1. Distinguish between
   Direction and Control

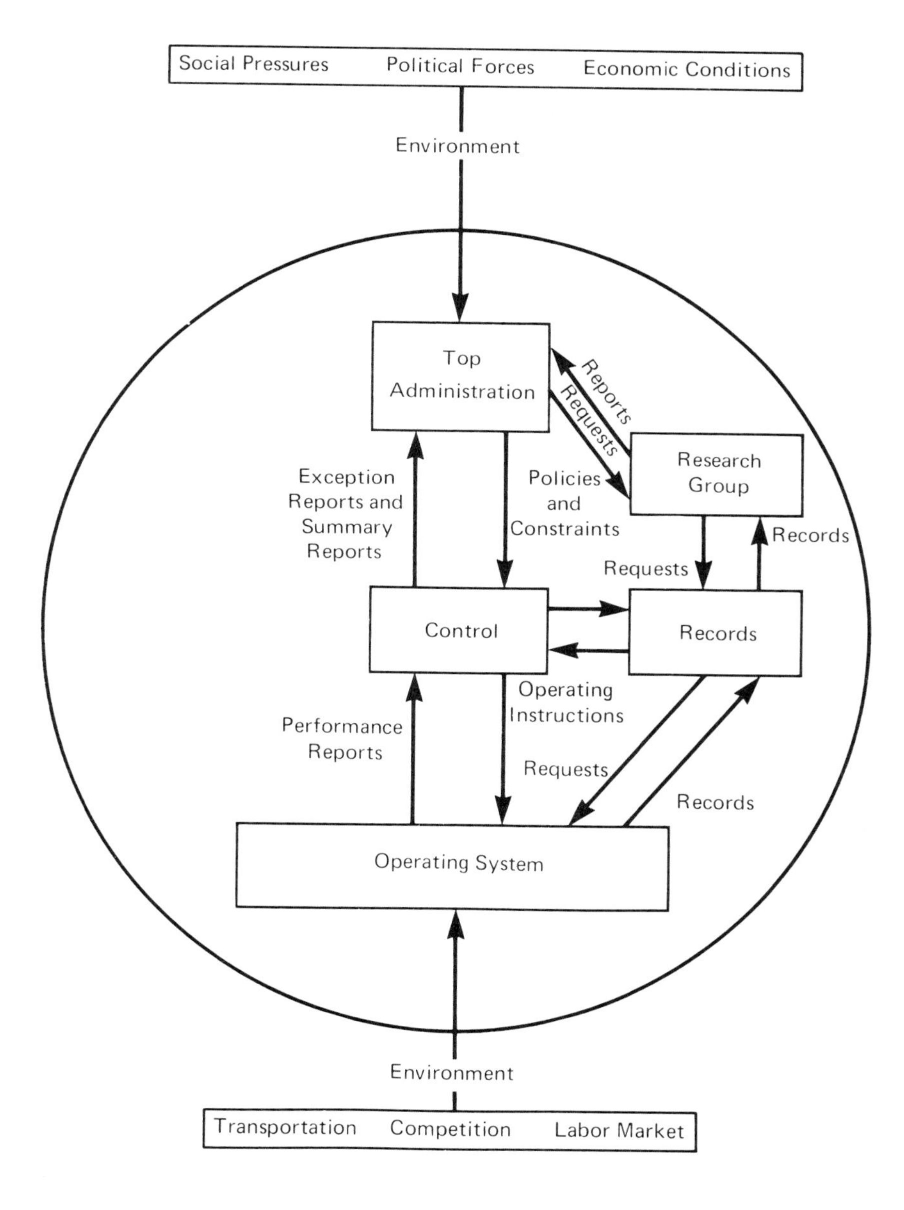
Social Pressures
Political Forces
Economic Conditions
Environment
Top Administration
Reports
Requests
Research Group
Exception Reports and Summary Reports
Policies and Constraints
Records
Requests
Control
Records
Operating Instructions
Performance Reports
Requests
Records
Operating System
Environment
Transportation
Competition
Labor Market

Figure 6–10

Operational Information and Exceptional Information
Information System and Management Information System

2. Discuss the interrelationship between administrative functions and an information system.
3. What types of information do top management usually require?
4. What are some problems that arise when using the exception principle for providing information?
5. Why should an information system be designed independently from existing information thresholds?
6. Under what conditions would the information system be triggered to provide exceptional information?
7. What are the cost components of maintaining records?
8. What is meant by the term mobility of information?

CHAPTER 6: SELECTED ANNOTATED BIBLIOGRAPHY

BITTEL, L. R., *Management by Exception.* New York: McGraw-Hill Book Company, Inc., 1964, 320 pp. A business-oriented book concerned primarily with the concept of management by exception. In the final chapter, the author relates the exception concept to operations research and information systems.

HEAD, R. V., "Management Information Systems: A Critical Appraisal," *Datamation,* XIII, No. 5 (May 1967), 22–27. Mr. Head is the founder of Software Resources Corporation and is a frequent contributor to the literature concerning the data-processing field. He provides an imaginative conceptual framework of the hierarchy of the data base for management information. The author emphasizes that system designers must come to grips with problem areas concerning the levels of the data base, specialized data bases, and management's "information threshold." An understanding of these problems is needed not only by system designers, but also by management. Industry trends are identified and briefly discussed under the headings of: application reworking, formalized systems planning, management science emphasis, regional information processing, and information management systems.

ROURKE, F. E., and G. E. BROOKS, *The Managerial Revolution in Higher Education,* Baltimore, Md.: The Johns Hopkins Press, 1966, Chap. III, pp. 44–67. This is a survey of 120 universities' use of institutional research. The questions surveyed include: who is most influenced by institutional research; who controls the projects; what projects are undertaken; and organizational problems. The authors predict that the primary mission of institutional research will become the study of academic programs and policies.

part three

ORGANIZATION OF DATA

The desired information discussed in Part Two is generated by processing data. However, for the processing to be efficient and effective, the data must be organized. Such organization of data is the subject of Part Three, Chapters 7–9.

Chapter 7 discusses the structure of data. It is hierarchial. The basic element of this heirarchy is the **character**. A set of characters constitutes a **field,** a set of related fields constitutes a **record,** and a set of related records constitutes a **file.** A set of files constitutes a **data base,** while a set of integrated files constitutes a **data bank.** In Chapter 7 these terms are all defined and examined.

In some cases data is long and inefficient to process. Sometimes, also, it is not unique and can lead to inaccuracies. To overcome these and other problems, data is represented by what is referred to as a **code.** Codes are defined, classified, and their advantages and limitations examined in Chapter 8.

The knowledge of the hierarchy of data and its coding enables us to discuss a related and important question: What data should be collected and processed? Some related questions are, How long should each data element be retained? When should it be updated? Who should make such determinations? These and other questions are discussed in Chapter 9, the final chapter of Part Three.

7

Basic Concepts of Data Organization

INTRODUCTION

Data must be organized so that it can be processed. This is somewhat analagous to the organization of a book. A book has a number of chapters, each organized into paragraphs; each paragraph has a number of sentences, each composed of words and punctuation; and finally, each word consists of letters. In the case of data organization, there is a data bank consisting of a number of files; each file has many records; each record is composed of data fields; and finally, each data field contains a set of characters. Thus, data is organized into a hierarchy of levels.

This chapter will examine the levels of data. Each level will be defined, its characteristics identified, and its relationships to efficient processing discussed.

CHARACTER

A **character** of data is the most basic of the data levels. It can be one of three of the following types:

1. Alphabetic (from A-Z)
2. Numeric (from 0–9)
3. Special Symbols (such as $,+,(,), etc.)

The set of special symbols available for printing output will vary with the printer. Each manufacturer of printers favors its own set. Furthermore, some printers allow lower-case alphabetic characters in addition to the upper-case alphabetic characters generally available. The various characters available are known as a **character set.**

DATA FIELD

Often one character is insufficient to express attributes that need to be recorded. In such cases, characters are combined. Whether single or combined, they form a **data field.** The value in the data field represents the attributes of a **data element.** It could be the number of cats, the social security number of a student, the age of an instructor, or an amount paid for travel.

The data element need not be quantitative. It could represent the name or address of a person, or his likes or dislikes. It could even represent ideas, anything whose attribute is worth recording. The attribute of a data element must be recorded in the data field assigned to the data element.

To illustrate a data element, one must first select a medium of storing data. The most common medium is a **data card,** also called the **Hollerith** card after its originator. This card has space for representing 80 different characters, each character in one of the 80 columns in the card. A commonly used character set is shown on a data card in Figure 7–1.

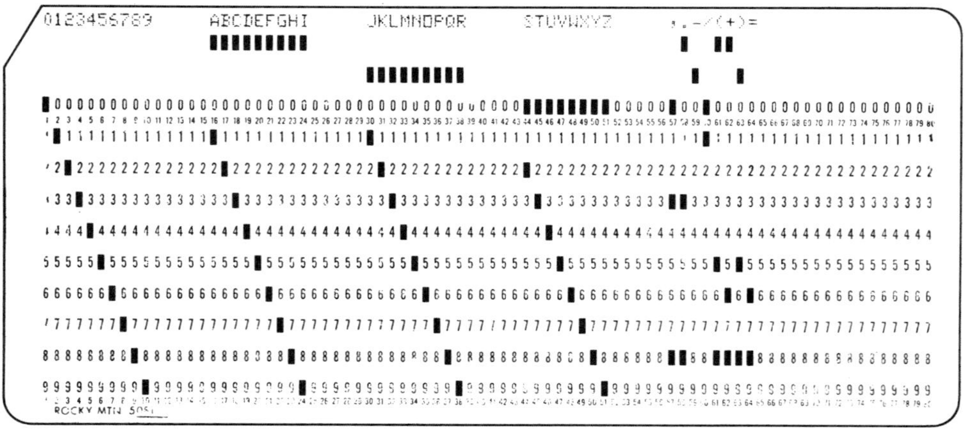

Figure 7–1. Data Card

Each character in Figure 7–1 is identified by its unique combination of punched holes in the card. When this card is read by special card readers, electrical pulses passing through the holes are recorded and the character corresponding to the card holes is recognized. Data so recognized by machines is referred to as **machine-readable data.** The transformation of written data into machine-readable data by punching prescribed holes on a card is achieved by using equipment called **keypunches.**

A sample data card will now be used to illustrate data fields and data elements. This is done in Figure 7–2 on the next page.

In Figure 7–2, three data elements are shown for illustration. These are social security number, name, and card type identification. Each data element has a specific data field assigned to it. In Figure 7–2 the social security number has a data field of card columns 1–9 (i.e. cc 1–9); name (cc 11–26); and card identification (cc 79–80). Every set of numbers in a field represents the data element assigned to that field. For example, any set of numbers in cc 1–9 in such a card represents a social security number. The data elements are separated by blank fields. The need and location of blanks is a matter of preference and design and will be discussed later.

The right-hand side of a card is often reserved for identification, such as semester, campus, or the identification of a specific card in cases of multiple cards. In Figure 7–2 the card is identified by a number. It could also have been identified by the type of the card, such as the identification "name," but a number takes less space and hence is more economical from the viewpoints of keypunching, storage, and processing. Such an abbreviated identification is referred to as a **code.**

The card code in Figure 7–2 is numeric. It could have also been a combination of alphabetic and numeric characters, referred to as an **alphanumeric** code or **alphameric** code. Such coding allows more permutations of characters but the numeric code has advantages of faster keypunching and processing. This and other topics of coding will be discussed in detail in the following chapter.

The data field location (such as cc 1–9) for a data element (the social security number) enables quick identification with no need for repeatedly identifying the data element. Thus, if it is desired to record data for a person whose name is R. Jones and who has a social security number of 987654321 on a campus coded 03, then all that is needed is to place the number 987654321 in card columns 1–9; the name Jones R. in cc 11–26; and the card code 03 in cc 79–80. (Why not code 3 in cc 79?)

Within a data field, the data cannot be placed just anywhere; it must go according to established conventions. For example, consider the code for the data field reserved for card identification. For a card numbered 25 there is no choice, 25 goes in cc 79–80. But with the number "3," where should it be

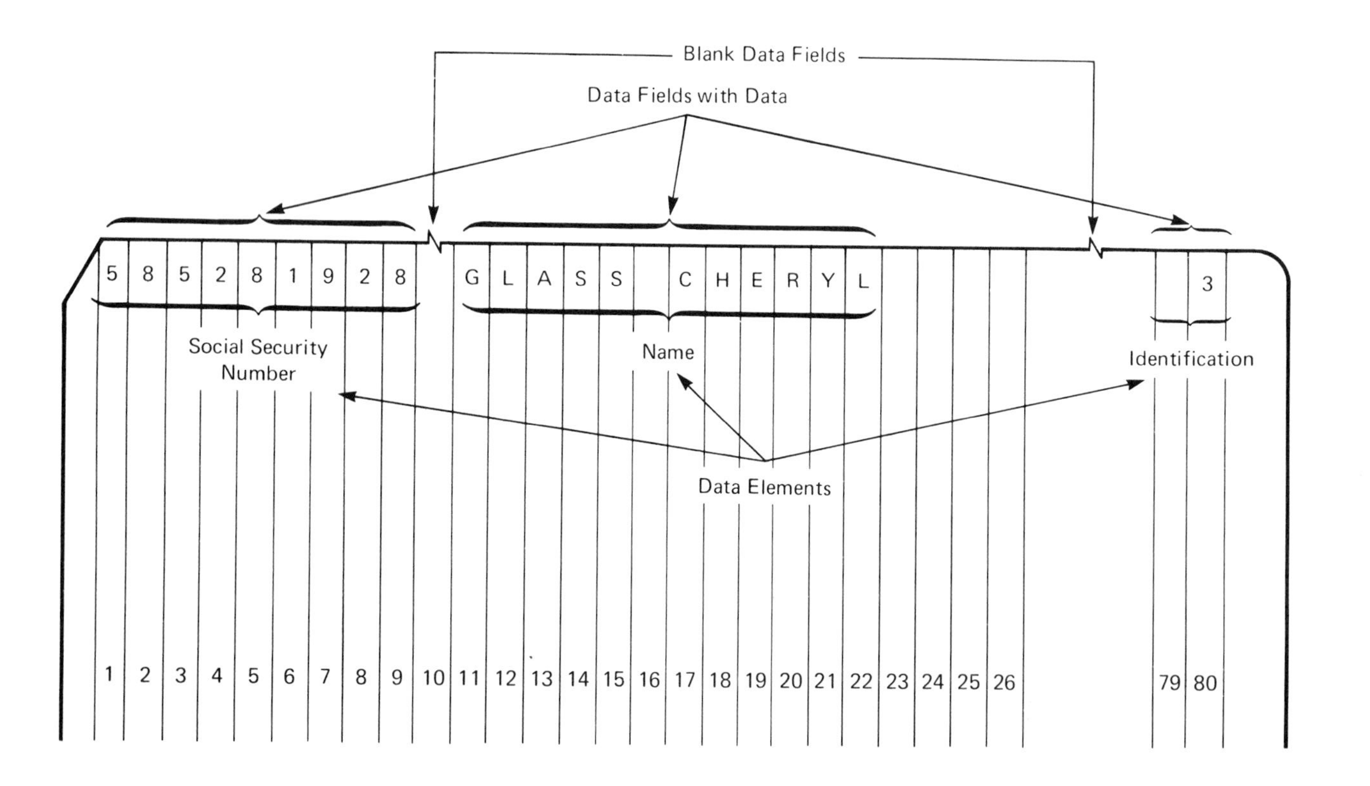

Figure 7–2. Illustration of Data Fields and Data Elements

placed? In cc 79 or in cc 80? If placed in cc 79 with a blank in the right-hand side, the blank could be mistaken for a zero in some computers and the number would then be read as 30. Instead, if the code 3 is placed in cc 80, no misunderstandings can arise, for an additional zero in front (leading zero) will have no effect since "03" has the same value as "3." Thus numeric data must be entered starting from the right which is referred to as **right-justification.** In contrast, alphabetic (and alphameric) data should start from the left and is **left-justified.** This is illustrated by Figure 7–3 (a). Alphabetic data could also be right-justified as is shown in Figure 7–3 (b). It is not only difficult to read but is also more difficult to process, compared to the left-justified data in Figure 7–3 (a). Right justification is therefore not the established practice.

C	A	R	T	E	R										
C	H	R	I	S	T	I	A	N	S	E	N				
C	O	X													
C	R	O	M	W	E	L	L								

(a) Alphabetic Data Left-Justified

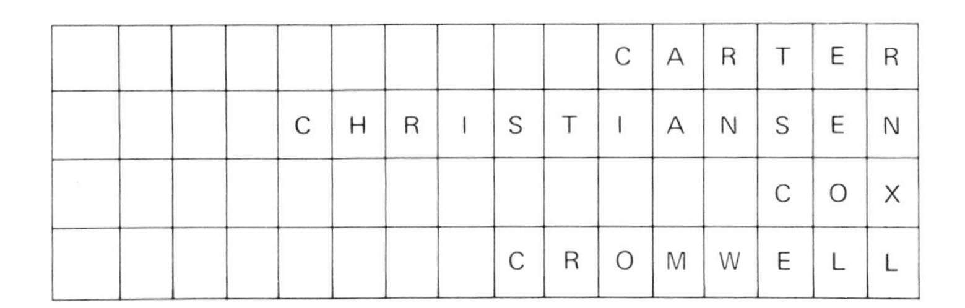

(b) Alphabetic Data Right-Justified

Figure 7–3. Alphabetic Data Entries

A data field can be divided into subfields. For example, a field representing a length may be divided into two subfields; one showing "feet" and the other identifying its corresponding "inches" of measure. Another example where subfields can be used is the field of a student or employee's birthdate. This field has three subfields as shown in Figure 7–4.

In Figure 7–4 an alpha code has been chosen for the subfield of month largely to illustrate the left-justification and the use of a trailing blank which is insignificant. Normally, the number of the month will be used to identify the month value. In the case of the subfield for the "day" of birth, the subfield is right-justified with a leading blank, or zero. In some computers, the machine representation for the two are not identical and hence a zero is required instead of a blank. Another problem with a blank is that it does not identify whether it was used on purpose or by error. For example, a blank followed by a "2" in the day subfield could have been an omission error. Insisting on a zero in place of the blank forces the issue and avoids omission errors.

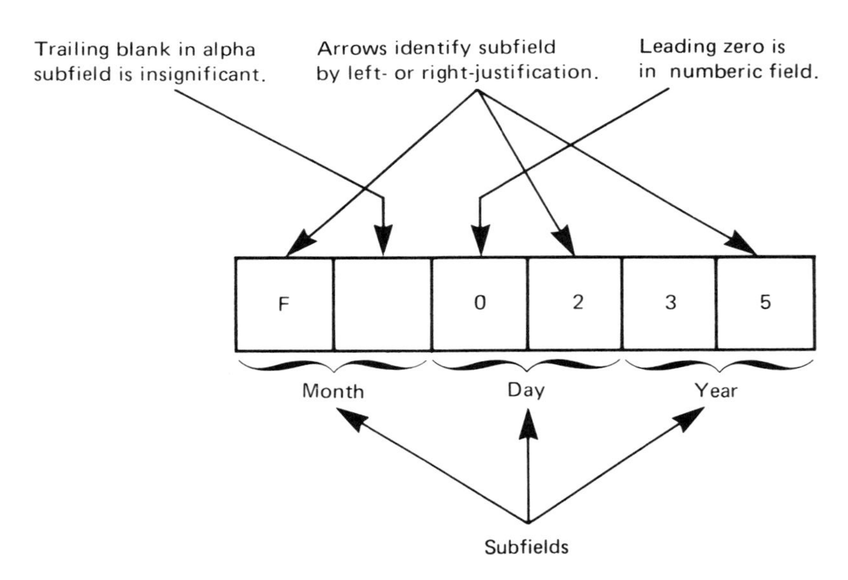

Figure 7–4. Subfields within Data Field of Birthdate

Why use subfields? There are at least two advantages. One is that subfields facilitate the data validity process and data preparation (a subject to be discussed further in Chapter 8). The second advantage is that subfields facilitate processing. It enables the processing of that part of the field which is relevant, while ignoring the rest. Thus, for example, suppose we need to calculate the age of a person correct to the year. We then need to look only at the subfield identifying the year and subtract it from the current year. The day and month subfield are ignored because they are irrelevant.

Another consideration of data location within a data field concerns data with decimal points. Consider the problem of recording a student's gradepoint average of "3.25." This could take four columns of a data card. However, it could be compressed into three data columns if we deleted the decimal point and had a convention on locating the decimal point. This convention is part of what is known as **formatting** and identifies both the width of the data field and the location of the decimal point. One type of formatting for decimal point values is called the **floating-point** format and is identified by the letter F, as shown in Table 7–1. The width (w) of the data field in the data card is indicated by a number which appears after the letter F. This number is followed by a decimal point and a number (d) which indicates the number of digits after the decimal point in the number.

Thus F4.2 is of the form Fw.d where w=width of the field, d=number of digits after the decimal point.

A number 8766 in format F4.2 would then be read as 87.66 since the value of d=2 and there must therefore be two digits after the decimal point. The formatting is specified in the computer program using the data. It enables the saving of a column of the data card otherwise used by the decimal point and is a good example of compacting and compressing data. The main reasons for compacting data are to reduce the costs of conversion, storage, transmission (if any), and the processing of data.

Another format identifies nondecimal numbers (i.e., integer numbers) and is referred to as the "I" format. It has the form Iw. Thus two numbers read under formats I2 and I3 in a string of numbers 98765 would be 98 and 765 respectively.

A review of the formats discussed above with more examples is shown in Table 7–1.

Table 7–1. Examples of Formatting Data

Data as Stored	Format Controlling Data	Data Value Used for Computation and Output	Comments
1234	I4	1234	No change.
004	I3	4	Leading zeros are insignificant as far as value is concerned.
56789	F5.2	567.89	The decimal point location is specified by the format.
56789	F5.3	56.789	Same as above.
003	F4.3	0.003	The leading zeros are significant.

There are other variations of expression within the two modes of formatting discussed, and another mode of formatting. Also, there are other methods of data compaction.[1] The purpose of this discussion, however, is not to provide the details essential to a programmer, but merely to introduce the concepts of formatting and data compaction necessary for an administrator using a data system.

RECORD

The format of a data element will determine the width of the data field. All data fields related to an entity can then be collected into what is referred to as a **record.**

A record could be a physical record such as the data card shown in Figure 7–2. Within a physical record are fields that relate to a logical entity or transaction, such as a student, a course offered, or an amount paid. These fields constitute a **logical record.** In Figure 7–2 the logical record is the physical record minus the blanks.

A logical record could contain one or more physical records. An example of such a record on magnetic tape created from two physical records (for the same person, i.e. same social security number) on cards is shown in Figure 7–5. This record includes identification data, such as the social security number which is entered only once; it excludes all blank fields on the original cards; it uses the card number identification to create the record but does not include it on the aggregated tape record itself; it includes all the statistical data on both cards; and finally, it has the identification of the data such as the semester identification, which, as with the social security number, is entered only once.

A logical record can have a **fixed** or a **variable length.** The latter occurs when the number of fields in a record is not constant but varies. Examples would be the record of courses taken by a student, or the record of degrees held by a faculty member. Each record may contain one or more fields. If, however, the number of fields used in creating each logical record is constant, the length of the record is fixed. This would make the record simple, but then it may consist of many blanks (because of non-existing values) resulting in wasted data storage space and processing. To overcome this problem, the record is allowed to vary in length in order to include all the relevant data. This raises a problem: how does one identify the end of the record? It is done by allowing a space between each record known as the **Inter Record Gap** (abbreviated as "IRG").

On a magnetic tape, the IRG is about ¾ of an inch wide. This is wider than the space required for many small records. Thus the space for overhead

[1]For a detailed discussion, see *IBM Record Compaction Technique,* Form E20–8252 (White Plains, N.Y.: International Business Machines Corporation, n.d.), 18 pp.

in record separation may often be more than that required for one of the records itself. This overhead can be reduced by having logical records processed in groups instead of individually. This grouping is referred to as **blocking.** Blocks are then separated by an IRG.

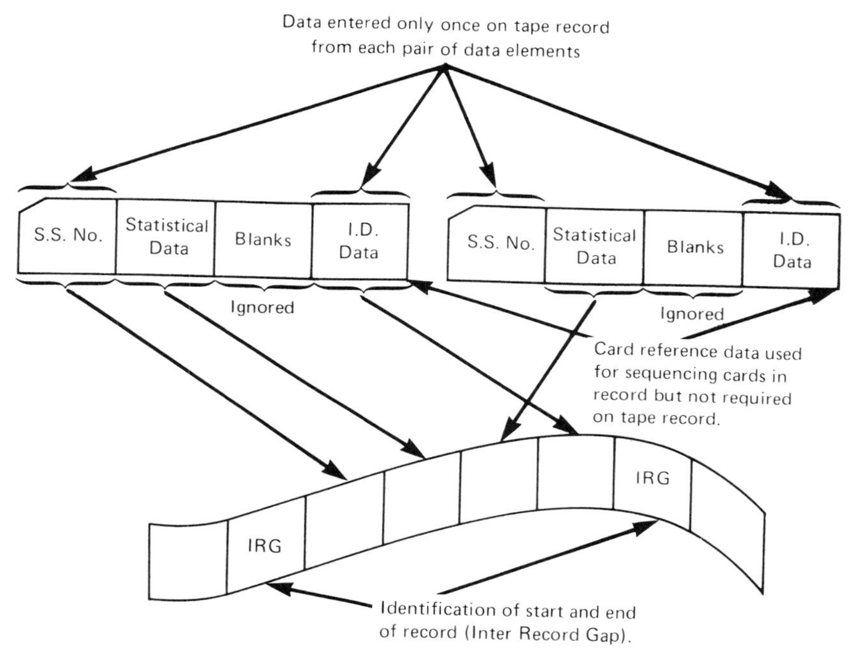

Figure 7–5. Illustration of the Transformation of Two Physical Card Records into One Logical Tape Record

A block of records can be of fixed or variable length. The fixed block has a constant number of logical records, each with the same number of characters in each record. In a variable block, the number of logical records as well as the number of characters for each record may vary. The specific values are identified in a prefix just before the records in a block. This is illustrated in Figure 7–6 where four logical records (R_1, R_2, R_3, and R_4) are shown in one block following the block description prefix.

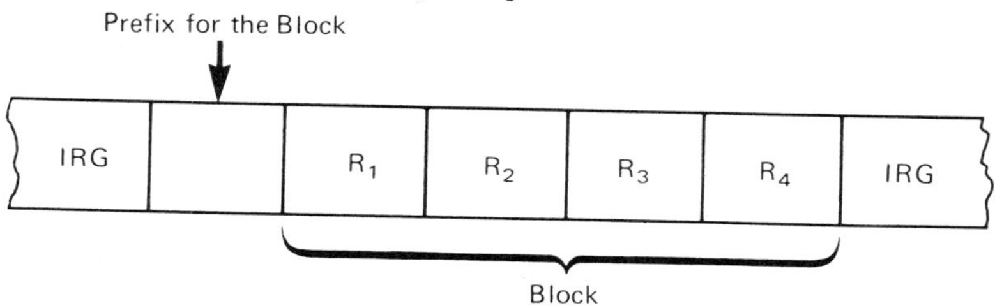

Figure 7–6. A Block of Records

FILE

A **file** consists of a set of records. When stored on a tape, it consists of a set of blocks of records, a set of IRG's that identify the end of each block, a header label, and a trailer label. The header label identifies data on file creation, file retention, and its serial and sequence numbers. The trailer label identifies the preceeding file and reel. It also provides control data on the file, including the number of records and the number of blocks in the file. This trailer label is followed by a mark identifying the end of file, referred to as the EOF mark.

The relationship of the EOF mark, the logical record, and the file labels are shown in Figure 7–7.

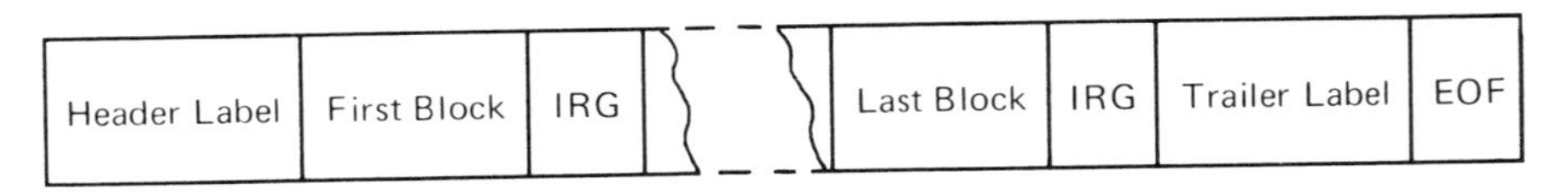

Figure 7–7. File Layout on Tape

A file can be classified in two ways: by type of data organization, and by function or use. The former classification includes sequential or random organization and is of great concern to the processor[2] but not as much to the administrator or user. The functional classification is of greater concern to the user. Each type in this classification will be discussed in terms of its characteristics, its uses, and by example.

A **Master File** is one which contains a set of basic records. It should be current at the time of processing and is made current through updating. This updating can be done from a file that has records on all transactions made since the last updating. This is called a **Transaction** or **Detail File.** It is temporary and transitory, and performs its main function at the time of updating.

As an example, consider a set of student files. The master file would typically contain basic data on students, such as names, identification numbers, dates of birth, academic records, courses being taken, and so on. During the semester, however, many students add and drop courses. These can be recorded on a transaction file. Periodically, or before the master file is processed, the transaction file is used to update the master file, after which the data on the transaction file is erased for recording future transactions. Keeping transactions separate from the basic data on the master file before updating enables faster processing of transactions.

For further economy of processing, the data fields on a master file can

[2]For such a discussion, see F. J. Clark, *Information Processing,* (Pacific Palisades, Ca.: Goodyear Publishing Company, Inc., 1970), pp. 176–79.

be selected for those more frequently used. These data fields constitute a summary record, and a set of such records is referred to as a **Summary File.** An example of this would be a student summary file. This would not include infrequently processed data, such as the name and address of relatives to be informed in case of an emergency, hobbies, and extracurricular activities.

Another important file type is the **History File,** used for recording historical information needed for calculating statistics, or for backup if the master file is lost or destroyed.

In a history file, there is the problem of the time period for which data should be retained. For example, should the data be included for students who left the institution five years ago, ten years ago, or more? There is a trade-off. The administrator may state "the longer the better" but the longer the data is maintained, the more costly it is in terms of storage and processing.

Another problem concerns the content of a history file. What data should be included? This subject will be discussed in great detail in Chapter 9 and, hence, will not be discussed further here.

DATA BASE AND DATA BANK

The next and highest level of data aggregation is the data base or data bank. These terms do not have a universally accepted definition but, generally speaking, a **data base** is a reference to a reservoir of data,[3] a set of data files, or just one large file,[4] as distinct from a **data bank** which is a set of integrated files.[5] Sometimes a data bank refers to a mass collection of data of the same type,[6] and sometimes the terms data bank and data base are used interchangeably.[7] In this book, the definition of a data bank as a set of integrated data files will be used.

The data bank has many advantages. It enables an institutional analysis that crosses functional and organizational lines. Because of the integration of data, the overlap and redundancy of data is eliminated, resulting in a reduction of the costs of data creation, validity testing, and maintenance. Control of data

[3]For this definition, see J. Gwynn, "The Data Base Approach to a Management Information System," in *Management Information Systems: Their Development and Use in the Administration of Higher Education,* eds. B. Lawrence and J. Minter (Boulder, Colo.: Western Interstate Commission for Higher Education, 1969), p. 10.

[4]J. Kanter, "The Ubiquitous Data Base Concept," *Data Processing Magazine,* IX, No. 5 (May 1967), 28.

[5]D. Sanders, *Computers & Management* (New York: McGraw-Hill Book Company, Inc., 1970), p. 80.

[6]E. A. Weiss, ed., *Computer Usage: 360 Assembly Programming* (New York: McGraw-Hill Book Company, Inc., 1970), p. 173.

[7]*Ibid.,* p. 74.

in its creation, maintenance, and access is greatly increased. The overlapping of programming is reduced but programming becomes more complex.

One important criticism of a data bank is that the user (an individual administrator) loses control over his data. He can neither define nor retrieve his data at will. He must accept a standard set of data definitions and an institutional set of procedures (such as those concerning updating and census dates—dates for which data is valid, such as ten days after registration for enrollment).

Another important criticism of the data bank is the concomitant complex problem of privacy of data. The data bank, it is argued, will enable unauthorized use of data that will infringe on the individual's right to privacy.[8]

There are technological problems too. These relate to the structuring of files, the identification and locating of data, and its fast and efficient retrieval. But these technological problems will no doubt also be overcome. Other technological developments, such as great reductions in cost of storage and processing, the ability to interface systems of different hardware manufacturers, and developments in programming languages and software will no doubt spur the trend toward data banks. Solutions to the problems of privacy of data will further encourage this trend.

SUMMARY AND CONCLUSIONS

In this chapter the hierarchy of data was discussed. The basic or lowest level of data is the character. Characters may be alphabetic, numeric, or special symbols ($,+, etc.). One or more characters comprise a data field. A data field is assigned to each variable, also referred to as a data element.

A data field may be divided into subfields to facilitate data preparation and processing. An example would be a data field for a date divided into subfields of month, day, and year.

All data fields related to an entity constitute a record for that entity. For example, a student's record will consist of data fields for his name, identification number, birth date, courses taken, gradepoint average, etc. There are several ways to form records discussed in this chapter, such as making them of fixed or variable length, and blocked or unblocked.

[8]For an excellent discussion of privacy and its relationship to security of data, see W. H. Ware, "Security and Privacy: Similarities and Differences," *AFIPS Conference Proceedings,* XXX (1967), 287–90. For another view of a computer scientist, see P. Baran, "Does the Interconnected Computer Network Pose a Hidden Threat to Invasion of Privacy," in *Conversational Computers,* ed. W. D. Orr (New York: John Wiley & Sons, Inc., 1968), pp. 195–205. For a more global view by a lawyer, see A. R. Miller, "The National Data Center and Personal Privacy," *The Atlantic,* CCXX, No. 5 (November 1967), 53–58. For a survey article, see L. J. Hoffman, "Computers and Privacy: A Survey," *Computing Surveys,* I, No. 2 (1969), 85–103.

A related group of records make up a file. There are several different types of files. Their characteristics, uses, and examples are summarized in Table 7–2.

A set of data or data files is a data base, while a set of integrated data files is referred to as a data bank. This subject will be discussed again in Chapter 9 as being one approach to data file design. Before doing so, however, it is necessary to discuss representations of data that make file processing efficient and effective. One such representation is a **code,** the subject of the next chapter.

Table 7–2. Comparison of Types of Files

Type	Characteristics	Use	Example
Master File	Contains basic information. Needs to be updated.	Provides basic information for processing.	Student File with basic data on students (including courses taken).
Transaction File or Detail File	Records an event or occurrence.	Provides latest information on changes for updating the Master File.	Courses added or dropped by students.
Summary File	A summary of a Master File.	For efficient and fast processing.	Short Student File.
History File	Provides relevant master and transaction data of past.	For backup and to provide historical statistical information.	Historical Student File.

KEY TERMS

Hierarchial Levels of Data
Character Set
Data Element
Data Field
Logical Record
Physical Record
Format
File
End of File
Blocking
Inter Record Gap
Header Label
Trailer Label
Data Base
Data Bank

REVIEW QUESTIONS

1. Distinguish between
   IRG and EOF
   Master File and Summary File
   Data Element and Data Field
   I and F Format of Data
   Physical Record and Logical Record
   Fixed Field and Variable Field
   Right- and Left-Justification
   Master File and Transaction File
   Alphameric and Alphabetic
   Header Label and Trailer Label
   Record and File
   Data Base and Data Bank
2. How does blocking affect the processing of a file?
3. Why is blocking not always used?
4. Describe how data can be put into machine-readable form. What are the characteristics of this data that makes it machine-readable?
5. Why should a data field have subfields? Give one example other than that given in the text.
6. Write the value of a student's gradepoint average in the I, F4.2, and F4.1 formats? What are the advantages and disadvantages of these three different representations?
7. Draw a diagram showing the hierarchy of data.

CHAPTER 7: SELECTED ANNOTATED BIBLIOGRAPHY

CLARK, F. J., "Files: Organization and Maintenance," *Information Processing.* Pacific Palisades, Ca.: Goodyear Publishing Company, Inc., 1970, Chap. X, pp. 173–89. The author has compiled from his lectures presented in a two-year data processing program in a text to provide readers with a broad foundation upon which they can build an in-depth understanding of data processing. Chapter 10 presents a brief and basic discussion of file organization and maintenance. After defining a file as an organized collection of records which has a common characteristic or function, the author explains how files are classified, types of files, and their maintenance. The flowcharts on file maintenance are helpful in understanding this area of data processing which the author believes is one of the most important activities in information processing.

DIPPLE, G., and W. C. HOUSE, *Information Systems.* Glenview, Ill.: Scott, Foresman and Company, 1969, Chap. VI, pp. 178–214. Mr. Dipple contributed his experience as a systems planner in industry and Professor House brought to bear his broad experience in education in the writing of this basic text on information systems. Included are two basic rules which are generally followed in the systematic recording of data. The levels of data are identified as the character, data item, record, and file. The data base concept is introduced and defined as the consolidation of all files or several files so that data elements required by two or more processing functions will not need to be repeated for each function.

IBM Data File Handbook (No. C20–1638–1). White Plains, N.Y.: International Business Machines Corporation, 1965, pp. 1–13. The basics of data files, their composition, organization, and processing are presented in this section. Those who have recently completed a basic course in data processing may find scanning of the material sufficient. The style of presentation is very formal.

KANTER, J., "The Ubiquitous Data Base Concept," *Data Processing Magazine,* IX, No. 5 (May 1967), 28–32. Management is built on accurate and timely information and the Central Data Base (CDB) provides it; however, the author suggests that management is prone to overlook three problem areas in implementing such a system. These are identified as the content, time, and file medium dimensions. To successfully implement the CDB concept these problem areas must be recognized and dealt with by management.

LEFKOVITZ, D., *File Structures for On Line Systems.* New York: Spartan Books, 1969, Chap. VIII, pp. 155–80. This book is designed to provide the programmer or systems analyst with basic principles and techniques for the organization of files in mass random access computer storage. Chapter 8 presents a discussion of on-line updating and maintenance of various file organizations. The techniques of file structuring for real-time update are categorized as: whole record addition, whole record deletion, deletion of keys, addition/deletion/modification of non-key data, and addition to keys. Processes for using each technique are presented in table form.

RUGGLES, R., "How a Data Bank Might Operate," *Think,* XXXV, No. 3 (May-June 1969), 22–23. A national data bank is needed to supply information about the operation of society and economic problems. Individual privacy would be protected, and violated only if the originating agency misuses the information.

8

Codes

INTRODUCTION

Codes are used for many purposes. During the Revolutionary War one lantern, hung in a prearranged steeple, indicated that the British troops were arriving by land and two lanterns meant that the movement was by sea.[1] A more elaborate set of symbols is the Morse Code used for transmitting messages over wire and for flashing lights across the seas. Other coded signals include a predetermined set of kicks under a bridge table or movements of the eyes used for transmitting secret messages in gambling or spying.[2]

Codes are also used in information systems. In this context, a **code** is a

[1]A. Kent, *Textbook on Mechanized Information Retrieval* (New York: John Wiley & Sons, Inc., 1962), p. 165.

[2]For more on this subject, see B. Kohn, *Secret Codes and Ciphers* (Englewood Cliffs, N.J.: Prentice-Hall, Inc., 1968), p. 63.

set of characters that identifies an attribute of a data element such that it achieves an advantage over the natural language identification.[3] The advantages of codes are discussed in this chapter, followed by a classificiation of code structures, a discussion on the selection of coding structures, and principles of code design. Some problems and issues concerning code structures are also discussed.

USES OF CODES

There are five main reasons for using codes. These are discussed below.

1. Codes are often an abbreviated equivalent of a natural language message and hence, they occupy less space than the uncoded data. This reduces the space needed for storing the data. For example, consider the following partial data record for a student: "Cheryl Glass who is a female, born in December 1947, is majoring in Philosophy." This record can be shortened by coding it. The name can be identified by the student's social security number 585281928; the sex can be coded as 2 for female (1 for male); the birth month can be identified by the number of the month which is 12 for December; the year of birth can be coded by the last two digits "47" (the last two digits are sufficient since it is unlikely that a person studying in the 1970s is born other than in the twentieth century); and finally, Philosophy can be coded as 1509, using the major codes developed by the U.S. Office of Education. The coded record will then appear as in Figure 8–1.

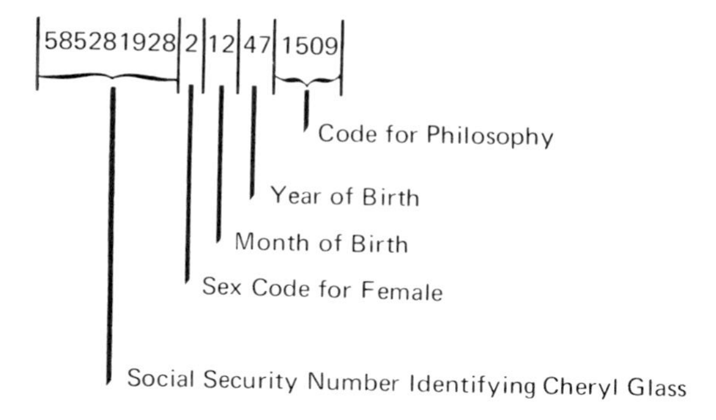

Figure 8–1

[3]For another approach, see G. W. Patterson, "What is a Code?" *Communications of the ACM,* III, No. 5 (May 1960), 315. Patterson states: "The most fundamental idea concerning a code is that of the existence of two languages, the source language (historically a natural language such as English) and the code language (usually made up of special signals created for the purpose at hand). . . . The code, properly speaking, is the system of rules that enables messages in the source language to be encoded into the code language."

This coded form requires only 18 data columns instead of the 78 columns of the English statement.

2. The use of a code saves time in recording the data in machine-readable form, such as keypunching it on a data card. It also saves time and sometimes equipment in transmission of data in cases where data is so transmitted.

3. Perhaps the most important advantage of a code is that it enables faster processing. For example, if one had to determine the number of females in a group of records like the one displayed in Figure 8–1, one would merely have to search for a "2" code in the tenth column from the left and add up the number of occurrences of such a code. The search time and computing time are both reduced by the use of codes, in comparison to the time required for processing alphabetic noncoded data. However, the time saved by codes in the processing and preparation of data must be weighed against the time consumed in preparing codes and using them. The net savings in many cases is still substantial enough to justify coding on economic grounds.

4. Another advantage of a code is that it provides a unique or near-unique identification. A near-unique code is the social security number. All social security numbers do not uniquely identify one person since a person can lose his number and obtain another. This reduces the usefulness of the code. Nonetheless, it is still advantageous to use this code. It eliminates the semantic vagueness of much of the uncoded information, such as names. Some students, faculty, and other personnel have the same last name, even the same first and middle initial. The problem of lack of uniqueness in names can be partially eliminated by use of the social security number. The non-uniqueness of the social security number can be completely overcome by using a "birth number," which is assigned in some states to each child at the time of birth. Such a number, however, is not as commonly used as the social security number.

A unique code is sometimes required as a linking element to link and integrate files. For example, a file of classes taught can identify a person by the course he teaches. By looking at the course, the person can soon be uniquely identified, even if his name is not unique. But if it is desired to find the cost of the course taught, then one must refer to a personnel file or a payroll file to identify the salary of the person teaching the course. For cross-referencing, the name of the person may not suffice since it may not be unique. A social security number or birth number code will provide the uniqueness necessary to link the files together.

5. Codes may sometimes appear in a final output. This is desirable when large amounts of data must be compressed onto one page. An example would be a schedule for classes offered. Some of the desired data for each class can be truncated, such as a long name of an instructor. Some data such as the title of courses are not easily truncated (e.g., "The History of Modern Mexican Philosophy from 1950–1970") and hence, they are abbreviated. But still there

is additional information that must be printed on one line such as the days and places where classes are held. In such cases, codes are used.

The use of codes in output design is of a secondary importance. The main use is that of facilitating the processing of data. Once processed, the coded data can be decoded for purposes of output reports. A computer program can look up the equivalent of each code in a table and print the decoded information. This is known as the Table Look-up method, which is part of the computer program. Also, the program can provide spacing, hyphens, or other symbols to make the output readable. Codes are thus an intermediate step between the document used as source data and the final output.

The conversion of data in the natural language to code characters according to a set of rules is referred to as **coding** or **encoding.** The person performing this operation is a **coder.** He uses a special form for this purpose called a **coding sheet.** The terms **coding, coder,** and **coding sheet** should not be confused with similar terms used in computer programming where a **code** is an abbreviated programming instruction. The person writing such programming instructions is also called a **coder** and uses **coding sheets.** He is sometimes differentiated from a programmer in that the latter does more than coding. The programmer designs the program and draws the flowchart to define the program logic.

Another use of the term **code** refers to a machine representation of the number system. One example is the binary system where 1001 is the binary representation of the number 9. Note that the coded message is longer than the uncoded data but it still is faster for processing in a computer.

Details on codes, coding, and coding sheets as used in programming and machine representation are beyond the scope of this book and will not be discussed any further. Coding as used in the development of an information system and very relevant to the user of such a system will be discussed below.

TYPES OF CODES

The coding systems most commonly used in educational data systems are as follows:

Classification Codes

These codes are used to classify types of a data element. An example of a classification code is the codes 1 and 2 used in Figure 8–1 to classify the sexes. The choice of the code is arbitrary in this case; it could have been 2 for male and 1 for female. Also, an alphabetic code can be used, such as M for male and F for female. An alphabetic code is more meaningful to the person coding and if printed on a report, it is more easily understood. But it may have the disadvantage of not being unique. Take the case of identifying the level of students by the first letter of the level. The letters F and S will suffice to identify the freshmen and sophomores, but this is only meaningful in a junior college. The codes would not work for a four-year college where an S code for a sophomore could be misinterpreted as a "senior." One suggested solution is to use a "C" for seniors (with the "S" reserved for sophomores). But there is no logic to it, and as a result some coders may confuse the codes and cause inaccuracies. One solution, then, is to use a two-letter code or a one-character numeric code.

Another example of the problem of alphabetic codes is the identification of the day that classes are offered. Both Tuesday and Thursday have the same first letter. How then, can the problem of non-uniqueness be overcome without losing the advantage of readability? One approach is to use the code "T" to identify both Tuesday and Thursday but to specify a subfield for each day of the week. Assuming that classes are held for six days a week, we may assign card columns 20–25 for the days of the week MTWTFS. The "T" appearing in column 21 is Tuesday and the "T" in column 23 is Thursday. Thus, each day of the week is identified unambiguously by a letter code without losing its readability characteristic.

Another important difference between numeric and alphabetic codes concerns their relation to processing. The numeric code has distinct processing advantages over the alphabetic code. In some data-processing equipment, the sorting of numeric data is twice as fast as for alphabetic data, because each alphabetic character is identified by two punches in a card as compared to the single punch necessary for numeric information. (See Figure 7–1.)

Since numeric codes and alphabetic codes have their own comparative advantages they can both be used together in a single code. Such a combination is referred to as an **alphameric** or **alphanumeric** code. Examples of such codes in every-day life are car license numbers and invoice numbers. Other examples of such codes are used in identifying persons. Various combinations of a person's name and address can be combined with a sequence number to form a unique identification. One coding system used by schools (and commerical banks) is to take the first five characters of the surname followed by the first and middle initials and then sequence all duplicated names by a two-digit number. Thus, for example, James Louis Samuelson becomes SAMUEJLO1 and John Lee Samuel becomes SAMUEJLO2.

Other examples of alphameric codes in educational data systems are the abbreviations for building and room identification. To identify a room uniquely one could have the room number follow the building code, which could be the first one or two letters of the building name. Thus, Room 23 in Darwin Hall could be coded D23 and Room 15 in Dorsey Hall would be coded DO15. These codes, however, can be misinterpreted. The second character in the code

DO15 could be interpreted as a digit zero which makes it Room 015 in Darwin Hall. The coding system must, therefore, be designed with great care to avoid such problems of misinterpretation.

Another reason for caution in designing alphameric codes (and this applies to alphabetic codes as well) is the danger of alphabetic characters forming undesirable permutations. Try using a five character code for abbreviating a faculty office which is in Soberville Hall, Room 20!

Block Codes

This coding type assigns a block of codes to each subclassification of a data element. For example, in some universities the course numbers 100–199 are assigned to freshmen courses, 200–299 to sophomore courses, and so on. Thus, a 353 numbered course is a junior-level course. The blocking enables the addition of codes without having to change all the other codes. For example, adding a sophomore-level course can be done (if there are numbers unassigned) without affecting other course codes and still achieve a meaningful code. This would not have been possible if all the courses had had a sequentially numbered code.

Group Classification

This coding system assigns subfields (parts of a data field) to each subclassification of a data element.

Examples of group codes are account numbers and codes used for inventory control. For example, an inventory code for a wooden chair with a straight back, side arms, and green leather upholstery in a classroom could be coded as 193015181. The code is a composite of groups of codes as follows:

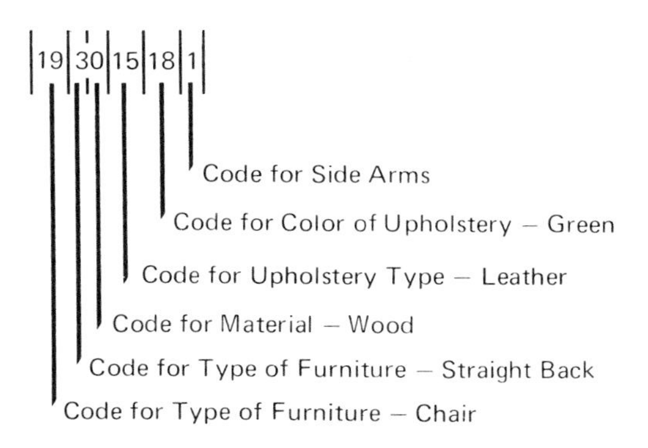

The block size for each subclassification should be designed so that additional codes can be added if needed. The same codes may be used for more than one subclassification and identified uniquely by their positions in the block.

The subclassifications facilitate the processing for purposes of statistical analysis and other computations, but a blocked code often results in a much longer code than a serial list for any given set of data elements.

Decimal Codes

Decimal codes are also used for subclassifications. The number before the decimal is the code for the data element classification, and the numbers after the decimal identify its subclassification. The best example of this coding structure is the DEWEY Decimal System used for classifying library books. One is shown below.

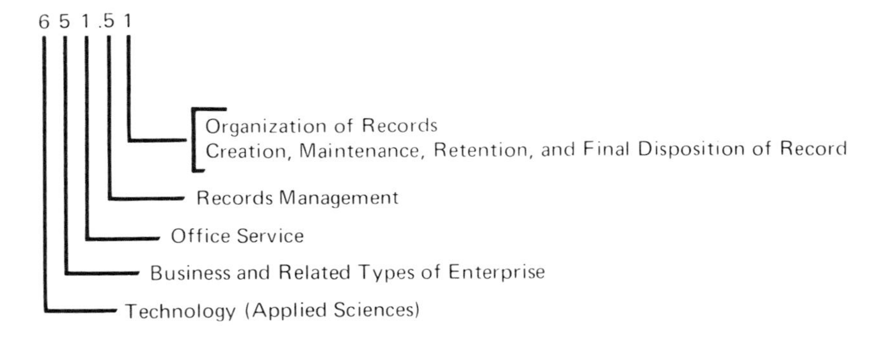

The decimal point in the code adds to its readability. It is irrelevant from the processing viewpoint since the subclassifications are under the control of the format.

SELECTION OF CODING STRUCTURE

The coding structure to be used for a data element must be chosen with great care since it affects many facets of an information system. Its effect on processing has been discussed. In addition, the readability of the codes has an important bearing on the rate of errors in coding and on the morale of the coders. Codes also have an important impact on the hardware and software components of an information system. Van Court Hare states this succinctly.

The selection of the particular code that will be used, even though unique, offers a classic example of economic trade-offs. On the one hand, some capacity or investment in facilities is required to transmit, process, and manipulate codes. On the other hand the capacity required in each of these phases of processing is affected by the choice of code format. In general, the shorter the code, the smaller the cost of transmission, storage, data entry, sorting and human handling. The longer code, however, requires less translation and 'look-up' capacity and processing and often provides greater versatility in data extraction, statistical analysis, and category combination.[4]

PRINCIPLES OF CODE DESIGN

Once a code structure is selected, codes must be assigned within the structure. Principles of designing these codes are as follows:

1. Logic in Assigning Codes

Codes must be logical and meaningful whenever possible. As an illustration, consider having to assign a numeric code for marital status. It is logical to have a "1" code to represent a single person while a "2" code represents a married person. The reverse set of codes would be confusing to some coders, resulting in inaccuracies.

2. Exhaustiveness of Codes

A set of codes should represent each possible attribute of a data element. When a set of codes is first designed, it is not always possible to anticipate all possible cases so it is wise to have a code for "other" cases. When the "other" category is large or includes subclassifications that must be identified separately, then the code should be revised accordingly.

3. Lowest Level of Aggregation

A code should, when possible, identify the lowest level of measurement or aggregation that might be needed (currently or during the lifetime of the coding structure).

An example may illustrate the point. Suppose that a state information system requires a report listing students by their levels. The two categories

[4]Van Court Hare, Jr., *Systems Analysis: A Diagnostic Approach* (New York: Harcourt, Brace & World, Inc., 1967) P. 494–95.

required are lower division and upper division. A four-year institution could then classify all its students by coding freshmen and sophomores as lower-division students and juniors and seniors as upper-division students. Later, however, if it is necessary to identify the freshmen as distinct from the sophomores, the former code will not allow this distinction since it is an aggregate of the two levels. This difficulty can be overcome by having separate codes for freshmen and sophomores (lowest level of aggregation) and combining them (aggregating) to identify the lower division students. Similarly, juniors and seniors could be coded separately but aggregated to identify upper-level students.

Another example is the case of courses offered at the senior level. A code for senior-level courses does not distinguish the senior courses recognized for graduate credit, a distinction important to the graduate dean. Coding senior courses for graduate credit separate from the senior courses not recognized for graduate credit provides the graduate dean with his level of aggregation (lowest level) without compromising the category of all senior-level courses which is required by the undergraduate dean. Hence, it is very important to design codes at the lowest level of aggregation.

4. Self-Checking Features

Some codes are long and need checking features to ensure that they are correctly transcribed and converted to machine-readable form. This is done by adding a check character that identifies errors in transcribing or data conversion. Examples of the check character will be discussed further under Control in Chapter 9. It is often used in educational institutions in addition to the social security number to ensure that the correct record is processed.

5. Expansion of Codes

A code should allow for expansion of the data attributes and for additional space that may be needed for a check digit or an additional attribute. Lack of planning for such needs at the time of code design can result in much extra reprogramming and restructuring of data files to incorporate such changes later. An example of such planning would be to allow a ten-character field for the social security number even though a check digit may not currently be in use.

6. Incorporation of Supplementary Information

In designing codes, it is sometimes possible to incorporate supplementary information without adding to the length of the code or compromising its other characteristics. An example is a code used to identify students. In designing this number code, the first three digits can be used to identify the year and semester of first enrollment. The latter four digits are sequential. The number is unique and yet identifies the date of first registration, which is valuable for checking as well as for preparing statistical reports.

PROBLEMS AND ISSUES WITH CODING SYSTEMS

The many types of coding structures discussed above and the numerous systems within each type suggest a problem: there are many different coding systems that can be used for the same problem. As a result, institutions of higher learning have different coding systems for the same data element: one for the institution, one for reporting to the State, and another for reporting to the U.S. Office of Education. These parallel coding systems lead to confusion and extra work.

There is one other important disadvantage: the different coding systems and the resulting classifications do not allow us to compare data among institutions in the country. This results in a tragic waste of information because it cannot be exchanged or compared. Some attempts to correct this situation are being made. The Henle Report[5] recommends coding systems for higher education and the U.S. Office of Education has contracted WICHE[6] to develop classifications that may be adopted by educational institutions across the country.

The problem of coding is closely related to the problem of definitions and classifications. Currently, some of the terms used in higher education (e.g., level of student and major) are not defined consistently among all institutions within the country. Even within some states, there is difficulty in finding a common definition of, say, the level of student, especially a doctoral student. Should all doctoral students be classified as a group or should doctoral students doing masters' work be classified as masters' students? Shouldn't doctoral students who have passed a comprehensive be classified separately from those who have not passed their comprehensive? Should doctoral students who are working on their dissertations be distinguished from those who have not started their dissertations? Or should the doctoral student be classified by a percentage of a prescribed workload? There is no agreement among institutions on this classification. The lack of standardized classification prevents accurate and meaningful statistical analysis on an inter-institutional basis.

[5]National Science Foundation, *Systems for Measuring and Reporting the Resources and Activities of Colleges & Universities,* NSF–67–15, 1967, 444 pp.

[6]WICHE stands for Western Interstate Commission for Higher Education. It has a Management Information System Project that is developing a Programming Classification Structure under contract by the U.S. Office of Education.

Another related problem with codes is the lack of a uniform identification code for a person throughout his student career. The social security number was mentioned earlier as being used for identification, with its problem of non-uniqueness. Another problem with the social security number is that it is used mainly in institutions of higher learning, not in high schools. Thus, a student's high-school performance cannot always be unambiguously and directly identified with his performance at a university.

One approach to this problem is the use of the birth number to identify each student. This is an eleven-digit code that not only identifies each student uniquely but also identifies within the code his year of birth and birth area.[7] This number, if used in all educational institutions, would give a unique identification not only through a student's educational life but even later when it could be cross-indexed to other governmental and business files (hopefully by that time we shall resolve the serious and important problems of privacy of data!).

There is another serious problem with coding: it is difficult to control and check. Some coding errors such as the use of a non-existent code can be detected by computer programs, which check each code against a list of accepted codes. (This will be discussed further in Chapter 16.) But if the code used is legitimate and is used incorrectly, it cannot always be detected. There is no mechanical way of checking such errors. One approach is to send a copy of the record to the person concerned and hope that he will conscientiously correct all errors. But what if the institution of last degree was some small university and was by mistake coded as Harvard University? Would the person be motivated to make the correction? If not, we have incorrect data as the result of incorrect coding.

The credibility of data is often directly related to the source of coding. Should the person doing the coding be the original source of the data (such as the student or instructor) or should it be a staff member with an expertise and training in coding? The administrator is tempted to make the student and the instructor do his own coding because it saves on coding personnel. But in some cases, this may be a penny-wise-pound-foolish strategy. This happened in one university that asked its students to code their residence status. That semester there was a 22 per cent error rate using this method and the university lost many thousands of dollars by collecting in-state tuition fees instead of out-of-state tuition.

Having the source of data do his own coding also leads to inadvertent errors. The coding structure is often misunderstood, or else the person coding does not care to search for the valid and relevant code.

Error rates can be reduced by hiring staff personnel to do all the coding. Alternatively, both the data source and the staff can do the coding. The data

[7]This is another example of providing supplementary information within a code.

source could do some coding (such as a self-coding admissions form), and the staff can provide the remaining codes, especially those relating to data that is important (such as residence codes) or complicated (such as major or discipline codes).

Coders should be persons able and trained in the coding structure and motivated as to the importance of their jobs. They must be selected and supervised with care. The coders' work must be regularly checked for errors on a statistical sample basis. The errors detected (and other errors reported) should be recorded, traced to the coder that made them, and, if the error rate is above previously set standards, the coder should be fired or relocated.

The administrator responsible for generating data must take the responsibility for supervising the coders, for specifying the classifications, and for working with the systems analyst in selecting the most suitable coding structure. As Paul Smith has stated: "Good coding is the very foundation of good machine systems; management should therefore review and understand the composition of the principal coding schemes."[8]

SUMMARY AND CONCLUSIONS

A code is a representation of an attribute of a data element. It is used in order to reduce the costs of transcribing data, preparing data in machine-readable form, transmitting it, storing it, and finally, processing it.

There are many coding structures. The important ones used in educational systems are as follows:

1. Classification codes
2. Block codes
3. Group codes
4. Decimal codes

The considerations in selecting a coding structure most suitable for a particular problem are its readability, its uniqueness, its capacity to classify, and its facility for processing. Within the coding structure, a code must be designed so that it is exhaustive, has an error-checking capability, has a capacity for expansion, and is compatible with other related coding structures.

Some of the problems in using codes are as follows:

1. A lack of universally accepted classifications and codes in education.
2. Lack of a universally accepted linking code that will trace a student through his entire educational career and link all relevant and related data.
3. Errors in coding (purposely or inadvertently) that cannot be checked. This

[8]P. Smith, *How to Live With Your Computer* (Scranton, Pa.: American Management Association, 1965), p. 81.

problem can be minimized by employing coders who are carefully selected and trained. They must be supervised by administrators who understand the need and structure of codes.

Coding in an information system must be carefully planned. Changes in codes often lead to extensive programming changes which can be expensive, time-consuming, and dislocating.

KEY TERMS

Code
Natural Language
Coder
Coding
Coding Sheet
Types of Codes
Alphabetic Code
Numeric Code
Alphameric Code

REVIEW QUESTIONS

1. Distinguish between
   Coder and Coding
   Classification Code and Decimal Code
   Block Code and Group Code
   Alphabetic Code and Alphameric Code
2. What are the principles of code design?
3. What are the disadvantages of using codes?
4. What attempts have been made to standardize codes and why?

CHAPTER 8: SELECTED ANNOTATED BIBLIOGRAPHY

Hare, Van Court, Jr., *Systems Analysis: A Diagnostic Approach.* New York: Harcourt, Brace & World, Inc., 1967, pp. 494–505. Examples are used to present some principles of coding for commercial use. Topics discussed include: code selection; block and serial codes; hierarchy of code structure; error detection and correction; code development; use of codes; and documentation. The discussion and examples are well suited for readers with a basic knowledge of coding.

Kent, Allen, *Textbook on Mechanized Information Retrieval.* New York: John Wiley & Sons, Inc., 1962, Chap. VII, pp. 163–95. The author presents what he believes are some emerging (circa 1962) basic principles of mechanized information principles. Although time has overtaken some of the material presented, graduate students, administrators, and the more technically oriented should find selected reading of some value. Chapter 7 is a particularly good treatment of codes and notation. The reasons for using codes and notations are given as: (1) to translate from a difficult-to-use source language to a language that is easier to use for a particular purpose, or purposes, (2) to decrease the amounts of space required to record information, (3) to supplement the information available in the source language, and (4) to distinguish between alternative ideas or words that are not easily distinguished in the source language. Each of these reasons are discussed in detail and summarized in tabular form.

LADEN, H. N., and T. R. GILDERSLEEVE, *System Design for Computer Applications.* New York: John Wiley & Sons, Inc., 1963, pp. 190–204. The authors have combined their practical experience in the EDP field to produce a book that both technical and nontechnical readers will find worthwhile. The cited portion of the book presents a discussion of 15 types of coding systems, some variations of each, and the advantages and disadvantages of the different codes. Also of interest is the discussion concerning the isolation of errors in the main code.

RANDALL, C. B., and S. W. BURGLY, *Systems and Procedures for Business Data Processing* (2nd ed.). Cincinnati: South-Western Publishing Co., 1968, Chap. XIV, pp. 204–17. The methods of coding and condensing information contained in source documents is well presented. Four considerations to keep in mind when constructing codes are offered, along with a brief discussion of several types of codes—block, group-classification, significant-digit, final-digit, mnemonic symbols, partial sequence, complete-sequence, and phonetic-index.

WARE, WILLIS H., *Digital Computer Technology and Design.* New York: John Wiley & Sons., Inc., 1963, Chap. III, pp. 1–26. This is the first of a two-volume work written as an introductory treatment to digital computer technology and design. The material presented has a mathematical flavor and will appeal more to the programmer and systems analyst. An excellent discussion of several types of codes is enhanced by the explicit examples of each code. The chapter is concluded with a listing of six code characteristics that the author believes should be considered in selecting a code.

9

File Design

INTRODUCTION

File design is concerned with the contents and locations of data fields in a file. It should follow a prescribed set of steps. These are shown in flowchart form in Figure 9–1. First, a design committee must be formed (box 2), which makes up a list of all data elements that may possibly be part of the file (box 3). The list is then circulated to interested parties for their reactions (box 4). These reactions and other relevant considerations are examined by the design committee. The benefits of including any one data element are weighed against its cost, and a list of data elements that will be in the file is determined (box 5). These data elements are then specified in terms of data organization, structure, and usage (box 6). Another committee is set up (box 7) to review the data file (box 8). The file design process is partially repeated if data elements must be changed (return to box 3) or specifications need revision (return to box 6). The review should be performed when problems concerning file design appear, or periodically after a predetermined delay (box 9), after which it recycles (to box 8) as long as the file is in existence.

The steps in file design outlined above will be discussed in detail below.

ORGANIZING FOR FILE DESIGN

The first step in file design as depicted in Figure 9–1 is the appointment of a committee charged with the responsibility of designing the file. For a simple functional application, this group would typically consist of the functional supervisor working with a systems analyst. For an integrated system or a complex application, the group would operate more formally and be larger in size. It should be representative of most or all of the large and important users. It should also have a balance in systems knowledge and experience. The larger the group the better the representation and balance, but this also increases the cross-contacts and tends toward inefficiency and interpersonal problems. There is a trade-off that must be resolved.

The users on the file design committee must be supplemented by a systems analyst and whenever possible a data specialist,[1] a person knowledgeable about the collection, analysis, and organization of data.

TYPES OF DATA ELEMENTS

Once a file design committee is constituted, it must work on specifying the contents of a file, that is, specifying the data elements to be included in the file. There are many types of data elements. Their identification will enable a better appreciation of why and when they should be included in a file. The broad categories of data elements to be discussed are statistical, control, checking, linking, identification, and others.

Statistical Data

Statistical data for an application could be of many types. Some would be basic to an application, such as the name, address, and age of a student or faculty member. This is sometimes referred to as a **basic statistical** data element. The record of an occurrence of an event related to the basic data element(s) is referred to as **transaction data.** Examples would be grades assigned by faculty, courses taken by students, and amounts paid against ac-

[1]For a detailed discussion of the functions of a data specialist, see *EDP Analyzer,* IV, No. 11 (November 1966), 12.

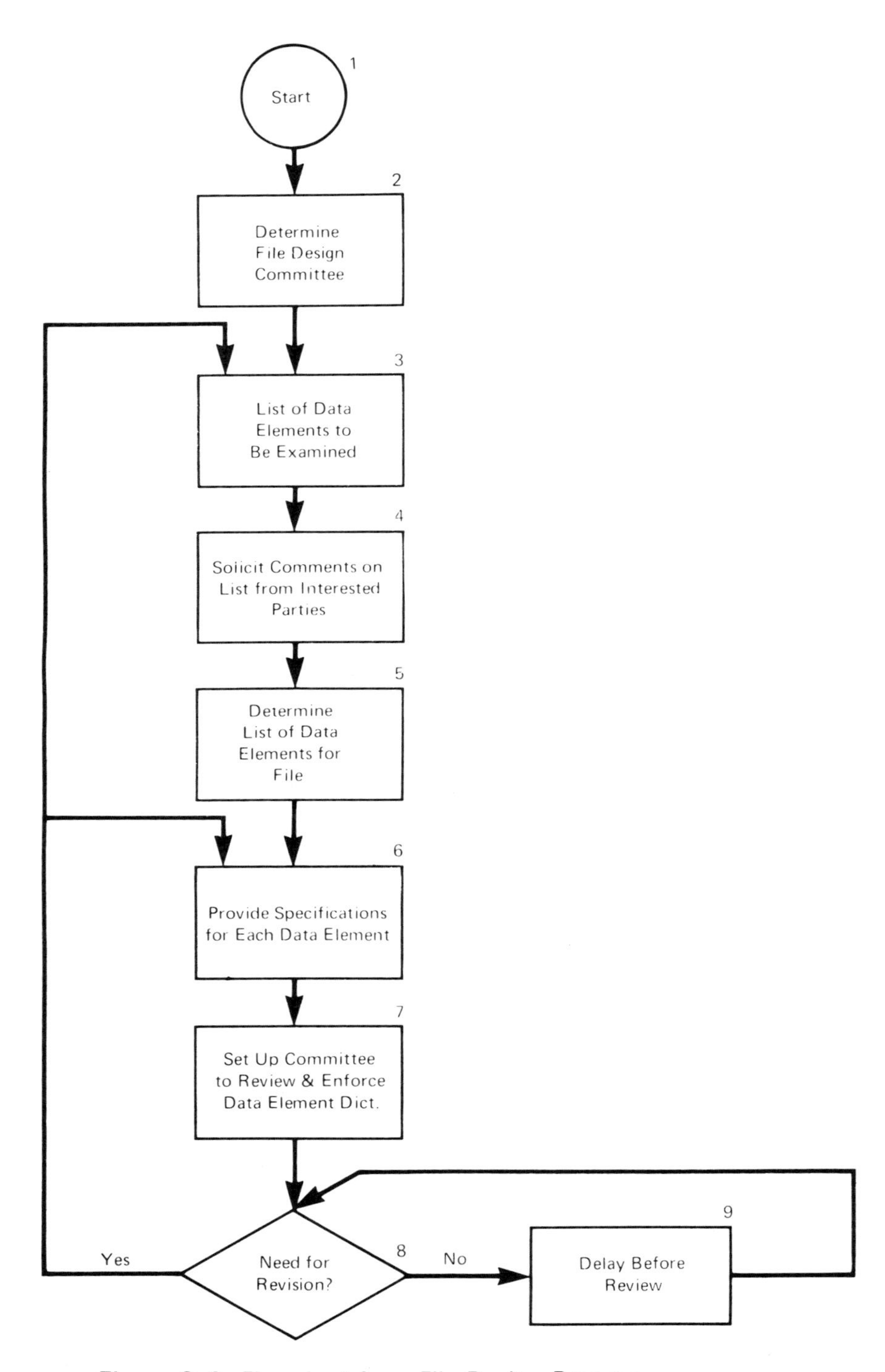

Figure 9–1. Flowchart for a File Design Process

counts receivable. Such transactions sometimes need to be traced. For example, invoice data in an automated system sometimes needs to be traced to the original invoice filed in a cabinet. This can be done by keeping the invoice number as part of the file. Such data is called **reference data.**

Data Elements for Control

In using data, there is always a danger that it is incorrect. The error may have taken place in recording, transcribing (an example would be the transfer from a document to a coding sheet), or in preparation (converting written data to machine-readable data). There are many techniques of detecting and correcting such errors, and these are discussed in Chapter 16 under quality control of information. Some of these techniques require additional data for checking, and this will now be discussed.

An error in data can occur either by an incorrect value of the data (such as a 17 instead of an 18) or because of a transposition (exchange of location such as a 71 instead of a 17). These errors can occur in a basic fixed data element that should not change, such as the social security number of a person; or a set of variable data elements, such as the fees paid by students or grades assigned to students. The former type of error is detected by a check digit and the latter is detected by computing and comparing totals. Each type of error detection will be discussed below.

Check Digit

A check digit is a digit calculated for a number consisting of several digits, according to a prescribed relationship based on the value of the digits in the number and their locational relationships. This digit is then attached to the number and every time the original number is used its check digit is calculated. If it does not coincide with the original check digit then an error is presumed to have occurred.

One technique of calculating a check digit is referred to as the Modulus 10, which detects changes in values of the digits in a number as well as a single transposition of two adjacent digits. The calculation of a check digit by the Modulus 10 method is as follows: take every odd digit and add them to produce a subtotal. Then every even digit is multiplied by "2" and the results are added to produce another subtotal. The subtotals are added and divided by "10." The remainder is the check digit.

An example of calculating a check digit is given below. It will then be tested for two types of errors: Case A will test for a change in the value of one digit and Case B will test for a single transposition. The number for which the check digit will be calculated is 123456789.

The number will be aligned in two rows separating the odd and even digits and the total will then be calculated.

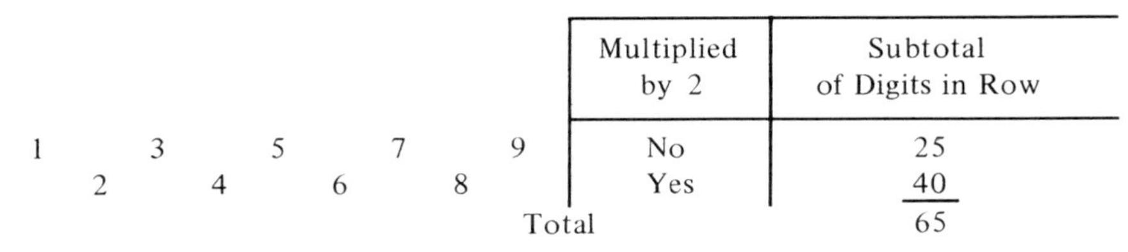

	Multiplied by 2	Subtotal of Digits in Row
1 3 5 7 9	No	25
2 4 6 8	Yes	40
Total		65

Remainder when total is divided by 10 = 5
Check digit = 5
New number = 1234567895

Now let us test the working of a check digit.

Case A: change value of first digit to 4 by error

original number	1	2	3	4	5	6	7	8	9	5
new number	4	2	3	4	5	6	7	8	9	5

original check digit

error in value

Calculation of a new check digit for Case A:

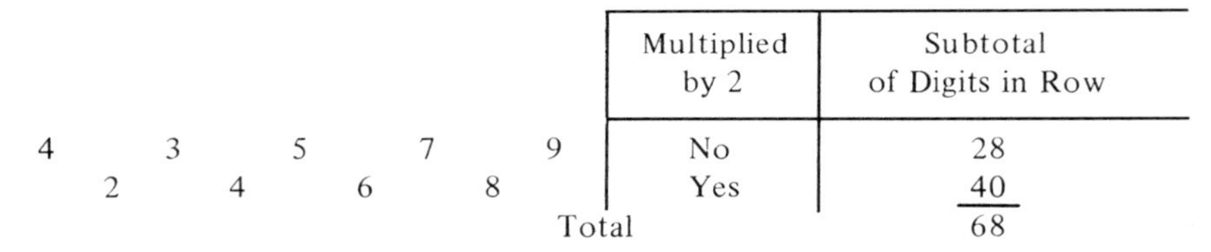

	Multiplied by 2	Subtotal of Digits in Row
4 3 5 7 9	No	28
2 4 6 8	Yes	40
Total		68

Remainder after dividing total by 10 = 8
New check digit = 8
Original check digit = 5

New check digit ≠ original check digit. Therefore, an error exists.

Case B: single transposition of the first and second digit in number

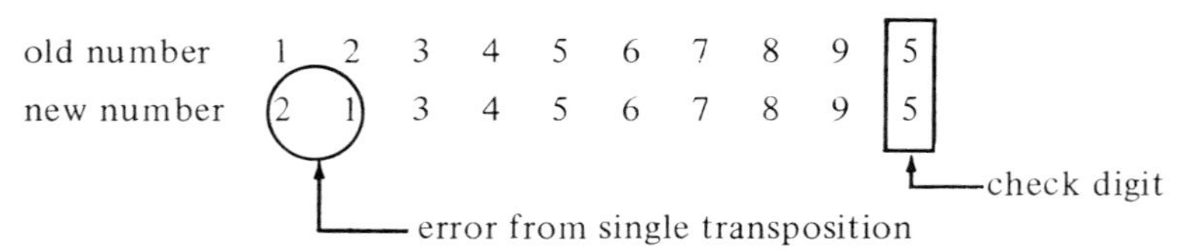

Calculation of new check digit:

	Multiplied by 2	Subtotal of Digits in Row
2 3 5 7 9	No	26
1 4 6 8	Yes	38
Total		64

New check digit = 4
Original check digit = 5

New check digit ≠ original check digit. Therefore, an error exists.

The reader should try a double transposition—that is, two digits exchanged with some other two digits, i.e., the number 3412 instead of 1234. The Modulus 10 method does not detect such an error, but there are other techniques, such as the Modulus 11[2] that do. These will not be discussed here because the purpose of this discussion is not an examination of all techniques of generating check digits but a demonstration of how the principle works.

The check digit can be used for checking numbers such as a social security number of a student. However, its use can create some problems: it adds one digit to the number, thereby increasing the difficulty of remembering the number; it also increases the storage space and time required for processing and adds to the data preparation effort. These costs must be weighed against the value of its ability to check for errors. When reliability is important, a check digit for an identification number must be seriously considered, especially if such a number is used frequently and is crucial to processing. An example of such processing in educational institutions is often the use of a social security number identifying a student registering for a course or receiving a grade.

Check Totals

Errors can also occur in data elements other than a long set of digits constituting a vital number. Such errors are detected among a set of data elements collectively. If the data elements are all alike, such as the fees collected from students, then a **subtotal** is calculated and recorded with the individual values. These individual values are then totalled by a computer program after the individual values are transcribed, converted, and transmitted. The computed subtotal is then compared with the subtotal provided with the original data. If the two subtotals do not agree, then an error is to be

[2]For a discussion of the Modulus 11 technique and its generation by a keypunch machine, see *IBM Bulletin,* No. G24–1022–1 (White Plains, N.Y.: International Business Machines Corporation, 1960), p. 6.

suspected and the data is not processed. If the data values are for different data elements, such as the date of a test and a score on the test, then these can nevertheless be totalled and referred to as a **hash total.** The fact that the data elements have different units does not prevent the checking technique which compares the original hash total with a similar computed total just before processing. If they do not agree, then the data is not processed.

Another commonly used total is a **batch total** which is the sum of subtotals in a collection, or "batch," of data. Again, such a total provided with data is compared with a computed batch total to check for accuracy. All these comparisons detect errors that may occur in transcribing, data conversion, and data transmission.

Linking Data Elements

The need for linking data elements was mentioned in the discussion on integration of files. The social security number of a student was cited as a data element that linked various files for purposes of student accounting.

Another example of the need of a linking data element arises in analyzing the utilization and cost of classrooms by departments. Some relevant data can typically be found on the Classes Taught File. For each class taught, this file includes data elements such as the name of the course, the instructor teaching it, the time and place where it is offered, and the units of credit offered for it. To calculate utilization and cost statistics one needs to know, in addition, the classification type of each room and its capacity. Such data elements could be made part of the Classes Taught File, but this would add to the cost of recording and checking such data since it is often available in another file, such as a Space File. Thus an alternative would be to get the additional data required from a Space File. This reference to another file, however, requires a data element that will be present in both files and can then link the two together. Such a link could be a unique room and building identifier, and is illustrated in Figure 9–2. The illustration is not to scale.

The function of linking can be performed by a data element only if it is part of the file that it must link. Furthermore, it must have certain characteristics. It must be unique or near-unique, it must be easily identifiable, and it must be easy to process. The two latter conditions sometimes cause a conflict of interest. For example, in the case of the linking element in Figure 9–2, the building name could be used as a linking element. It is easily identifiable and meaningful to the supplier of the data. However, the data can be long, and is alphabetic. From the viewpoint of processing, a numeric code is then preferable. The trade-off cannot always be resolved in the interest of either the supplier of the data or the processor, in which event both the name and the code for the building are data elements to be included in the file, the code then performing the sole function of a linking data element.

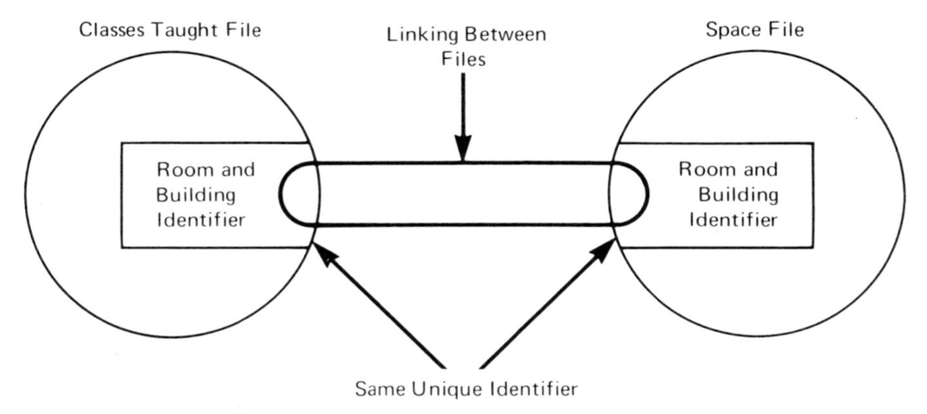

Figure 9–2. Illustration of a Linking Element

The linking discussed thus far concerns horizontal integration; that is, the integration of different files for a given time period. But there is another type of integration: longitudinal integration that is done over a period of time. In the case of a college student, the longitudinal integration could go backwards into his school file and forward into his alumni file. These files must then be linked by a linking data element if the other data elements are to be related for analysis.

Identification Data Elements

A set of data to be processed needs to be identified in terms of the entity to which it belongs, the time period to which it is related, and its relationship to other data elements. For each case, a data element is used as an identifier. These are discussed below.

The entity to which a set of data belongs poses no problem with a small institution doing only its own processing. But in cases where the processing of more than one institution (including a branch or other campus) is done in one place, the institution whose data is being processed must be identified. This is typically done by an institutional (or branch, or campus) code.

The time period for which data is processed in an educational institution is typically a semester (term or quarter). This can be identified by a code. The year of the semester should also be identified to provide uniqueness.

The file to which a data element belongs must be identified. This can be done by a file code. In cases where the data element is part of a physical record and there is more than one physical record in one logical record, then the relationship of any one physical record to other physical records must be identified. In the case of data cards, these can be numbered sequentially by a card number.

Examples of the above data elements will be given later in Table 9–1.

Other Data Elements

Other data elements sometimes found in a file include trailer and overflow identification, checkpoint data, data needed for processing such as an alpha-sort number, security and frequency codes, and codes identifying the type of processing needed (e.g., delete or add data element). These data elements are not of direct interest to the administrator and hence will not be discussed further.[3]

DETERMINATION OF FILE CONTENT

The types of data elements discussed above must be examined for relevancy in the design of any file. A list of data elements must be prepared (box 3 Figure 9–1) and circulated to all interested and affected persons in the organization (box 4 Figure 9–1). Their suggestions for additional data elements must be added to the original list. The list must then be examined carefully in order to identify and eliminate redundancies or inconsistencies. Data elements must also be examined for feasibility. Sometimes a data element is not measurable (such as the propensity to riot); is not available (such as data on the rank and salary of first employment after graduation at the time of graduation); is not always reliable (such as the distribution of faculty effort when stated by a faculty member); or is not legal to collect (such as the race and religion of a student). Each data element that remains after the scrutiny discussed above must be examined for its cost-benefit ratio. The inclusion of a data element on a file has a cost[4] which includes the components of collecting, recording, conversion to machine-readable form, storing, and processing. This cost must be weighed against the benefits of having the data element on the file. The benefits include that of contributing to needed information or to reliability and back-up.

Before determining the cost of a data element, one often has to determine the width of the data field to which it is related. As an illustration, consider a name as a data element. The cost of having a name on a file depends on the width of the field, which in turn depends on whether it is the surname and the initials or the full name spelled out. This determination is, therefore, a prerequisite to the selection of data elements.

A benefit-cost analysis would quickly exclude some data elements such

[3]For a discussion of this topic, see *IBM Data File Handbook,* No. C20–1638–1 (White Plains, N.Y.: International Business Machines Corporation, 1965), pp. 5–6.

[4]For one approach to costing the collection and conversion of a data element, see R. R. Brown, "Cost and Advantages of On-Line DP," *Datamation,* XIV, No. 3 (March 1968), 40–43.

as letters, memos, and other text material. Other data elements have a high benefit-cost ratio and are essential, such as a linking or identifying data element. For the remaining data elements the benefits may be difficult to evaluate. Difficult decisions must then be made, largely by the administrator for he alone is the best judge of the value of a data element in terms of its contribution to information.

The benefit-cost ratio approach is an ideal approach. In practice, however, this approach is not always followed, especially in institutions where processing is a service function. The choice is more a function of the power exerted by the person wanting the data element. This pressure must be resisted by the File Design Committee.

The final determination of a list of data elements for a file (box 5 in Figure 9–1) may look something like the sample record of a faculty personnel file presented in Table 9–1.

The record shown in Table 9–1 is part of a logical record. This is indicated by the fact that the physical card record has a card number (item 23). Other physical records belonging to the same logical record can be recognized by their location, that is, their position following the first physical record to which they belong. The *first* physical record then becomes the **header.** This technique is used extensively in scheduling students at registration. Cards which identify the courses taken follow a header card which identifies the student taking those courses.

An alternative method of identifying all physical records as belonging to a logical record is to have the identification data element for the logical record in each physical record. This method uses up more record space but it enables machine processing to do the assembling of the physical records into a logical record. This method is also less prone to manual human errors.

A study of the record in Table 9–1 will reveal that it does not include any name and address. There could be one of many reasons for this. One could be that the name and address are not necessary to the output of this file. For example, it may be a statistical file for a State Commission of Higher Education analyzing its faculty where the names and addresses of individuals are irrelevant. An identification number is necessary (item 3 in Table 9–1), but only as reference data for checking the validity of data or for follow-up studies. The identification may be a social security number or a pseudo-identification number, with the equivalence table between the pseudo-number and the individual a carefully guarded secret. Such measures are often taken to protect "privileged" information. These measures were taken by the American Council on Education for the questionnaire study on incoming freshmen.[5] The equivalence table in this case is stored with a service bureau in a foreign country.

[5]For details of this case, see *Computerworld,* IV, No. 9 (March 1970), 1, 8.

Table 9–1. Sample List of Data Elements for a Personnel File

Data Element No.		Card Column	Comments
1.	Institutional Code	1-2	
2.	Campus Code	3-4	
3.	Identification Number	5-13	
4.	Check Digit	14	
5.	Unassigned	15-16	
6.	Sex	17	
7.	Birthdate	18-23	
8.	Place of Birth	24-25	
9.	Birth Place Classification	26	
10.	Unassigned	27-28	
11.	High School State	29-30	
12.	High School Graduation Year	31-32	
13.	Unassigned	33-41	
14.	Year of First Appointment	42-43	
15.	Title Position in First 1 Appointment	44-45	
16.	Title Position in First 2 Appointment	46-47	
17.	State of Residence in First Appointment	48-49	
18.	Nature of Prior Employment	50-51	
19.	Year of Termination of First Appointment	52-53	
20.	Year of Second Appointment	54-55	
21.	Title of Second Appointment	56-57	
22.	Unassigned	58-78	
23.	Card Number	79	Should be "1"
24.	File Type Code	80	Should be "4"

Another reason for not having the name and address on the record shown in Table 9–1 is that names and addresses are "variable" type data and should be kept separate from "fixed" type data. This is, in fact, the case with the physical record in Table 9–1. All the data elements therein are "fixed" in that they would not change except for special cases, such as if an instructor gave the wrong data to start with and discovered it later. Such data is recorded, checked, and stored only once and its alteration thereafter carefully controlled.

Other data elements in the record in Table 9–1 are identification data (items 1,2, and 24); a check digit (item 4); and statistical data (items 6-9, 11-12, and 14-21). Some data fields (items, 5, 10, 13 and 22) are unassigned and are strategically scattered throughout the record in order to allow for expansion in the file. Such allowances for growth enable the addition of data elements adjacent to related data elements without having to restructure the record. For example, suppose that future plans call for the addition of a data element of five card columns to identify the name of the high school of graduation. This data element can then be assigned card columns 33–37, which would keep it adjacent to other data elements (items 11 and 12) concerning high school of graduation and would not require any restructuring of the record.

SPECIFICATION OF DATA ELEMENTS

The determination of a list of data elements for a file must be followed by detailed specifications for each data element. The considerations in such a detailed specification are listed below. A sample of detailed specifications of one data element is shown below. A set of such detailed specifications for each data element is then referred to as a **data element dictionary** and provides the basis for all computer programs using that file.

Name of data element
Literal description (description in words)
Variable name (abbreviated identifier)
Location of data element
- In physical record
- In logical record
- In file

Data description
- Format
- Character composition
- Required or optional

Level of accuracy
Access level
- Origination
- Output
- Update and change

Life cycle of data element
- Time and frequency of origination
- Time and frequency of update
- Time for purging

Example of Specification of a Data Element

Name of data element:	Date of birth
Literal description:	Same as above
Variable name:	DOB-PER
Location of data element:	cc 18–23 Card #1 File #4
Data description:	312 Month/Day/Year • Leading zeros are mandatory • The last two digits only of the year must be recorded in the subfield for year Example: 8th of March 1926 must be recorded as 030826 • This data element is *required.*
Level of accuracy:	This data element must be recorded with great accuracy since it may be used as a basis of promotion, tenure, retirement, and insurance payments.
Access level:	• Must be entered only by Personnel Office • Can be inquired only by level 1[6] • Cannot be changed except by procedure B.[6]
Life cycle:	• Entered once from Form 526 • Altered only by procedure B • Purged only when entire record is purged

The above examples are self-explanatory except perhaps for the variable name. This is an abbreviated identifier of the data element and must be used for all abbreviated references, especially for references in the program. The programming language used will restrict the format of the variable name and within these constraints it may be possible to make the variable identifier meaningful and readable. From the design viewpoint, however, it is critical that the variable identifier be unique for all data elements. In an integrated system, special care must be taken to ensure uniqueness not just for the file in which the variable appears but for all the files in the integrated system, or else computational results may be other than what is desired.

ORGANIZATION OF FILE REVIEW

The preparation of the data element dictionary is the termination of the first phase of file design. The second phase is that of maintaining and controlling the data element dictionary. This function must be performed by a group

[6]These codes are explained in detail in the data element dictionary and not shown here.

of persons organized in a committee, such as a Data Element Review Committee. The desirable structure of this committee will be discussed but within the context of the functions that need to be performed. These functions are as follows:

1. Minimize the data elements in the dictionary while keeping it simple, comprehensive, efficient, and flexible. Such a task requires the careful weighing of the benefit and cost of each data element that is a candidate for addition or deletion. Changes to the dictionary can result in high programming costs as well as procedural and administrative costs. These can be disruptive to the organization and expensive in resources, especially in an integrated system.

An example of a disruptive effect of changes in data elements occurred in an institution where the author was once consulting. The Registrar at the time of registration decided not to collect a data element because she no longer needed the output generated. A week later it was discovered that the data element that was dropped was essential input to a report required by the Dean of Students. But this discovery was a week too late. The students generating the data element had left the registration lines and the data had to be collected by correspondence and by many hours of manual searching of files. This problem would not have arisen if the Registrar (or any other user of an integrated system) was not allowed to make unilateral decisions about data elements. Such decisions must only be made by the institution-wide review committee on data elements.

The problem could also have been averted had the relevant tools of analysis been used. For example, an input-output matrix associating every data element with every output it helps generate would have identified the Dean of Students as a user of the dropped data element. Other tools of analysis, such as indexes, a catalog,[7] and an automated data dictionary[8] can also help in controlling and efficiently maintaining the data element dictionary.

The control exercised by the Review Committee is concerned with the overall file design and need not restrict subsystems from defining specialized data elements that are of little or no interest to other segments of the institution. This can be done even with existing data elements by assigning blocks of codes for specialized use. Such locally defined data elements must, however, be compatible with and within the overall file design. The monitoring of this is one of the functions of the Review Committee.

2. Responsiveness to a need for change in the data element dictionary is another function of the Review Committee. Such needs for changes may be

[7]For a detailed discussion of this subject, see W. B. Stevens, "The Concept of the 'Data Analysis and Control Catalog' for Management Information Systems," *Computers & Automation,* XVII, No. 4 (April 1968), 40–42.

[8]For a discussion of this topic, see "Processing the Corporate Data Base," *EDP Analyzer,* VIII, No. 4 (April 1970), p. 10.

a result of a change in organizational goals, in the power structure of the organization, or even a change in an administrator's ability to use an information system. The users of the information system must be regularly queried for their reactions to the adequacy of the data element dictionary. A mechanism for getting such feedback must be initiated and maintained.

3. Needed changes to the data element dictionary must be made promptly and explained adequately to all affected personnel. A system of easy and efficient updating needs to be designed and maintained. All documentation outdated as a result of the changed data element dictionary must be withdrawn and purged from the system.

The functions discussed above must be performed by a Review Committee composed of a data specialist and two or three administrators. The latter should preferably be members of the file design committee to provide continuity, but primarily they should have the following: the authority (formal or informal) to set standards and enforce them; the ability to resist proposals for changes that are not in the interests of the overall system; the ability to prevent unilateral changes by administrators; and finally, the ability to rule in cases of conflict of interest between users.

The task of the Review Committee is continuous and lasts as long as the information system is in existence. This is reflected in the diagram of Figure 9–1. The task of the Review Committee is recycling from an evaluation (box 8) back to listing new data elements (box 3), or changing specifications of existing data elements (box 6), or elsewhere in the file design cycle. This recycling can be triggered by a dissatisfied user or periodically by the Committee itself (box 9). Such periodic reviews result in responsive actions, along with enforcement of standards for controlling and maintaining the data element dictionary.

SUMMARY AND CONCLUSIONS

This chapter is concerned basically with defining the contents of a file in terms of data elements and in specifying each data element. This requires that a list of essential data elements be prepared and each data element be specified in terms of its meaning, data element name abbreviation, format, level of access, and location in file. The set of such specifications constitutes a data element dictionary.

Such a dictionary provides the basis for storing the data prior to its processing, a subject that is technical and hence will not be discussed in this book.

The data element dictionary must be periodically reviewed, controlled, and maintained. This is the responsibility of a Data Element Review Committee. It should set up mechanism to receive feedback from users of the dictionary on its adequacy, make the necessary modifications to it, and inform all concerned about any changes.

KEY TERMS

File Design Committee	Hash Total
Basic Statistical Data	Batch Total
Transaction Data	Linking
Reference Data	Benefit-Cost Analysis
Check Digit	Data Element Review Committee
Check Totals	Data Element Dictionary

REVIEW QUESTIONS

1. Distinguish between
   Statistical Data and Reference Data
   Check Digit and Check Totals
   Fixed Data and Variable Data
   File Design Committee and Data Element Review Committee
2. How can errors in data transposition be detected and corrected?
3. What are the essential characteristics of data elements used for linking?
4. How and why is benefit-cost analysis applied to file design?
5. What functions are performed by the Data Element Review Committee?

CHAPTER 9: SELECTED ANNOTATED BIBLIOGRAPHY

BOGUSLAW, R., *The New Utopians,* Englewood Cliffs, N.J.: Prentice-Hall, Inc., 1965, Chap. II, pp. 29–46. The new utopians are those professionals who are more commonly known as system engineers, computer programmers, and operations researchers. The author conceptualizes these new utopians as "social engineers" who in their quest for maximizing solutions have ignored the "human engineering" dimensions of the problem and its solution. In Chapter 2, the author seeks to explain the meaning of the word "system" by discussing the systems concept from five different viewpoints: the connective idea; the idea of control; the interdisciplinary idea; the big picture idea; and the organism idea. Reading of this entire book is highly recommended. Boguslaw has a delightful style and a refresing approach.

"The Corporate Data File," *EDP Analyzer,* IV, No. 11 (November 1966), 1–12. Here is an analysis of the development of the corporate data file. Because of the continual flow of data between files, the files must be designed using compatible data definitions—field lengths, locations of decimal points, locations of fields within a record, and so on. Included in the article are several good tables which summarize the probable features and some likely contents of the corporate data file and some of the information desired about data definitions. Some techniques, such as using design sessions, are discussed as means to develop consistent compatible data definitions and format.

"Creating the Corporate Data Base," *EDP Analyzer,* VIII, No. 2 (February 1970), 13. This is the first in a series of four reports on the major aspects of the CDB (corporate data base). This issue discusses the investigation, design considerations, and conversion planning aspects of creating the CDB.

GWYNN, JOHN, "The Data Base Approach to a Management Information System," in *Management Information Systems: Their Development and Use in the Administration of Higher Education,* eds. J. Minter and B. Lawrence, Boulder, Colo.: Western Interstate Commission for Higher Education, 1969, pp. 9–15. Institutional management continues to express a desire for more relevant information —they don't want volume, they want relevancy. To insure that relevant information is available in the data base, Mr. Gwynn suggests an initial fact-finding period, culminated by an intensive effort in one area, will yield operational experience on a data base which can grow to include data for more areas. Included in this article is a list of nine factors that characterize the administrative data processing environment that should be considered in a relevant data base, and a survey of the experience of Stanford University in its effort to build mechanized data bases.

IBM Form and Card Design (No. C20–8078). White Plains, N.Y.: International Business Machines Corporation, 15 pp. The first section of this manual presents some useful guides for form design while the second section is devoted to card design. Both sections are well illustrated and give the basic steps for both form and card design.

KAUFMAN, F., "Data Systems that Cross Company Boundaries," *Harvard Business Review,* XLIV, No. 1 (January-February 1966), 141–55. All businesses are involved in constant interconnection and intercommunication with other organizations. Thus, company boundaries are not the only, or even the most meaningful, system boundaries. The author gives examples of going beyond conventional "total systems." thinking, and foresees paperless clearing-houses. Worthwhile studying are the illustrations of: how computers communicate with each other; an airline data processing system; a central retailing system; and an account billing and payment system.

"Organizing the Corporate Data Base," *EDP Analyzer,* VIII, No. 3 (March 1970), 14. This informative article provides an overview of file organization in three distinct parts, (1) data structures, (2) storage structures, and (3) access methods.

"Processing the Corporate Data Base," *EDP Analyzer,* VIII, No. 4 (April 1970), 13. This installment on the CDB discusses the current status of data management systems. To illustrate the state of the art, the Mark IV data management is described.

STEVENS, WILLIAM B., "The Concept of the Data Analysis and Control Catalog for Management Information Systems," *Computers and Automation*, XVII, No. 4 (April 1968), 40–42. The article suggests a technique for controlling the data collected during studies leading toward a Management Information System. The concept is identified as the "Data Analysis and Control" (DAC) technique and is based on establishing a file of descriptions of all data to be used in the system through a series of interviews with management and an analysis of the existing system. Four benefits of using DAC are given, (1) provides a discipline for the data collection and analysis functions, (2) provides control of the data, (3) provides a powerful tool for simplifying data correlation and analysis, and (4) assists in computer programming and systems documentation.

part four

DEVELOPING INFORMATION SYSTEMS

The tools of analysis discussed in Part One, the introduction to information systems in Part Two, and the discussion of data organization in Part Three provide the necessary background for Part Four: the Development of an Information System. This subject concerns the orderly transformation of a need for information into an information system that meets this need in an efficient and effective manner.

Since this part of the book is long and important, it has been summarized in Chapter 10. The chapter also gives an introduction to the content and organization of each of the chapters that follows. Before doing so, however, it is desirable to introduce a few new terms and review some old ones.

A Glossary in Prose

INTRODUCTION

This is an attempt to introduce information systems terminology in a meaningful context.[1] The narration will also serve the purpose of giving a partial preview and summary of the chapters to follow.

Many of the terms in italics are defined formally in the glossary at the end of the book or are discussed in the following pages of the text. Some terms have already been defined and are repeated for review or continuity.

The discussion in this glossary is brief and, as a consequence, it tends to oversimplify. A reader may, therefore, decide not to read the glossary and to move to the next chapter. In that case, he will not lose any continuity of presentation.

[1]For a prose glossary on computers that is more technical than this one (and highly recommended), see J. Caffery and C. J. Mosmann, *Computers on Campus* (Washington, D.C.: American Council on Education, 1967), pp. 187–93.

THE DEVELOPMENT OF SYSTEMS

Most educational institutions have information systems whose main function is to provide information when it is needed, where it is needed, and in the form in which it is needed. To achieve this, the development of an information system must be carefully planned and executed. This development is performed in *stages* and consists of a set of jobs called *activities.*

The first group of activities, or stage in the development process, is a *feasibility* study which examines alternatives for practicality within organizational *constraints.* A constraint is a force that places a limit on what is possible.

Once an alternative is chosen as being acceptable to the administrator, the *user* of the system, the next stage in the development process is for him to define his needs more specifically. To achieve these needs, a system is *designed* and then *implemented.*

There are many types of information systems. The earliest were manual systems which were followed by electrical accounting machines, more commonly referred to as *EAM equipment.* These were superseded by *computers,* which are electronic machines capable of performing complex operations with data. These operations are performed very quickly, accurately, and automatically. But computers must be instructed precisely as to what operations are to be performed and the sequence in which they are to be performed. These sets of instructions are called *programs.*

There are many *programming languages* in which programs are written. One group of such languages is called *machine languages,* also referred to as *lower-level languages.* The programs in machine language are a set of instructions stated in coded numbers that are directly recognized by the machine. Other programming languages are more like the English language and are referred to as *higher-level languages.* These are more independent of a particular machine than are machine languages. Their usage often reduces the *conversion costs* that result from changing from one computer to another. An example of such a high-level language and one most commonly used for information systems and business data processing is *COBOL.* Languages used mainly for scientific programming are *ALGOL, MAD, APL,* and many others. There are some languages that are often used for both scientific and business data processing. Examples of these languages are *FORTRAN* and *PL/1.* Programming languages are used to communicate with a computer and are distinct from languages used to communicate between people, which are known as *natural languages.*

This book is concerned largely with computer-based information systems. It will not discuss systems that are entirely EAM oriented, but will be concerned with EAM equipment inasmuch as it is used to support computer processing. Among such equipment is the *keypunch* which punches holes in a *data card* to correspond to data according to a specific coding system; a *verifier* that identifies errors in keypunching; a *reproducer* that reproduces cards with possible variations in the locations of specific sets of holes in them; a *sorter* that classifies cards according to desired data classifications; and a *collator* which merges data cards—that is, combines two similarly sequenced sets of cards into one set. These devices are concerned with preparing data that goes into the computer and are, therefore, referred to as *input equipment.* Devices that handle data coming out of the computer are called *output equipment* and include a *printer* that prints output; a *decollator* that separtes the carbon sheets from multiple sheets of paper, called a multiple *ply* paper; and a *burster* that breaks the perforations between sheets in order to separate them. These devices, except the printer, are also referred to as *off-line* devices because they are not connected to the CPU (Central Processing Unit), the unit that performs the computational and control functions in a computer.

When devices are in direct communication with the CPU, they are referred to as *on-line* equipment. Examples are printers and terminals that receive input or produce output directly from the CPU. These may be *typewriter terminals* or *CRTs* (Cathode Ray Tubes). A *CRT Terminal* looks much like a television set sitting on top of a typewriter. The terminal may be physically part of the computer, in which case it is called a *console.* It can also be located remote from the computer, in which case it is said to have *remote access;* it is connected to the computer by direct cable or by telephone. In cases of telephone transmission, there is a need for converting voice signals of the telephone into data acceptable for the terminals. This is done by a *data-phone* with a *data transmission set.* The data-phone in this case performs the function of an *interface* between the terminal and the telephone lines. Interfaces are also required between the computer and its *on-line peripheral devices.* Examples of on-line peripheral devices are a *printer* that prints output, a *plotter* that plots output graphically, a *card reader* that reads punched cards, and an *optical scanner* or *optical reader* that recognizes marks and special characters on documents. The characters can be of different styles and sizes, referred to as *fonts.*

The equipment discussed above is called *hardware.* Different combinations of equipment are referred to as *configurations* of equipment. The selection of the best equipment configurations is part of the system design stage in the systems development process.

In contrast to hardware, there is *software,* which is the set of computer programs. A program instructs the computer on the *algorithm* to be used, that is, the specific computing procedure to be followed in order to achieve the desired output. Such a program is sometimes called an *applications program.* In contrast there is a set of programs that translates and interprets the applications programs from a higher-level language into machine language. These are called *compilers, assemblers, translators,* and *interpreters.* Other computer programs govern the scheduling of *jobs* (user's programs that have been processed by the computer), and automate the relationship of the computer and its peripheral devices. These are called *monitors* or *supervisors.* Still other computer programs perform "household" duties of automating the operations of the computer and performing frequently required functions, such as *listing* an information file. These are called *utility* programs.

The compilers, assemblers, translators, interpreters, monitors, supervisors, and utility programs are collectively referred to as *systems programs* and are frequently provided with computer equipment by the manufacturers. These programs are distinct from *applications programs* that are typically provided by the user. Collectively they constitute what is known as *software.*

Systems programs and techniques are referred to as *operating systems.* The operating system along with the hardware configuration is unique for most computer systems. This is why programs run on one system are not easily run on another. If two computer systems can run the same set of computer programs they are considered *compatible* with each other. One system can then serve as a *backup* for the other in the event that one breaks down.

This book is addressed to the administrator in education. Typically, he will not be concerned with systems programs and techniques related to hardware or operating systems. He is, however, interested in the successful operations of the information system. To achieve this he must participate actively in the design of the *output,* which is the result he will receive, as well as the *input,* which is the data and resources that are put into the system. The hardware and software of the system should then produce the desired results. The interrelationship between man and the machine system (hardware and software) is governed by a set of instructions referred to as *procedures.*

Part of system design, especially of an information system, is concerned with the structuring and storing of data so that it can be efficiently and effectively processed. This is known as *data management* or *file management.* It is concerned with a *data base,* also called *data bank,* which consists of a set of *integrated* files. A *file* is a set of records; a *record* is a set of *data elements;* a data element is something with a value worth recording. Each data element is represented by a *data field,* which is a set of *data columns.* On a *data card,* there are 80 data columns, each representing a *character* of data. *Data* is the record of a fact or event which, when selected and processed (individually or with other data), is called *information.*

Input data and programs to be processed are stored on a *storage* or *memory device.*

There are many types of memory devices. One is called *core.* It is part of the computer equipment and is referred to as *primary storage* or *internal storage.* An *external* memory device example would be a *magnetic tape* similar to that used for recording songs. It is more suitable for recording data that is to be processed and retrieved *sequentially.* An example would be a payroll or student grade processing at the end of a semester. If the processing is to be done on an individual basis, data must be processed and retrieved in *random* order. The memory device appropriate for such *random processing* is a *disk* which is similar to a phonograph record. The tape *(magnetic* or *paper tape)* and the disk are referred to as *auxiliary, secondary,* or *external storage.* They supplement the *internal* core *storage.*

Most data changes. This change is recorded as a *transaction.* A file containing all transactions is called a *transaction file* or *detail file.* It changes the original data on the *master file.* The reflection of new transactions is referred to as *updating,* and periodic updating of a master file is referred to as *file processing.* The deletion of irrelevant data is referred to as *purging* of data.

After the input, output, files, and procedures are designed, the design specifications are implemented and the new system is then *tested.* This consists of a comparison of existing performance with desired performance. Often they do not match. Problems may exist with the computer programs. These are detected, located, and corrected, which is referred to as *debugging.*

Performance is again compared with desired performance. Once the system appears to perform as expected, it is then *documented,* which is the process of stating all relevant facts about the system. This documentation includes: *flowcharts* and *decision tables,* which specify the logic of the *decision rules* and show the flow of data and information. The documentation and programs are then deposited in a *program library* and are handled, maintained, and controlled by personnel referred to as *librarians.*

After successful testing and documentation, the system is implemented and then evaluated. The evaluation should be based on both efficiency and effectiveness. *Efficiency* refers to the relationship of output and input. *Effectiveness* refers to the successful achievement of critical factors of performance set by the user. Examples of critical factors are *accuracy,* which is freedom from error, and *timeliness* which concerns the time availability of information.

Computer operations have many *modes* of operation. One is *batch processing* which involves the collecting of jobs into a batch before they are processed. Another is *on-line time-sharing* where the user is serviced when his turn comes up. However, because of very fast processing speeds the user is serviced almost instantly and has the illusion of having the machine all to himself and *dedicated* to his use. Many educational institutions have time-sharing systems, if not for administrative purpose, then for educational services.

Some educational institutions allow their students to run their computers. This mode of processing is called *open-shop,* in contrast to the *closed-shop* situations where the computer room is closed to all but professional personnel responsible for operations, known as *computer operators.*

There are many other professional personnel involved in the development of systems. The most important of these is the systems analyst. In developing a complex system, there is often a *team* of *systems analysts* also referred to as *systems designers* and *systems engineers.* Among them, the team members have an expertise in analyzing and synthesizing systems; in *Operations Research* and *Management Science,* which is the use of mathematical and statistical techniques for finding the optimal (best) solution; in industrial engineering; in applications programming; and in data management. The team of systems analysts also has some knowledge of computer hardware and operating systems, and calls on *hardware and systems programming specialists* for help when needed.

The systems analyst sometimes does his own computer programming and sometimes he assigns this responsibility to a *programmer,* who is a professional at writing programs. If the logic and flow of the program is specified in detail, then the actual writing of the program is done by a lower-level programmer, called a *programming coder.*

Another person referred to as a *coder* is a clerk who represents lengthy data by abbreviated *codes.* The codes may be *alphabetic, numeric,* or a combination of alphabetic and numeric symbols called *alphanumeric* or *alphameric.*

The use of coding to reduce the size of data is one of many types of *data compaction* techniques. The data, after being *recorded* in written or coded form, is then *converted* to symbols that can be read by a machine. Data once converted in this way is referred to as being *machine-readable.* An example is a data card with punched holes, also referred to as a *Hollerith card* named after the person who invented data cards in their present form in 1889.

If data conversion is done on a keypunch, then it is done by a *keypuncher.* The cards are sometimes also processed on EAM equipment by a *TAB operator.* Other professional and technical personnel involved in systems work are the *systems programmer,* who writes systems programs, and the *control clerk,* who checks and controls the quality of output. The checking should be done after each *run* which is a computational attempt with a set of data. If the output meets the prescribed standards, it is distributed to authorized personnel.

The *run-time* may be a few seconds or a few minutes. But developing a system that will produce a desired run of a few seconds on a computer often takes many days, months, or even years.

With modern computers, the run-time is very small compared to the *response-time,* which is the time elapsed from the moment the input starts being read to the moment the output is produced. It includes the time required to wait before the computer *Central Processing Unit* is available, and the time for reading and printing. In information systems, the time spent in input-output operations is typically very large compared to the time spent on computations, and hence it delays the operations. Such a computer system is referred to as being *input-output bound,* as opposed to scientific machines that are limited on computing capabilities and are referred to as being *compute bound.*

In addition to the response-time, there is also time spent in preparing input and time spent in the control of output and its distribution. These are, relatively speaking, the more time-consuming and error-prone operations, since they are very *people intensive;* that is, these jobs are mostly done manually by people.

One other time concept concerns *lapse time.* It is the time that it takes from the start of a job to the finish, and not necessarily the time actually spent on the job. For example, an administrator may take ten minutes to make a decision, but it may take him three weeks of preparation to make it. The lapse time is then three weeks and ten minutes. Similarly, the lapse time for preparing computer programs is much longer than the actual time spent in *writing* a program, since it includes the hours often spent in waiting to use the computer for debugging. These long lapse times for administrative decision-making and program preparation are the reasons why the development of information systems takes so long and why they must be planned with adequate *lead-time.*

Systems personnel, user personnel, hardware, software, procedures, and input data constitute the basic components of a system. The resources are organized in to specific jobs and activities, the collection of activities being known as a *project.* The activities of the project must be *sequenced* and *scheduled* and these must be controlled for the timely completion of the project. This is done by a *project leader* or *project manager* who is responsible for the planning, organizing, and implementation of a systems project.

10

Introduction and Summary of the Development Process of an Information System

This chapter is largely a summary of the remaining chapters in this part of the book and is concerned with the process of developing an information system. Each development consists of a set of stages that must be carefully planned and executed. These stages will be examined in detail in the eight following chapters of Part Four.

The stages of development are summarized in this chapter with special emphasis on their interrelationships. This is followed by a discussion of the need for an understanding of the development by different levels of administrators, the need for their participation in the development process, and finally, a discussion of the organization of the chapters that follow.

THE DEVELOPMENT PROCESS

The "gross" stages of system development are shown in the network diagram in Figure 10–1. Each stage consists of a set of activities, which are

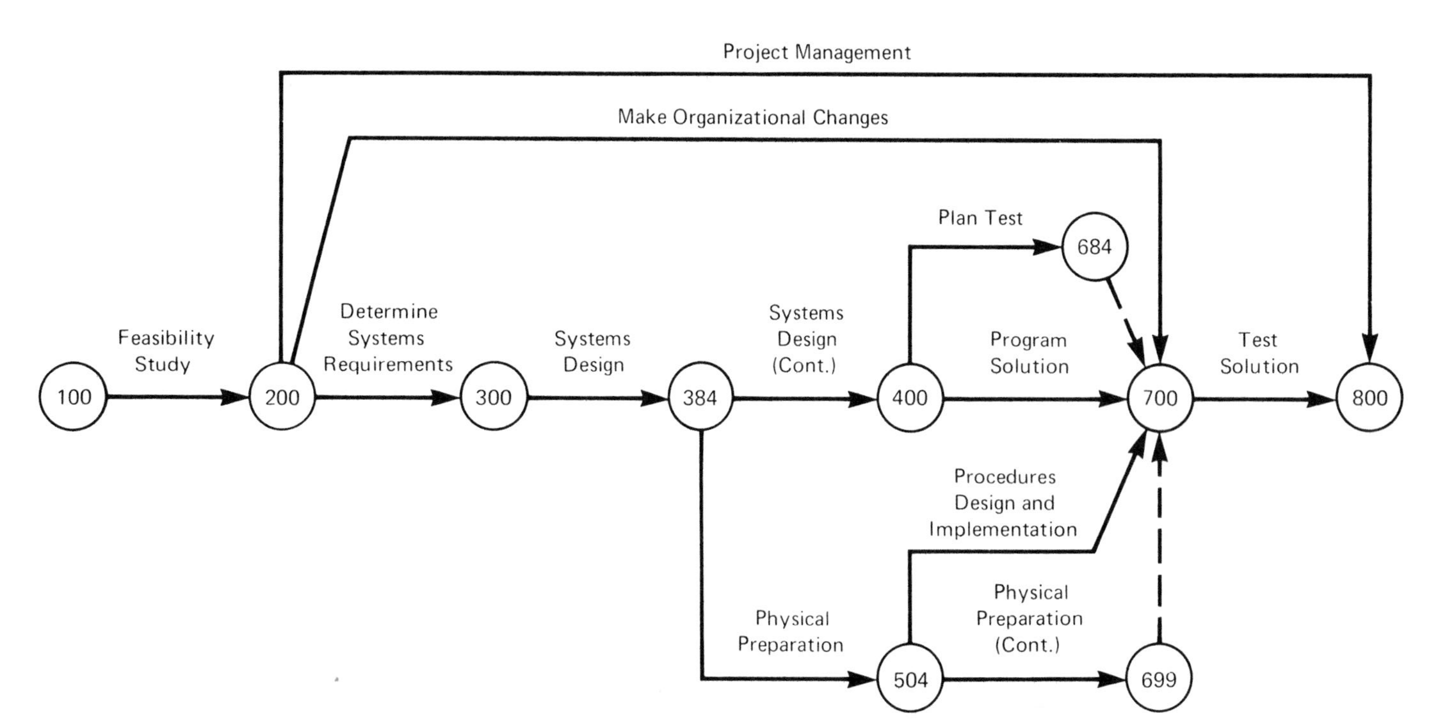

Figure 10–1. Overall Network Diagram for the Development of an Information system

displayed and discussed in detail in the following chapters. The stages are summarized below:

Feasibility Study

The first stage in the systems development cycle is the feasibility study (activity 100–200 in Figure 10–1). This is the examination of possible alternate solutions to the systems development problem and the checking of these solutions for constraints of technology, resource availability, and organizational structure. For each solution that satisfies the constraints (and is feasible) the costs are compared to the benefits. If the costs are greater than the benefits or if the organization cannot afford the resources required, then the development process is terminated. If the benefits are equal to or greater than the costs, then one of these solutions is chosen for implementation.

Determining Systems Requirements

Following the decision to implement a solution, the problem needs to be defined more precisely and completely than it was in the feasibility study. This is shown as activity 200–300 in Figure 10–1.

In this stage, the objectives, policies, and constraints of the user must be stated completely and in operational terms. These statements are the responsibility of the user (the administrator).

Design of the System

The systems requirement statement is the basis on which a systems designer creates and designs the system (activities 300–384 and 384–400 in Figure 10–1). He produces a "blueprint" which will be the basis for the production of the new system.

The design is a set of detailed specifications for each component of the system. The main components are the following:

1. Physical Preparation
2. Procedures
3. Program Solutions
4. Organizational Changes

Each of these design specifications is produced and implemented in parallel and then assembled into a complete system. These stages will now be discussed briefly.

1. Physical Preparation

The physical preparation for a system is mainly the selection and installation of equipment. This usually involves technical decisions made by specialists and consultants, but these decisions often concern the administrator, inasmuch as equipment requires a large commitment of funds (one-time and recurring costs), as well as an allocation of space. The physical preparation activities are shown as 384–504 and 504–699 in Figure 10–1. They start after the prerequisite design work is done, which is shown as activity 300–384.

2. Procedures

A procedure provides information on how, why, and when a job is to be performed. Most systems have procedures which must be designed and tested carefully because they often determine both the effectiveness and the efficiency of the system. The prime responsibility for the implementation of procedures is that of the user, who must eventually use the procedures. The set of activities on procedures is shown as 504–700 in Figure 10–1 and is done after the prerequisite physical preparation (activity 384–504) is completed.

3. Program Solutions

One of the design specifications is concerned with the output and solutions that the new system must generate. Sometimes manual methods are used to arrive at solutions. In many cases, however, the problem may be complex enough to require the use of a computer. In this case the computer must be instructed as to how to produce the desired solution. These instructions are called a **program.**

The computer programs are written by professional programmers. It is important, however, for the administrator to know programming capabilities and limitations, and their relationship to the overall systems development process.

The set of activities on programming is shown as 400–700 in Figure 10–1.

4. Organizational Changes

New systems often require that jobs be performed differently and by different personnel. This may require structural changes in the organization, and may result in displacement and unemployment. The adjustments to the systems changes must, therefore, be carefully planned and patiently implemented. The failure to do so will result in organizational resistance and the failure of the new system.

A related set of activities concerns orientation and training. Personnel using the new system must be trained and the administrators involved must be oriented as to the "how" and "why" of the new system. This orientation and training requires selection of personnel, preparation of educational media, and the conducting of the orientation and training sessions.

Organizational changes have a long period of gestation. Hence, the changes must begin soon after the feasibility study. This is shown as activity 200–700 in Figure 10–1.

Testing the Solution

Once the solution is programmed, procedures prepared, physical preparation completed, and organizational changes implemented, the system is ready for testing. The testing must be carefully planned before it can begin.

There are many approaches to testing. The new system could be tested in parallel to the old, or it could be tested by a pilot system on a small scale. Testing could also be done in different stages and at different levels. Statistical techniques enable the testing of sample data, from which inferences can be made about the whole system. This inference, or the results of the testing of the population, is then compared with the specifications stated in the Determination of the Systems Requirement stage. If unsatisfacoty, the system is redeveloped. If satisfactory, the system is then ready for operation.

The testing activity is shown as activity 700–800 in Figure 10–1. It is preceded by a planning activity shown as 400–684. 684–700 is a dummy activity.

Project Management

A systems development with a large number of interrelated activities is organized as a **project.** Its activities must be planned, scheduled, and controlled if it is to be completed within the desired time and within the resources allocated for the project. To accomplish this, project management techniques such as the GANNT chart, the Critical Path Method (CPM), or the Program Evaluation and Review Technique (PERT) are used.

Project Management is often initiated if a solution is selected in the feasibility study, and continues until the end of the testing phase. This is shown by the activity 200–800 in Figure 10–1.

The Redevelopment Cycle

The development process examined thus far has been concerned with all the stages of development, from the initiation of a system study to the time the system becomes operational. Once the system is operational, it is evaluated.

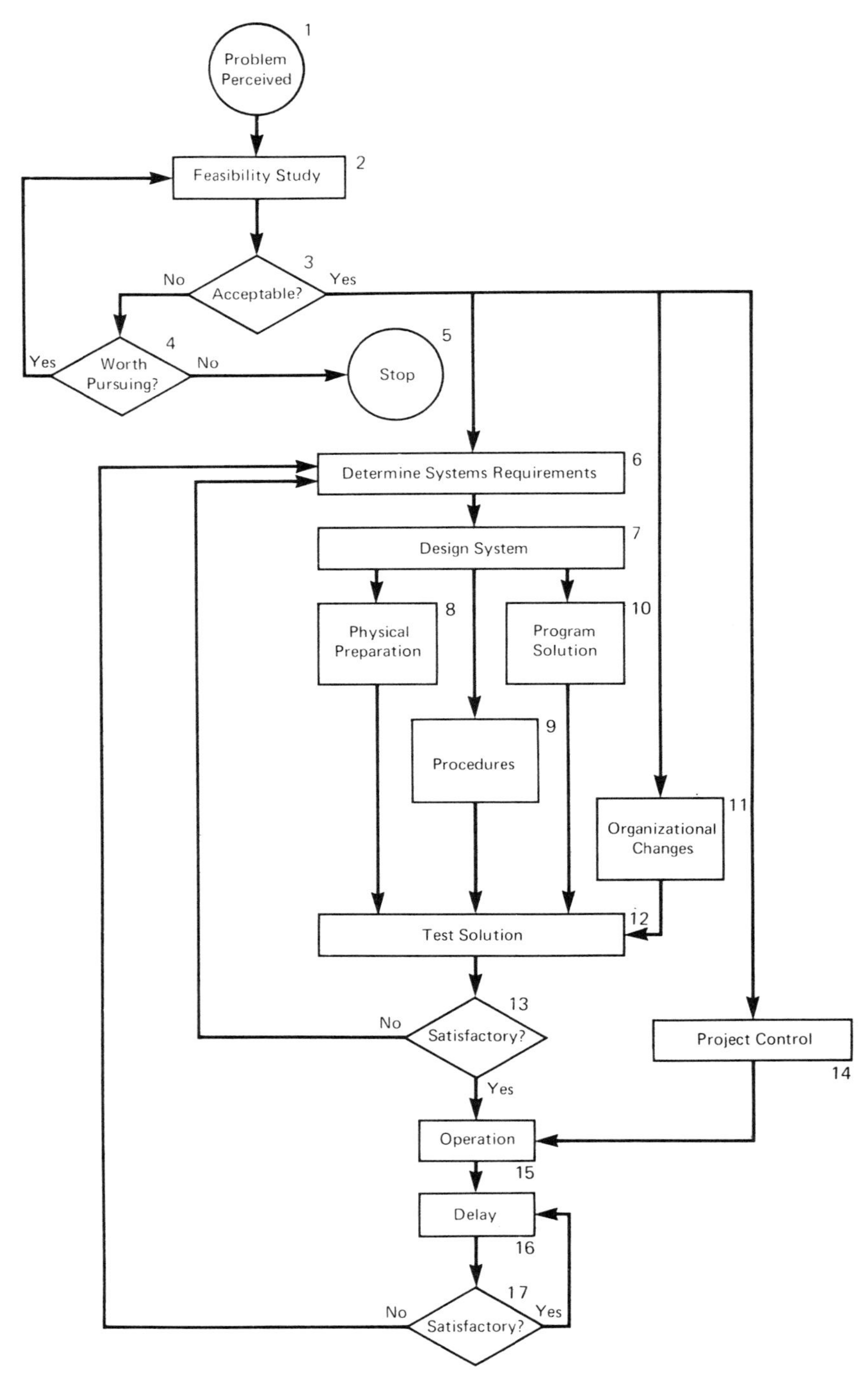

Figure 10–2. Flowchart of System Development and Redevelopment Process

If the evaluation proves that the system is unsatisfactory and the resources for redevelopment are available, it is redeveloped. Once redeveloped the system is re-evaluated; the cycle of evaluation and redevelopment continues as long as the system is in existence. Such a redevelopment cycle is a subject not discussed in great detail in this book. However, the relationship of the redevelopment cycle to the initial development process of Part Four will be identified and summarized in this chapter.

The redevelopment process starts with a logical decision: is the system satisfactory? Logical decisions (as explained in Chapter 2) cannot be identified by a block diagram or a network diagram but can be shown in a flowchart. Also, some of the stages of initial development shown in Figure 10–1 involve logical decisions. (Is the proposed system feasible? Are the test results satisfactory?) All these decisions can best be depicted in a flowchart and are shown in Figure 10–2.

The perception of the need of a new system (circle 1 in Figure 10–2) may come from the administrator or the systems analyst. The need initiates a feasibility study (box 2 in Figure 10–2). The proposed system is tested for feasibility (box 3). If unsatisfactory (NO exit from box 3), it is examined for potential of further study (box 4). If the proposed system is totally unfeasible, then the effort is terminated (circle 5). An example of this case would be where the minimum resources required for a minimum system are more than the resources available. If, however, there is a possibility that another systems design would be feasible, then another feasibility study is conducted (box 2) and the process recycles (from box 4 to box 2 and then to box 3 and back to box 4) until the proposed study is either considered to be feasible (YES exit from box 3) or terminated (at circle 5).

If the feasibility study is approved (YES exit from box 3), then the stages of determining system requirements (box 6) through the testing of the solution (box 12) and the parallel set of activities on organizational changes (box 11) are executed. These correspond to the activities shown in the network diagram in Figure 10–1 and will not be discussed further. If the test proves unsatisfactory (NO exit from box 13 in Figure 10–2), then the process may recycle to redetermine systems requirements (box 6) or to some other stage in the development cycle (not shown in the diagram for sake of simplicity). If, however, the test proves satisfactory then the system becomes operational (box 15). Up to this point the development is controlled by the project control personnel (box 14).

During the operational phase the system is evaluated (box 17) after a prescribed time delay (box 16). If the system is satisfactory (YES exit of box 17), then there is another prescribed delay (box 16) and another evaluation cycle. If, however, the system is found unsatisfactory (NO exit from box 17), then the redevelopment cycle starts again. It may recycle to the systems requirement determination (box 6) or in some cases may even initiate a new feasibility study (box 2), depending on the nature of the problems involved.

NEED FOR UNDERSTANDING THE DEVELOPMENT PROCESS

There are many administrators in education (and managers in business) who are disappointed in their information systems[1] and complain about the large gulf between what was promised and what has been achieved. Two reasons contribute to this credibility gap: first, systems analysts often promise more than they can produce; second, the administrator (and the business manager), in their ignorance of information systems, often expect too much. They think the information system, especially a computer system, is a magic machine that will produce whatever is requested instantly. This misconception on the part of the administrator and the over-enthusiasm of the systems analyst reinforce each other, resulting in a feeling by the administrator of being let down. He can reduce, if not eliminate, this possibility by participating in the development of his system. A knowledge of system development and his participation in it will not only ensure that he is not oversold but will also reduce the danger of his levels of expectation being exaggerated. Furthermore, an administrator's knowledge and participation in the development of his system is the only way for him to ensure that he gets the information he really needs.

Part Four of this book, is designed to provide the administrator (reader) with a basic knowledge of system development. Hopefully he will use it.

PARTICIPATION BY ADMINISTRATORS

A theme that will be repeated throughout this discussion on system development is that administrators must approve and be involved in the various stages of development. The question that arises is, what level or levels of administration should approve and be involved in which functional level of system development? Generally speaking, the answer is that personnel should be involved in the development of a system when it concerns their functional level, and administrators must approve the development of systems one level below them, except in the case of top administrators, who must also approve systems at their own functional level. This general set of rules is shown diagrammatically in Figure 10–3.

[1]In Tom Alexander, "Computers Can't Solve Everything," *Fortune,* LXXX, No. 5 (October 1969), 126, the author indicates that many businesses have been oversold or have overbought computer information systems.

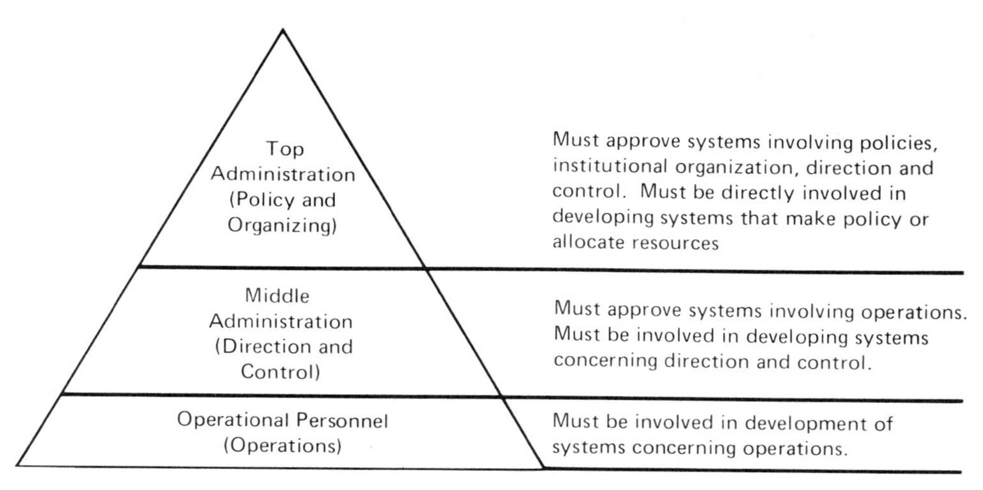

Figure 10–3. Levels of Administration and Other Personnel for Different Types of Systems

In addition, the development must be approved by the appropriate institutional committees responsible for coordinating such developments (to be discussed later).

Figure 10–3 implies that systems which only affect operational matters do not need the approval of top-level administrators. An example would be the case of a housing office that spends $20,000 per year in assigning rooms to students. If its functions can be automated within the $20,000 per year annual allocation, then top administration need not be involved, since the system does not involve institutional policies or additional institutional resources. The approval of the middle-level administrator (such as the Director of Housing) in this case would be sufficient. However, if the system requires additional resources (even on a one-shot basis), affects institutional policies or the organization, violates institutional constraints, or creates interdepartmental rivalries, then the approval of top administrators becomes necesssary.

The importance of participation in systems development by the administrator in education corresponds to the importance of participation by managers in business and industry. This necessity of manager participation has been borne out by empirical evidence from a survey done by Garrity, who studied 27 companies in 13 different industries that used computerized information systems. Garrity identified two groups of companies: one group that was unmistakably successful in its use of computer systems, and another that had marginal success at best. In analyzing the characteristics of success of the "lead" companies, Garrity observes that

> executive management devotes time to the computer systems program in proportion to its cost and potential and in relation to the executives' other responsibili-

> ties. This time is spent not on the technical problems, but on the management problems involved in integrating computer systems with the critical management process of the business. In particular, top management time is spent in reviewing the plans and programs for the computer systems effort and then in following up on the results achieved.
>
> Through formal progress reviews (taking place at least quarterly), lead company executives ensure that the computer effort focuses on high-leverage applications. They also see to it that current projects are proceeding on schedule. On projects that are not panning out, they look for the trouble spots and institute corrective action. In short, the lead company corporate executives are *personally* involved in making the computer pay off . . . in every lead company and in two-thirds of the average companies, the computer executive is no more than two levels below the chief executive. (In one-third of the average companies, however this executive is three levels down). From this it would appear that so long as the computer executive is positioned high enough to have corporate stature (i.e., within two levels of the chief executive), the computer systems effort can succeed —*provided,* of course, he plays an effective role and is given the kind of top management leadership already discussed.[2]

Even at the operational level, top management has an important influence on the degree of participation. Garrity states:

> Obviously, the close involvement of operating management is essential if a company is to apply computer systems effectively to inventory management, equipment scheduling, demand forecasting, and the like. The lead companies have achieved it by a combination of factors, including productive missionary work by the technical staff. But top management's attitude seems to be the principal ingredient. Where top management has fostered a tradition of effective line-staff relations, where top management has created an atmosphere favorable to an innovating, inquiring approach, operating executives have been much more willing to participate in the effort. Indeed, in some cases they have been the prime movers.
>
> But over and above this indirect encouragement, top management in most lead companies has specifically spelled out to operating executives the corporate commitment to the computer effort, its objectives, and operating management's responsibility for achieving the anticipated return. One operating manager commented: "I did not volunteer to be a guinea pig for the computer. But the message came through loud and clear. I was expected to use the computer and show results."[3]

The decisions made by administration on matters of information system development would be made by either individuals or groups of administrators. Group decision-making is often preferred because it has the advantage of better representation of the many departments in the organization that are

[2]John T. Garrity, "Top Management and Computer Profits," *Harvard Business Review,* XLI, No. 4 (July-August 1963), 10.

[3]*Ibid.,* p. 12.

most affected by systems changes. This representation will not only improve the probablilty of organizational acceptance but will ensure a more equitable distribution of systems effort in the organization.

Group decision-making on system development in education should include faculty members. This not only ensures faculty representation (they are important users of an information system) but often draws upon a source of competent and knowledgeable personnel.

The composition of the group deciding on information systems development could vary, depending on the functional nature of the system and the importance of the system. In some institutions, it is a standing committee that maintains the continuity necessary for developing integrated systems, especially of the operate-now-integrate-later type systems. The name of such a committee varies from institution to institution. The name used in this book will be the "Systems Development Policy Committee." The emphasis here is on policy-making, overall coordination, and surveillance, rather than the detailed user specification and detailed implementation which is done by an ad hoc **design committee** or a **development committee.**

ORGANIZATION OF PART FOUR

The relationship between stages of development and the chapters in the book are shown in Figure 10–4. This flowchart diagram will appear at the start of each chapter. The stage of development to be discussed in the chapter to follow will be shaded in the diagram so that the reader can see its relationship to the rest of the development process.

Each stage of development discussed in the following chapters consists of a set of activities. These activities will be discussed in detail and shown in a flowchart or a network diagram. In the case of a large set of activities, small groups of these activities will be examined in partial network diagrams. At the end of the chapter, the partial network diagrams will be aggregated into one network diagram.

The material is sometimes repeated. However, when repeated it is either in a different format (a flowchart converted to network) or at different levels of aggregation (for network diagrams) and is designed to offer reinforcement of the material presented.

The main theme of this part of the book is that information system development is not an exact science, and yet there is a set of steps which, when followed, will greatly improve the chances of achieving an effective and efficient system. Optimal systems and even good systems do not just happen. They are the result of careful planning and execution. They are costly. They often affect the entire organization in important ways. To achieve them, the administrator must participate actively in their development. The knowledge required for such participation is the subject of the chapters that follow.

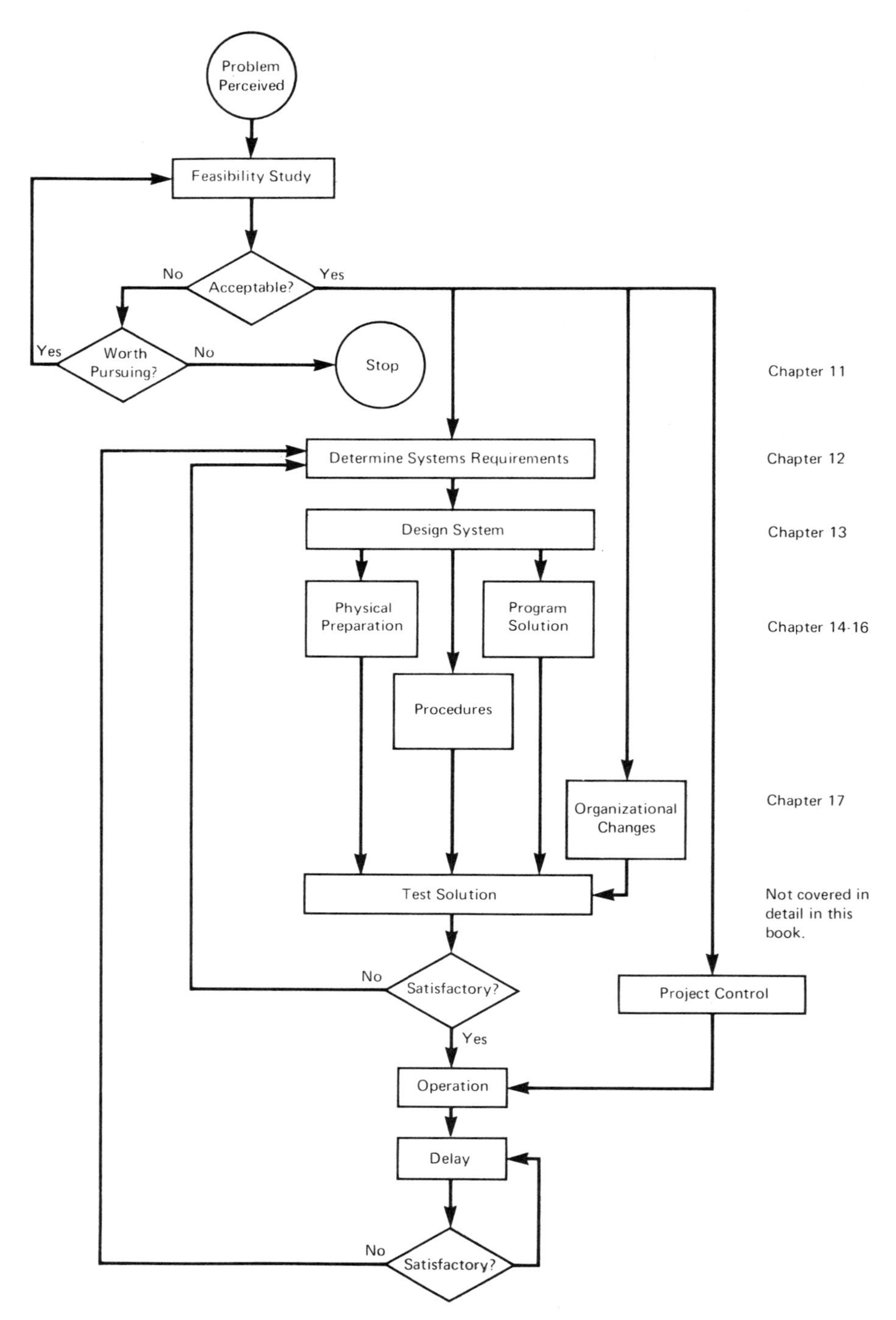

Figure 10–4. Flowchart Showing the Correspondence Between the Stages of Development and Chapters in this Book

KEY TERMS

- Development Cycle
- Redevelopment Cycle
- Feasibility Study
- Systems Requirements
- System Design
- Physical Preparation
- Procedures
- Program Solutions
- Organizational Changes
- Testing the Solution
- Systems Development Policy Committee

REVIEW QUESTIONS

1. Distinguish between
   Development Cycle and Redevelopment Cycle
   Technical Constraints and Organizational Constraints
2. What are the interrelationships among the "gross" stages of system development?
3. What are the responsibilities of the system designer and the administrator during system development?
4. Why should organizational changes start early in the system development?
5. What are some approaches to testing the solution?
6. What is the main theme of this chapter and of this part of the book?
7. What is the purpose of studying the existing system prior to implementing a new system? Is this widely accepted?
8. What two general stages can the development process be divided into?
9. What is the purpose of a steering committee in system design?

CHAPTER 10: SELECTED ANNOTATED BIBLIOGRAPHY

BLUMSTEAD, A. R., "The Designs Approach to an Educational Data System," *AEDS Journal,* I, No. 2 (December 1967), 57–66. A good overview of the development process applied specifically to education.

MCDONOUGH, A. M., and L. J. GARRETT, *Management Systems: Working Concepts and Practices.* Homewood, Ill.: Richard D. Irwin, Inc., 1965, Chap XV, pp. 199–209. This is an excellent review and summary of management systems. Systems may be thought of as ladders that ease the climb toward goal accomplishments and that effective management information systems can alleviate the impact of organizational and managerial changes. A summary diagram for management systems and the accompanying explanation provide a review of the authors' concept of management information systems.

ORLICKY, J., *The Successful Computer System.* New York: McGraw-Hill Book Company, 1969, Chap. VII, pp. 135–50. A good summary and review of the information system development process. The "phases" discussed are: programming, supporting procedures, education, conversion planning and development of auxiliary procedures, file cleanup, program testing, debugging, and conversion.

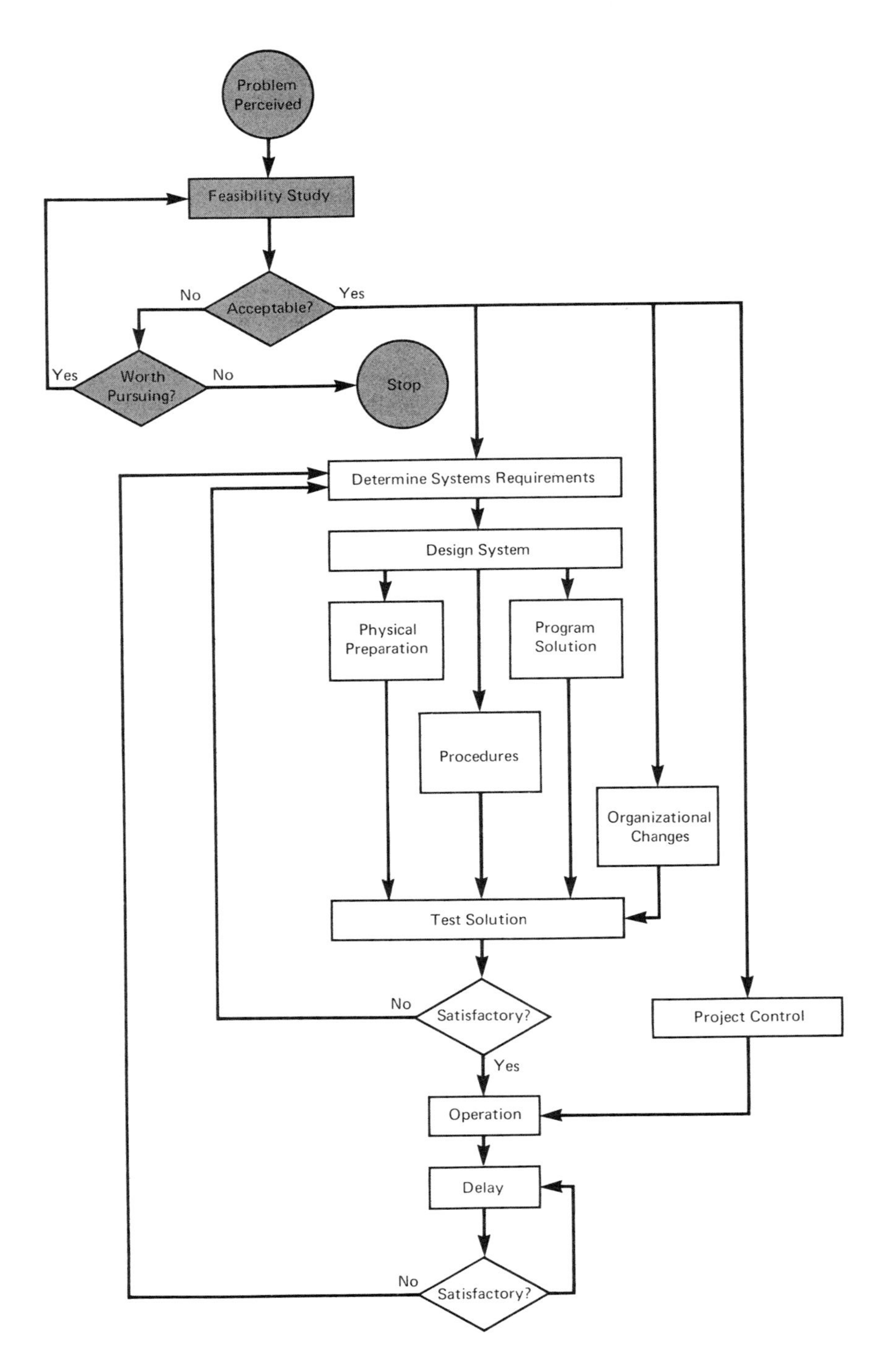

Problem Perceived
Feasibility Study
No
Acceptable?
Yes
Yes
Worth Pursuing?
No
Stop
Determine Systems Requirements
Design System
Physical Preparation
Program Solution
Procedures
Organizational Changes
Test Solution
No
Satisfactory?
Yes
Project Control
Operation
Delay
No
Satisfactory?

11

Feasibility Study

INTRODUCTION

This chapter will examine the nature and scope of the feasibility study and its four phases, and will include some observations on the duration of the feasibility study. The material is discussed from a college administrator's point of view and emphasizes his role in the feasibility study.

The four main phases of feasibility study are:

1. Organizing for the feasibility study
2. Search for a solution
3. Feasibility analysis
4. Choice of a solution

Each phase will be discussed with the help of a flowchart. In the summary section, a flowchart showing all the phases and their interrelationships is provided.

NATURE AND SCOPE OF A FEASIBILITY STUDY

Whenever an information system change is proposed or a new information system is to be installed, a feasibility study must be performed in order to determine whether or not the desired objectives can be achieved within existing constraints. The study should propose a new system identifying the costs of the proposed changes (monetary *and* organizational costs) and computing the benefits of the new system. Based on this information, the administrator should decide either to implement the proposed changes or to discontinue the study.

The feasibility study postulates a new system. The system may fail in the testing phase of the implementation. There is always that risk and uncertainty. But, without a feasibility study, the risk and uncertainty are much greater. The feasibility study, if properly conducted, greatly reduces and sometimes entirely eliminates this risk. Since it identifies and anticipates problems that must be solved, it thereby greatly improves the chances of success of the proposed system.

The term **feasibility study** is used differently in different professions. For example, the term **feasibility** has a special meaning to an operations research person who distinguishes a **feasible solution** from an **optimum solution.** If a proposed systems change were to be studied using an operations research model, the feasibility study would be performed to examine the feasibility of achieving an optimum solution. To the computer scientist, the feasibility study is performed to determine the feasibility of acquiring computer equipment. Once computer equipment is acquired, its applications are sometimes called **applications studies.**[1] To the systems analyst, a feasibility study is concerned with the practicality of a proposed systems change. It is this approach to feasibility studies that will be discussed in this chapter.

Feasibility studies should be performed whenever a possible system change is expected to have a major impact on the institution. Examples of such a change would be the installation of a faster data processing system (such as a computer system to replace an EAM processing system), the reduction of high clerical burden (such as payroll or accounting systems), the expansion of an existing system to take advantage of advanced technology (such as time-sharing terminal systems), or the redesign of an existing system to make it more responsive to changing needs. In cases of complex or major system changes, the feasibility study itself would require considerable resources and hence could be performed in stages: a preliminary study, followed by a detailed study only if the preliminary study proved successful.

[1]R. H. Gregory and R. L. Van Horn, *Automatic Data-Processing Systems,* (Belmont, Ca.: Wadsworth Publishing Company, Inc., 1960), Chap. XVI, pp. 528–57.

PHASES OF A FEASIBILITY STUDY

For all the above-cited types of feasibility studies, there is a sequence of four phases that must be followed. These are discussed below:

Phase One: Organizing for a Feasibility Study

The first phase in any feasibility study is organizing for the study itself. A flowchart representation of this phase is shown in Figure 11–1. Each event or activity in this diagram will be discussed below in the sequence of its occurrence in the diagram.

Phase One is initiated by the recognition of the need for a systems change (box 2 in Figure 11–1). This initiation may come from the administrator and is usually due to one or more of the following reasons:

1. Changes in organizational goals, plans, and needs.
2. Changes in organizational structure (such as a change of a top administrator) or availability of resources (such as funds required for implementing a new system).
3. Change in environment (such as the need for additional information by government agencies).
4. Changes in technology that may now make some systems feasible which were previously not feasible.

The initiative for making a feasibility study may also come from systems personnel. Systems personnel are more often aware of the potential benefits of system change, especially those arising from changes in systems technology. Also, they can often identify systems changes that are closely related to other changes currently implemented, where the benefits are often very high for small incremental costs. Furthermore, systems personnel can identify systems changes necessary for the development of related subsystems of the overall system. This is especially true in cases where the operate-now-integrate-later approach to information systems development has been adopted.

Once the problem has been recognized, it is defined and formulated (box 3 in Figure 11–1). This is followed by appointing personnel to make a study of the feasibility of achieving the proposed systems change (box 4 in Figure 11–1).

The qualifications required for personnel to perform the feasibility study are as follows:

1. Knowledge of systems techniques. Whether this is a knowledge of operations research, statistics, computer science, information science, or a combination of these, will depend on the nature of the problem. A knowledge of computer systems (hardware and software) is useful, especially if the systems change

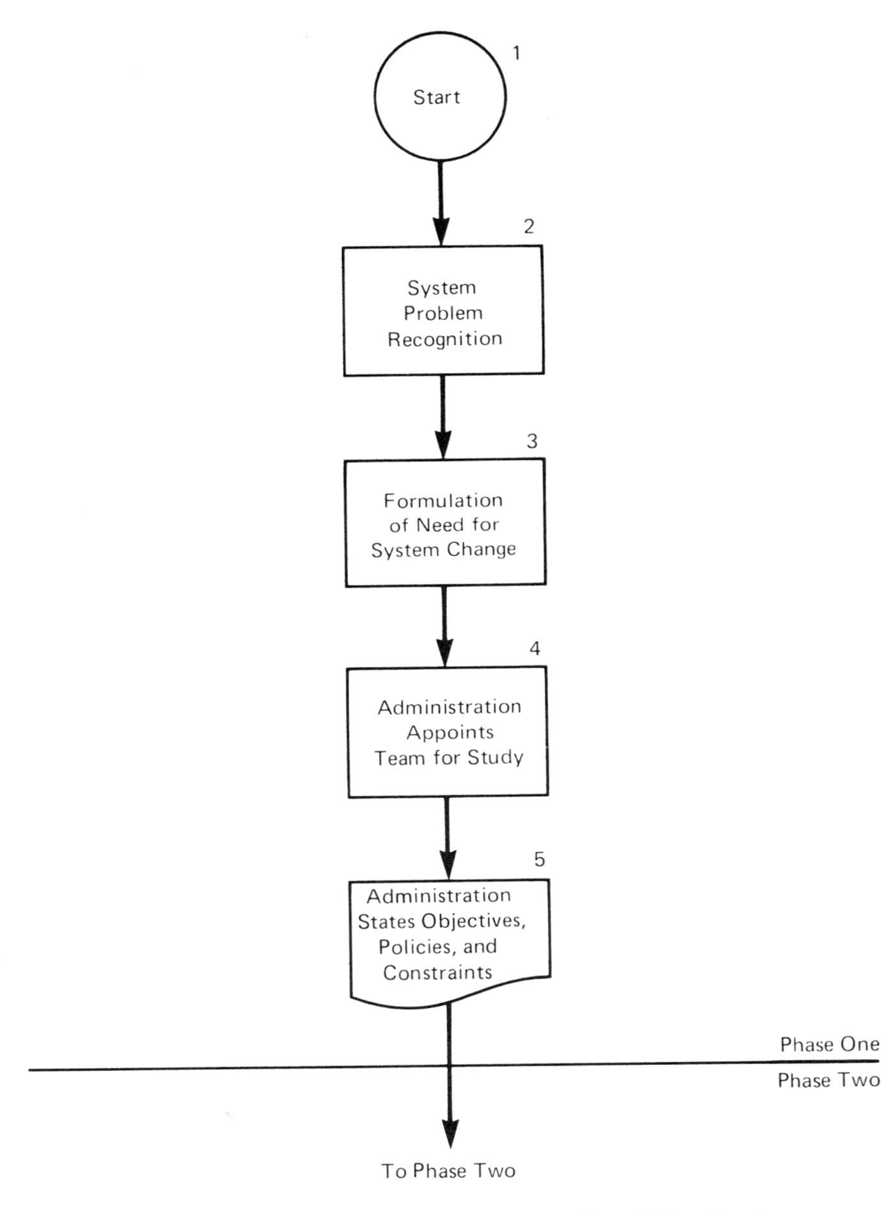

Figure 11–1. Phase One: Organizing for Feasibility Study

involves designing a large or complex information system. A specialist in computer systems is not essential, but an understanding of the potentials and limitations of computer systems is helpful in making full use of technological developments.

2. The ability to work with people. The effect of projected system changes on people is often real, or it may exist only in their imaginations. In either case, people may feel threatened and manifest their feelings by not cooperating with the feasibility study group. Sometimes they are openly hostile. Working in this environment requires tact and an understanding of people.
3. An understanding of the organization, its structure, its philosophy, its objectives and policies, and finally an understanding of its operations.
4. An ability to see the overall picture and yet be willing to work with details where necessary.
5. A position in administration. This provides the status and authority sometimes necessary to get cooperation at different levels of the organization in order to collect information necessary for the study.
6. Experience in projects of the type being considered.

The above qualities are seldom found in one individual and hence a team of people is appointed to perform the feasibility study. The team approach has the advantage not only of meeting most, if not all the requirements listed above, but also of enabling a division of labor. It also adds to the objectivity of the study.

Sometimes the qualities required of a team (e.g., experience in this type of project) are not available in the organization, in which case consultants should be used. This further adds to the objectivity of the study.

The size of the team usually varies between two and eight. The larger the team, the better the objectivity and the greater the chance of finding the desirable qualities among the members. However, a larger team has greater cross-contacts between individuals in the group and increases the probability of personality conflicts that can delay reaching decisions.

The team to conduct the feasibility study must be selected with great care and its members must be assigned sufficient time for the performance of their duties. Lack of time and lack of competent personnel often lead to failure, not only of the feasibility study but of the project itself, since the recommendations of the study, if accepted, become the basis for implementation of the project. This foundation work, therefore, must be done with care.

A team leader must be chosen whose duty is that of effectively completing the study within constraints specified by the administration. To do this he must have administrative experience and the ability to work with and inspire people. He must be knowledgeable of administrative goals and policies so that he can guide the team in interpreting the organizational environment. It is also desirable that this person be a member of the administration. Experience has shown that the higher the level of the administrator the greater the chances of success.

After the team has been appointed, the next and last step in this phase is for the administration to state the objectives of the study and to specify related policies and constraints (box 5 in Figure 11–1). This step should be done after the appointment of the team so that it can ask for clarifications of previous statements on the subject (box 2 in Figure 11–1) and query the decision-makers about relevant variables. This query process gives the team the opportunity to confirm its interpretations of the organizational environment and to have the objectives stated in operational terms. The operational definition is difficult because administrators tend to state objectives in general, ambiguous terms such as "more information," or "faster reporting." The team must determine what "information" and how "fast" is fast enough. More precisely: should the response time be one hour or one day, two days or two weeks? The administrator must specify his objectives, even though this may be a time-consuming and agonizing process. That is his responsibility and is in his interest. If he does not do so, then the team or the system analyst does so by default.

Sometimes the administrator argues that he does not know what can be realistically achieved and hence will not state the goal to be achieved. Such caution is not recommended. The administrator should state his goals and if they are not feasible he will be so informed. He can then scale down his goals accordingly.

A good example of a seemingly unrealistic goal stated by an administrator was the case of the SABRE system, initiated in 1954 by American Airlines.[2] The company realized they were losing money because of the lack of timely information on the availability of seats on their airplanes. Their objective, therefore, was for a reservation clerk anywhere in the U.S. to be able to get accurate information on schedules and seat availability on any airplane a few seconds after a query was made. Such fast response was technologically impossible at the time and yet it was achieved in 1963 and is now taken for granted in the airline industry.

Fast response is also important in the educational environment. Take the case of grade reporting. In many institutions of higher learning the response time is very important, especially if there are only a few days between semesters. The fast preparation of grade reports is important to students, advisors, and administrators. The students and advisors wish to know what courses the students have failed because this determines the courses that have to be repeated and other courses in series that can or cannot be taken. The administrators need to know the academic performance of each student in order to determine which students are to be put on probation and which are to be suspended. If the grade reports are not available in time for these decisions to be made, it results in the changing of many student programs, in considerable

[2] R. W. Parker, "The SABRE System," *Datamation,* XI, No. 9 (September 1965), 49–52.

psychological and other hardships on students, and in much paperwork for the administration. Fast response in this case, therefore, is crucial. The objective could be stated in operational terms: grade reports must be mailed or made available at the Registrar's Office no later than 24 hours after the deadline for returning grades. Even if this objective is not immediately attainable, it should still be stated and would then serve as a goal for future attainment.

Sometimes the goals can be achieved in the short run, provided the necessary resources and support are available. An example of this situation arose in one experience of mine. I witnessed a registration at a medium-sized university which used a computer system for registration. The information system did not operate according to expectations. The students stood in line for up to ten hours in order to register. It was estimated that the average wait was over three hours. The faculty felt disgraced and the press deplored the situation. The President received messages from the Board of Trustees, friends in the community, and irate parents. The President responded. He called his systems personnel and set his goal for the next registration: average waiting time of 20 minutes and a maximum of 60 minutes. The President was questioned about constraints, especially constraints on the availability of administrative secretaries to work peak hours during the registration. In reply, the President offered his own personal secretary during peak loads. The next registration was held and all students were clocked-in and clocked-out of the registration system. The average time was 21.4 minutes and the maximum was 48.2 minutes. This case study is an illustration of what can be achieved when the objectives are clearly stated, resources are available, and there is top administrative support.

The feasibility study team must ensure that all constraints are specified. Administration must specify the resources that will be available for the project and the organizational changes that are possible or not possible. This defines the feasible space of solutions that must be searched.

In cases of large systems projects, the administration must state its policies concerning the problems of unemployment and displacement resulting from the study. Without such a policy, valuable personnel who would not necessarily be displaced may feel threatened and leave the organization. Other personnel who would be displaced may leave before the new system is installed while they are still needed. In many cases, the best personnel leave the earliest thereby disrupting the conversion to the new system.

Personnel policies stated tactfully and well in advance could reduce these problems. Policies related to reclassification of jobs, retraining, and transferring personnel can often alleviate the fear of unemployment.

Finally, the statement by administration must give the team all the authority to cross departmental boundaries when necessary to collect information. This authority must come from at least one level higher than the personnel involved. In cases of complex systems changes, the authority should come from the top administrator.

At this point, Phase One of the feasibility study is terminated and Phase Two, the search for a solution, is initiated.

Phase Two: Search for Solutions

A flowchart of the steps in phase two is shown in Figure 11–2. Each of the events in the figure will be discussed below.

The first step in the search for a solution is to study the existing system and to collect and analyze all relevant information on the environment (box 6). This may be familiar to some members of the team but a detailed understanding by all team members is desirable. Without such an understanding, it may not be possible to evaluate current performance and to determine what changes are required.

The above approach is not supported by all systems analysts.[3] One group argues that a detailed study of the existing systems will prejudice and bias one's view. What this group proposes is a "fresh" approach unaffected by the existing system, which may need a complete change.

To a great extent, the choice of approach depends on the objectives and constraints stated by the administration. They may wish to retain the existing structure and allow some changes, or they may encourage a fresh look and allow large system changes. In either case there is the problem of deciding on the detail and depth of the analysis of the existing system and the extent of the collection of data and its relevancy. If the feasibility study is to be followed by an implementation of its recommendations, then, of course, all the analysis and data collected in the feasibility study will be useful. But there is the possibility that the study will be discontinued, in which case all the investment in this stage will be lost.

The stage of studying the amount of information to be collected and analyzed (boxes 7 through 10) is of a general nature and should only include that which is needed for the broad survey type of analysis necessary to make the decision on whether or not to proceed further with the implementation of the study. However, it is often difficult to decide on the amount of information to collect for short-term and long-term considerations. For example, consider a feasibility study where only one item of information from the permanent record card of each student is necessary, but for the implementation of the system being studied, three data elements (items) for each student are required. When collecting the one item for the feasibility study, it is very tempting to collect all three elements since the marginal cost of acquiring the additional information is very small (the largest portion of cost is the fixed cost, which is constant no matter how much data is to be collected). Collecting data on

[3]For one view of this approach, see D. F. Heany, *Development of Information Systems* (New York: The Ronald Press Co., 1968), p. 165.

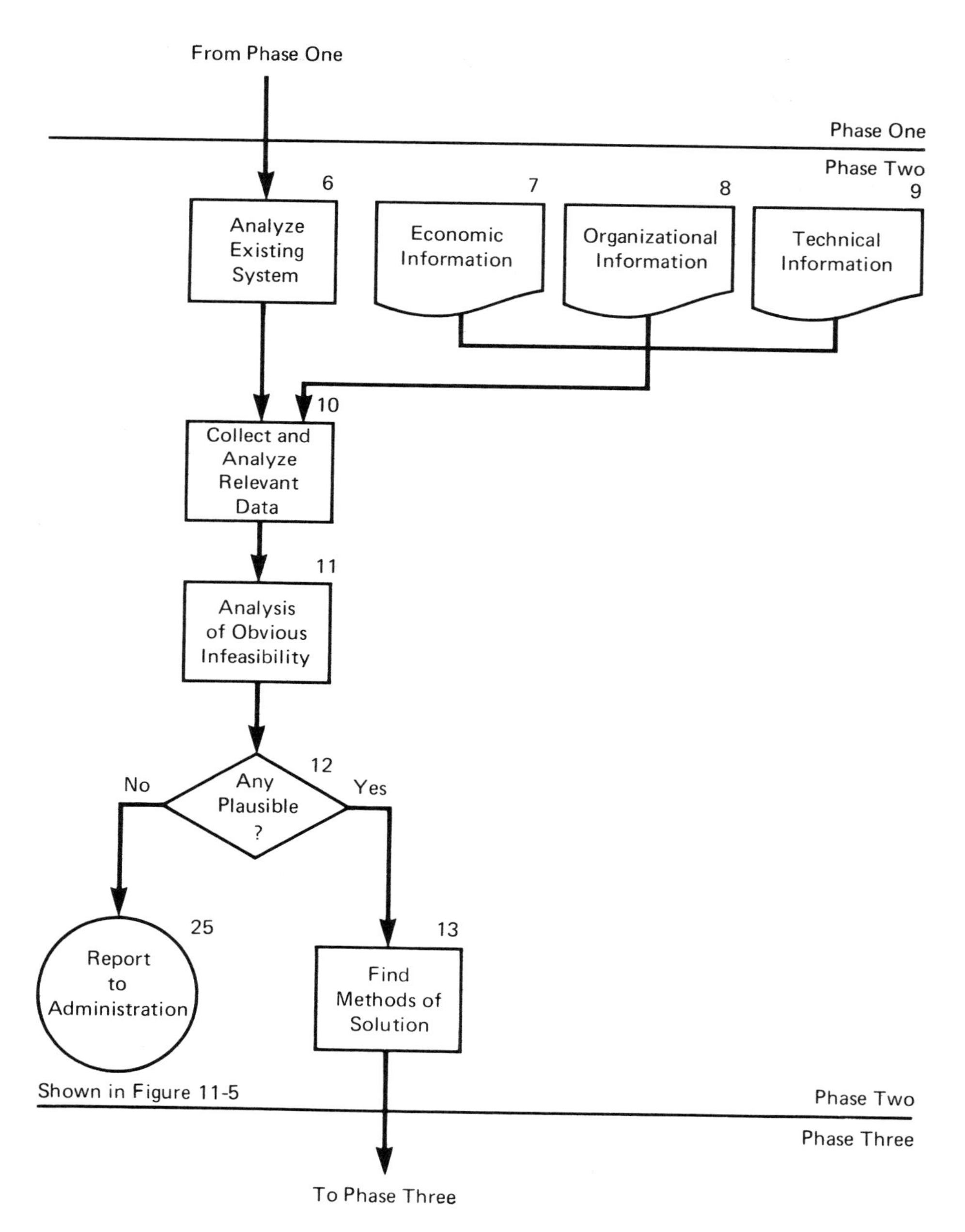

Figure 11–2. Phase Two: Search for Solutions

the three items will increase the cost and time of the feasibility study (short-run) but decrease the total cost of the project (long-run if the project is implemented). Hence, there is a trade-off between short-term and long-term costs. The final choice is a function of the time and cost constraints of the feasibility study, the magnitude of incremental costs, and the probability that the project will be implemented. This is just one example of many of the difficult decisions the feasibility team must make.

When collecting the relevant information, the team may find obvious reasons for there being no feasible solution (box 11). Consider the case of an objective of operating a terminal system with $10,000. In analyzing economic information they may discover that the minimum equipment cost for such a system is in the range of $30,000. In such a case, it is a waste of time to pursue the study any further since it is obvious that there is no feasible solution. It is, therefore, not necessary to perform the next phase of the feasibility study. Instead, the team should report its finding to administration (the No exit from box 12 to circle 25) who must then make the decision to terminate the study or restate its objectives and constraints.

If, however, the team finds no obvious glaring reasons for the project being unfeasible, it then proceeds to determine alternative solutions (the YES exit from box 12 to box 13). These solutions will then be examined for feasibility in Phase Three, the next phase.

Phase Three: Feasibility Analysis

Phase Three of the feasibility study is shown in Figure 11–3. It is the formal testing of the feasibility of the alternate solutions derived in Phase Two. These alternatives are tested (box 14) against constraints (boxes 15–18). The three main constraints (economic and financial constraints, organizational constraints, and technological constraints) correspond to three main feasibility tests: economic and financial, organizational, and technological. Each of these will be discussed in turn below.

Economic and Financial Feasibility

Theoretically, economic feasibility is a simple concept. The expected benefits must exceed or equal the expected costs in order for a project to be economically feasible. Again, theoretically one can calculate the cost part of the equation, though in designing information systems, the costs are often underestimated.[4] One reason for this is that the user's requirement is almost

[4]Ninety percent of all computer installations failed to keep within their budget and time schedule. D. Brandon, "The Need for Management Standards in Data Processing," *Data and Control Systems,* IV, No. 9 (September 1966), 27.

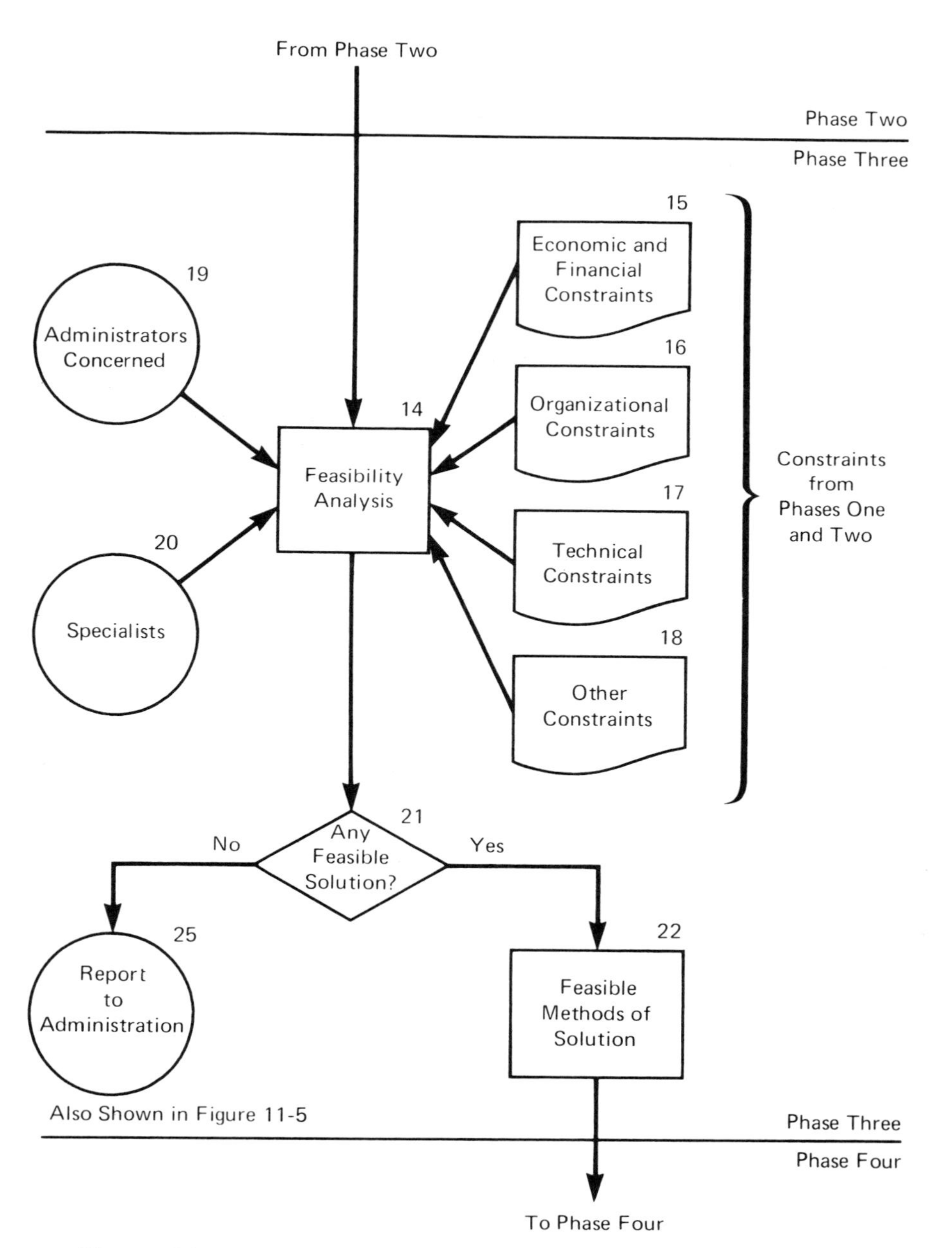
From Phase Two
Phase Two
Phase Three
15
Economic and Financial Constraints
19
Administrators Concerned
16
Organizational Constraints
14
Feasibility Analysis
Constraints from Phases One and Two
17
Technical Constraints
20
Specialists
18
Other Constraints
21
Any Feasible Solution?
No
Yes
25
Report to Administration
22
Feasible Methods of Solution
Also Shown in Figure 11-5
Phase Three
Phase Four
To Phase Four

Figure 11–3. Phase Three: Feasibility Analysis

always understated and invariably increases along with the development of the project. The other reason is that analysts often underestimate costs.

The benefits of information systems can, in some cases, be measured. For example, the benefits of an automated information system that eliminates the need of secretaries can be measured in dollars. Unfortunately, most of the benefits of information systems cannot be measured in a satisfactory quantifiable form. Examples of these variables are the accuracy and timeliness of information. How, for example, can one measure the value of grade reporting within a day versus a week; or the value of information necessary for better advisement of a student; or the value of fast response to bibliographical information and selective dissemination of information on new books by a faculty member or a student? One cannot satisfactorily measure these variables nor can one impute a benefit to them. One approach to this problem is to compute the expected cost of the system and let the administrator decide whether or not the expected benefits are worth that cost. For example, the systems change may have an expected cost of $5,000. The administrator must then weigh the expected benefits against the expected cost of $5,000 and make his choice.

If a proposed system is economically feasible, then its cost must be compared with the financial constraints (funds available) for its financial feasibility. Often a proposed system with a high benefit-cost ratio is economically feasible but is not financially feasible.

Organizational Feasibility

Organizational feasibility is concerned with testing for organizational constraints. One example would be a case where the information systems change may require the combining of two departments into one. The administrator responsible for the proposed absorbed department may seriously object and the top administrator may not be willing to intervene. The departmental administrator's resistance constitutes an organizational constraint on this solution alternative.

Other examples of organizational constraints on feasibility are the judgment (and it can be only a judgment with no proof) that the system, if implemented, would not be used or that it would be resisted to the point of being ineffective. Or, the person responsible for the new system may not have the qualities necessary for it to be viable. These qualities may be the willingness to accept experimentation; operate in an atmosphere of change; take risks of mistakes in system design; make changes in procedures and personnel; and finally, have the technical and administrative ability to be responsible for the changed system.

Organizational nonfeasibility could result even at the lowest organizational level—such as the secretaries. They may be unable to perform the proposed new jobs or resist having to change their existing methods. For example, they may resist or be unable to prepare data by mark-sensing forms instead of typing, or by using a terminal instead of cards for preparing input data. Organizational nonfeasibility may result at all levels of organization. There are, however, three areas of support which are most important: top administrators, operational administrators, and systems personnel.

The support of top administration in implementing large and complex information systems is absolutely essential. Without such support, the study should be continued with the utmost caution. However, top administrative support, if not accompanied by operational administrator support and systems personnel capability, should be considered inadequate and hence organizationally not feasible. But, if the systems personnel are not capable, and there is support at both the top and the operational level, then the situation can be corrected. Consultants could be hired to fill the gap and used to select, hire, and train systems personnel. Another possible situation is one where the support of top administrators is accompanied by a high level of system personnel but with no support at an operational level. This situation would be considered organizationally not feasible by some, but feasible by the more courageous. In the latter case, the study should proceed with some caution and with an extra effort at overcoming the weakness in the situation. If the top and operational level of administration are systems oriented, and experienced systems personnel are available then this will lead to the most effective and efficient system.

Table 11-1. Decision Table for Testing Organizational Feasibility

	Rule 1	Rule 2	Rule 3	Rule 4	Rule 5	Rule 6	Rule 7	Rule 8
Top Administrative Support	N	N	N	N	Y	Y	Y	Y
Operational Administrative Support	Y	Y	N	N	Y	Y	N	N
Experienced Analysis Available	Y	N	Y	N	Y	N	Y	N
Discontinue Study		X	X	X				X
Hire Consultants (assume available)						X		
Train Analysts						X		
Continue Study with Caution	X						X	
Continue with Enthusiasm					X			

The organizational feasibility rules discussed above can be stated in the form of a decision table. This is shown in Table 11–1.

The availability of systems personnel is the least important because it is a **derived** variable, inasmuch as systems-oriented top administrators and operational administrators will attract good systems personnel. If attracted for some other reason (such as the academic program) they will not be retained for long. The demand for systems personnel is much greater than the supply and will remain so for some time. They would rather move than fight nonsystems oriented administrators.

In higher education, the operational administrators most concerned with systems development are the Registrar and the Business Officer. If they are biased against information systems or unequal to the job, then important potential areas where a system could be effective are organizationally not feasible—unless corrective action is taken. Three approaches to this type of situation are suggested by Newman, Summer, and Warren:

> 1) Change the job e.g., withdrawing a duty from one position and assigning it to another position, adjusting the degree of decentralization, and providing additional assistance where a man is weak; 2) Change the incumbent, perhaps through counseling and training; and 3) Remove the incumbent, either by transfer or dismissal action.[5]

Organizational feasibility may require the merging of two departments (such as the Office of Admissions and the Registrar) or the expansion of the duties of one officer. For example, it may require an increase in the duties of the Registrar and a corresponding increase in the Registrar's salary so as to attract and retain a person who can perform the additional responsibility resulting from system changes, especially changes involving advanced information technology.[6]

Technological Feasibility

Sometimes a solution to a problem is not feasible because we do not have the technology to solve the problem. Examples include our lack of mathematical or statistical techniques to determine optimal solutions in some decision-making situations, and the lack of equipment to perform certain types of operations (such as machines that read handwriting).

[5]W. H. Newman, C. E. Summer, and E. K. Warren, *The Process of Management* (2nd ed.) (Englewood Cliffs, N.J.: Prentice-Hall, Inc., 1967), pp. 272–73.

[6]For another example of organizational infeasibility, see McKinsey and Company, Inc., "Unlocking the Computer's Profit Potential," *Computers and Automation,* XVIII, No. 4 (April 1969) 28.

Other Feasibility Considerations

Sometimes there are constraints other than economic, financial, organizational, and technical. An example is the time constraint. A case study illustrates this.

A university administrator needed a set of computer reports on grading practices and enrollment predictions. His systems group stated that it was economically, organizationally, and technologically feasible but that it would take at least three weeks. This, however, violated a constraint: the time constraint, as the job had to be ready for an Accreditation Committee visiting on campus in a week. The project was, therefore, not feasible and not implemented.

The administrator, or would-be administrator, can learn from this case. The lesson is the fact that computers are fast, but they need programming instructions on what to do with the data. The data collection and the programming of instructions are still generally manual and slow. They must be planned well in advance to ensure the availability of results when needed.

Feasibility Decision

The feasibility decision in Phase Three is the result of deliberations by the feasibility study team. They may call upon administrators and specialists for advice and counsel (circles 19 and 20 in Figure 11–3).

Sometimes there are a number of alternatives that are feasible but not all simultaneously, often because of the lack of sufficient financial and personnel resources. The feasibility study team must then select among these alternatives and rank them in terms of recommended priorities. An example of this problem would be the feasibility of the automation of one out of many departments. In selecting the department to be automated, it must give some weight to the department that is the source of basic data needed by other departments in the organization. Also, one department may be preferred because it is small and isolated and its automation could provide experience in systems change without adversely affecting the rest of the system in the event of miscalculations. Such experience is valuable to both systems and organizational personnel. Other considerations include the systems designers' preference to start with small jobs with a high pay-off and a high probability of success. These are situations where the work is repetitive, has a high volume, and is being done by clerks.

Systems designers also prefer jobs where their assignment is well designed and unambiguous and there is adequate time for planning and implementing the change. They avoid areas with potential emotional resistance, whether it be at the administrative or secretarial level.

The choices between alternative system implementations are often not simple because of the many considerations involved. But rankings and priorities must be assigned and the highest ranked feasible set of solutions selected (YES exit from box 21 of Figure 11–3). If there are none, this is reported to administration (NO exit box 21 of Figure 11–3).

Phase Four: Choice of Solution

Selling the Product

The fourth and last phase of the feasibility study is shown in the flowchart of Figure 11–4. It largely concerns the administrators who must make the final decision. To help them make the decision, the feasibility study team must present their recommendations, but before doing so other related information must be collected and prepared (box 23).

The information from the feasibility study necessary for the administration to make a final decision must include the following considerations:

1. Statement of objectives and scope of study
2. Identification of alternatives with preference rankings.

For each alternative, the following information must be provided:

1. Resources required
   - 1.1. Developmental
     - 1.1.1. Equipment
     - 1.1.2. Personnel
     - 1.1.3. Space
     - 1.1.4. Other
   - 1.2. Recurring
     - 1.2.1. Personnel
     - 1.2.2. Other
2. Anticipated consequences of proposed project
   - 2.1. Organizational changes
     - 2.1.1. Structural
     - 2.1.2. Personnel
     - 2.1.3. Procedures
   - 2.2. Informational changes
   - 2.3 Anticipated problems
3. Limitations of proposed project
4. Benefits of project
   - 4.1. Economic
   - 4.2. Organizational
   - 4.3. Overall systems
   - 4.4. Other
5. Time schedule
   - 5.1. Time schedule of project
   - 5.2. Priority reassignment of other jobs
6. Summary

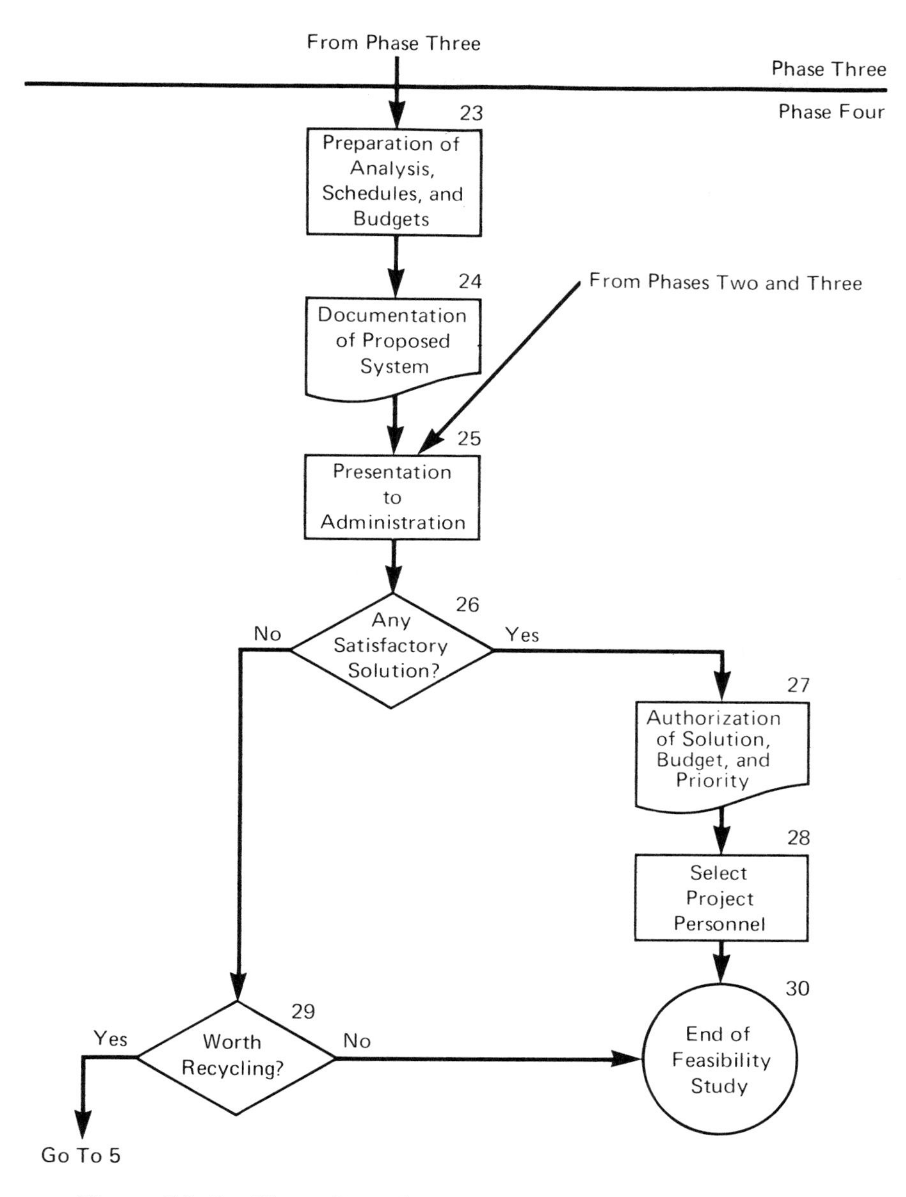

Figure 11–4. Phase Four: Choice of Solution

The above information should be supported by examples of output and performance figures from other case studies.

Buying the Product

It is the administrator's responsibility to ensure that all relevant variables are specified and that the estimates are checked. For example, the budget estimates should be checked for reasonableness. In this checking process, administrators in institutions of higher learning can find experienced help among their faculty. This is a rich resource that administrators have not learned to use. Faculty members in the Schools of Business and Industrial Engineering may well provide the necessary resource. Alternately, outside consulting help can be used. In all cases, administrators must allow for overruns on estimates and delays in their schedules because this has been the history of systems changes, especially in the area of computer installations.

Administrators have to rely on systems personnel for making time and cost estimates, and systems personnel often hedge in doing so. They claim that their job is developmental, often untried and full of uncertainties, and that they cannot make predictions or estimations with accuracy. There is a point in this assertion but it is often exaggerated. Even in the development of information systems and programming for computer systems, one can make fairly good predictions. In recent years, the profession has developed some experience in this matter and many business firms exist solely by developing programming systems. They have developed techniques and rules for predicting costs and generally remain within their estimates.[7] Systems personnel in educational institutions can learn much from experience in these industries as well as from their own past performance.

Administrators must carefully study their feasibility study report and search for bias and omitted considerations, such as the organizational impact. They should look with caution at studies that dismiss organizational impact as unimportant. Many systems changes have organizational implications, especially on future job classifications and employment. These implications must be recognized and plans for their solutions carefully studied.

Decision on Feasibility Study

The final decision involves weighing all the costs and benefits (box 26). Only the administrator can make this judgment and in doing so he must impute values to the many intangible benefit variables. He must estimate the effect of the many conflicting and compensating factors and evaluate the

[7]See "Managing the Programming Effort," *EDP Analyzer,* VI, No. 6 (June 1968), 1–8.

trade-offs. He alone can determine the contribution of the proposed new system to organizational goals and to the effectiveness of the organization.

In selecting systems projects to be implemented, administration must maintain a balance between short-range and long-range significance of the project as well as between subsystems and total system implementation. There is typically a tendency to spend all of one's systems effort in putting out local short-range "brush-fires" and neglecting the overall long-range planning needs.[8] This problem can be overcome by allocating system personnel exclusively for long-range systems planning, but it requires top-level commitment of resources.

In some cases the administrator may not find any of the proposed solutions to be acceptable. To facilitate an acceptable solution becoming a feasible one, he may have to relax the constraint on the system or else scale down his objectives. This decision would require recycling (YES exit from box 26 in Figure 11–4 to box 5 in Figure 11–1).

If there is an acceptable solution (YES exit from box 26) then this choice must be accompanied by certain decisions that are necessary for implementation (box 27). This includes authorization of a budget, time schedule, necessary policy and procedural changes, and sometimes a reassignment of existing priorities of systems effort.[9] In some cases, statements concerning organizational policies on personnel are necessary. This subject is discussed in Chapter 17.

In the system authorization document, top administration must take actions necessary to ensure that the promised benefits of the new system are fully realized. There are many cases on record where, in the feasibility study, a department head will support the claim of savings such as the replacement of clerks, but after the system is implemented the savings disappear. The replaced clerks do unproductive work and are part of what the economist calls **disguised unemployment.** This can be prevented if the top administrator sets a date when the funds representing the promised savings resulting from the new system will be withdrawn from the department concerned. This action has two important effects. One, it ensures that the savings from the new system are realized; and two, it motivates the department concerned to cooperate with systems personnel so that the proposed project can be completed effectively and in time.

The final step in this phase is to appoint a project leader to be responsible for the implementation of the project (box 28). The qualities of the project

[8]For examples of this attitude, see J. Rosenzweig, "The Weapon Systems Management Concept and Electronic Data Processing," *Management Science* (Series A), VI, No. 1 (January 1960) 149–64.

[9]In systems work, there is often more demand for resources than the supply of resources. The assigning of these resources is thus an important and often difficult choice.

leader must include proven experience in administering such projects. This appointment is very important and must be made with great care. Furthermore, he must be given the authority needed to carry out his responsibility.

In addition to the project leader, it is desirable in cases of complex projects to have a User and Administrative Committee to help the project leader in interpreting institutional policies and in clarifying users' needs. Whenever necessary, this committee could also monitor the progress of the project at determined check points. With the project personnel appointed and their responsibilities clearly specified, the feasibility study is terminated.

DURATION OF A FEASIBILITY STUDY

The feasibility study may take a few days if the systems change is a simple one. In cases of complex systems changes, such as the SABRE system installed by American Airlines, it could take up to four years.[10]

The duration of the feasibility study is a function of (determined by) the complexity of the problem being considered; the availability of systems personnel and administrators concerned (for example, academic department chairmen and faculty are not all available during summer); the state of documentation of the existing system; the amount of detail analysis to be used after the feasibility study is implemented; the number of departments involved in the study; the urgency for the project; and finally, the systems orientation of personnel involved.

The feasibility study should not be rushed at the expense of quality and thoroughness because it is not only the basis for the decision on implementation but is also the basis for design and evaluation after the decision is made to implement it. It must, therefore, be taken seriously. Additional time spent on the study may well contribute to the project being relevant and effective.

SUMMARY AND CONCLUSIONS

A feasibility study is primarily a fact-finding effort that provides the information necessary for the decision on whether or not to implement a proposed systems change. The secondary function of the feasibility study is to provide the basic data necessary for the design, evaluation, and scheduling of the project if implemented. A side-effect advantage of the feasibility study is that it forces an examination and investigation into the problem, resulting in the identification of related problems and areas of potential benefits from systems changes.

[10] R. W. Parker, "The SABRE System," *Datamation,* XI, No. 9 (September 1965), 49–52.

A feasibility study can be viewed as having four phases: the organization of study, the search for solutions, the feasibility analysis, and the decision on implementation. Steps in each of these phases and their interrelationships are shown in flowchart form in Figure 11–5.

The feasibility analysis is of three types: economic feasibility, organizational feasibility, and technological feasibility. In some cases, these would not be performed in sequence. For example, in a study involving some types of equipment the technological decision must be made before its economic and organizational feasibility are examined. In other cases, these three feasibility analyses can be done in parallel, or simultaneously. The approach used will largely depend on the nature and complexity of the problem. The greater the complexity of the proposed systems change, the more formal and thorough should be the feasibility study.

A feasibility study may find a system proposal not feasible for one of many reasons. The most frequent is financial: the necessary funds are not available. The next important reason is economic: the costs exceed the benefits. Non-economic reasons are constraints such as time, the lack of necessary organizational environment, or the technological inability to achieve the objectives.

Figure 11–5 shows the two important documents generated by the study which will be used later if the project is implemented. One is the systems proposal (symbol 24) identifying what can be achieved and the resources required for it. This is the commitment of the systems personnel. The second important document is the authorization of the project, (symbol 27) which is the commitment of the administration to the project. This authorizes the resources available to the project and states the policies required to make the procedural or organizational changes necessary for project implementation.

Figure 11–5 identifies three important decision points. Two are taken in by the feasibility study team where a recommendation may be made to discontinue the study, either as a result of information collected (box 12) or as a result of the formal feasibility analysis (box 21). The third decision point is taken by the administration (box 26) and is the final one. If the decision is to discontinue the study when the project should have been implemented, then the institution has lost an opportunity for benefits from systems change. If the decision is to implement the study when it should have been discontinued, then there is a loss of resources and perhaps even an organizational disruption that was unnecessary.

Feasibility studies are costly and time-consuming but they are necessary. If properly conducted, feasibility studies reduce the risk of wrong decisions in systems changes. Sometimes feasibility studies fail to reduce risks and to anticipate problems. Some common reasons for such failures are:

1. A crash approach which does not allow sufficient time to adequately perform all the phases of the study.

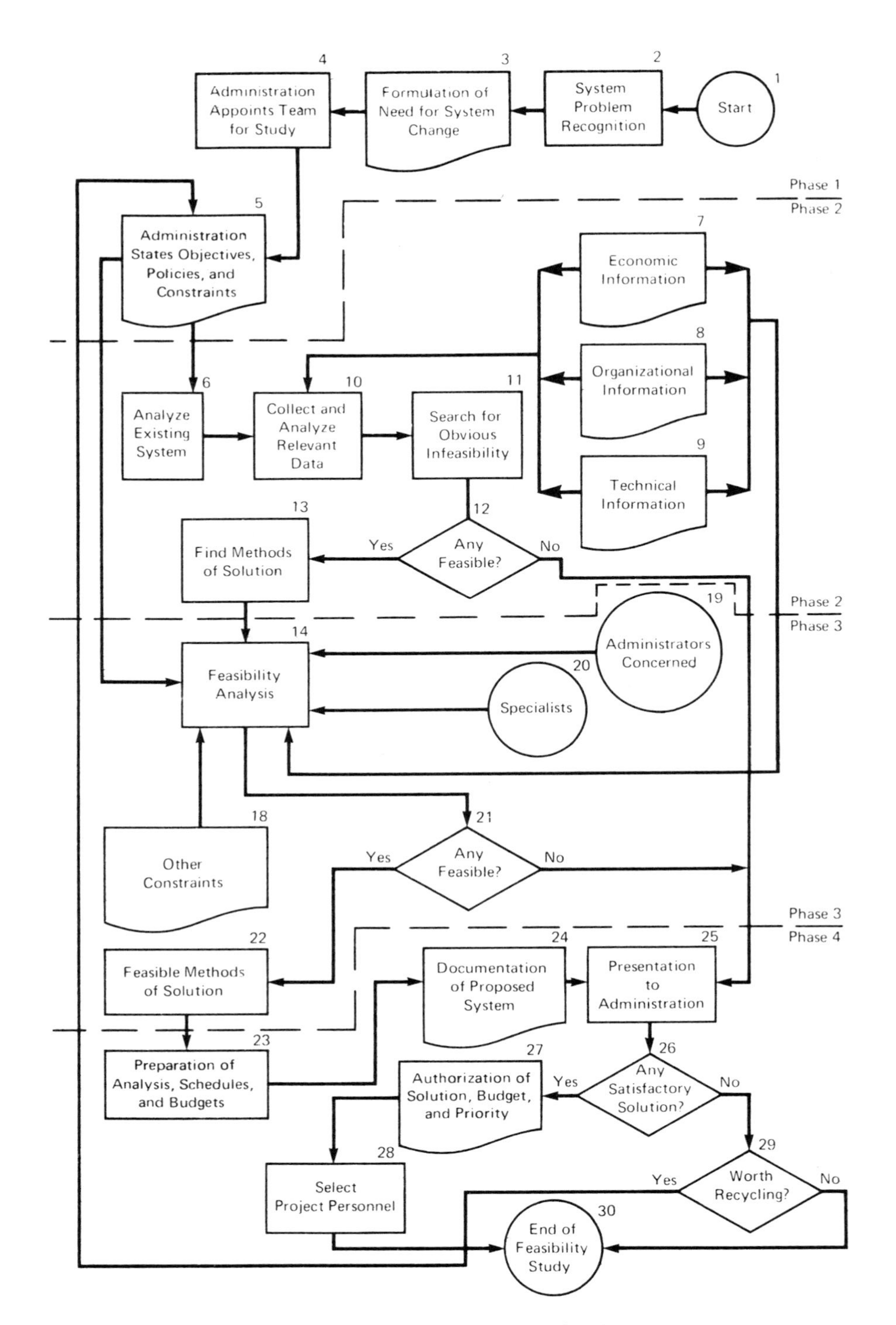

Figure 11–5. Flowchart for Feasibility Study

2. A non-integrated approach that does not consider the role of the project and system change in the long-range plans of the institution or its systems master plans.
3. Poor leadership and poor staffing (sometimes inadequate time assigned to study) of feasibility team.
4. Failure to adequately specify objectives, constraints, and problem areas.
5. Lack of organizational support.
6. Estimation errors. These may be errors in estimating organizational resistance, problem difficulty, resource requirements, and organizational impact.

The implications of a system change are never fully predicted in the feasibility stage of a systems change, especially in systems changes involving electronic data processing (EDP). This is borne out from business experience and is applicable to education. A study of 11 business firms by Vergin and Grimes shows that

> despite lengthy pre-installation studies, no firm was completely successful in foreseeing all the major and minor benefits and disadvantages that follow the installation of the computer. This, in fact, may be nearly impossible. Since any given factor may be extremely important in one firm and not even exist in another, the experience of others does not provide a complete guide for the firm planning EDP.[11]

KEY TERMS

Feasibility Analysis
Economic Feasibility
Financial Feasibility
Organizational Feasibility
Technological Feasibility
Feasibility Report

REVIEW QUESTIONS

1. Distinguish between
   Organizational Feasibility and Economic Feasibility
   Objectives and Constraints
   Economic Constraints and Financial Constraints
   Feasible Solution and Optimum Solution
2. Why are the objectives and constraints specified after assigning a team to study the proposed change?
3. Why do some system analysts not study the existing system prior to studying alternate solutions?

[11] R. C. Vergin and A. J. Grimes, "Management Myths and EDP," *California Management Review,* VII, No. 1 (Fall 1964) 61.

4. When is a nonfeasible system aborted?
5. What are the "outputs" of the system feasibility?
6. When should feasibility studies be conducted?
7. What information should the administration provide to the system designers and when?

CHAPTER 11: SELECTED ANNOTATED BIBLIOGRAPHY

ALEXANDER, TOM, "Computers Can't Solve Everything," *Fortune,* LXXX, No. 5 (October 1969), 126–29, 168–71. This is an excellent reminder that computers have limitations which must be kept in proper perspective. The author discusses tendencies of computer usage, the gap between computer capabilities and their use, and problems arising in the development of computer applications.

ASIMOW, M., *Introduction to Design.* Englewood Cliffs, N.J.: Prentice-Hall, Inc., 1964, Chap IV, pp. 18–23. Although written specifically for engineers, the concepts presented are applicable to the design of any system and can be easily grasped by the non-engineer. Chapter 4 includes an excellent treatise on the relationships among the stages of the feasibility study which is supplemented by a flowchart showing inputs and outputs of the feasibility study phase of development.

AWAD, E. M., *Business Data Processing* (2nd ed.). Englewood Cliffs, N.J.: Prentice-Hall Inc., 1968, Chap XXV, pp. 421–44. Managers and administrators can use this as a general guide for what to include in the feasibility study. Topics include personnel and technical qualifications for a project team, team responsibilities, human engineering considerations at feasibility study time, cost-analysis, and general factors to consider when studying the feasibility of computerized systems.

DIEBOLD, J., "Bad Decisions on Computer Use," *Harvard Business Review,* 47, No. 1 (January-Feburary 1969), 14–28, 176. Diebold presents fairly specific considerations in determining a cost-benefit ratio for a management information system. The benefits of a management information system are categorized and the relationship between personnel and hardware costs discussed. Included are the results of a survey showing the computer's share of plant investment and seriousness of the communications gap between management and computer personnel.

GLAZER, R. G., "Are You Working on the Right Problem?" *Datamation,* XIII, No. 6 (June 1967), 22–25. Managers and administrators can help to insure that their computer will contribute positively if a detailed analysis of the company and economics is undertaken. This is a more global approach to the feasibility study and its component studies.

GREGORY, R. H., and R. L. VAN HORN *Automatic Data Processing Systems* (2nd ed.). Belmont, Ca.: Wadsworth Publishing Company, Inc., 1963, Chap. XVI, pp. 526–629. This is an introductory book to business data processing and does not require previous knowledge of electronic computing systems. A feasibility study guide for selecting a course of action in a feasibility study is provided in a decision-table format. Each step of the feasibility and application studies is discussed in some detail to include the relationship among the steps. For those with a good EDP background, a reading of the summary at the end of Chapter 16 should be sufficient.

OPTNER, S. L., *Systems Analysis for Business Management.* Englewood Cliffs, N.J.: Prentice-Hall, Inc., 1960, Chap. V, pp. 105–15. Questions which should be asked by management at feasibility study time are proposed. The author presents a generalized outline for the conduct of the feasibility study.

SANDERS, D. H., *Computers in Business: An Introduction.* New York: McGraw-Hill Book Company, 1968, Chap XII, pp. 253–78. A very readable, nontechnical and basic treatment of computer data processing is presented in textbook form. In Chapter 12, the author examines (1) the essential nature of feasibility studies, (2) the prerequisites to a successful study, and (3) the steps in the feasibility study approach. A feasibility study is made by an organization to determine the desirability of using a computer to achieve specific objectives and, with this purpose in mind, Dr. Sanders proceeds to discuss and summarize: common pitfalls to be avoided; common feasibility study objectives; data-gathering questions; questions for analysis and design; factors in equipment selection; and factors to consider in equipment acquisition.

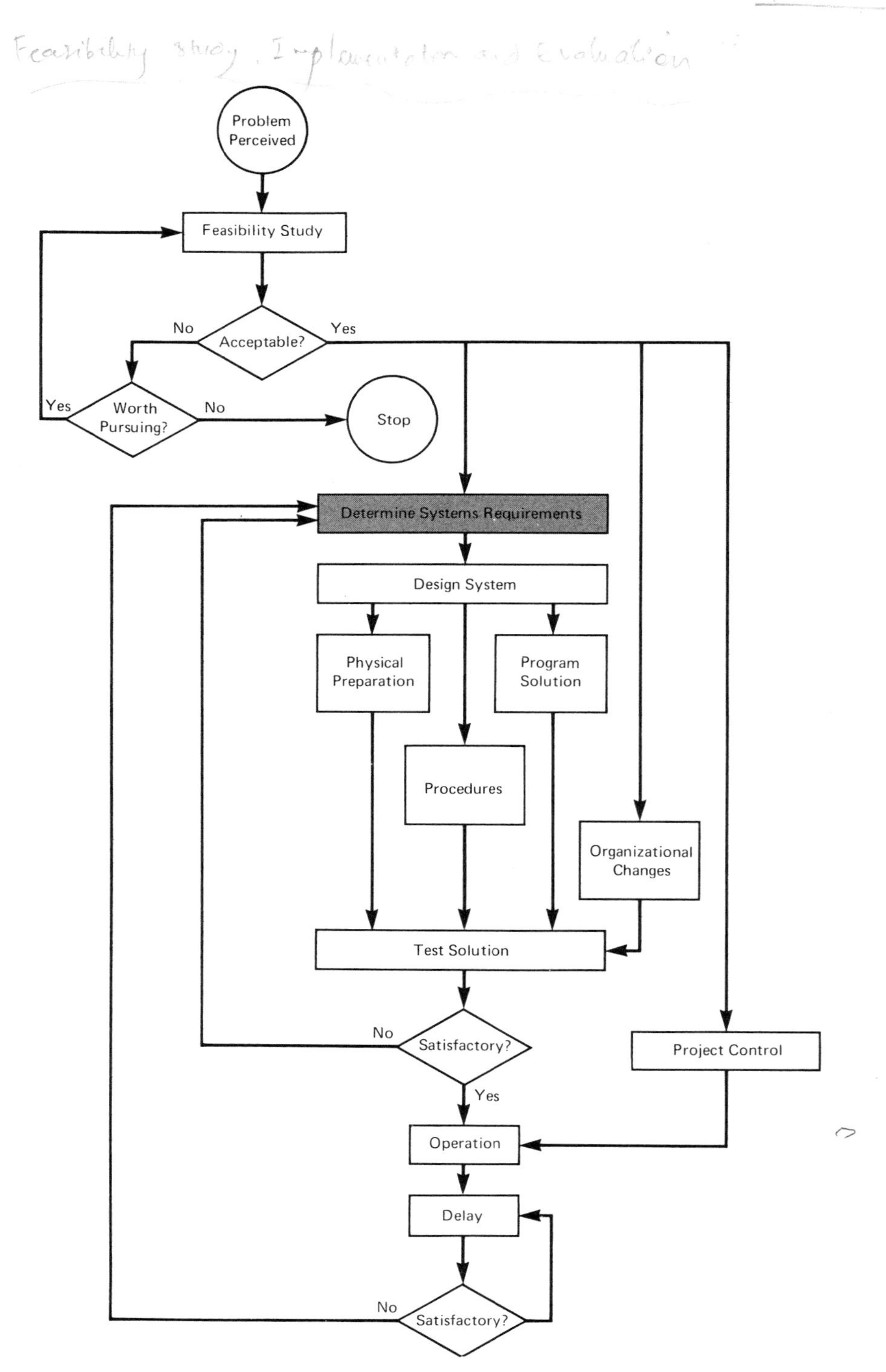

Problem Perceived
Feasibility Study
Acceptable?
No
Yes
Worth Pursuing?
Yes
No
Stop
Determine Systems Requirements
Design System
Physical Preparation
Program Solution
Procedures
Organizational Changes
Test Solution
Satisfactory?
No
Yes
Project Control
Operation
Delay
Satisfactory?
No

12

Determining Systems Requirements from the User's Viewpoint

If we agree that a computer can do anything we instruct it to do, then why isn't it obvious that the failure of a computer to deliver the hoped-for output is the fault of the one issuing the instruction?

E. D. Dwyer[1]

INTRODUCTION

This chapter is concerned with determining the requirements of a new system from the user's viewpoint. The requirement specifications are the instructions issued by the administrator as to the performance expected of the new system. It is actually an extension of the work done in the feasibility study,

[1]Quoted in J. Rosenzweig, "The Weapon Systems Management Concept and Electronic Data Processing," *Management Science* (Series A), VI, No. 1 (January 1960), p. 150.

which was concerned with stating the objectives to be achieved by the new system. This statement is usually in general terms, but for purposes of actually designing the system it is necessary to restate these objectives in greater detail and completeness.

As an example, consider in a university the designing of an information system that will automatically determine each student's scholastic standing after the grades are processed at the end of each semester. Such an information system identifies the students who should be put on probation, suspended, or withdrawn from the institution. The statement on the rules concerning scholastic standing is usually published in the university catalogue and this is all that is needed in the feasibility study stage. But this generality is insufficient for designing an automated system. What is needed is a complete set of decision rules identifying actions for each set of conditions, such as those stated in a decision table. The implicit rules which are unstated in the catalogue must be clarified and must all be unambiguously and quantitatively specified.

In looking at an information system there are two viewpoints. One is that of the administrator and manager—those who actually use the output of the information system—and the other is that of the systems analyst. The latter may wish to specify requirements of the system that will ensure it meets the standards set by the user in an effective and efficient manner. These are the **means** to achieve the user's requirements which are the **end** product. The **means** will be the subject of the following chapter. The production of the **end product** is the topic of Chapters 14–17.

In determining user's requirements, the systems analyst may contribute to systems specifications, but to a large extent this is the stage in which the user expresses himself and identifies his needs. The systems analyst is the coordinator, the catalyst, and the documentor.

Organization of Chapter

The main steps in this stage of systems development are identified in Figure 12–1. Some of these steps will be discussed in the sequence in which they appear. Others will be discussed in groups of related activities. These are not performed at one time, but alternate with other sets of activities. Hence the discussion is according to the sequence shown in Figure 12–2.

A network diagram of the activities shown in the flowchart in Figure 12–1 will appear in the Summary and Conclusions.

SOME DEFINITIONS

Before proceeding further with this chapter, it may be wise to define a few terms that will be used repeatedly in the following pages.

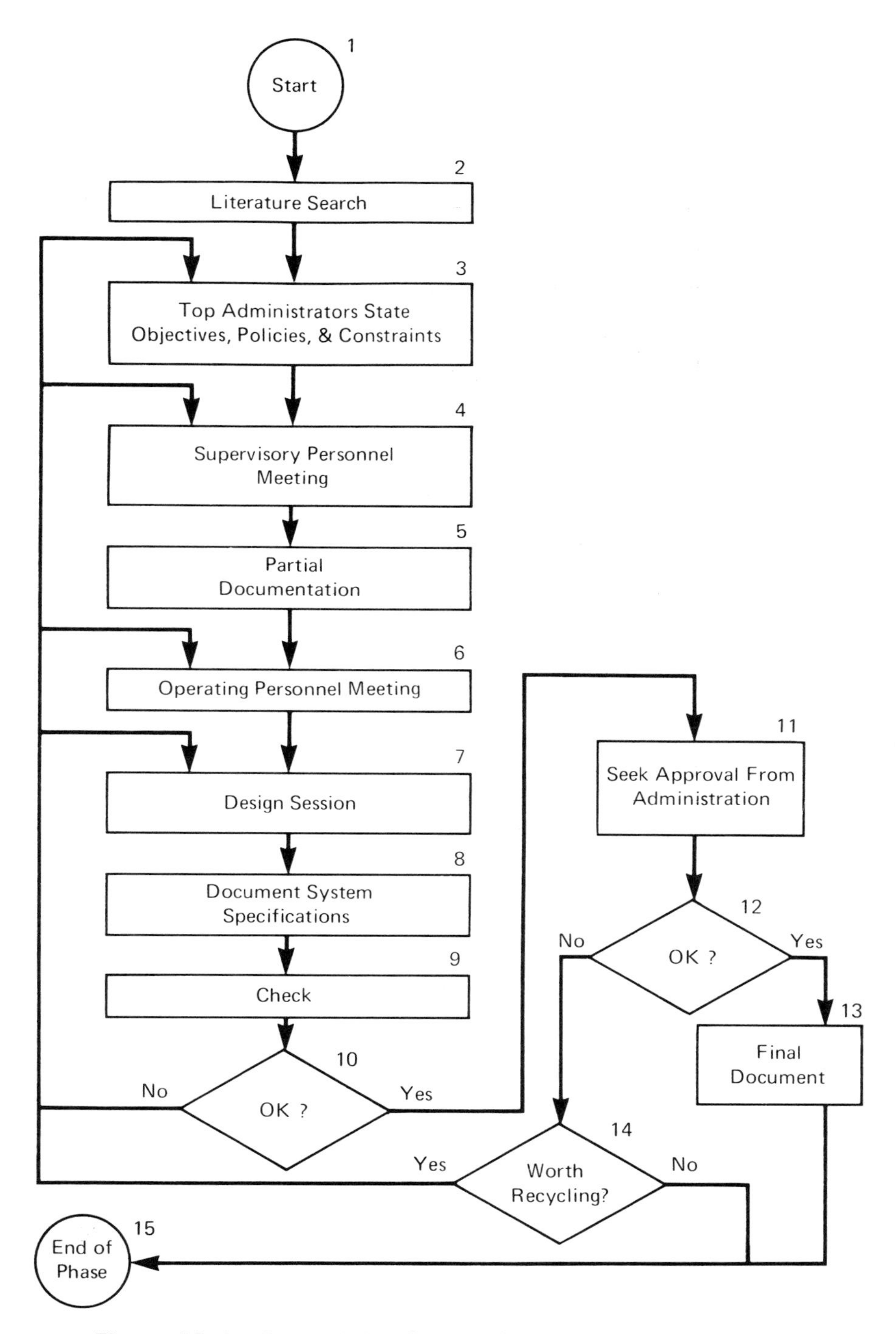

Figure 12–1. Determining System Specifications

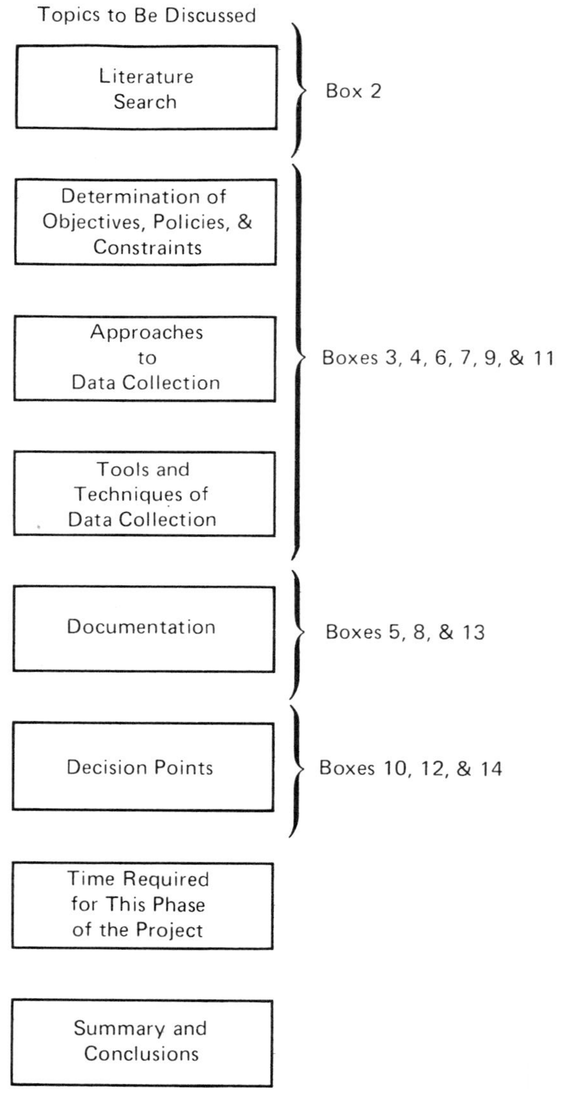

Figure 12–2. Sequence of Topics to be Discussed in This Chapter

Systems User

A Systems User is a person who has a need for information related to his job. In an educational institution he is typically an administrator at the top, control, or operational level. Sometimes the ultimate user is a worker or a clerk, but his need must be expressed through his supervisor.

Requirement

As defined by Rosove,

> a "requirement" . . . may be defined as a characteristic which a system or one of its elements should possess if the system is to accomplish a given objective.
>
> Requirements statements, in their totality, at all system levels and in all functional areas tell us *what* the system is supposed to do in both qualitative and quantitative terms, rather than *how* it is to do it. It is the function of system design, by contrast, to answer the question: how?[2]

In the context of system development a **requirement** from the systems designer's viewpoint is often the same as an **objective** from the point of view of the user. Hence, these two terms will be used interchangeably in this text.

Systems Personnel

Systems Personnel are persons who perform the technical functions in creating a new system or modifying an existing system, so that the systems requirements specified by the user are met.

Development Team

A group of users and systems personnel who help in the development of an information system.

LITERATURE SEARCH

This step is conducted largely by systems personnel. For them, it is the opportunity to learn about system changes in other institutions similar to the

[2]Perry E. Rosove, "The System Requirements Phase," in *Developing a Computer-Based Information System* (New York: John Wiley & Sons, Inc., 1967), pp. 67–68.

one being studied. Also, it is an opportunity to learn about the organization being studied, its stated objectives, size, the nature of its products, its operations, and its organizational structure. Some of this is in print and can be found in annual reports, catalogues, and publicity material. This information must be supplemented with observations and the questioning of administrators by the systems analysts. An attempt should be made to identify the informal organization and the informal power structure. This helps to identify the decision maker(s) at different levels of the organization who must participate in determining the systems requirements.

In this phase, the systems personnel must learn the vocabulary of the user personnel, and throughout the study they must ensure that a word or a term means the same thing to all concerned. Lack of agreement on terminology is often a source of much confusion, inaccuracy, and wasted effort. Definitions must be clarified and agreed upon very early in the project.

For example, consider the system change on student scholastic standing reporting. A crucial variable is the GPA (gradepoint average), or more specifically, the cumulative GPA. Is this GPA the same as the total GPA, the final GPA, or the overall GPA? Do all these terms mean the same thing? Does this GPA include transfer units and, if so, are there any conditions on the type and number of courses to be transferred, and the institutions recognized for such transfer purposes? All terms and conditions must be clarified and must, whenever possible, be compatible with terms used in the profession. Fortunately, some such terms have been agreed upon and published in glossaries and booklets on definitions[3] and should be used whenever available.

There is also the problem of definitions of terms used by systems analysts. The profession is yet too young and changing too rapidly for a settled body of definitions. Some glossaries have been developed and some terms have been defined by professional organizations. An example appears at the end of this book. However, there are still many terms such as *real-time systems* and *total systems* that have different meanings to different people. It is important for the administrator to recognize this situation and attempt to keep up with different and changing definitions.

The clarification of definitions, and orientation in the organization prepares systems personnel for their meetings with the administrators. The administrators, on their part, must also prepare to meet with systems personnel. They must review and update their knowledge on information systems. They should also participate in educational programs for systems change—a subject discussed in Chapter 17.

[3]Office of Education, *Definitions of Student Personnel Terms in Higher Education,* EO–50083, 1968, p. 60.

IDENTIFYING USER'S OBJECTIVES, POLICIES, AND CONSTRAINTS

The user's requirements and constraints must be identified at each level of administration. As shown in Figure 12–1 on p. 000, this is done at the top administrative level (box 3), at the supervisory level (box 4), at the operational level (box 6) with an intermediate step of documentation (box 5), and at all levels combined in a design session (box 7). The design session enables an overview of the interrelationships between each level of administration and at the same time provides an opportunity to identify and resolve conflicts on systems specifications between the different levels. The design session as a method of data collection will be discussed later under the tools and techniques of data collection.

User's Objectives

Administrative considerations include organizational objectives, policies, and constraints. The latter term has already been defined. Objectives and policies will be defined according to Anthony where " 'objectives' are what the organization wishes to accomplish . . . and 'policies' are guidelines that are to be used in the choice of the most appropriate course of action for accomplishing the objectives."[4]

Stating Objectives and Policies

Stating objectives is difficult for administrators even if they are not reluctant to share this information. Yet, it is necessary that this be done. Information systems should be uniquely designed for an organization. They are meaningful only in the context of the goals and objectives of the organization.

The importance of defining objectives on the performance criterion is emphasized by McKean.

> There is a great danger of forgetting, or at least neglecting, the significance of criteria-selection. If extreme care is not exercised in this part of the task, all the researcher's ingenuity and scientific tools may be wasted in deriving right answers to the wrong questions—which are sometimes diametrically wrong answers to the real questions.[5]

[4]R. N. Anthony, *Planning and Control Systems: A Framework for Analysis* (Boston: Harvard University, 1965), p. 16.

[5]R. N. McKean, "Sub-optimization Criteria and Operations Research," in M. Alexis and C. Z. Wilson, *Organizational Decision Making* (Englewood Cliffs, N.J.: Prentice-Hall, Inc., 1967), p. 165.

Theoretically goals and objectives are clarified in stated policies. In practice, however, policies are often not too helpful. Laden and Gildersleeve make the following observation:

> Policy that governs a particular course of action is riddled with exceptions and is so fuzzy as to be subject to several interpretations, all of which have been used at one time or another in the history of the operation. . . . Too much information is available for some processes. Not enough is available for others.[6]

Policy information can sometimes be found in manuals. But often manuals either do not exist or when they do exist are outdated. The missing information is usually crucial, for that is what caused them to be outdated in the first place. Thus, systems personnel have a difficult time determining systems objectives—both long-range and short-range. They must determine how the system project fits into the organizational plan, and then detect the ambiguities in policies and demand clarity and precision for them. They must draw out the unwritten policies, the unstated goals, the biases and preferences, as well as the priority rankings of the administrator. The more the administrator and the systems analyst cooperate in this process, the more relevant the systems specifications will be.

Basic to the question of goals and objectives is the value system of the decision-makers. This includes the decision-makers' preferences, priority rankings, biases, and prejudices. In some systems projects these must be stated if a relevant and meaningful solution is to be found.

Perhaps an example will illustrate the point. Consider the objective in a university to be that of reducing the queueing line of students during registration within specified limits. This is a classic problem in Queueing Theory and can be solved, provided we know the value of the different cost coefficients. One cost coefficient would be the hourly waiting cost of a secretary servicing a registration station. This value is known: the wage rate of the secretary. The other cost coefficient is that of a faculty member waiting an hour to advise. Is this cost the monthly salary of the faculty member divided by a standard number of working hours a month or divided by the hours spent on campus a month? Neither cost value, however, may represent the psychic cost of the waiting faculty. What, then, is the cost of a faculty member waiting an hour? Similarly, what is the cost of a student waiting? To the university, the monetary cost is zero. But the social cost is not zero. Even to the institution, the cost in terms of public relations and the effect on the image of the institution is definitely not zero. But what is the trade-off between making a faculty member wait as opposed to making a student wait? What is the trade-off between students waiting and a saving in overtime for secretarial help? These

[6] H. N. Laden and T. R. Gildersleeve, *System Design for Computer Applications* (New York: John Wiley & Sons, Inc., 1963), p. 228.

are difficult questions to answer! But they must be answered by the administrator or else the systems personnel will answer them by default. Systems personnel are not always in a position to make such choices. The administrator alone must make these determinations and should not let this responsibility be exercised by default.

Specifying Constraints

The concept and need for identifying constraints is illustrated in Figure 12–3.

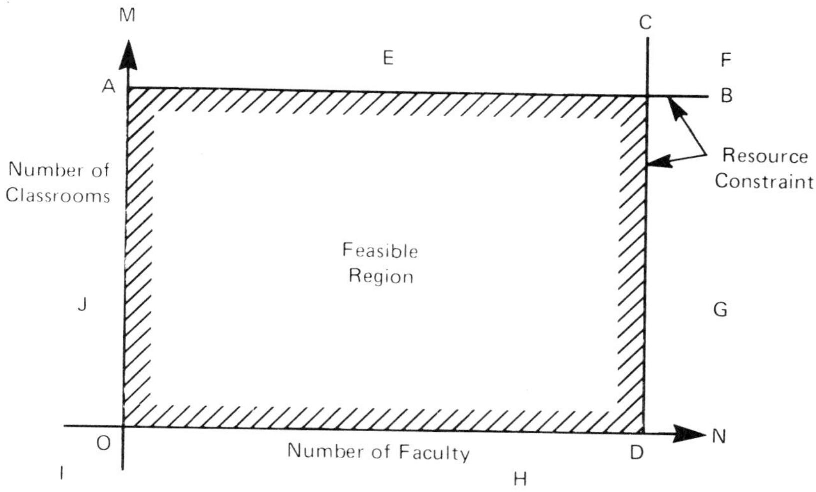

Figure 12–3. Illustration of Constraints

Only two resource constraints are considered for simplification of the illustration. These are the number of classrooms and the number of faculty available. The values of resource availability constitute constraints on the system and are shown by the lines AB and CD respectively (OA and OD are the available number of classrooms and faculty respectively). Any solution requiring more resources than those available is not feasible. Examples are points E, F, and G. Points H, I, and J are also not feasible since they require negative resources which is meaningless. In general, all points with negative resource values and points that require more resources than those available are not feasible. Other points are feasible and correspond to the inside of the space bounded by the X and Y axes (OM and ON respectively) and the resource constraints AB and CD (the boundary lines). This is the shaded area in Figure 12–3 and is called the **feasible region.** Its demarcation reduces the area for a solution. It saves wasted effort in considering solutions outside the feasible area. This illustrates the importance of identifying constraints.

Constraints are mostly resources such as funds, personnel, and equipment. Those required for an information system project should have been approved in the previous stage of the feasibility study. However, there may still be constraining problems of acquiring these resources. For example, additional personnel and equipment may have been approved but there may be a lead-time in their acquisition imposing a timing constraint. Another example of constraints are state or federal laws concerning minimum wages and maximum hours of employment. All such constraints must be clearly specified so that the system can then be designed within the constrained feasible space.

Performance Specifications

Objectives, policies, and constraints as they relate to user's requirements must be specified in operational terms as desired performance levels. Some relevant considerations are summarized in the following list:

Output
- Content
- Format
- Quantity
- Availability
- Response Time
- Frequency
- Distribution List
- Retention

Processing
- Decision Rules
- Accuracy
- Ratio or Absolute Range
- Significance of Results
- Capacity
- Current
- Future

Input
- Source
- Media
- Procedures
- Validity Checks

Security
- Access to
- Input
- Origination
- Maintenance
- Decision Rules
- Output

- Nature of Access
- List of Those Allowed Access
- Control of Access
- Identification
- Hardware
- Software
- Audit
- General or Specific
- Internal or External

Back-up System

- Items Needing Back-up
- Nature of Back-up
- Procedures
- Maintaining
- Activating

The considerations of output, processing, input, and security have been discussed earlier and will be discussed further in Chapter 13 on System Design. The considerations of back-up will be discussed below.

Back-up System

Another determination of performance concerns the dependence of an organization on the system working without serious breakdowns. Consider a computer used for an information system in a university which breaks down for a day in the middle of registration. Is that an event that can be tolerated? If not, then a back-up system capability must be designed. Similarly, what happens if the input data is physically destroyed or "lost" during computer processing? Can it be recreated at the source or must the system have the capability of regenerating such losses? A solution to this problem is to keep back-up data, but this adds to the cost of the system. The systems personnel must estimate the costs and the administrator must decide whether or not the back-up is worth the cost.

Example of System Specification

The various criteria of information systems specifications can be illustrated by a sample set of specifications, as shown in the following outline:

1. Output
   1.1 This information subsystem determines the scholastic standing of all students and generates copies of the student's academic record for advisory purposes. The main output is to have the contents and format as shown in Attachment A.[7]

[7] All attachments referred to in the set of specifications do not appear in this book but would be with the detailed job specifications.

- 1.2 The supplementary output desired is listed and briefly described in Attachment B.
- 1.3 Response time after grade report deadline:
  - 1.3.1 Ideal: less than 24 hours.
  - 1.3.2 Average: less than 48 hours.
  - 1.3.3 Unacceptable: more than 72 hours.
- 1.4 Distribution: according to list only, see Attachment C.
- 1.5 Frequency of distribution: for specifications see Attachment D.
- 1.6 Retention: data to be kept for longitudinal studies up to ten years.

2. Processing
   - 2.1 Accuracy.
     - 2.1.1 GPA calculations correct to 3 decimal places.
     - 2.1.2 Error rate.
       - 2.1.2.1 Error no more than an average of one record in 1000 records during each year.
       - 2.1.2.2 % error in computed values is to be no more than 0.3%.
   - 2.2 Capacity: 10,000 students currently, 15,000 students maximum in five years with a straight line growth rate assumed.
   - 2.3 Timeliness: the output must be available soon after each end of semester.
   - 2.4. Procedures: for other processing specifications, see Attachment E.
3. Input
   - 3.1 Data to be generated internally at processing center from grade reports.
   - 3.2 Validity program to detect required data that is missing, check for ranges of acceptable data, and perform validity checking of computations.
   - 3.3 For other input specifications see Attachment F.
4. Other Design Specifications
   - 4.1 Security.
     - 4.1.1 Security and access during processing must be restricted to "authorized" processing personnel and those on the list in Attachment C.
     - 4.1.2 Check on *all* student-employee grade records once every academic year.
   - 4.2 Back-up.
     - 4.2.1 Data: the data required for the processing of this system should be considered "vital." A back-up must be available in the thermostatically controlled vault of the Registrar's Office for regenerating the data in the event of willful or accidental destruction of the Computer Center.
     - 4.2.2 Equipment: no back-up will be required in the event of a breakdown of the computer and processing equipment.
5. Resources Required
   - 5.1 Equipment: no more than available.
   - 5.2 Processing: no charge—service by the Computer Center.
   - 5.3 Personnel: work to be absorbed by existing staff.

5.4 Supplies: $550 fixed costs at time of approval of this document, $1100 recurring costs/year for preprinted forms.

6. Testing Conditions.
New system to run parallel to current manual system for one semester and be approved by Dean Smith before release to operations.

The example used above is of a relatively simple system, but for illustrative purposes it suffices. It identifies all the important performance criteria that must be specified. It identifies the data inputs that must be accepted, the resources that should be available, the operations that must be performed, the administrative constraints that must be observed, and the output that must be produced. This document (along with the attachments specifying the details) now serves as the job description for design personnel. It is a statement of what the user expects and what the system must deliver. It is a continuation of the work done in the feasibility study and provides the framework for the detailed design work—the subject of the next chapter.

DATA COLLECTION

The system specifications, such as discussed above, involve interaction between systems personnel and all levels of administration, with top-level administrators to determine their objectives and constraints, and with middle and supervisory personnel to determine operational specifications. In the flowchart in Figure 12–1 (p. 223) these system specification activities and their documentation correspond to boxes 5 and 8, and are preceded by meetings with administration, boxes 3, 4, 6, and 7. It is in these meetings that all the necessary data is collected.

The approaches to data collection are many. The three main approaches being traditional, innovative, and hybrid. These approaches will now be examined, and followed by a discussion of the tools and techniques of data collection used in them.

The Traditional Approach

The oldest and still the most common approach is for the systems personnel to carefully analyze and study the current system. The main thesis of this approach is that the system team cannot contribute to the specification and design unless it intimately knows the organizational and operational environment to be changed. Furthermore, it is argued that detailed fact-gathering and analysis provide information needed in the design stage, identify problem areas and areas of potential gains, and finally, give clues to system solutions.

Some considerations to be examined in this approach are shown in the list below.[8] Its degree of detail identifies one disadvantage of the approach: it can become a very time-consuming job, especially in an institution that has accumulated many forms but no updated documentation on procedures. In one organization of 300 persons, it took 10,000 man-hours (an equivalent of approximately five man-years) to collect the necessary information.[9]

RELATED WORK

What related work is being done?

How is it being done?

PREPARATION AND PROCESSING

Who originates source data?

Who prepares documents?

How often is processing performed?

How long does it take?

Where is the processing performed?

Who performs it?

What equipment and supplies are used?

How many copies are prepared? Who receives them?

Is there unused processing capacity?

What is the volume of documents (maximum, minimum, and average)?

What has been the historical growth rate?

FORM AND TIMELINESS OF DOCUMENTS

Is document in a useful form?

What are its limitations?

Is exception reporting used?

Can two or more documents be combined?

Is greater accuracy needed?

Can lesser accuracy be tolerated?

Is faster reporting desired? Is it needed

USE OF DOCUMENTS

Who receives the document?

Does the document initiate decision? What decision? By whom?

Is there a part of the document that is ignored or rarely used?

What additional information is needed?

What processing is performed by the user of the document?

[8]Adapted from G. B. Davis, *Computer Data Processing* (New York: McGraw-Hill Book Company, Inc., 1969), p. 468. Used with permission.

[9]"Managing the Systems Effort," *EDP Analyzer,* VI, No. 7 (July 1968), 4.

What is the flow of the document?

STORAGE AND RETRIEVAL

Is the document retained? How? For how long?

What are the procedures for retention and purging?

How often is data purged and updated?

How often is it retrieved?

What are the procedures for retrieval?

How large is file (in number of records and average size per record)?

What is growth rate for file?

Is there a *need* for integrating different files? Which files?

COST

What is the cost of processing the document?

What is the change in cost resulting from a change in frequency or accuracy of processing?

How much of present costs of processing will be eliminated by computer processing?

What is the cost of storage and retrieval?

Another important argument for the traditional approach is that one must understand the existing system in order to design a new system to at least match current performance. This is important because many administrators want what they currently have and hopefully a little more, but not necessarily all they should get. They are "satisfiers" and do not even attempt to approach the optimum solution. There may be one of two important reasons for this attitude: one is that the administrator is not willing to try something new and unknown to him, and instead wants to continue with the pattern of decision-making and processing that has now become a habit; the second reason may be that the administrator did not plan ahead, and with the new system about to be implemented, he does not want to go through the time-consuming process of analyzing his present and future needs and specifying a future system. Being pressed for time he specifies the new system as matching the old one.

Because of one or both of the above reasons, we have many instances in education, even in business, where information systems are not taking advantage of system technology. There are still many card and noncomputer systems that duplicate manual systems, and many computer systems that merely duplicate the card and non-computer data processing systems. The equipment they have is doing the job done by equipment of the previous generation of technology. The results are a tragic loss resulting from inefficiencies. What is needed is a fresh look at system needs, and the use and exploitation of current systems technology to optimize performance.

The Innovative Approach

This approach does not study how the organization currently performs. Unhampered and uninhibited by current procedures and practices it specifies what is desired, even though this may seem idealistic and unobtainable.

Heany calls this approach the **logical** approach and explains it thus:

> Other equally talented designers try not to get too close to in-place systems lest this compromise their objectivity. To identify with operating people or with the designers of the current system might, in their judgment, channel their thinking. Instead, these designers concentrate on logical methods of satisfying the posed requirement. They try to be uninhibited . . . , to consider all conceivable ways of deriving the information. In this, they argue, ignorance of details of how things are actually done is a blessing in disguise. They feel free to experiment with novel ideas which an individual more knowledgeable in the ways of the business might dismiss as impractical.[10]

One set of consequences of the innovative approach is that it could lead to many changes in policies and procedures, as well as to changes in organizational structure. These approaches could be risky and might not appeal to administrators other than the daring and innovative.

The Hybrid Approach

Another approach is a combination of the above two approaches: the innovative approach followed by the traditional approach. The hybrid has some of the advantages of both approaches. It is uninhibited by the existing system until the new system is tentatively specified. The tentative specifications are then checked to make sure the new system more than matches the current system.

The disadvantage of the hybrid approach is that it compounds one disadvantage of the traditional approach: it can be very time-consuming and costly.

A variation of the hybrid approach is to use the traditional approach but supplement it with some of the more recent innovative tools for data collection, such as the ADS[11] which will be discussed later in this chapter.

The choice of approach for data collection is a function of the nature of the problem, the resources (money and personnel) available, the orientation of administration, and the attitudes of the systems personnel. The traditional

[10]D. F. Heany, *Development of Information Systems* (New York: The Ronald Press Company, 1968), p. 65.

[11]This is an acronym for Accurately Defined System.

approach is the most commonly used. Accordingly, it has been the basis of the flowchart in Figure 12–1 on p. 223.

TOOLS AND TECHNIQUES OF DATA COLLECTION

To collect data of the type discussed above, various tools and techniques are used. Those to be discussed below are interviewing, design sessions, the Study Organization Plan, and the ADS method.

Interviewing

Interviews have been used very extensively as a means of data collection in the social sciences. There are many variations, such as structured and unstructured interviews. Both should be used in specifying user requirements. Structured interviews result in answers to a predetermined set of questions, while unstructured interviews are more impromptu and spontaneous. Structured interviews provide the essential answers the systems personnel must have; being predetermined they ensure that nothing important is left out and they are not very time-consuming. Unstructured interviews can be time-consuming, but they provide insights that result in better systems design.

Systems Design Sessions

Systems design sessions are variations of the "bull-sessions"[12] that have been used successfully in business and industry. A session consists of a group of people discussing a problem and generating ideas as a result of the cross-fertilization of thoughts from different backgrounds and training.

The participants of the design sessions are administrators, systems personnel, and specialists, including consultants when needed. In some cases when students are directly involved, they too should participate. The side effects of such meetings are better "involvement" in the project of the parties concerned, as well as a better appreciation of the interrelationships of the system.

The design session could be held repeatedly and at different points in the system development. In Figure 12–1 (p. 223) it has been held after meetings with operational personnel, but it could also be held after individual meetings

[12]This is sometimes referred to as "brain-storming" or "synetics." For a further discussion of this subject, see W. J. J. Gordon, *Synetics, the Development of Creative Capacity* (New York: Harper & Row, 1961), p. 180; and T. Alexander, "Synetics: Inventing by the Madness Method," *Fortune,* LXXII, No. 2 (August 1965), 165, 168, 190–98.

with supervisory personnel, or after the meeting with top administrators. The strategy depends on the problem and nature of personnel involved.

The design sessions should be conducted after careful planning and preparation. The participants should be carefully chosen, a suggestive and provocative agenda prepared, and all relevant documents made available with adequate time for study. For complex systems projects the design session may last from two days to two weeks. Experience has shown that the sessions are more productive if they are held away from work and constant interruptions.[13]

Design sessions on systems changes tend to result in flowcharting. Photographing these flowcharts from a blackboard before they are erased provides good preliminary documentation.

The design session (as well as other bilateral meetings between administrators and systems personnel) provides the occasion to exchange reservations, concerns, objections, and differences of opinion. The administrators in these meetings must ensure that the systems objectives and organizational policies are not compromised unnecessarily. Furthermore, it is their responsibility and in their interest to ensure that the systems personnel get a good conceptual understanding of the problem.

The administrators and systems personnel must also size each other up so that they may take support from each others' strengths and compensate for each others' weaknesses. Exaggerations must be deflated, differences in design philosophies must be understood and appreciated, and a lack of realism must be compensated for.

Study Organization Plan

The Study Organization Plan (referred to as SOP) is a systematic methodology of collecting information and designing a new system as practiced by the International Business Machines Corporation. It was originally designed for "breakthrough" types of information systems projects and was used with great success. Though its use has been largely in business and industry, its application to educational organizations is valid.

The SOP consists of three phases:

Phase 1. Understanding the Present System
Phase 2. Determining Systems Requirements
Phase 3. Designing New System

Phases 1 and 2 correspond to this chapter and Phase 3 to the next chapter in this book. Phase 1 is concerned with "the determination of what is done in the existing system, using what inputs, with what resources, and to achieve

[13] "EDP Design Sessions," *EDP Analyzer,* I, No. 5 (May 1963), 7–10.

what results. Information is collected and organized into a meaningful pattern to permit an accurate understanding of the business as it presently operates and reacts to its environment."[14] Phase 2 "reviews the input of these basic questions about the new system. What must it do? How well must it do it? What resources have management specified be used? To answer these questions and to arrive at a valid set of systems requirements, Phase 2 blends known facts about the present system with projections concerning the future."[15]

The SOP method involves the completion of a number of forms: the Resource Usage Sheet showing the resources (personnel, equipment, and materials) consumed by each organizational unit; the Activity Sheet identifying the inputs, outputs, and file usage of each activity; the Operation Sheet listing the volumes and lapse times of each operation; the File Sheet specifying each file's characteristics; the Message Sheet identifying recorded or unrecorded communications entering or leaving an operation; the Input-Output Sheet showing the input-output specifications; the Required Operation Sheet recording details of operational elements within flowchart diagrams; and Resource Sheets providing quantity and cost data on each resource used.

The SOP method[16] is in the traditional approach of data collection. Like other traditional approaches, it is very time-consuming and costly, but it is systematic and thorough. Its detailed data does help analyze bottleneck areas and recognize areas of potential efficiency and effectiveness. It also provides a sound basis for the design activity to follow.

The ADS Method

ADS stands for the "Accurately Defined System."[17] It was originally designed by the National Cash Register Company. It claims a precise definition of what the new system must perform so that the design phase may then follow.

The ADS method uses five forms for collecting the necessary data. These forms are on outputs, inputs, data files, computations, and the logic involved. They are designed to ensure consistency among data fields; to identify relationships of input, computation, and output; to assure completeness of relevant information; to ensure validation of rules and ranges of values; and, finally, to specify the boundaries of the system.

[14] *IBM Basic System Study Guide,* Form F20–8150 (White Plains, N.Y.: International Business Machines Corporation, 1963), p. 2.

[15] *Ibid.*

[16] For a discussion of the SOP Method, Phase 1 and 2, see *IBM Study Organization Plan, The Method Phase I and Method Phase II,* No. F20–8136–0 and F20–8137–0 (White Plains, N.Y.: International Business Machines Corporation, 1963), p. 38 and p. 27 respectively.

[17] For a further discussion of ADS, see *EDP Analyzer,* VI, No. 11 (November 1968), 4–6.

Other Instruments of Data Collection

Other instruments of data collection are the flowchart, network diagrams, decision tables, and the process flowchart. All the above instruments have been discussed elsewhere except the process flowchart. This is shown in Figure 12–4 on the following page.

The process flowchart of the type shown traces each step in the process and identifies the time it takes and the volume involved. An analysis of the chart will quickly identify bottlenecks in the process as well as duplicated and redundant steps. This then suggests areas of potential savings in time and effort.

As an illustration, consider step 3 of correcting incompleteness. The time required for this step could, perhaps, be reduced if the form used were redesigned or supplemented by instructions for completion. Alternately, perhaps the faculty completing the forms need a training session or perhaps a "talk" by the chairman or the Dean on the importance of filling out the gradesheet completely. This matter should be further examined by the administrator involved.

A "talk" to faculty by department heads could also help in reducing the time spent in waiting for unreturned gradesheets (step 10). Alternately, this waiting period could be reduced if the department chairmen and Deans take the responsibility for their respective faculty returning grades on time. Or the waiting period could be eliminated by substituting all missing grades with a special incomplete grade, thereby not delaying the processing of returned grades. Or perhaps the grades could be processed in batches, thereby delaying the processing of only those grade reports affected by the delayed grades. These and other alternatives should be examined. The intensity of the search for an alternative will depend on the need for reducing the time spent in the current process and the desire for efficiency. The process chart does help in identifying the steps where the time of processing can be reduced or eliminated.

DOCUMENTATION

Many of the instruments of data collection, such as the SOP and ADS methods, are essentially techniques of documentation. The other instruments of data collection, especially the interviewing and design sessions, should be documented. This must be done soon after the event while memories are fresh and should be verified by the individuals involved. In addition, the documentation should be integrated periodically as shown in boxes 5, 8, and 13 of Figure 12–1 (see p. 223).

The need for documentation cannot be over-emphasized. It should be a complete recording not only of all the commitments made, but also of all

PROCESS CHART WORK SHEET

Please read instructions on other side before completing this form.

Job: Grade processing at end of semester Page 1 of 1

Charted by: Hussain Date: Nov. 1969 Current Method

Step Number	Details of Step	Delay	Operation	Transportation	Storage	Check/Control	Time Required	Number	Comment
1	Receipt of grades & logging	○	●	□	△	▽	2-3-4 m		
2	Check for completion	○	○	□	△	▼	1-2-3 m		Completed by faculty
3	Incompleteness corrected	○	●	□	△	▽	1/2-12 -50 m		
4	Delayed 'til batch is collected	○	○	□	▲	▽	1-5-8 h	100	
5	Sent to computer center by courier	○	○	■	△	▽	5-10-15 m		
6	Optically scanned	○	●	□	△	▽	10 m		
7	Cards checked	○	●	□	△	▽	5-15-30 m		
8	Cards started in batch	○	○	□	▲	▽		500	
9	Unreturned grades traced	○	●	□	△	▽	1-5-15 m		
10	Waiting for unreturned grade sheets	●	○	□	△	▽	0-2-15 h		
11	Special operation on unreturned grade sheets	○	●	□	△	▽	5-10-15 m		
12	Optical scanning	○	●	□	△	▽	10 m		
13	Cards checked	○	●	□	△	▽	5-10-15 m		
14	Cards checked for completion	○	●	□	△	▽	5-8-15 m		
15	Send grades to computer room	○	○	□	▲	▽	3-5-6 h		
16	Processing of grades	○	●	□	△	▽	3-4-5 h		
		○	○	□	△	▽			
		○	○	□	△	▽			
		○	○	□	△	▽			

Abbreviations used d = days h = hours m = minutes

Figure 12–4

definitions used and assumptions made in order to avoid misunderstandings later.

OTHER ACTIVITIES

The stages of system specifications discussed above are iterative, considering each level of administration one at a time and continually making changes as new relevant information is uncovered. Furthermore, the data should be checked for factual content, statistical accuracy, and conflicts with the stated systems proposal and objectives. The steps in stating systems specifications are difficult and slow. But the project team must patiently and methodically reconcile the terminological and definitional differences and resolve the conflicts of interest among the users.

The systems specification must then go through a series of decisions of approval. The first such decision is by the systems project team itself (box 10 in Figure 12–1, p. 223). If needed information is found missing, the job recycles to the relevant point in the flowchart (box 3, 4, 6, or 7 in Figure 12–1). This process must keep recycling until it is satisfactory, then it goes to the administration, who, if dissatisfied, can also recycle the process (boxes 3, 4, 6, or 7 in Figure 12–1). If the administration does not consider it worth recycling (box 14 in Figure 12–1), then this phase or the project are terminated (circle 15 in Figure 12–1).

The termination of the project in this phase could be a result of dissatisfaction with the systems specifications, or it could be the result of a reevaluation of the project in the light of changed environmental conditions, such as the unavailability of expected resources; change in assumptions made during the feasibility study; a change in priorities; or a change in administrators. Only if the administration still decides to implement the project and is satisfied with the systems specifications (box 12, Yes exit in Figure 12–1, p. 223) will the document on systems specifications be finalized (box 13 in Figure 12–1). This phase of the project is then terminated. The resulting final documentation which is prepared in this phase represents the "bill-of-goods" that the user wants from the new system and forms the basis for the next stage of development, the design stage.

SUMMARY AND CONCLUSIONS

The stage in the development process after the feasibility study is the specification of the user's requirements. It is in this stage that the administrators at different levels must ask themselves what information they need, as well as why, how, and when they need it. These questions are diagnostic questions that must be answered before the treatment phase, which is the design and detail specification phase, the subject of the next chapter.

The activities in the user requirements phase are shown as a flowchart in Figure 12–1 on p. 223. The same activities are shown in a network diagram in Figure 12–5.

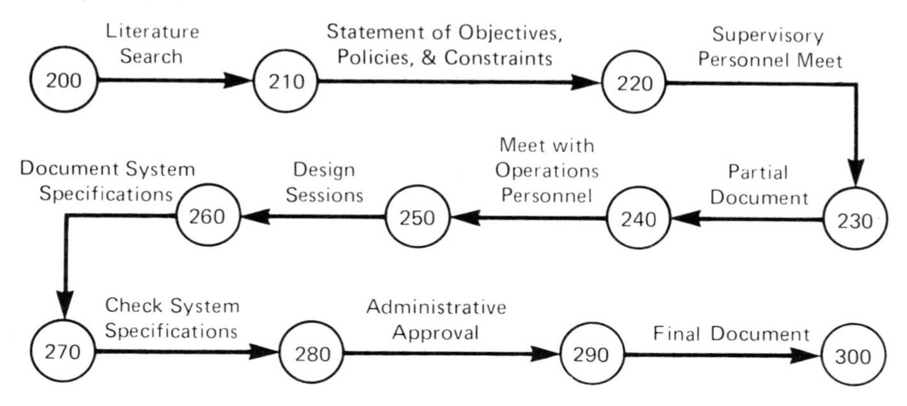

Figure 12–5. Network Diagram for Determining System Specifications

The specification of user's requirements consists of identifying the objectives (and policies), constraints, assumptions, environment, and requirements of the system. These are shown in Figure 12–6.

Tools and techniques used in collecting data on user's requirements that were discussed were as follows:

1. Interviews
2. Design Sessions
3. SOP
4. ADS

In defining the system's requirements, the user sometimes tends to be a perfectionist in defining the system completely and accurately. This may become an infinite process since the needs of the user are forever expanding and changing. The other extreme is equally dangerous. A system defined hastily could lead to an ineffective system. A judicious middle ground must be found.

The system requirements determined must specify the following:

1. Objectives, goals, and criteria of performance
2. Outputs to be produced

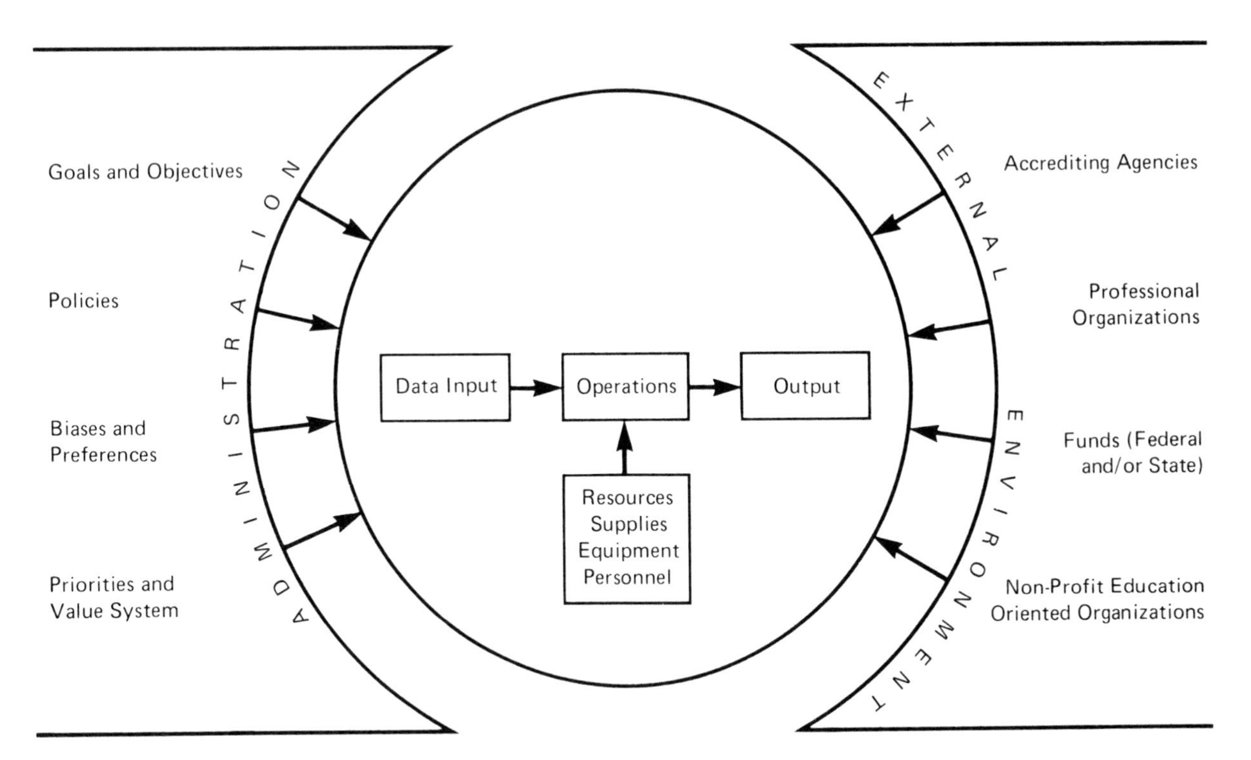

Figure 12–6. Components of System Affecting System Specifications

3. Inputs to be used
4. Processes to be performed
5. Resources to be available
6. Procedures to be followed
7. Organizational and other constraints to be met

The documentation of the user's requirements are presented to management. If approved, they become the basis for the detailed design of the system, the topic of the next chapter.

KEY TERMS

Requirements
System User
Systems Personnel
External Environment
Feasibility Region
Objective Functions
Data Collection Instruments
Data Collection Approaches

REVIEW QUESTIONS

1. Distinguish between
   Literature Search and Study of Existing System
   Objectives and Requirements of an Information System
   System Requirements and User Requirements
   Structured Interview and Unstructured Interview
   SOP and ADS
   Innovative Approach and Hybrid Approach
2. What function can a "feasibility region" perform?
3. Why should objectives, constraints, and policies be stated explicitly?
4. What factors should be considered in selecting an approach to data collection?
5. What activities should occur between the feasibility study and the determination of system requirements?

CHAPTER 12: SELECTED ANNOTATED BIBLIOGRAPHY

GLANS, T. B., et al, *Management Systems.* New York: Holt, Rinehart and Winston, Inc., 1968, Part III, pp. 191–282. The authors' collective experiences come from the International Business Machine Corporation, Rich Products Corporation, and the State University of New York at Buffalo. This is a presentation of the philosophy and methodology used to determine systems requirements. Included are detailed discussions of goal and activity alignment, system performance measurement, and system requirement documentation. Also discussed are decision tables, activity models, quantitative requirements, and the dynamic use of forms.

GROSSMAN, A., and R. L. HOWE, *Data Processing for Educators.* Chicago: Educational Methods, Inc., 1965, pp. 39–58. This is a readable checklist which could be used by educators as a general guide in the initiation of a data-processing study. Specific, nontechnical suggestions are given in the areas of scope of the study, document collection and coding, grid chart analysis, and file and source document analysis.

HERTZ, D. B., "Developing a Computerized Management Information System," *Management Review,* 55, No. 4 (April 1966), 61–65. This is a very generalized handling of the topic and is recommended only as a guide to administrators. Included are some desirable characteristics of an information system and some pointers on how to help insure successful implementation of the system. Also included is an introductory discussion of the implication of computers on decision-making.

"Overall Guidance of Data Processing," *EDP Analyzer,* VI, No. 8 (August 1968), 1–12. This article discusses the role of executive leadership and the importance of executive attitude in data processing. Advantages and disadvantages of current approaches are discussed. Desirable qualities in overall guidance and four alternative approaches are listed. Recommended for managers involved in data processing.

ROSOVE, P. E. *Developing a Computer-Based Information System.* New York: John Wiley & Sons, Inc., 1967, Chap. III, pp. 67–93. The focus of this book is on the human factor and the interdependence of the human factor with other elements in the system development process. The book is written by personnel of the Systems Development Corporation who have extensive experience in the development of large-scale, computerized information systems for defense. Readers can profit by reading the material contributed by personnel having first-hand experience with complex information systems. Several development strategies are introduced, but Rosove emphasizes deductive strategy and planned evolution of the system. The purpose of the requirements phase is to determine the need for the system, identify system's users, and to define the users' information needs.

SWANSON, R. W., *Introduction to Business Data Processing & Computer Programming,* Belmont, Ca.: Dickenson Publishing Co., 1967, Chap. XIV, pp. 198–218. This book grew out of a university course taught by Mr. Swanson, but also reflects his practical experience as a project engineer. It is directed to those individuals having had little or no previous exposure to the subject of automatic data processing. The author suggests that in determining system requirements, the first order of business should be to develop the descriptive requirements for inputs, processes, outputs, and resources, and then develop the necessary quantitative data such as volume and time. The logical relationships between the desired output and the available input can be established using one of several approaches; however, the most popular approach is to study the existing system.

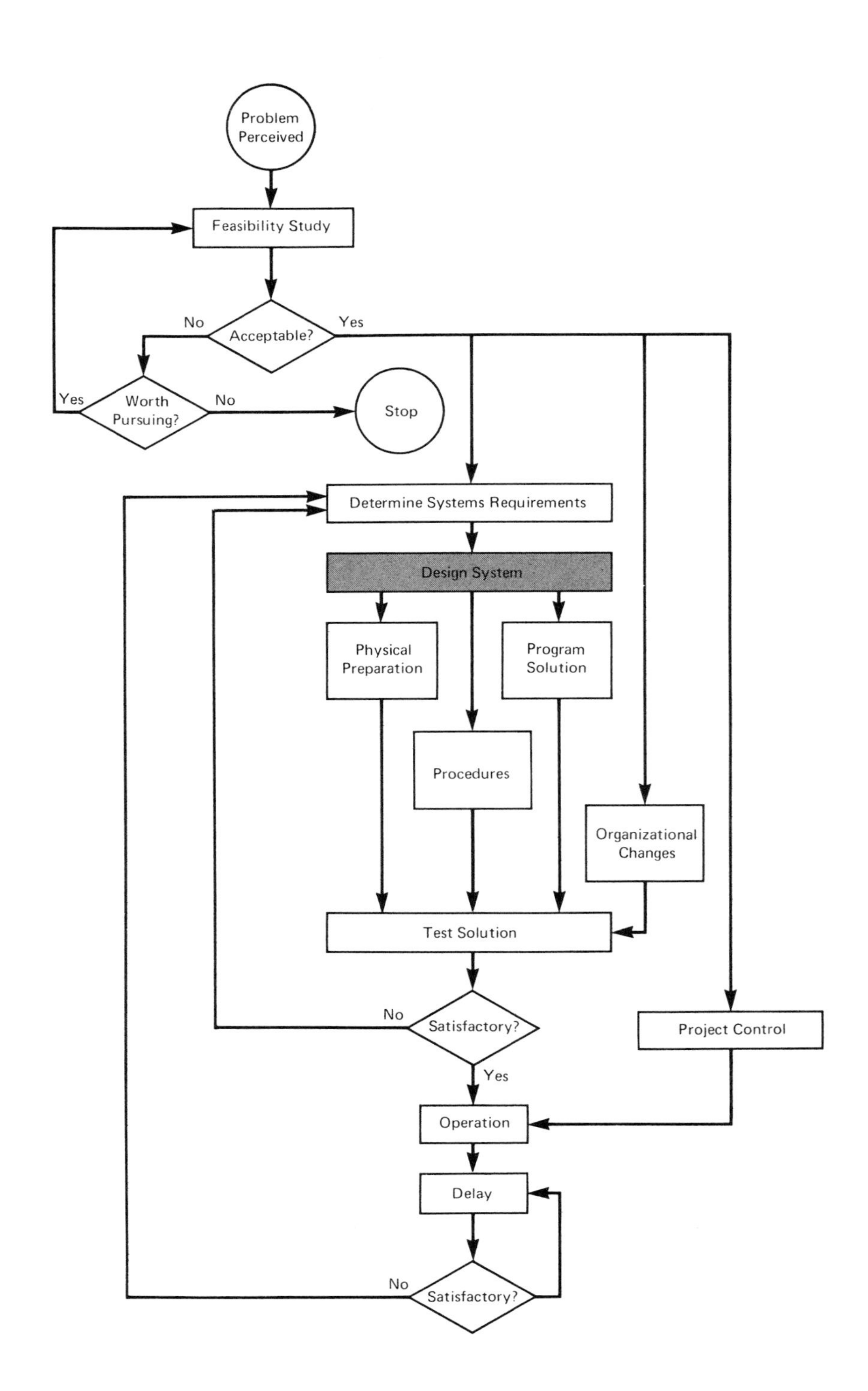

Problem Perceived
Feasibility Study
Acceptable?
No
Yes
Worth Pursuing?
Yes
No
Stop
Determine Systems Requirements
Design System
Physical Preparation
Program Solution
Procedures
Organizational Changes
Test Solution
Satisfactory?
No
Yes
Project Control
Operation
Delay
No
Satisfactory?

13

Design of a System

INTRODUCTION

This chapter is a continuation of the discussion in the previous chapter. Having determined the gross specifications from the user's viewpoint, it is now necessary to specify the details of design for the construction of the system. The designing of a system is much like the building of a house, where the architect works from his client's specifications of the general layout—the location of doors, windows, closets, electrical outlets, and other elements the client considers necessary. The architect then produces a blueprint showing the precise location of each element in relation to the others, its dimensions, and the materials to be used in each case. The architect also specifies the standards for the operations to be performed by the construction crews, bricklayers, plumbers, electricians, and other workers. In the design of an information system, the development team acts as the architect. Starting with the statement of the user's requirements, the development team specifies the detailed systems layout: the inputs, output, flow of information, and their interrelationships. It is also necessary to set standards for the personnel required, forms to be used, equipment to be utilized, and the input data needed. Finally, the systems development team must specify the system test specifications, the operational specifications, the computer programming specifications (in cases where computer programming is used), and the role of the new system in the overall systems plan for the organization. These are the topics of this chapter. Also discussed are the overall systems plan and documentation standards.

The specifications of operational standards and hardware discussed in this chapter are the basis of physical preparation and procedures to be discussed in Chapters 14 and 15. The use of specifications of output and input, file design, quality and control, and programming are the subject material of Chapter 16, while the testing standards specified are the basis for the testing phase of development (not discussed in this book).

The activities in this stage of system development are largely sequential, hence they will be identified by a network diagram rather than a flowchart. These will be discussed in groups of related activities and identified in partial network diagrams. At the end of the chapter a composite network diagram of all the activities in this stage of development will be displayed.

OVERALL SYSTEMS PLAN AND SYSTEMS PLANNING SPECIFICATIONS

Only the systems (or subsystems) to be designed are typically examined during the feasibility study stage. But after the user's requirements have been specified, they must be reviewed in the context of the overall systems plans—both short-range and long-range.[1] The overall systems plans must be reviewed for each systems change proposed in order to eliminate redundancy, overlapping, and a tendency to deviate from the path leading toward the efficient and effective achievement of organizational objectives. If necessary, corrective action must be taken and adjustments made.

The overall systems planning activity is shown as activity 300–310 in Figure 13–1. The resulting document is then sent to all personnel involved. They will be identified later, after their role in the project is discussed.

There is another planning activity that must be performed. This concerns

[1]For a definition of planning, see R. N. Anthony, *Planning and Control Systems: A Framework of Analysis* (Boston: Harvard University, 1965), p. 16.

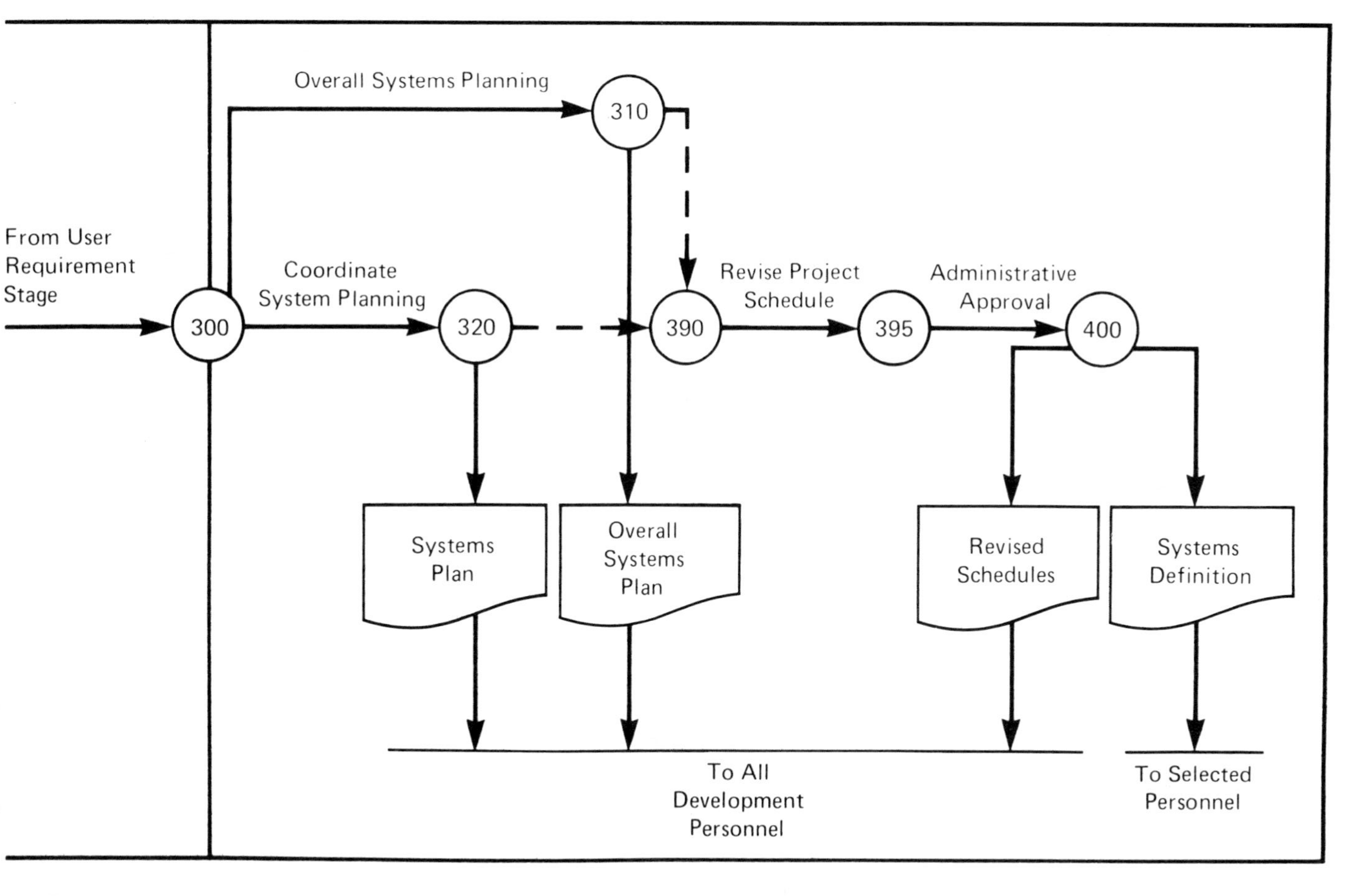

Figure 13–1. Partial Network Diagram Showing Systems Plan and Systems Activities

the plan for the system being designed, showing the interrelationships and interfaces between activities involving different departments, agencies, and personnel. This activity is shown as 300–320 in Figure 13–1. The document generated by this activity must be distributed to all personnel involved with the system, to facilitate relating their roles to the other activities.

Parallel to activities 300–310 and 300–320 are other activities which will be discussed later. After the completion of all these parallel activities, the project schedule is revised if necessary. This is shown as activity 390–395. (The activities 310–390 and 320–390 are dummy activities.) The revised schedule and the systems definition specifications are then presented to the administration for its approval. The specifications will be modified if necessary until the administration approves them (activity 395–400). This stage is then terminated and the next stage of design implementation is initiated.

The activities parallel to 300–310 and 300–320 referred to above will now be discussed. Two of these relate to operational and hardware specifications.

DETERMINING OPERATIONAL AND HARDWARE SPECIFICATIONS

Operational and hardware specifications are closely related, in the sense that operational standards must be specified before hardware needs can be specified. This relationship is shown in Figure 13–2. The details of hardware specifications are beyond the scope of this book but are the subject of much writing elsewhere.[2] The details of computer hardware are very technical, and educational administrators would not be expected to be knowledgeable in this subject. They can treat hardware as a black-box. But the development team, if necessary, with the hardware specialist, would specify the hardware characteristics and standards necessary to meet the user's requirements. This information is then used in the physical preparation stage to acquire the hardware needs, and in the testing stage to ensure that the specified hardware standards have been met.

Even if an organization has its own computing system, there is often a need for operational and hardware specifications, especially input or output equipment specifications. An example of this would be scanning equipment, which has been used effectively in education for scheduling students, grading, collecting housing data, and for research. If used for scheduling and grading, the hardware and operational specifications may look like the following:

[2]For an example see *IBM Management Planning Guide for a Manual of Data Processing Standards,* No. C20–1670–1 (White Plains, N.Y.: International Business Machines Corporation), pp. 26–27.

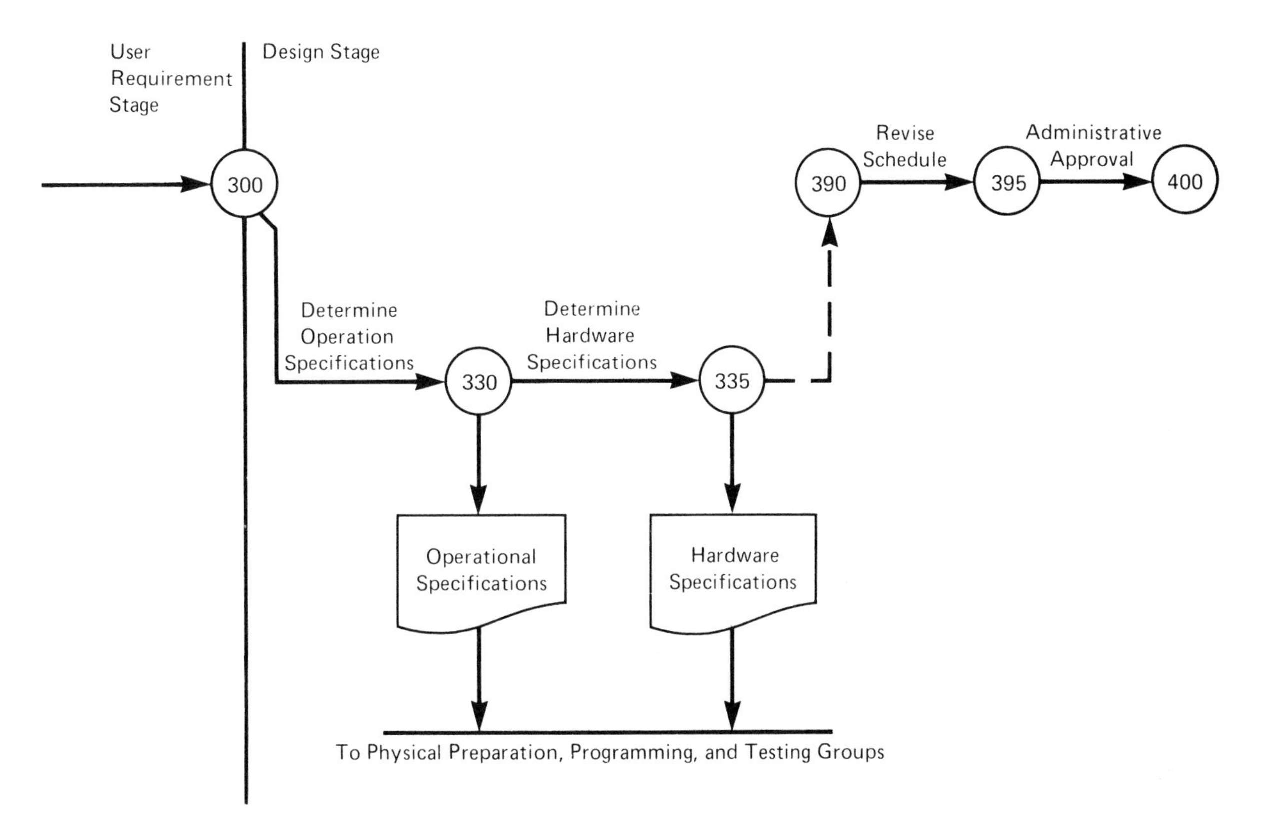

Figure 13–2. Partial Network Diagram Showing Physical Preparation Specifications

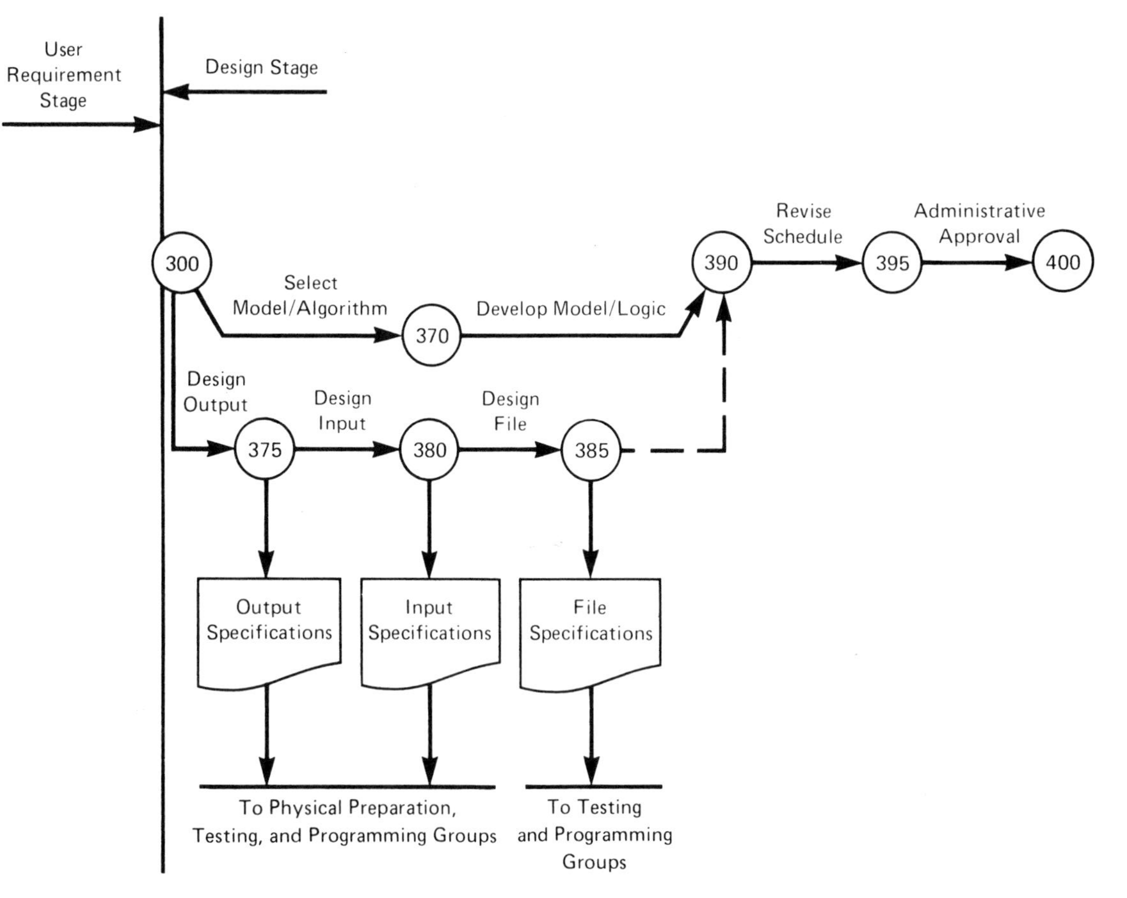

Figure 13–3. Partial Network Diagram Showing Input Through Output Activities

Operational Specifications

The operational specifications for the example on scanning needs may be somewhat as follows:

Speed $>$ (more than) 1600 documents/hour
Error rate $=$ 1/10,000 markings
Maintenance $\ngtr$ (no more than) 24 hours at any one time

The activities of operational and hardware specifications generate a document that is used for physical preparation (to be discussed in Chapter 14) and in the testing phase (not discussed in this book).

Hardware Specifications

An example of hardware specification for the problem examined above may appear as follows:

Cost $\ngtr$ (no more than) $4,000/year
Capability $=$ Read markings on document and convert to cards at least 400 markings per document. Document size should be about 8½" x 11". Medium darkness of marking should suffice.

Selection and Development of the Model

A set of activities parallel to hardware activities is concerned with the solution. It requires the selection of the model or algorithm to be used, followed by the development of the model and the logic. These are shown as activities 300–370 and 370–390 respectively in Figure 13–3. In some information systems there may be no model selection involved but the decision-making logic may have to be specified. This could be done in the form of a decision table, which then provides the basis for programming the solution.

INPUT PROCESSING AND OUTPUT SPECIFICATION

In a functional sense, input and processing come before any output. But from a design viewpoint, the order is reversed. It is necessary to know the output requirements first because these determine the processing and the input that are required. Similarly, the input design must come before the file (needed for processing) is designed because the input determines the records which constitute the file. These interrelationships are shown in Figure 13–3. The activity for designing the output (300–375) precedes the input design activity

(375–380) which in turn precedes the designing of the file (380–385). In some cases, a preliminary file design is necessary before the input is designed. Not all possibilities are shown in Figure 13–3.

Output Specifications

Problems in Output Specifications

The output should be specified as a joint effort between the systems personnel and the user, within or outside the development team, depending on the composition of the team. The systems personnel should identify the output that can be produced and the user determine what output he wants. The incremental cost of information is relatively small at the design stage compared to producing that information all by itself later. An analogy would be the cost of including a public-address system in a building while it is being built rather than after the building is constructed. It is, therefore, very important for the user to anticipate all his needs (current and future) during the system design stage, and preferably in the previous stage—the determination of user's requirements. This is the responsibility of the administrator concerned with the system, for he alone can best project his needs. Time and effort to state needs at this stage are well spent.

In stating his needs the administrator should not overspecify and demand information that is "nice to have" but is unnecessary. Unnecessary information can be a burden and have a negative benefit. It can "crowd-out" the needed information, thereby making it difficult to find and use such information. There is also the cost of producing the information, maybe not to the administrator but certainly to the institution. The system development team must weigh the benefits of output against its costs before they determine what output is needed.

The designing of output is shown as activity 300–375 in Figure 13–3. This subject will be discussed in the next section.

Output Content and Format

The details of content of the output may have already been specified as part of the user's requirements. If not, then the details must be specified now. For example, the input variables, parameters, and output variables for each computation required for the output should be specified, along with their spatial relationships if these are desired on the output. Requirements such as totals, subtotals, and figures in absolute values or percentages must also be specified.

One characteristic of good output is that it can be understood and accurately interpreted by any user, even one who has not participated in the development of the system and is ignorant of the environment. This characteristic in an output can be checked by asking the following questions: Is the output to be produced readable? Does it have an adequate, unique, and meaningful title? Are the different types of reports easily accessible? Are the pages identified? Are all the abbreviations and codes used in the output adequately identified? Are the assumptions identified? Is the period for which the data is relevant identified? Is the output dated? In cases of runs on the same date, is the run number identified? Is the output complete? Is it accurate? Is the output easy to store and retrieve?

If the answers to any of these questions are not in the affirmative, then the output design needs further study and additional specifications. The questions posed above may seem trivial, but in many systems it is the consideration of seemingly small and inconsequential matters that makes the information system design effective.

Perhaps some illustrations may emphasize the point. In one university, the information system produced a class schedule. Its use resulted in many students attending the wrong class or being in the wrong room. On analysis of the output, it was found that the room information, corresponding to the course which was in the first column, appeared in the tenth column from the left. In using the schedule and in aligning the corresponding information the students' eyes moved one line upward or downward. The result was an ineffective use of output. The problem was corrected by reformatting the output and keeping the more relevant information, such as room number, in the left-hand columns, and the lengthy and less consequential information, such as the title of the course, in the right-hand columns. Further solutions to this problem were to group lines with spacing between the groups and to have horizontal lines printed in the spacing to help the eyesight keep on a horizontal row of information.

In a similar situation of scheduling, students wishing to take English 101 ended up in a class of Engineering 101. The source of error was the ambiguous use of an abbreviation "Eng" for both English and Engineering. There are numerous such examples unique to each situation. There are no rules to avoid them, except perhaps to take great care in output design and to check and recheck the design. Attention should be paid not only to the results but also to its "packaging" so that it can be used easily, readily, and effectively.

Other output considerations are discussed elsewhere in this book: user's requirements of output were discussed in Chapter 12.

The output specifications, once determined, are sent to the personnel involved in programming, physical preparation, and testing. They are also prerequisites for the next set of activities to be performed, i.e., the design of input.

Input Specifications

As with output, there is input data that is "nice-to-have." It is tempting to collect such data with the expectation that it will be useful later because the incremental cost of additional input is often very small compared to the expected benefits later on. One should be cautious in collecting too much data and yet it is important to collect data in the lowest level of detail that is needed or will be needed later.

As an example, consider the case where one has to produce statistical data on classes offered by an undergraduate institution and classify them by lower-division and upper-division courses. To do so requires information on each class offered and identification as to whether it is an upper-division or lower-division course. However, in collecting this information, it would be no more difficult to identify the course as being freshman, sophomore, junior, or senior, and then aggregate this information as part of the processing. This aggregation (combining) relationship could be expressed as follows:

LOWER DIVISION = FRESHMEN + SOPHOMORES
UPPER DIVISION = JUNIORS + SENIORS

The two above expressions, incidentally, are valid computer program instructions that could provide the information needed on lower- and upper-division courses and yet have the ability of dividing it further into freshman, sophomore, junior, and senior. The extra cost of programming is trivial compared to the additional information provided, and hence it would be wise to collect the more detailed information. If this possibility is not considered in the design stage and the information of the detailed breakdown is needed at a later date, it would require redesigning the system and considerable extra work. One cannot disaggregate (separate into components) so easily as one can aggregate. Therefore, one must collect data input at the lowest level of aggregation that will eventually be needed.

The example emphasizes the necessity for a careful examination of not only current but future needs. The administrator is in the best position to do that. He must then compare the value of additional detail with the cost and determine whether or not the additional data should be included in the file.

An input-output grid is used by a programmer to identify logically similar reports (such as reports 3 and 4 in Table 13–1) and is also used in maintenance of programs. The grid is also useful for the user and systems analyst because it identifies the consequence of not collecting any one data element. For example, in Table 13–1, data element 2 is crucial, data element 3 is little used, and data element 5 is never used. The effect of input data on output is graphically portrayed.

Table 13–1. Input-Output Grid

	Report 1	Report 2	Report 3	Report 4	Report 5	Report 6	Report 7	Report 8
1. Name	X		X			X		
2. Social Security Number	X	X	X	X	X	X	X	X
3. Sex				X				
4. Marital Status			X		X			
5. Date of Birth								
6. Units Taken			X	X				
7. Units Earned			X	X				
8. Level of Student			X	X				
9. College of Student					X	X		X
10. Major of Student						X		
11. Other Data	X	X					X	X

The determination of output and input (activities 300–375 and 375–380 in Figure 13–3, p. 254) enables the design of the file (activity 380–385 in Figure 13–3). This work is primarily done by the systems analyst. Its study does not greatly concern the administrator beyond a general appreciation of the topic as discussed in Chapter 8.

The specification of the file is an important document in determining a solution, a subject to be discussed in Chapter 16. Another specification that is a prerequisite for determining a solution is the quality, control, and programming specification. Its discussion will now follow.

QUALITY, CONTROL, AND PROGRAMMING SPECIFICATIONS

Quality and Control Specifications

Quality and control are related because the function of control is to ensure specific levels of quality. This is achieved by setting up quality standards and ensuring that they are met.

Control is exercised with each system component such as input, output, and processing. These aspects are therefore discussed, with the design of each. There is, however, one important aspect of control that affects all components of the system, the **audit trail.** Its need must be specified in the design stage because the decision on this will affect the programming stage which follows.

Li discusses the concept of an audit trail as follows: "An audit trail in an accounting system is analogous to a series of road signs in a highway system; both are designed to provide information such that one can easily find one's way out from any point in the system."[3] The accountant tests the process of data flow in a system by "tracing selected transactions through an *audit trail*."[4]

Unfortunately for the auditor, the computer has eliminated all the detail recording which was done in the manual processing of his audit trail. But as McRae points out, the computer, "if used intelligently, permits the auditor to carry out a more thorough audit with rather less effort than he has expended in the past."[5] McRae continues the accountant's view:

> A computer does not pose *additional* problems, but it does pose *different* problems. The focus of the audit is moved from one set of operations to another. For example, in auditing a manual accounting system we tend to stress arithmetical accuracy and posting figures from one set of documents to another. When auditing an EDP system we concentrate more on verifying the input documents and seeing that the subsequent procedures are carried out as planned. We are more concerned with checking the system than with checking the individual items being processed by the system.[6]

The concept of the "trail" can be used by an administrator in a school, college, or university. He may wish to trace every student grade entry on a student grade record, just as the accountant wishes to trace transactions, to

[3]D. H. Li, *Accounting Computers Management Information Systems* (New York: McGraw-Hill Book Company, Inc., 1968), p. 297.

[4]*Ibid.,* p. 296.

[5]T. W. McRae, *The Impact of Computers on Accounting* (London: John Wiley & Sons, Ltd., 1964), p. 158.

[6]*Ibid.,* p. 159.

ensure control over the process of grade-record flow for each student. This would also enable the administrator to check students' records which may for some reason be suspect or need to be traced for checking.

"Trailing" has a cost. The administrator, therefore, must weigh the costs against the benefits before determining whether or not he should specify trailing as a requisite of the system.

The Business Manager usually wants an audit trail. In some states, the auditing of public institutions is mandatory and hence many educational institutions have auditors, most of whom insist on an audit trail. The institution, then, has no choice. The auditor should be involved in specifying his needs.

The control and quality specification activity is shown as 300–365 in Figure 13–4. It generates a document that is sent to the testing personnel who make sure that the quality standards set are met by the new system. The document is also sent to the programming group so that these capabilities can be programmed.

Programming Specifications

Programming specifications are required by the programming group. These should include information concerning the program to be written, the capability and features of each program, and the choice of the programming language(s) to be used. This is shown as activity 300–360 in Figure 13–4.

The administrator and the development team have little, if any, role in the programming details. They should, however, specify the standards the programmer must follow. Some of these standards are quite universal and would already be part of the processing center's standards, or could be found in a standard textbook or manual.[7]

Most of this work is technical, but the administrator should be interested in ensuring that the standards facilitate the interchangeability between programmers and the independence of individual programmers. Also, the standards should ensure a uniform product that is efficient and effective. The standards should also be such that the final product and the programmer's performance can be measured and evaluated from both the systems designer's and the user's viewpoint.

Part of the work of the programmer concerns testing, documentation, and operations. These would be described in the respective specifications concerning these activities.

[7]D. H. Brandon, *Management Standards for Data Processing* (Princeton, N.J.: D. Van Nostrand Company, Inc., 1963), Chap. IV and V, pp. 69–149; and *IBM Management Planning Guide for a Manual of Data Processing Standards,* No. GC20–1670–1 (White Plains, N.Y.: International Business Machines Corporation), pp. 45–59.

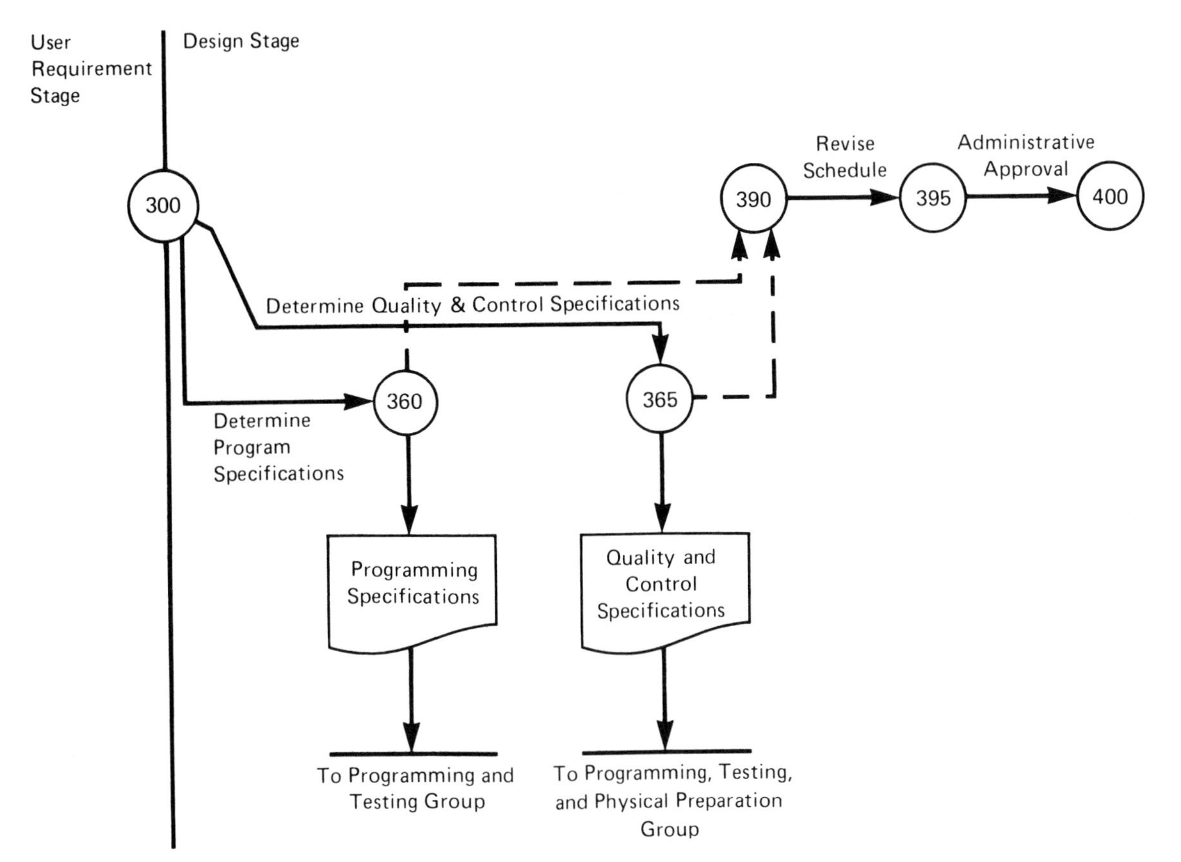

Figure 13–4. Partial Network Diagram Showing Programming and Control Specifications

ORGANIZATION, TESTING, AND DOCUMENTATION SPECIFICATIONS

There are three miscellaneous matters that remain to be specified. These are organizational change specifications, testing specifications, and documentation specifications. These activities, shown in Figure 13–5, will be discussed in turn below.

Specification of Organization Changes

A new system may require changes in organizational structure. More common though, are the problems of manpower and personnel availability.

Personnel are an important factor of production which must be specified. However, not all the needs for personnel are known at this point of the development process. For example, personnel needed for the operation of equipment are not known since equipment may not have been selected yet (in cases where additional equipment is required). When this need is determined, its specifications must be sent to persons responsible for manpower planning.

Meanwhile, most other manpower needs are known. For example, the needs of programmers can generally be estimated even though programming details have not been specified. Similarly, the need for input preparation personnel (unless input equipment is to be selected) can be determined and specified. Training Activities

There is another type of manpower needed: not additional manpower but existing manpower trained differently. This might include office workers and even certain levels of administrators. Some new information systems require a knowledge that must be acquired if the system is to operate effectively and efficiently. This must be specified and the personnel responsible for education and training be so informed.

Another aspect of manpower specification concerns the retrenchment of existing personnel. This problem is more serious in educational institutions that are state-supported, where personnel cannot be fired so easily and must be relocated or absorbed by attrition. This will be discussed further in Chapter 17. Its solution often requires a long gestation period and hence must be specified as early as possible. The activity of specifying personnel needs (300–355) is shown in Figure 13–5. The resulting document is sent to the persons responsible for organizational changes.

Testing Specifications

Problems of testing (like those in other activities of the development process) must be examined during the design of the system. This is especially true of on-line systems and is pointed out by Martin as follows:

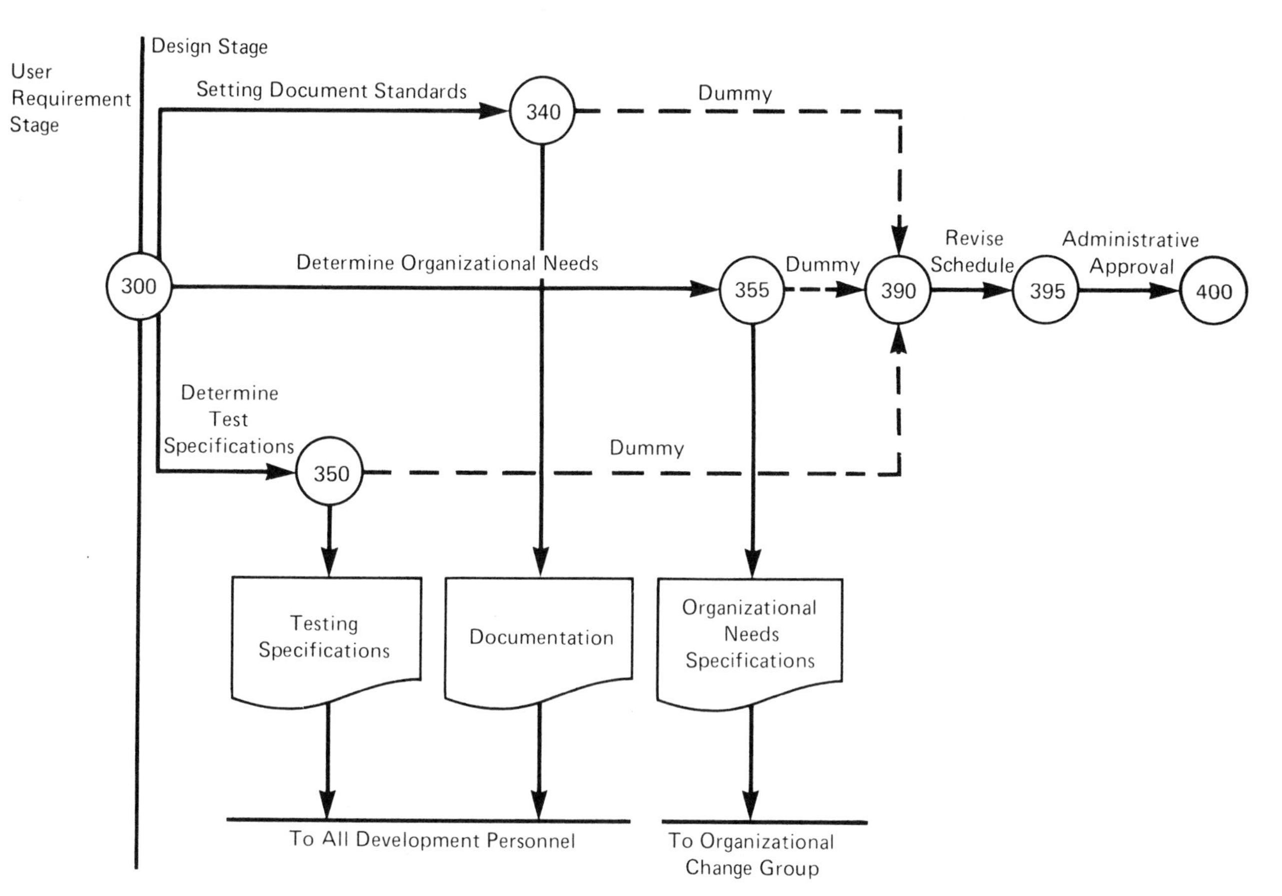

Figure 13–5. Partial Network Diagram Showing Documentation Standards, Testing, and Training Activities

> (Testing) cannot be separated in any of its phases from the design, implementation and maintenance of the system. This is probably the most important single principle of success in real-time testing. A design policy that aims only at the perfect running system and ignores its suitability for testing is unrealistic and will lead to chaos at installation time.[8]

One design policy that makes a system suitable for testing is modularity, a subject that will be discussed further under programming for a solution in Chapter 16.

As part of the design of an information system, one must specify the standards and requirements of testing. These include the choice of an approach to testing the system. One approach is a **pilot study.** In it, the new system is designed and tested on a small scale, and only after it is found to be successful is the full-scale system implemented. This reduces and localizes the losses and disruption that may result from errors in the design of the new system.

As an illustration, consider a large school system or a multi-campus university. In it, the new information system could be tested in one school or on one campus. Only if it proves successful is the new system extended to the other schools or campuses.

When a pilot study is not feasible (as in cases of one school or a one-campus university), the administrator may decide to have a **parallel** run or a **dry** run. This involves the testing of the new system in parallel with the old system. This approach (like the pilot study) has the advantage of giving the administrator an opportunity to observe the new system and assure himself that it meets his performance standards before he gives up his current system. The administrator may insist on this approach if he is skeptical of the new system, or is skeptical of anything new, or if the consequences of system failure may be so great that he may not be willing to take the risk of anything going wrong. Examples of the latter case would be the implementation of a new scheduling and sectioning system or payroll preparation.

There is, however, a price that must be paid for the added assurance. Both approaches take more time and require more manpower. Also, the two systems running simultaneously often leads to confusion to both the user (administrator) and the user's user (the student). All these factors result in considerable organizational strain.

Sometimes a parallel run is not feasible. In such an event, the new system could be simulated.[9] In any event, whichever choice is made, there is a cost. The administrator must weigh the cost of testing with the consequences of no

[8] J. Martin, *Programming Real-Time Computer Systems* (Englewood Cliffs, N.J.: Prentice-Hall, Inc., 1965), p. 253.

[9] For a good discussion of this subject, see *EDP Analyzer,* "Data Processing Planning via Simulation," VI, No. 4 (April 1965), 1–13.

testing and the danger that the system may fail to perform. In automated information systems, this possibility is always finite. McRae points out that with automation the "errors occur less frequently" than in manual systems, "but those errors which do occur are less likely to be detected."[10] One unidentified variable, one unstated decision rule, one transcribing error, or one incorrectly stated programming instruction and the entire system can function incorrectly.

To reduce the probability of systems failure the development team must specify the conditions of testing. One approach would be to test the system with a **factor of safety.** The concept of the safety factor is old and important in engineering. For example, a bridge designed for a peak (maximum) rolling load of five tons but a factor of safety of two will be tested under ten tons of rolling load. This allows for unexpected conditions up to double the normal peak load. In an educational institution, an information system may be designed for an expected maximum of 10,000 students and a response time for a certain set of reports of 24 hours. With a factor of safety of 2 in both cases, the system will have to be tested for 20,000 students and a response time of 12 hours. This allows for unexpected circumstances and gives the administrator an added assurance against failure. He can now argue that if the system can operate with a safety factor of two then it surely can operate under "normal" expected conditions.

The magnitude of the safety factor should be specified by the development team after weighing the benefits of the safety factor against the incremental cost due to it. This is another subjective judgment the development team must make.

Another specification of the testing phase concerns the person responsible for testing. Much of the testing will be done by the systems designers but it is desirable to have someone from the outside perform the final testing. He will not take things for granted, as systems designers tend to do, and will be more objective.

The testing specification activity is shown as 300–350 in Figure 13–5. The testing phase as well as other phases should be documented after their completion. These documentations must follow specified standards if the system is to be maintained effectively after it is operational. These standards of documentation will now be discussed.

Determining Documentation Specifications

The specifications for documentation consist of determining standards that must be followed in documenting a system.

[10]McRae, *The Impact of Computers on Accounting,* p. 158.

The term standards has been defined earlier. The term **documentation** now needs to be defined. For the purposes of this book, the definition given by Gray and London is very appropriate.

> Data processing documentation can be defined as an organized series of descriptive documents relating to all aspects of systems development and operation. A document is further defined as a written record of the completion of a phase of work. Within the broad definition of documentation as given above, a further breakdown of types of documentation may be made. Basically documentation may be categorized into *development documentation* and *control documentation.* Development documentation is descriptive of a system itself, i.e., a system's operating performance characteristics, tools and materials. Development documentation is therefore the means of communicating information about the system.
>
> Control documentation on the other hand is concerned with communicating information about resources used to develop the system; it is therefore primarily concerned with project development organization, with personnel, time, materials and money.[11]

To the above definition should be added one more characteristic of good documentation as suggested by McDonough and Garrett, "the overall set of evidence of choices or decisions made throughout the study of a system."[12]

Administrators should be interested in both types of documentation: developmental and control. The latter is important for auditing the project and evaluating it. The former is necessary for the operation and use of the system. It is often composed of a set of four manuals: The Systems Manual which provides general information of system objectives and systems information; the Programmer's Manual which provides all pertinent information concerning the programs used; the Operator's Manual which enables the operator to run the programs; and finally, the User's Manual which should give the user all the information he needs to effectively use the system.

The documentation package, if properly prepared has many advantages. These are:

1. It is a record and evidence of all the commitments and expectations. Memory can lapse with time but written documentation provides evidence.
2. It is useful in routine evaluation of the project.
3. Documentation is very useful in initiating and training newcomers to a system, as well as useful for administrative review, both at the organizational and the systems level.
4. Documentation is essential for the maintenance of the system, i.e., changing

[11] M. Gray and K. London, *Documentation Standards* (Princeton, N.J.: Brandon Systems Press Inc., 1969), p. 9

[12] A. M. McDonough and L. J. Garrett, *Management System Working Concepts and Practices* (Homewood, Ill.: Richard D. Irwin, Inc., 1965), p. 73.

the system to allow for changes in administrator's needs or changes in the system environment.

5. In some organizations there is only one person knowledgeable of the system. The existence of documentation in such a situation makes the organization less vulnerable to persons leaving or being relocated or reassigned to other duties.
6. Documentation facilitates the auditing and control of an information system.

Some of the above advantages make documentation not only desirable but essential to system effectiveness. It is, therefore, important that the administrator ensure that documentation is completed and done according to specified standards. In the area of information systems, this is especially difficult because programmers and systems analysts have a reputation for disliking documentation and for procrastinating in completing it. They argue that they are either busy with another project and do not have the time for documentation or that they will document the system only after it has stablized. In one sense, a system seldom stabilizes because it is constantly evaluated and redesigned. Thus documentation tends to be indefinitely postponed. This problem can be overcome by insisting that the documentation of the system be completed before other projects are started.

The problem of undocumented systems is more serious in educational environments where much systems and programming work is done by students. Often they do not have the professional loyalty that many full-time employees have. Students (only a little less than professional programmers) are very mobile and often leave in the middle of a project without any documentation. This then requires that the system be redesigned and reprogrammed.

Documentation is disliked because it is dreary work and is time-consuming. Some companies will contract a system job for a 20% reduction in cost if no documentation is required. This may be very tempting for an institution but it is a "penny wise pound foolish" proposition. Documentation is too important to be compromised.

The importance of documentation and the fact that it is not a popular activity makes it important to control. This can be done by setting up documentation standards and insisting that they be followed.

Many systems groups and data processing installations have their own standards on documentation. The systems development team must examine them for their adequacy to the system and, where necessary, supplement these standards to meet their unique requirements, especially with regard to the user's manual. The standards of documentation should include the following considerations:

1. Documentation must be divided into different manuals so that each group of

personnel involved may use what it needs without holding up the rest of the documentation.

2. Each manual must contain a prescribed set of material.
3. The presentation of the manuals, especially the user's manual, must be at different levels: abstract, detailed, and summary.
4. The manuals must use prescribed forms so as to have a standard format as well as to ensure the recording of essential information.
5. The timing of the completion of the documentation must be specified. Documentation loses its value if it is not available when needed. The dates of documentation completion must be included in project planning charts.
6. Testing standards for the documentation must be specified. Often persons who prepare the documentation have lived with the system so long that they take things for granted and do not include these. This problem can be overcome by having people unfamiliar with the system operate it on a test basis. Incompleteness, inadequacies, and ambiguities will soon identify themselves.
7. The control of documentation should also be specified. The place where the documentation is kept and the persons authorized to use and modify it must be specified.

The person responsible for documentation must provide a continuity to the function and must have the authority necessary for its control. Procedures for its revision and an assurance of its validity must also be established.

The documentation specification activity is shown in Figure 13–5 on p. 264. The documentation standards should be sent to all personnel involved in the system development. This would include project management personnel, programming personnel, physical preparation personnel, operational personnel, testing personnel, and also the personnel responsible for organizational changes.

Most of the documentation will be done by the systems personnel. Since it is typically not done by the administrator, the techniques and details of documentation will not be discussed further in this book.

SUMMARY AND CONCLUSIONS

This chapter is conceptually a continuation of the previous chapter. Both specify the system specifications. There are, however, two main differences, that of detail and that of responsibility. The last chapter specified the overall specifications, and this chapter provided the details of the same gross specifications. The gross specification statements as discussed in the last chapter are largely the responsibility of the user. It is his needs that are specified. The detail specifications are provided by the systems development team, in particular the systems analyst. These details must be checked and sometimes even initiated by the user. Again, both parties (the user and the systems analyst) must work closely together to ensure that the real objectives of the system change are fully achieved.

The design activities discussed in this chapter are the coordination of the systems plan and the specifications of the operational needs; the hardware needs; the design of output, file, and input; the programming needs; the quality and control requirements; the selection and development of the model; the personnel needs; and finally, the testing specifications. The partial network diagrams of groups of these activities were shown in Figures 13–1, 13–2, 13–3, 13–4, and 13–5. The combined network incorporating all the partial networks is shown in Figure 13–6. This is a generic network diagram for the design phase. Individual systems designs will deviate somewhat. In smaller systems, some activities will be eliminated (e.g., hardware needs) and others combined (e.g., programming and testing).

The product of this stage of the development process is a set of specification documents that will be the basis for the other stages and phases in the development process. These documents and their further use in the development process are shown in Figure 13–7.

The last activity of this stage of development, as shown in Figure 13–6 is revising the schedule (activity 390–395). This is often necessary since the detailed design specification may require adding activities or adjusting time estimates to complete activities. The revised schedule, along with a summary of system definition (which is an aggregation of the specifications documents discussed earlier), is then presented to the administration for its approval (activity 395–400). This approval step is desirable because it keeps administration current with the development of the system change and at the same time gives all parties an opportunity to check on their assumptions and on systems objectives.

The approval by administration of the system definition is then followed by the implementation of the design specifications. The implementation phase to be discussed first is that of physical preparation.

KEY TERMS

System Design
Specifications
Input-Output Grid
Audit-Trail
Quality and Control
Pilot Study
Parallel Run
Simulation
Safety Factor
Documentation Package

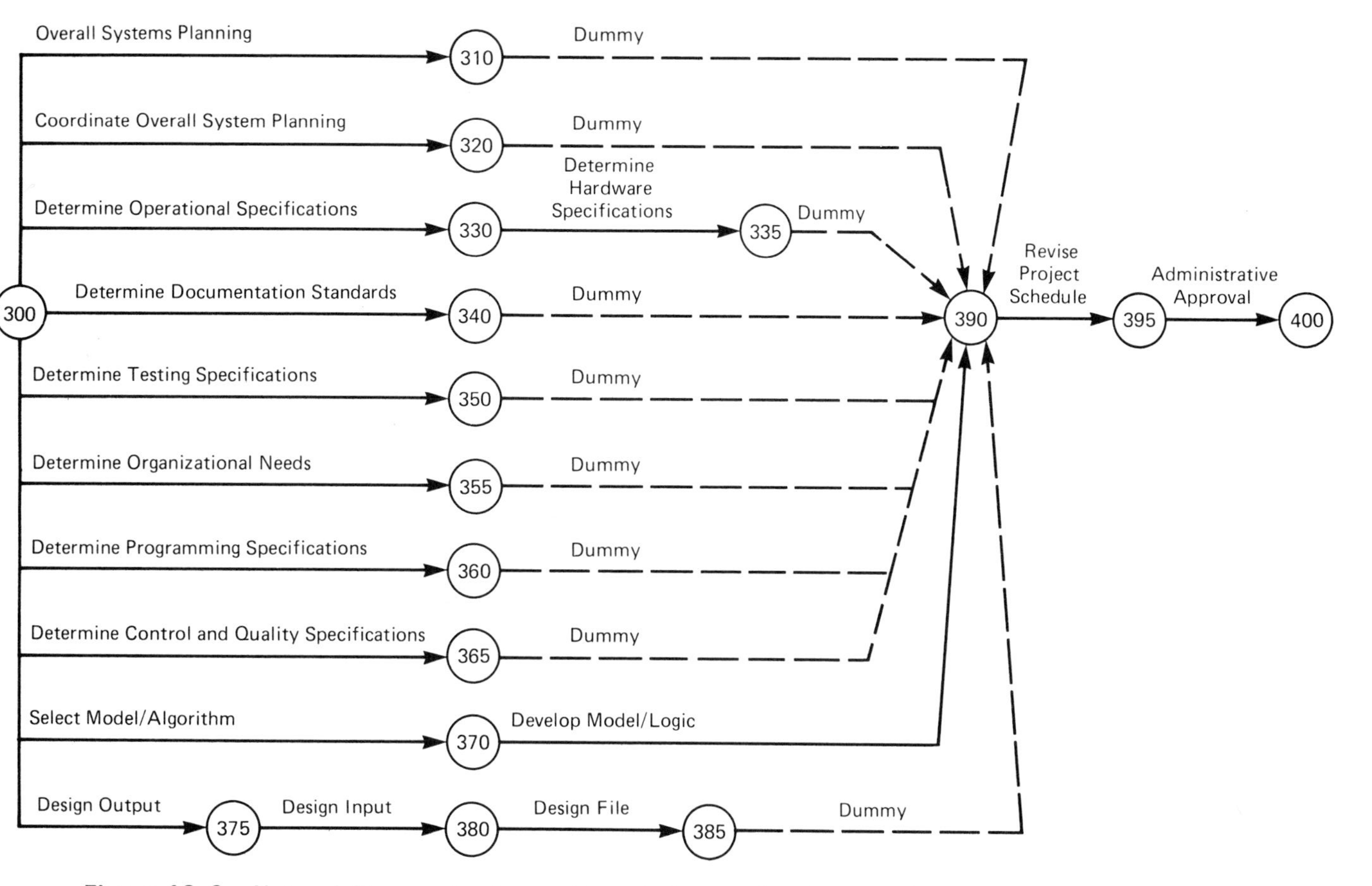

Figure 13–6. Network Diagram for Design Stage in System Development Process

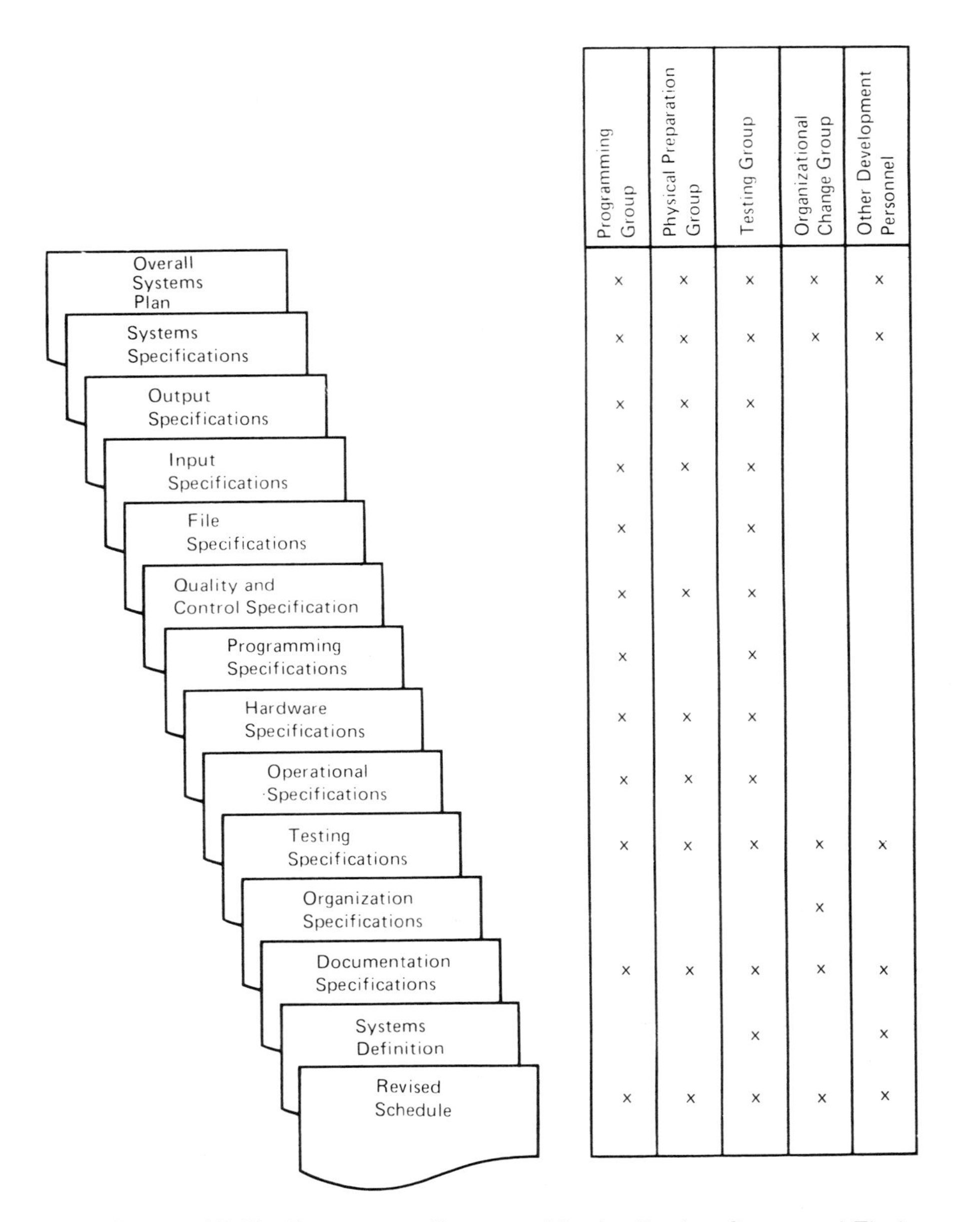

Figure 13–7. Documents Generated in the Design Stage and Their Users

REVIEW QUESTIONS

1. Distinguish between
   Development Documentation and Control Documentation
   Pilot Run and Parallel Run
   Operator's Manual and User's Manual
   Gross Specifications and Detailed Specifications
   Operation Specifications and Hardware Specifications
2. What are the advantages of having a good documentation package?
3. What specification documents result from this stage of the system development process?
4. What design activities are carried out in the design phase?
5. What is the relationship of the audit trail to control and to programming?
6. Under what conditions are development of programming specifications dependent upon hardware choice?
7. When should documentation of the system occur?

CHAPTER 13: SELECTED ANNOTATED BIBLIOGRAPHY

General Design Considerations

ASIMOW, MORRIS, *Introduction to Design.* Englewood Cliffs, N.J.: Prentice-Hall, Inc., 1962, Chap. I and III, pp. 1–6, 11–17. Although this book, the first in a series constituting a reference source for instructors and students in engineering courses, is written by a professor of engineering, the non-engineer/scientist will find the material easy and rewarding. The philosophy of design discussed in the first chapter and the methodology of design outlined in Chapter 3 are applicable to the design of information systems. Chapter 1 concludes with a listing of 14 design principles and Chapter 3 discusses 7 phases of a design process.

CHAPIN, N., *Introduction to Automatic Computers* (2nd ed.). New York: D. Van Nostrand Company, Inc., 1957, Chap. XII, pp. 269–87. In writing this basic textbook, Dr. Chapin shares with readers his experience as a respected data processing consultant. In the discussion of output data, the author discusses seven major areas to be considered in specifying the output to be produced—(1) the use and form of output data, (2) the information content, (3) the timing of the availability, (4) the format, (5) the distribution, (6) the reliability requirements, and (7) the cost and flexibility of the means of producing the output data.

LADEN, H. N., and T. R. GILDERSLEEVE, *Systems Design and Computer Appreciation.* New York: John Wiley & Sons, Inc., 1963, Chap. V, pp. 76–97. This gives a moderately detailed discussion concerning what to specify as fields in a data item, the order by which they should be recorded, considerations of format, and the number of characters allocated to each field. Presents computer characteristics that strongly influence data design, objectives to be considered in item design, and the trade-offs between using fixed variable item size.

Rosove, P. E., *Developing Computer-Based Information Systems.* New York: John Wiley & Sons., Inc., 1967, Chap. IV, pp. 94–137. An information system of people and equipment provides the manager with the means to receive and transmit information. The design of an information system starts with specifying the users' requirements and continues through the recommendation on design continuation. The iterative nature of the design phase requires management to repeatedly make decisions on whether or not to continue the design effort.

Auditing

"Auditing Fast Response Systems," *EDP Analyzer,* V. No. 6 (June 1967), 1–12. A general discussion is presented on the changes in auditing procedure caused by new, fast response systems, procedural and operational checks, revisions for the audit trail, and testing programs that check internal controls. References are given to in-depth articles for auditing an EDP system.

Conway, B., "The Information System Audit," *Management Review,* LVII, No. 3 (March 1968), 37–48. The information system audit may be used by managers as a technique for controlling the planning, implementation, and operational phases of the information systems development. The author calls upon his experience as an International Business Machines Corporation senior systems consultant to present a clear and nontechnical discussion of the planning and conduct of the audit. He also cautions the audit team to be aware of two major kinds of risks: (1) that the system or parts of it will not work, and (2) that the amount of resources committed to this particular system may leave other systems' work vulnerable to failure.

McRae, T. W., *The Impact of Computer on Accounting.* London: John Wiley & Sons, Ltd., 1964, Chap. VI, pp. 158–89. The author's purpose in writing this book is to interest accountants in what can be done with computers; however, one need not be an accountant to profit from the material presented. Chapter 6 deals with the topics of audit and control. Problems connected with the audit and control of EDP systems are raised along with some suggested solutions. Four techniques to audit the system are suggested and discussed: the black-box approach, job simulation, audit in depth by statistical sampling, and audit of the job file directly. The chapter concludes with a brief explanation of several self-checking devices under the headings of automatic machine checks and programmed checks.

Warder, B., "An Auditor Looks at Data Processing," *Journal of Data Management,* V, No. 2 (February 1967), 16–19. The author, a CPA himself, identifies and offers answers to two questions that he believes are going to be foremost in an external auditor's mind when he is auditing company procedures: (1) does an adequate audit trail and do adequate controls exist in EDP operations? and (2) how can the client's computer be programmed to assist in reducing the time required for the audit, ascertaining that the records are correct, and improving the reliability of audit tests? An audit trail is defined as the ability to trace a source document through to its final resting place in the financial statements.

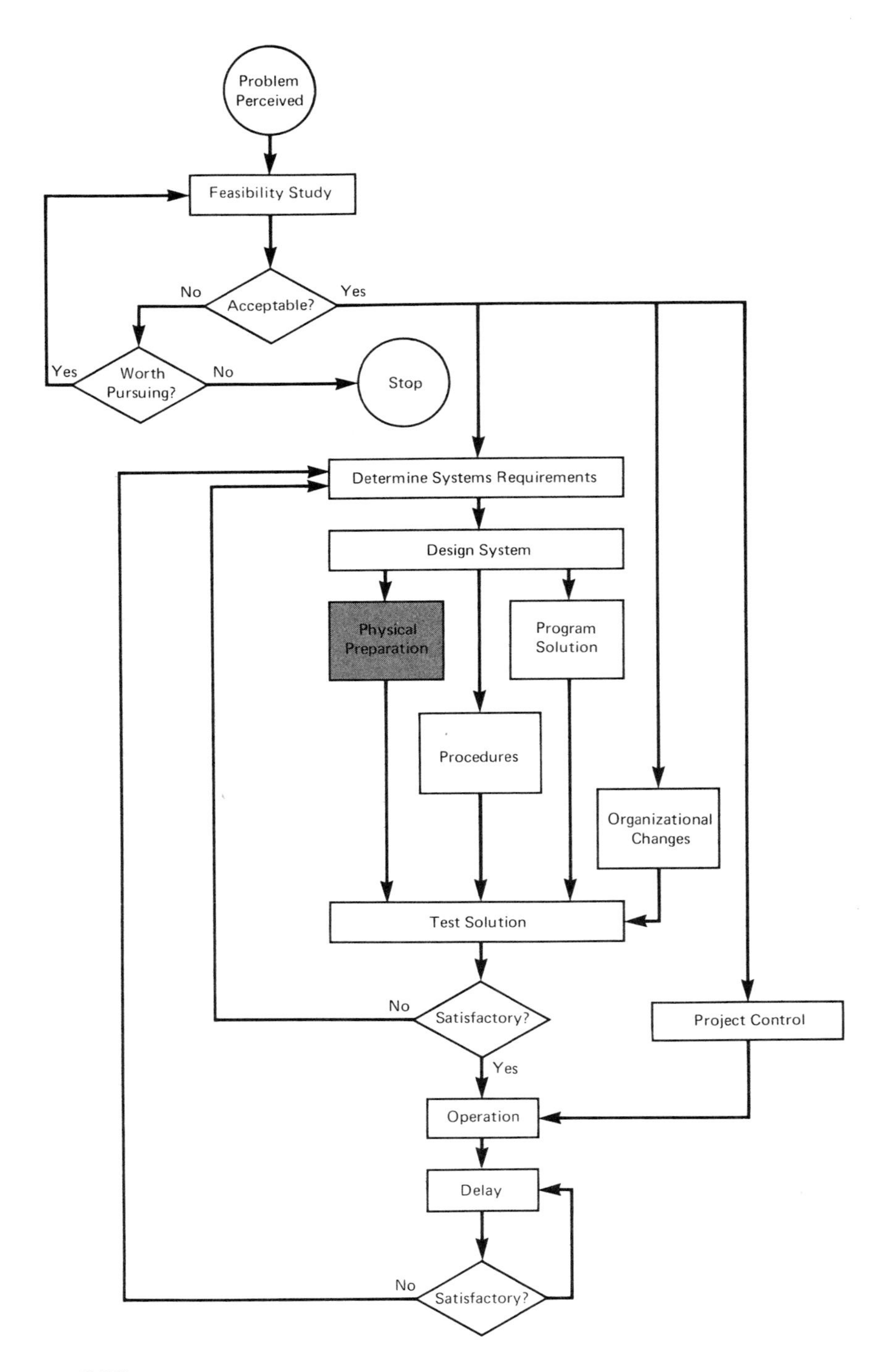
Problem Perceived
Feasibility Study
No
Acceptable?
Yes
Yes
Worth Pursuing?
No
Stop
Determine Systems Requirements
Design System
Physical Preparation
Program Solution
Procedures
Organizational Changes
Test Solution
No
Satisfactory?
Yes
Project Control
Operation
Delay
No
Satisfactory?

14

Physical Preparation

INTRODUCTION

Physical preparation includes the selection of equipment and related activities, as well as the design of forms necessary for the operation of the system. Most of the discussion concerns design, and as such this chapter is closely related to Chapter 13. However, unlike Chapter 13, the activities in this chapter on physical preparation need not be completed before the programming stage. Instead, they are both performed in parallel along with activities concerning procedures (to be discussed in the next chapter). These are shown in Figure 14–1.

The structure of this chapter will be similar to that of the previous chapter. Groups of activities will be discussed and illustrated in partial network diagrams, then the aggregation of the partial networks will be presented in the Summary and Conclusions section at the end of the chapter.

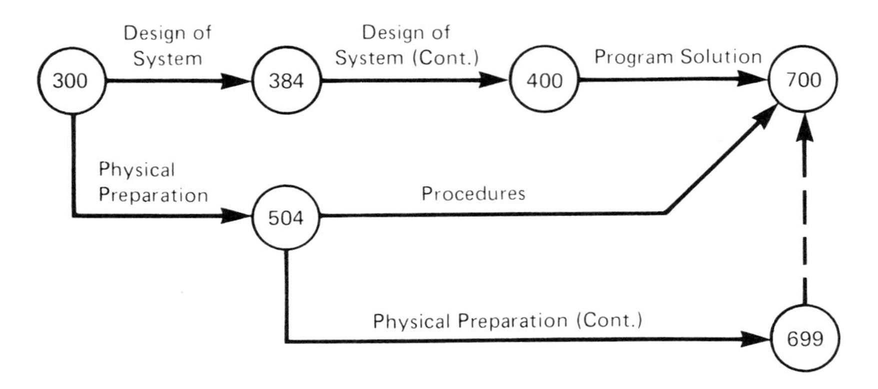

Figure 14–1. Relationship Between Design, Solution Determination, and Physical Preparation

EQUIPMENT-RELATED ACTIVITIES

Introduction

In this chapter no attempt will be made to discuss the details of selection and installation of equipment such as a computer system. There are two reasons for this exclusion. First, this subject is very specialized and technical. One manual lists 222 activities[1] for the critical path diagram of a computer installation. These details would normally be handled by specialists in hardware and the systems personnel working with the manufacturer. They are typically not of interest to the educational administrator.

The second reason for excluding the discussion on hardware is that many information systems studies do not require a computer installation. In many situations the computer system is already operative, and only changes or additions to the system are necessary. In some cases there may be a computer system but no information system. This seldom happens in business, but does occur in educational institutions where the academic departments use a computer for instruction. The administrator who uses the computer system does not have to go through the decision-making process of selecting and installing the computer, and therefore he does not need to know the details of equipment selection and installation. However, the administrator should know the gross steps and considerations involved in acquiring equipment, since he may need some equipment of his own (such as data preparation or output terminal equipment), and also because equipment is such an important and crucial component of many information systems. Furthermore, computer systems are

[1] *IBM Management Planning Guide for a Manual of Data Processing Standards,* No. C20–1670–1 (White Plains, N.Y.: International Business Machines Corporation, n.d.), p. 13.

frequently exchanged for more advanced computer systems. The administrator should, therefore, know some of the problems involved in equipment selection, installation, and conversion. The main activities related to equipment will be discussed, followed by a discussion of the interrelationships of these activities with other developmental activities, along with some observations on the nature and importance of equipment conversion.

Activities

The basic activities related to equipment are shown in Figure 14–2. These are initiated by the operational and hardware specifications generated in events 300 and 335 respectively, discussed in the last chapter. These prerequisites are indicated by dummy activities 330–555 and 335–555 respectively in Figure 14–2. They are followed by the study-of-equipment activity, 555–560. This can be a lengthy and complex process depending upon the nature of the equipment and the magnitude of the funds involved. The study would require that detailed technical specifications be stated and sent to manufacturers for bids. The request for bids may include **bench-marks,** a typical mix of jobs for which manufacturers are asked to present performance figures. This enables comparisons to be made between different equipment manufacturers as well as between different configurations within the products offered by one manufacturer. The evaluation of different configurations is often difficult because of the many intangibles involved. The trade-offs are difficult to make, for instance, between a combination of proved and unproved equipment; a manufacturer with a reputation for good service and support compared to a newcomer to the industry; software and systems support; as well as between numerous features that are available or almost available. But the selection of equipment must be made largely by equipment and hardware specialists, (activity 560–570 in Figure 14–2). This decision must be approved by top administrators, especially in cases where the choices involve a cost more than the already approved funds, and in cases where the choice may have other unexpected organizational impacts.

The selection of equipment is followed by placing an order (activity 570–575); the preparation of a site (activity 575–580); the installation of the equipment (activity 580–585); and the testing of equipment (activity 585–700). This testing should meet all the relevant standards for equipment performance set in the design stage discussed in Chapter 18.

Other Equipment-Related Activities

The equipment-selection activity has many important relationships with other activities in systems development. This activity generates an equipment-

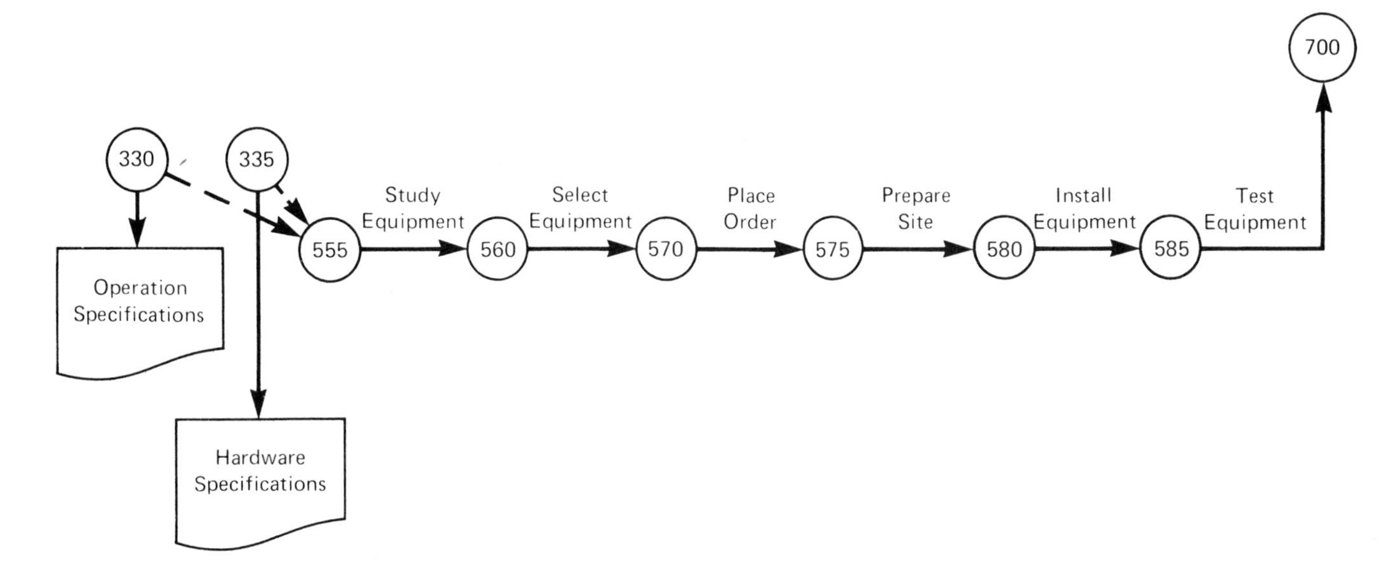

Figure 14–2. Partial Network Diagram for Equipment-Related Activities

configuration document (shown with activity 560–570 in Figure 14–3) which is very important to the programming activities. It also leads to the study and specification of manpower requirements, (activity 570–595 in Figure 14–3) and the generation of a document used in manpower planning. This document is the possible basis not only for the hiring and firing of personnel, but also for orientation and training, a subject to be discussed in Chapter 17.

A parallel activity to manpower specifications is the schedule information resulting from the hardware selection (570–590 in Figure 14–3). This information is used by the project manager for planning, scheduling, and control of the project.

There are other possible related activities not shown in Figures 14–2 and 14–3. For example, suppose that the new equipment configuration includes new input equipment, such as mark-sensing equipment, or new output equipment such as terminal units. This information will become a prerequisite for the input design and output design activities respectively. Also, if the equipment is to be operated by the user, then operational procedures must be written and personnel trained to operate the equipment. Relevant changes in the network diagram must be made by the project manager.

Conversion

The changing of operations from old equipment to new equipment is often referred to as equipment conversion. Such conversion, like file conversion, can be time-consuming, costly, and strenuous. Many equipment conversions require reprogramming. If the programming is converted to a higher-level language from a symbolic language, it may take three-fourths of the original programming time; if converted from a higher-level language of a second-generation machine to a higher-level language of a third-generation machine, the additional work may take about 5 percent of the time required for the original program.[2] These programming conversion factors will be a function of the complexity of the program; the equipment configuration; the languages used; and the competence of the programmers. But in almost all cases of computer conversion, there is reprogramming involved. This type of programming, if it does not involve redesigning, is considered a mundane job. Along with the uncertainty associated with conversion, this results in conversions being unpopular with programmers.

Chapin discusses the problems of equipment conversion.

> Typically the conversion period is one of strain and disruption in the organization. Work loads are much higher than normal because the old system must still

[2]R. L. Harmon, R. C. Aubuchon, and D. C. Mengersen, "Planning Successful Conversions," *Ideas for Management, 21st International Systems Meeting* (Cleveland, Ohio: Systems and Procedures Association, 1968), p. 77.

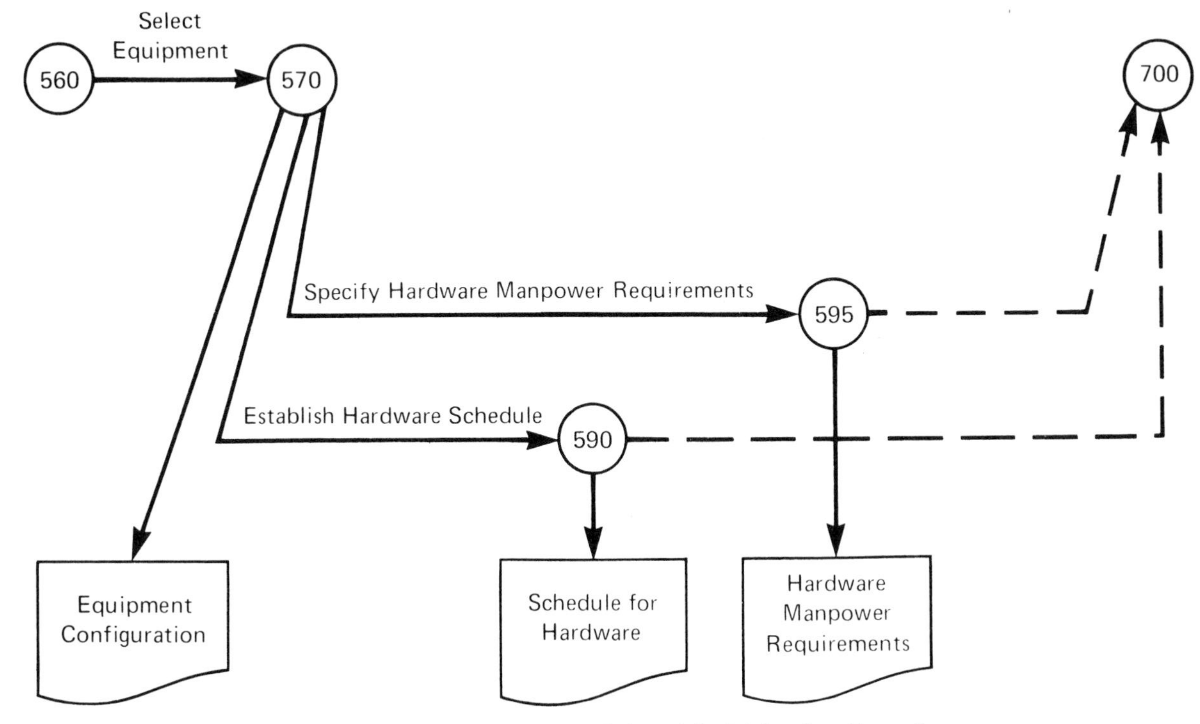

Figure 14–3. Partial Network Diagram for Equipment-Related Activities (continued)

be made to function until the new system is functioning satisfactorily. This means that in effect two systems must be operated together. During the conversion periods, things rarely proceed as they should. Unforeseen difficulties crop up and must be disposed of, often under great pressure of time. Mistakes are made, cost mounts up rapidly as overtime is paid and as work is redone, and customer service may be unavoidably affected. Then, there are always the last-minute changes. Regardless of how thorough a job has been done in all the preceding stages, something surely will have been found to have changed enough to require changing the program.[3]

Although conversions are unpopular and surrounded with uncertainty, they are also moments of opportunity; occasions for system redesign. The reasons for wanting to redesign are many. First, computer equipment changes bring with them greater capability, and to make maximum use of this capability sometimes requires reprogramming and redesigning of the system. Second, the need for redesign may be initiated by the user. His cycle of needs may correspond to the cycle of hardware changes. The cycle of user's needs is part of the evolving process of maturing user and maturing systems personnel. Having succeeded in one system, they wish to expand and incorporate increasing demands for more services and more sophistication. The third reason for redesigning is an economic one. If the system is not redesigned along with the equipment conversion then two conversions may be required: an equipment conversion followed by a file conversion. To do both together may in some cases be a better allocation of resources as well as a less disrupting alternative for the organization.

Whatever the reason, redesigning, along with equipment conversion, is a complex task that must follow a systematic development procedure such as the one discussed in this book.

FORM DESIGN ACTIVITIES

Another aspect of physical preparation of a system is the development of forms required by information systems. This is shown in Figure 14–4. There are two functional types of forms that are examined; input forms and output forms. Other forms, like those used in operations, are not of direct interest to the administrator and will not be discussed.

The output form design would typically start before the input form design, since its working document, the output specification, is prepared first. The prerequisite output specification for the output design activity (500–505 in Figure 14–4) is shown by the dummy activity 375–500, where event 375

[3]N. Chapin, *An Introduction to Automatic Computers* (2nd ed.) (New York: D. Van Nostrand Company, Inc., 1963), p. 359.

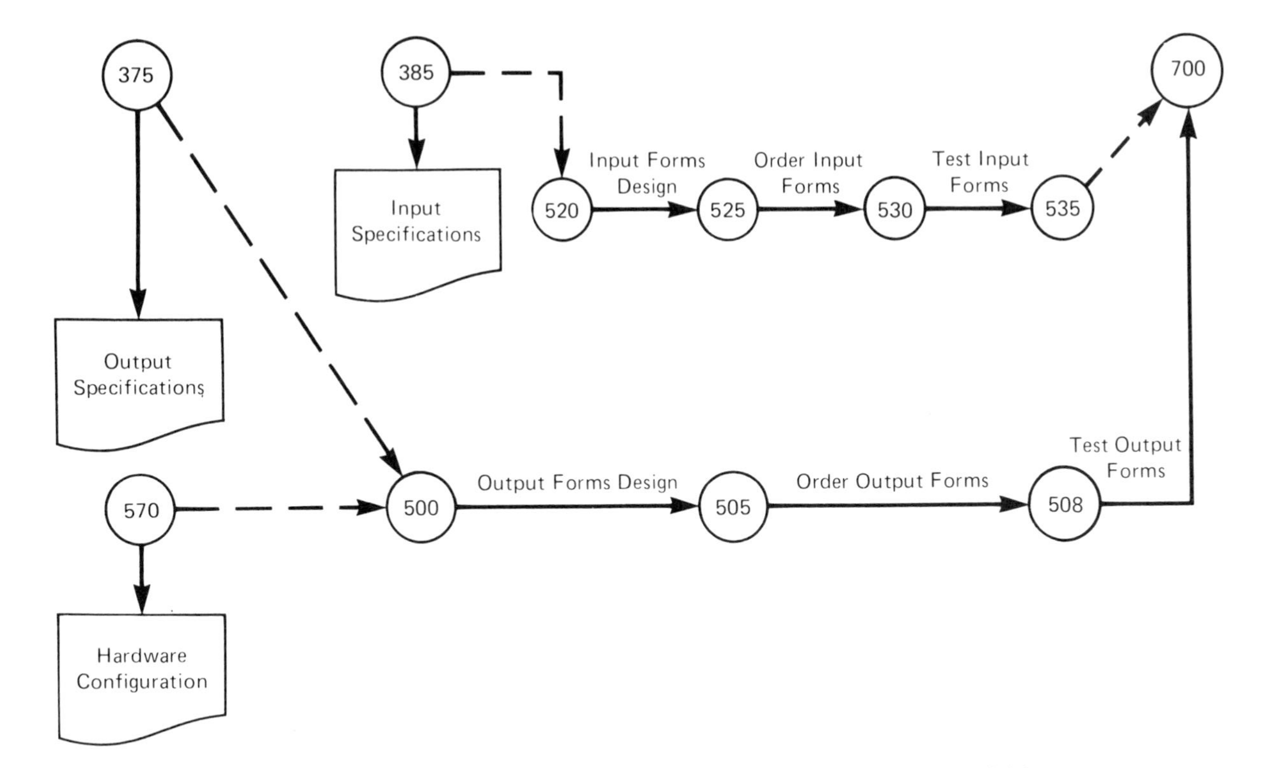

Figure 14–4. Partial Network Diagram Showing Form Preparation and Related Activities

generates the output specifications. Another prerequisite is the equipment configuration selection which is done in event 570. This prerequisite is shown by the dummy activity 570–500 in Figure 14–4.

Form Design

There are principles of design that apply to all forms. Some important ones are: the forms must be unambiguously titled and worded so that they cannot be misinterpreted; the colors of the forms should be chosen for emphasis and ease of reading (light brown and light green print have been found empirically to be easy on the eye); the print must be spaced to facilitate reading; related data should be grouped together to minimize backtracking of thought; and the sizes of the forms should be such that they can be put in standard binders and file cabinets. There are other principles of form design that apply specifically to the design of input or output forms. The output form design was implicitly covered in the discussion on output design (in Chapter 13). The design for input forms will be discussed below.

Input Form Design

New forms are often designed because the currently existing forms are found to be inadequate. An attempt should then be made to incorporate the inadequate forms in the new forms. This is important because forms are costly not only to print but also to store and control. There is a tendency in some institutions to add to forms without adequately controlling their number and use. Such a situation leads to such cases as one institution accumulating 3,100 different forms,[4] and another using 28,000 different forms.[5]

The design of forms is an art. Some problems are unique to each form, though there are rules developed by people in the computer field that apply to many of the forms designed. These can be used as a checklist and are shown below.[6]

1. Are the instructions for completing the form adequate and easily understood?
2. Is the code (if used to complete form wholly or partially) identified so that errors can be traced?

[4] C. L. Bateman, "Forms Control," *Ideas for Management, 1967 International Systems Meeting* (Cleveland, Ohio: Systems and Procedures Association, 1967), p. 16.

[5] R. R. Tekulve, "Simplification Through Forms Design," *Ideas for Management, 14th International Systems Meeting,* II (Cleveland, Ohio: Systems and Procedures Association, 1961), p. 106.

[6] C. B. Randall and S. W. Burgly, *Systems & Procedures for Business Data Processing* (2nd ed.), pp. 235–36. Copyright © 1968 by South-Western Publishing Company. Reproduced by permission of the publisher.

3. Is there sufficient space for completing information without crowding?
4. Are the questions worded unambiguously?
5. Are the questions in proper sequence to avoid confusion?
6. Are lines to be filled in by typewriting spaced to conform to typewriter spacing?
7. Is the vertical alignment on forms to be typewritten such that clerks can use the typewriter tabular-stop device?
8. Does the form provide larger spaces for handwritten data than typewritten data?
9. If the form is to take information from or pass information to another form, does it show items in the same order as the other?
10. Does the form have all recurring items printed so that only variable values need to be filled in?
11. Is all known information preprinted?
12. Have all fact-gathering data been included?
13. Have the data been so arranged that backtracking is unnecessary?
14. Is the form designed so that no information is lost when the form is filed or bound?
15. Is the form printed on the size and weight of paper that meets the requirements of the form without being more expensive than necessary?

It is difficult to over-emphasize the importance of form design. An ambiguously worded question or even a badly sequenced question can cause inaccuracy. In one institution a student being admitted was asked numerous questions about himself and one question about his father. The question after the father's name was: date of high-school graduation? This question was meant by the form designer to identify the student's high-school graduation date but it was misunderstood. Many students entered their father's date of high-school graduation.

Another example of a misunderstanding arose with the date of birth. One student entered 3/1/42. It was interpreted as the first day in March 1942, but the student was born on the third day of January 1942. He was a foreign student coming from the British Commonwealth. Their convention for writing dates is day/month/year.[7]

Such problems always arise. They cannot always be anticipated but they can be minimized. This particular date problem could have been detected if a stratified sample of students (including foreign students) was used to test the form. Another way to have avoided the date inaccuracy would have been to use boxes, as in Figure 14–5.

[7]Convention proposed for interchange of data between data systems is Year/Month/-Date. For details, see *Communications of the ACM,* XIII, No. 1 (January 1970), p. 55.

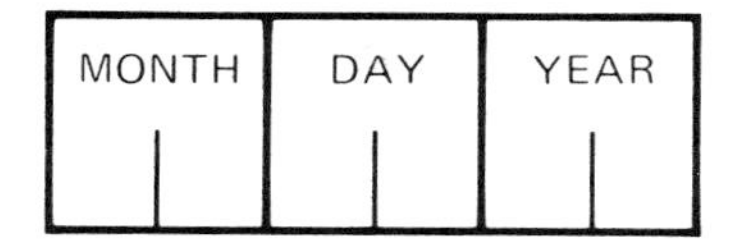

Figure 14–5. Entering of Date

Boxes eliminate dangers of reversing the order (though there is still the danger that a student may put Mo indicating Monday as the day of birth). This problem can be overcome by an example, or by instructions on completing the form. Boxes also eliminate problems of misinterpretation of written data. For example, the numbers 51 and 57 are not always distinguishable if written continuously. If the numbers are put in boxes, the danger of misrepresentation is reduced. The Germans identify their seven with a dash on the stem. Such conventions are used commonly by data-processing personnel. They use a dash to distinguish a Z from a 2, and a slash to distinguish the number 0 (zero) from the letter O. (This latter convention is unfortunately the opposite of the practice in the military).

The box technique has other advantages. It can keep units separate, such as cents from dollars, and can also ensure that all digits of a number are entered, such as the nine digits of a social security number. An empty box assigned to a social security number can be detected more easily by a glance than a missing number in a string of nine members written on a line.

Boxes are also used for coding. Some forms have a space reserved on the right-hand column with boxes used by a coder to code information written on the left-hand side of the form. The form is then used as a document for direct keypunching.

Another variation of the use of boxes is to use one box to check the existence of a condition. One such example is shown in Figure 14–6.

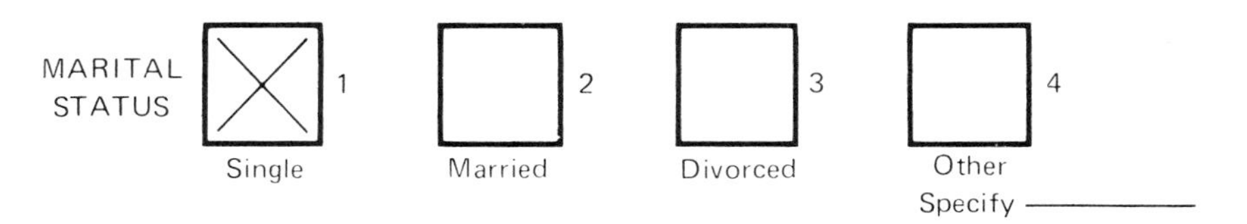

Figure 14–6. Illustration of Use of Boxes for Checking

The checking of a box identifies the existence of the corresponding condition. For example, in Figure 14–6, the person completing the form is single. When this form is converted to machine-readable data, it will be recorded as a "1," the code stated to the right of the box identifying single persons.

A box identifying "other" categories is a catch-all for cases that were unexpected, and ensures the exhaustiveness of all possibilities. It is important to insist that all "other" cases be specified. There are two reasons for this. One is that the specification sometimes identifies the entry as not really an "other" category but as a difference of perception between the form designer and the person completing the form. For example, a student or a faculty member who is "separated" may not consider himself either married or divorced and so will consider himself in the "other" category. Such a specification of the entry will enable it to be modified to conform to the categories stated on the form, which in this case could put the entry among the "married" persons.

Another reason for the "other" category specification is to enable the identification of categories that were overlooked by the designer, or categories that have become important since the form was originally designed. In such cases, the form must be redesigned and the new, important category be assigned a category and code of its own.

The entries in boxes (and other parts of a form) should be carefully explained, perhaps by examples, on another part of the form or on an instruction sheet. If not, errors may result. As an example of the problem consider the entries of dates in Figure 14–5. Inaccurate entry examples are shown in Figure 14–7.

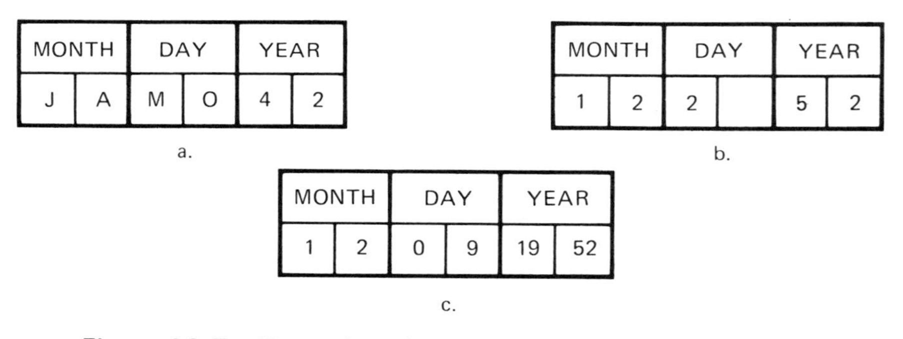

Figure 14–7. Illustration of Incorrect Entries

The problem in Figure 14–7(a) is that the month and day are identified by the starting alphabets rather than a number. Figure 14–7(b) has one number in the day boxes. The entry may have been a "2" but will be interpreted as a "20." The problem in Figure 14–7(c) is that the year boxes have been misused. All these problems could be overcome by the redesigning of the boxes as shown in Figure 14–8. This figure also shows examples of correct entries that could be part of the instructions for completing the form. There is still no guarantee that the form will be completed correctly, but at least the chance of error has been reduced.

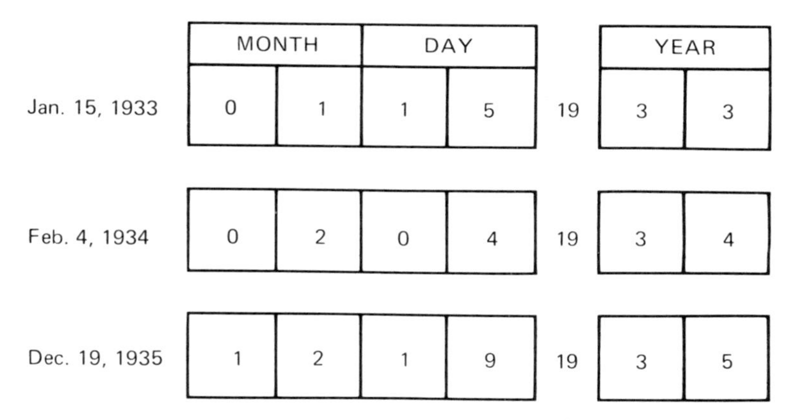

Figure 14–8. Examples of Completing Data Boxes

Another use of boxes in the design of input forms is for marking by special pencil. These marks, if made on specially designed cards, can be read directly by machine and are referred to as **mark-sensing.** This technique eliminates any further data conversion to machine-readable form, and thereby reduces the processing time and inaccuracies in processing.

Mark-sensing can also be done on specially designed sheets. They have been used for collecting grades, scheduling, inventory control, fee analysis, housing assignments, and extensively by the ACT.[8] The ACT uses mark-sense sheets for scoring tests as well as for collecting basic data. The low error rate when used by high-school students is encouraging for administrators in higher education where the student body should be better able to follow instructions and complete the forms.

Mark-sensing requires special equipment features on card reproducers for mark-sensing cards and special equipment for reading mark-sensing documents. The latter is not yet available commercially at prices that enable it to be commonly used. But this equipment and other equipment capable of reading typed documents will soon become more available at lower prices. This may make input preparation not only faster and more accurate, but also cheaper than existing techniques.

SUMMARY AND CONCLUSIONS

In this chapter, two important aspects of physical preparation were discussed; activities related to equipment, and the development of forms.

Equipment selection, installation, and testing were discussed, but only at

[8]ACT is the abbreviation for the American College Testing Program.

a very gross and general level. The details are beyond the scope of this book. In the discussion, references were made mostly to computer input and output equipment as it relates to the development process. The discussion applies, however, to other equipment, such as supporting peripheral equipment and communication equipment.[9]

The designing, testing, and control of forms is a very important component of information system design. It can significantly affect systems performance because it can affect the accuracy of input and the effective use of output. Form design is an art, and its practice is the specialty of form designers. Many institutions cannot afford such specialists, in which case the systems designer, with help from the user, must design the forms.

Forms should be designed so that they are unambiguous and complete; easy to understand and interpret; and finally, so that they have a format, color,[10] and print that make them easy to read and easily convertible to machine-readable data. One technique used successfully in designing forms is the assignment of specified boxes for data.

The equipment-related activities are shown in a network diagram in Figure 14–9. One important set of related activities is excluded; those related to procedures. This is the topic of the next chapter.

KEY TERMS

Equipment Configuration Document
Conversion
Form Design
Box Technique
Mark-Sensing
Bench Mark

REVIEW QUESTIONS

1. Distinguish between
   Equipment-Related Activities and Form-Related Activities
   Conversion and Redesign

[9]For a survey of some basic input-output equipment, see Appendix B.

[10]The importance of the color of a form is illustrated by the following case history. One large university used two forms in its admissions process—one to inform students that they had been admitted, the other to inform them that they had not been admitted. Both forms were white continuous forms with the printing of name and address done on a computer printer.

In one run, the operator used the wrong form, admitting some students who had not been accepted. The error was detected after the letters were mailed. Fortunately, these were traced from the listings and the errors were corrected.

Needless to say, the color of one set of forms was changed in order to reduce the probability of such an error reoccurring. This case study illustrates the serious implications of a seemingly unimportant principle of form design.

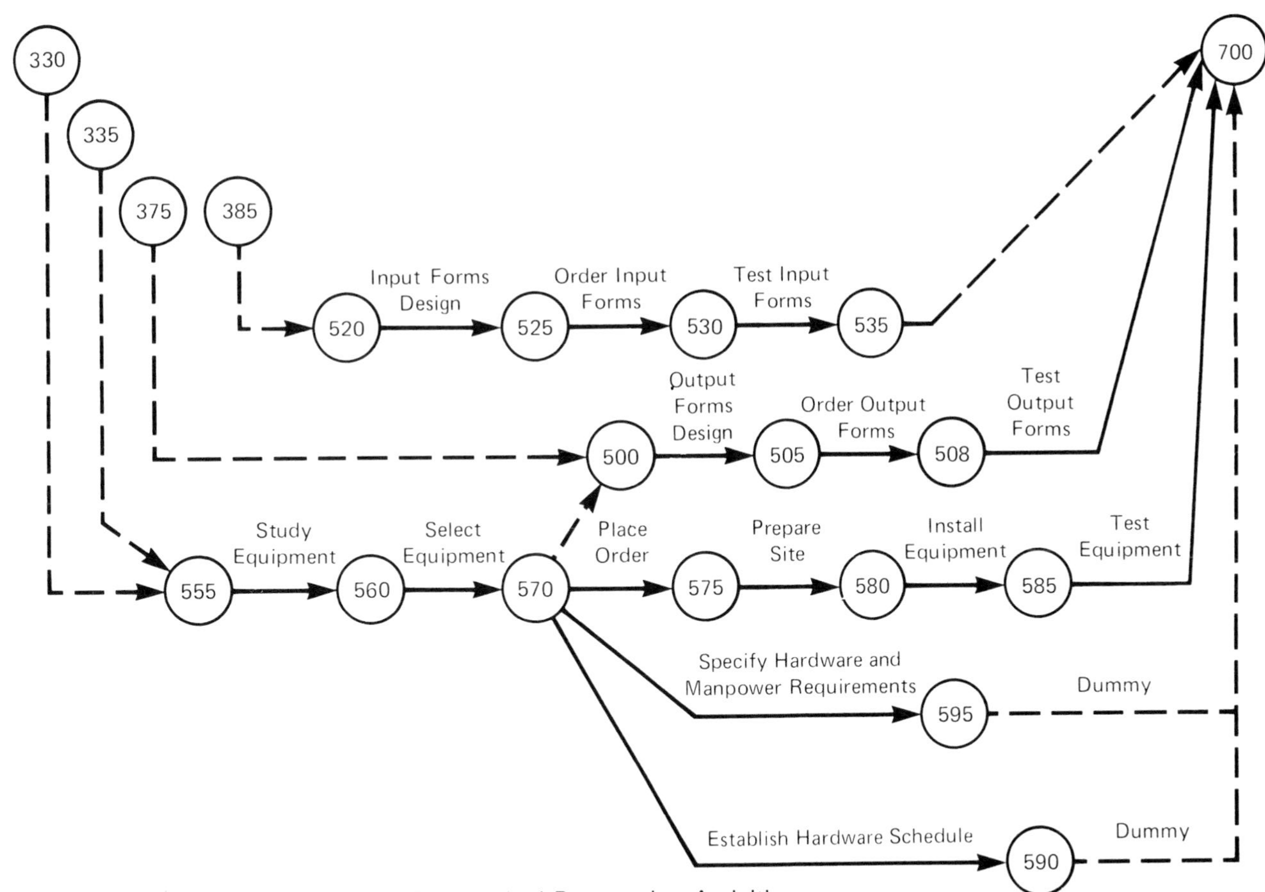

Figure 14–9. Network Diagram for Physical Preparation Activities

Functional Forms and Operational Forms

2. How can you minimize the danger of receiving inaccurate data?
3. What are the reasons for redesigning the current system with an equipment conversion?
4. What are the principles of form design?

CHAPTER 14: SELECTED ANNOTATED BIBLIOGRAPHY

IBM Form and Card Design (C20–8078, No. S–8083). White Plains, N.Y.: International Business Machines Marketing Publications, 1964. Systems designers and user managers alike can use this as a guide for the design of forms and card layouts. Included are discussions of form size and spacing problems. Card design considerations include field size, data sequences, relevant machine characteristics, and techniques that assist in card design.

KAISER, J. B., *Forms Design and Control.* New York: American Management Association, Inc., 1968, 173 pp. Presented in general terms are the rudiments of form design. Techniques to aid in proper form design, multipart forms, and typical errors in form design are discussed. Included are considerations and uses for master cards and detail cards. Specific examples are given in the appendices.

KANTER, J., *The Computer and the Executive.* Englewood Cliffs, N.J.: Prentice-Hall, Inc., 1967, Appendix A, "Considerations in Installing a Computer," pp. 103–6. Ten guidelines for developing proper planning and control techniques are presented for managers. Each point is excellent; however, the discussion of each is only enough to serve as a base for further study.

LADEN, H. N., and T. R. GILDERSLEEVE, "Source Document Considerations," *System Design for Computer Applications.* New York: John Wiley & Sons, Inc., 1963, Chap. IX, pp. 177–213. The authors list considerations for source document formats, the encoding of forms, and card design. Realistic methods of form design and rules for optimal equipment utilization are given. Other topics include automatic generation of machine-coded documents, self-checking numbers, and paper-tape design.

MYERS, G., "Forms Design & Control," in *Systems and Procedures* (2nd ed.), ed. V. Lazzaro. Englewood Cliffs, N.J.: Prentice-Hall, Inc., 1968, pp. 182–213. Dr. Myers is manager of Systems and Procedures for the Aerospace Group of General Precision, Inc. This treatise is aimed at managers who must ensure proper form design. Techniques and specific considerations for ensuring proper form design and use are discussed. Also included are discussions on optical character and magnetic character recognition.

OLSEN, J. L., "Forms Design & Control," *Ideas for Management.* Cleveland: Systems & Procedures Assn., 1962, pp. 36–89. Mr. Olsen is Assistant Director of the Methods Department of Liberty Mutual Insurance Companies and a member of the faculty at Northwestern University. His article is an excellent and detailed treatise of the subject in meaningful terms. The organization of a "forms control team" and each member's responsibilities are discussed. Excellent examples and case studies are presented.

RANDALL, C. B., and S. W. BURGLY, *Systems & Procedures for Business Data Processing* (2nd ed.). Cincinnati: South-Western Publishing Co., 1968, Chap. XVI on Form Design, pp. 235–52. C. B. Randall is Director of Management Information at North American Rockwell Corporation; S. W. Burgly is Dean of Curricular Administration of Point Park College. The design forms are presented in step-by-step fashion beginning with a checklist for form evaluation and ending with specific considerations for forms used with IBM 402 and 403 accounting machines.

ROSOVE, P. E., "The Installation Phase," in *Developing a Computer-Based Information System,* ed. P. E. Rosove. New York: John Wiley & Sons, Inc., 1967. Chap. IX, pp. 279–309. Mr. Rosove describes the general characteristics and objectives of the installation phase. Three main reasons for the importance of the installation phase are listed and discussed—the need for the test and verification of system design concepts in an operational environment, the need for the psychological acceptance of the system by the user, and the need for the development of an operational capability. The author believes that the following sequence of activities must be conducted during the installation phase: (1) instruction of the users on system characteristics, (2) conduct of a trial use period by users, (3) test and verification of the system design, (4) detection and correction of errors, inadequacies, and gaps, and (5) development of an operational system capability. Much of the discussion in this chapter is based on Mr. Rosove's experience with the military's SAGE system.

WEISER, A. L., "Automatic Data Processing Systems—Physical Installation Considerations," *Computers and Automation,* XVIII, No. 12 (November 1969), 44–49. Weiser's purpose is to familiarize business executives responsible for equipment purchasing with installation considerations. Included is a brief but comparatively detailed outline and discussion of 16 considerations, such as space requirements, site selection, safety, and delivery.

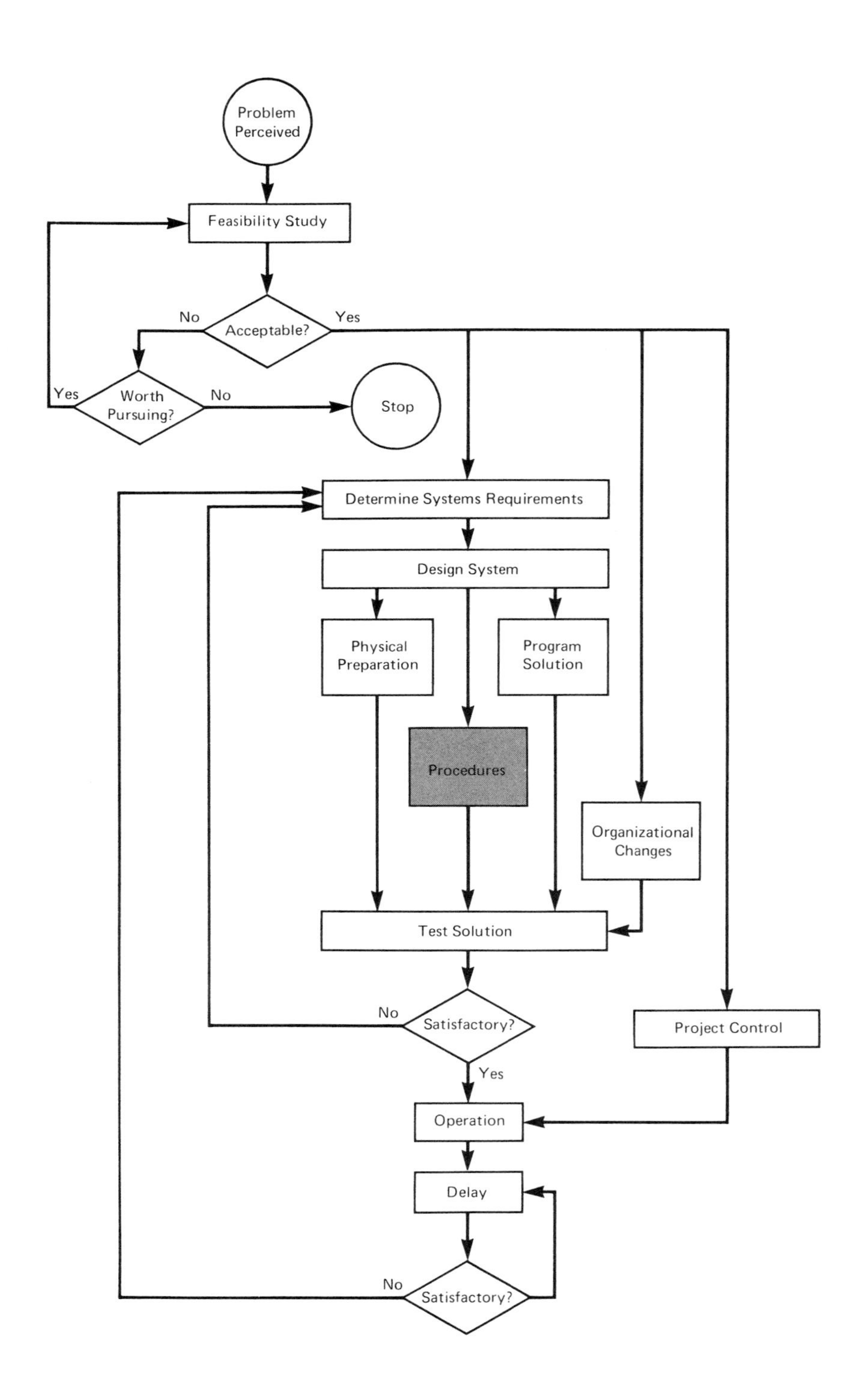

Problem Perceived
Feasibility Study
Acceptable?
No
Yes
Worth Pursuing?
Yes
No
Stop
Determine Systems Requirements
Design System
Physical Preparation
Program Solution
Procedures
Organizational Changes
Test Solution
Satisfactory?
No
Yes
Project Control
Operation
Delay
Satisfactory?
No

15

Procedures: Their Design, Production, and Control

INTRODUCTION

Forms and equipment discussed in the previous chapter are instruments and components of an information system used in operations. There are related operations that must be performed in a specific way and in a prescribed sequence in order for the system to operate as intended. This set of events has to be explained and responsibilities for it have to be assigned to personnel. This is done by a set of instructions called **procedures.** They provide the link between what has to be done and who does it.

According to Johnson, Kast, and Rosenzweig, a procedure (or method)

> tells how to do the job, what processes to use, and other general information about the job. The procedure is task-oriented; it normally is written as a formal document segmenting the tasks to be performed. The primary purpose of the procedure is instructional in nature. It is not designed or intended to represent

job flow except with the task covered, or to relate the task at hand with those preceding or following.[1]

Friedman defines procedures as referring

> to a predetermined sequence of actions which should be taken to carry out some task or job, specifying what shall be done, how it shall be done, who shall do it and when . . . system procedures provide a link among the men, machine, and computer programs within the system, a link which can be used to orient and educate the users before the system is installed and operated, and which will guide them when it is put into use.[2]

The above definitions identify two aspects of procedures: the descriptive and the prescriptive. The latter aspect of procedures is emphasized in the definition given by Sondel.

> Procedures take the form of initiative language in the prescriptive mode, systematized by systemic language in the formative mode. To say this differently, the prescriptors are arranged as a means-end pattern.
>
> Each means-end design is calculated to reach a desired goal-state. Each means-end design falls generically under the broader means-end pattern of the system. Each means-end design is synchronized and coordinated with every other such means-end design, such that the goal-state of the system will be effected.
>
> But the means-ends hypothesis is a speculative model. In operational procedures we can never be sure what fortuitous circumstances have contributed to success or failure. We do the best we can . . . [3]

Sondel's definition suggests the heuristic character of designing procedures. They are heuristic in the sense that they are exploratory methods of solving a problem and are improved by evaluation and experience.

The cycle from procedure design to evaluation can be traced in a flowchart, as shown in Figure 15–1. It starts with the design of procedures (box 1) (which is preceded by relevant specifications stated in previous stages of the development process) which are then written up in a **Procedures Manual** (box 2). This is often a part of the **User's Manual** and can be written by a technical writer or the systems analyst. The Procedures Manual should be written in such a way that the text is clear, concise, and unambiguous. It should be motivating, emphasizing the importance and need for the operation whenever appropriate.

[1]R. A. Johnson, et. al., *The Theory and Management of Systems* (2nd ed.) (New York: McGraw-Hill Book Company, Inc., 1967), p. 116.

[2]L. A. Friedman, "Design and Production of System Procedures," in *Developing Computer-Based Information System,* ed. P. E. Rosove (New York: John Wiley & Sons, Inc., 1967), pp. 201, 203.

[3]Bess Sondel, "Systems and Procedures: Semantic Dimension," *Ideas for Management, 18th International Systems Meeting* (Cleveland, Ohio: Systems and Procedures Association, 1965), p. 127.

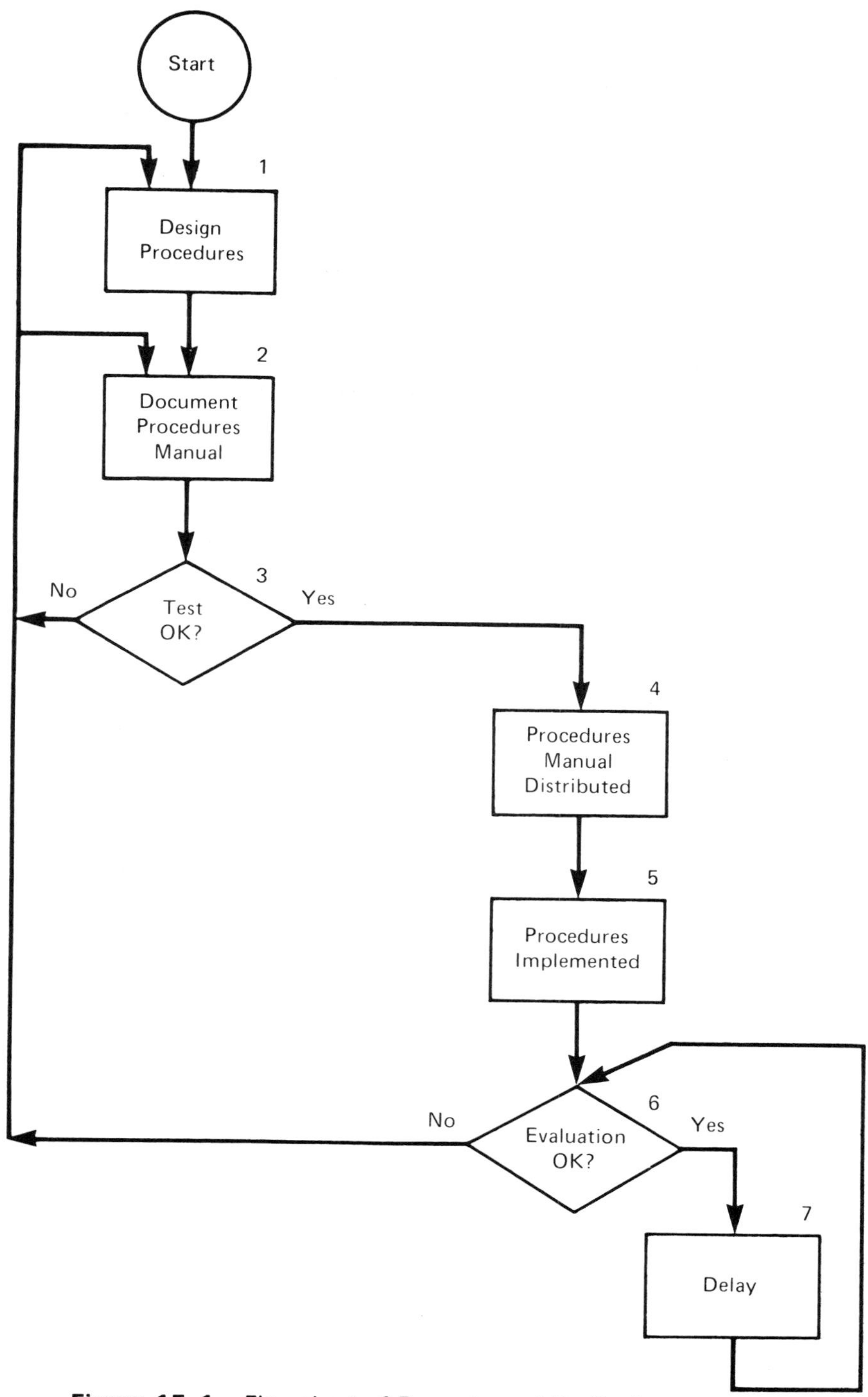

Figure 15–1. Flowchart of Procedures Life Cycle

The Procedures Manual should be personnel-independent whenever possible. It should not name individuals, but refer to positions in the organization. Some individuals require special procedures to overcome deficiencies or to take advantage of special capabilities and these should be added as the necessity arises. Procedures should be specific but flexible enought to allow for exceptions.

The Procedures Manual, once written, must be tested (box 3 in Figure 15–1). Preferably, this should be done by a person who would use the procedures and, if possible, by one who did not help design the procedures in order to provide objectivity in testing.

In situations where the procedures are related to other subsystems, the testing may have to await the completion of the design of the whole system. Often, however, procedures such as those concerning input card preparation can be tested in isolation and in parallel with the rest of the system. If the procedures are found unsatisfactory and do not meet the criterion of operations (such as response time, maximum error rate, etc.) then the procedure must be redesigned (box 1) or rewritten (box 2) depending on the nature of the problem. If the test is found to be satisfactory, then the Procedures Manual is distributed to the personnel involved (box 4). In the distribution of Procedures Manuals great care must be taken to withdraw old and outdated Procedures Manuals. This is very important; many system problems have arisen because of the use of outdated procedures (especially of outdated and non-existing codes).

The withdrawal of outdated procedures cannot be done without a record of the distribution list. This is an important reason for maintaining the distribution list. It is part of the procedure control that is necessary for effective systems operations.

Following the distribution of the Procedures Manual, the procedures are implemented (box 5) and become operational. During the operations of a system, the procedures should be evaluated (box 6). This should be done explicitly and periodically on a sample or population basis to ensure that the procedures are being understood and followed, and that the objectives for which they were designed are being achieved.

An implicit evaluation of the procedures would result from complaints or errors traced to them. Whether explicitly or implicitly, if the evaluation is found to be unsatisfactory, the process is recycled to the design stage (box 1) or documentation (box 2) of procedures. If the evaluation is found to be satisfactory, then there is a predetermined delay (box 7) whereafter the procedures are reevaluated (box 6).

Some of what is shown in Figure 15–1 is not part of the stage of the initial development process discussed in this part of the book. The discussion (boxes 5,6, and 7) relates to procedures during and after implementation of the system. They are shown here for purposes of continuity of the discussion on procedures.

The design and testing of procedures are shown as activities 540–545, 545–550, and 508–510 in Figure 15–2. Perhaps the design of procedures (activity 540–545) can be further explained in the context of an example. The problem to be discussed is the design of procedures for input control at the office of admissions in an institution of higher learning. The purpose of the example is two-fold: to illustrate a procedure in an information system and to discuss input control.

PROCEDURES FOR INPUT CONTROL—AN EXAMPLE

The procedure design is shown in a flowchart in Figure 15–3. The sending, receiving, and checking of the admissions form is shown in boxes 2, 3, 5, and 6. The accumulation of a batch of 50 forms before they are processed is shown in box 4, which is an example of the timing of the decision-rule being specified. The number of forms in the batch is a decision that the administrator must make, since the delay resulting from the batch-size rule will affect public relations and may even result in loss of registration. This is a good example of how procedures that may seem unimportant and trivial can have a significant effect on the organization. It is, therefore, important that the administrator pay attention to the steps in procedures and make the value judgments when necessary. If he does not do so then by default the judgment will be made by the system analyst who may not be qualified to make such a decision.

Once accepted, the admission form is coded by the coding clerk (box 7), and is held until a batch of 100 is collected (box 8). This batch size is typically a function of the time it takes to "set-up" for the job and the time it takes to perform it. If the "set-up" time to start a job is high compared with the recurring time (for instance, a ten-minute average set-up for an average of one minute to process), then the batch size would be larger to compensate for the set-up cost than in a situation with a lower set-up compared to processing time (such as a two minute set-up time for a ten-minute processing time).

Once the specified batch is accumulated, it should be logged (box 9) and sent to the Processing Center or Computer Center, abbreviated as PC (box 10). The logging of batches is an important control function to ensure that no batch gets lost and that it is processed within a specified time.

The coded sheets are then keypunched and verified (box 11) and are checked for validity by a computer program (box 12). If the validity run is satisfactory (Yes exit of box 13) then the data is ready for processing (box 14) and one branch of the procedure is terminated (circle 27).

If the validity program finds one or more errors (No exit in box 13), then the results are sent to the Admissions Clerk for correction (box 15). In this procedure the entire batch must be error-free before any data in the batch is processed. No weight is given to the number of errors in a record, the number of records in error, or the significance of the error. Again, there is a decision

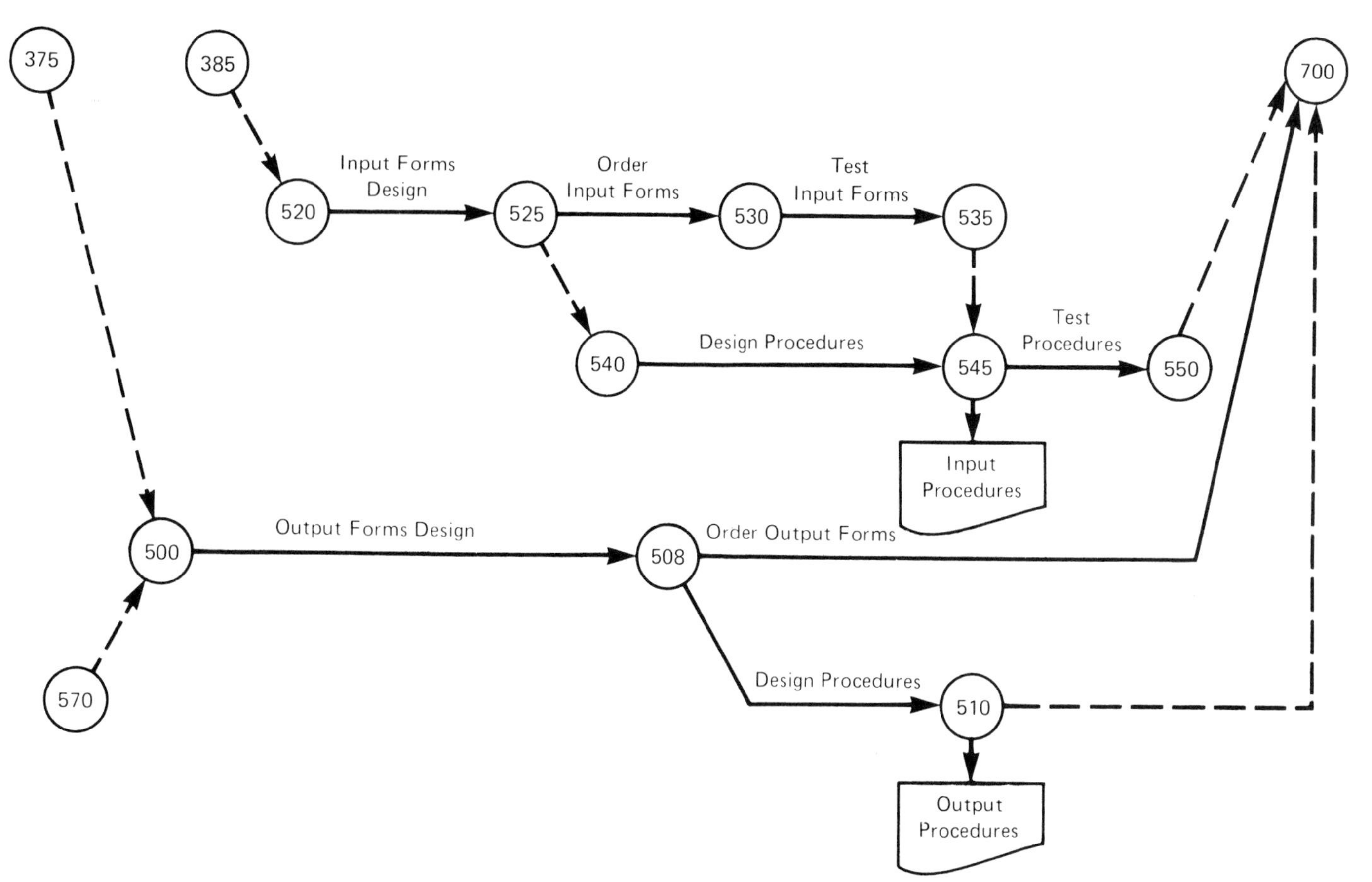

Figure 15–2. Partial Network Diagram Showing Procedure Activities with Related Activities

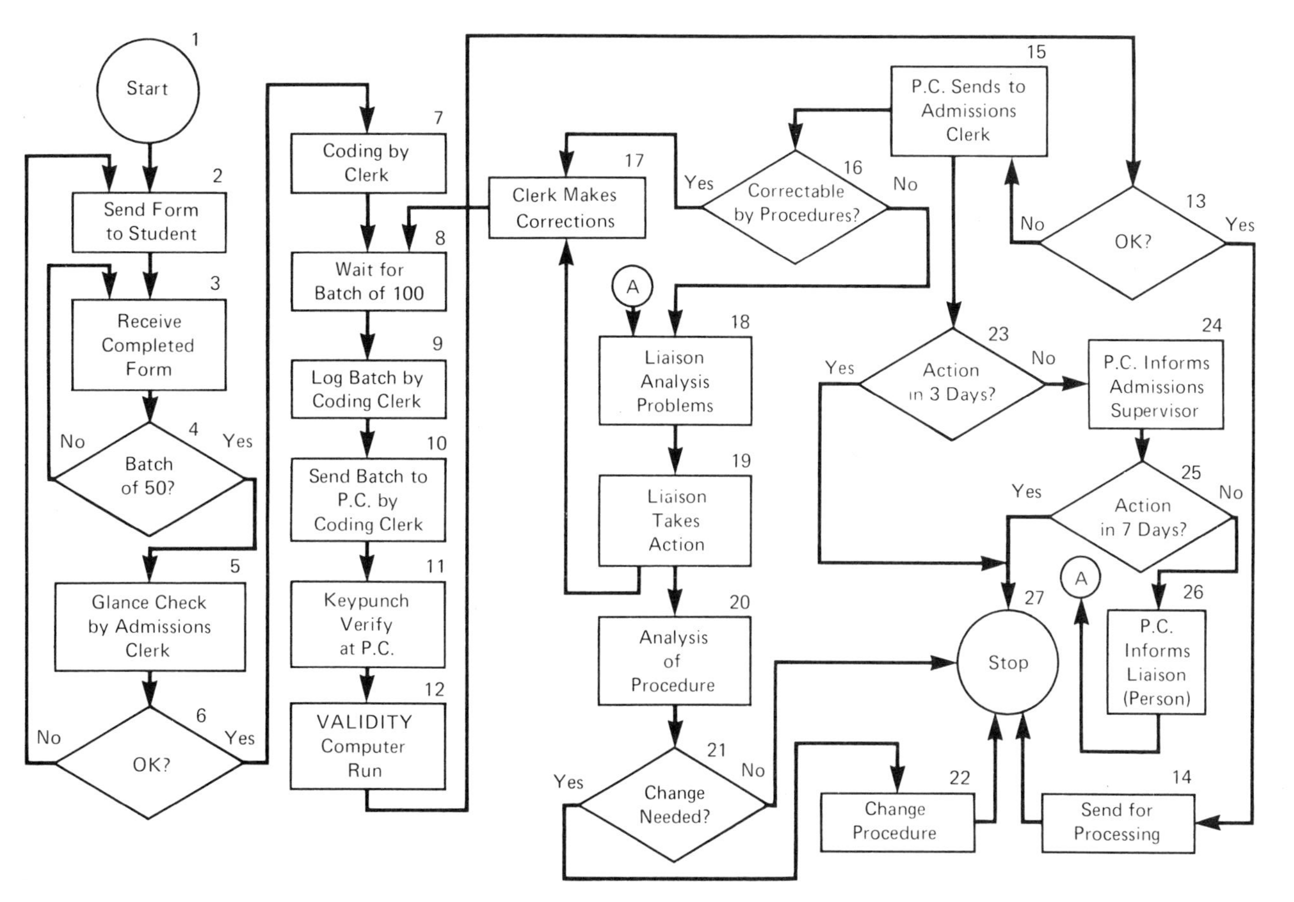

Figure 15–3. Flowchart Showing Procedures for Admissions Input Preparation

here that could cause delays in processing. An institution with a high demand for admission may be able to afford such a procedure, whereas another institution could not afford it. A similar problem may arise in a business office which does not process a batch of 100 incoming checks because of one unacceptable check. This would deprive the institution of the funds from the remaining 99 checks. An alternative would be to process those that are acceptable and correct the errors in those remaining.

The Admissions Clerk examines the error(s) for those that can be corrected by the procedures specified (box 16). If the error(s) can be corrected (box 17), the data is recycled for processing by waiting for a batch (box 8). If the error is not correctable by these procedures and if the procedures specify that it be examined by the liaison person, then this is done (box 18). The liaison person may be the admissions clerk supervisor or a person in the office who is knowledgeable in data processing and is responsible for liaison and handling exceptions. The liaison person determines what action must be taken (box 19), and communicates it to the Admissions Clerk. The error is then corrected (box 17) and recycled.

The error should be analyzed by the liaison person in consultation with his supervisor and the systems analyst (box 20) to decide whether or not the procedure needs changing (box 21). If changes are necessary, they are made and a new procedure initiated (box 28), and this analysis is terminated (circle 27). If no change is necessary, then this analysis process is also terminated (circle 27).

Another part of the procedure concerns the follow-up on corrections that have to be made. This part of the procedure starts with the results of the VALIDITY run being sent to the Admissions Clerk (box 15). This information is logged by the Processing Center and no action is taken if corrections are made in a specified period—in this case it is three days (box 23 and circle 27). If not, follow-up action is taken, and the supervisor of the Admissions Clerk is notified (box 24). Again no follow-up action is taken if corrections are made in the specified period which in this case is seven days (box 25 and circle 27). If corrections are not made in the specified time, then the liaison person is informed (box 26), the reasons for the delay are analyzed (box 18), and the process recycles until completed.

This discussion of the procedure of input preparation is only a partial illustration of the entire input control procedure. Many details have not been included. For example, the control steps after logging the batch (box 9) or the steps that the admissions clerk must take for making corrections (box 17) have not been specified. Forms to be sent to the student as well as forms for coding and logging, the format of delay instructions, and the needed documents have not been identified. In a Procedures Manual the above should all be identified and explained.

The purpose of Figure 15–3 is to demonstrate some of the important contents of a procedure. It does explain what job must be done, who does it, and when it must be performed. The "why" and "how" are to be explained along with other details in the Procedures Manual.

The procedure that states the time period in which the job must be performed adds a time dimension to the specified sequence of events. These could be specified in time units, such as in boxes 23 and 25, or in units of processing, such as in boxes 4 and 8. In addition, an upper or lower boundary could be specified. For example, there may be a deadline date specified for the processing of admissions forms whereupon the batch values and specified days of waiting are overruled.

The procedure shown in Figure 15–3 can be considered to have three main parts: (1) the steps for normal operations (boxes 1–17); (2) the exceptional problem evaluation (boxes 18–22); and (3) the follow-up of delays (boxes 23–26). Parts (2) and (3) provide the detection of deviation from expected performance and its correction. This closes the control loop. It further facilitates an evaluation which will result in procedural changes, when necessary, in order to improve the efficiency and effectiveness of the system.

PRINCIPLES OF PROCEDURE DESIGN

As mentioned earlier and implied in the previous example, the design of procedures is heuristic. There is no mathematical algorithm for designing procedures. There are, however, some principles of procedure design that should be followed. These are:

1. Personnel must be assigned to jobs in accordance with their capability, responsibility, and authority. Thus a clerk should not be assigned data processing duties of which he or she is not capable, nor should he or she be allowed to make value judgments for which he or she is not authorized. Also, motivation must be considered in assigning personnel.
2. In designing a procedure, human considerations must not be overlooked. Whenever possible, the procedures must not be monotonous, and the job should allow for job enlargement.
3. The boundaries and the domain of each person's responsibility regarding each job should be well specified. For example, in Figure 15–3 the Admissions Clerk must be told through the procedures what errors to correct (box 16) and how to correct them. If errors other than those specified do occur, then the clerk notifies the liaison person who also must have stated decision rules on what has to be done. Actions for unexpected situations should also be specified, such as "consult your supervisor" or "consult the systems analyst." The rules must be well defined, yet they must allow for flexibility of action. Priorities should also be specified. The degree of specificity of procedures will vary with the nature of the environment and its response to external disturbance. As Friedman puts it, "In general, the more disturbances which enter

the system, the greater the need for external control by human beings over these perturbations, and the greater the need for system procedures to 'program' the human being enabling him, to exercise this control (thereby closing the loop)."[4]

4. Procedures should be standardized whenever possible, especially different procedures performed at the same time by the same person. Sometimes, procedures have to be different because of the nature of the problem, such as the processing of regular students and extension students. In such cases, the different processings should be assigned to different persons. If there is a constraint on the number of persons available, then the processing should be staggered in time so that they can be kept separate. This will avoid switching between different procedures for the same job which can cause much confusion, resulting in inaccuracies.
5. Procedures should allow for feedback and evaluation. Statistics should also be maintained on the frequency of errors by type of error so that information useful in tracing errors and in the evaluation of procedures is available. For example, statistics on high error rates resulting from incorrect coding could be traced to a coder who is poorly trained or incapable of meeting the operational standards.
6. The relationship between procedure design and program design has not been shown in the partial network diagram in Figure 15–2. It is implicitly a coordinating function that the systems designer must perform. He must identify situations where a programming change can simplify the procedures. In one university the equivalent of three full-time employees were involved in tracing and resolving errors. This work was reduced by a third as a result of a change in the validity output so that it would identify an error and trace it to a source document. Various listings in different sorting order are often helpful for reference and checking and can save much manual effort. They can also improve morale. Every effort must, therefore, be made to ensure that operations in which the human has the comparative advantage are assigned to people, and operations that can be better done by machine are done by a computer.

   Another example of the comparative advantage of machine over human processing is the operation of replacing a large number of old cards with updated cards (known as **merging**). If the order of the cards (records) is crucial then human processing will most likely result in errors due to the wrong cards being pulled or inserted and cards put in the wrong order. This problem can be overcome by using machines for merging. This will not only add to accuracy of operations but will also save manual labor.

Sometimes constraints on development effort will not allow all operations to be automated, even if this is the logical thing to do. On other occasions it is difficult to decide on trade-offs between extra programming or extra procedures, such as one that will improve morale. Often an administrator may

[4]Friedman, "Design and Production of Systems Procedures," p. 205.

want to eliminate a procedure in order to reduce manual effort by using computer processing, which may cost more effort, even on a recurring basis. This often happens when he is not paying for the processing cost but is paying for the manual cost. Such a choice is a poor economic one for the institution but a good one for the administrator in charge of the manual effort. The responsibility for avoiding such choices often falls to the systems designer and the development team who must look for such situations and decide in terms of improving the whole system. System personnel must also identify situations where human operations will be more effective and efficient than computer operations.

PRODUCTION AND USE OF PROCEDURES MANUALS

Based on the general principles discussed above, procedures should be designed (activities 540–545 and 508–510 in Figure 15–2 on p. 300); tested (activity 545–550) (output procedures are not yet tested since output is not yet available); and documented (shown as a document symbol with events 510 and 545). These documents constitute a Procedures Manual. It should include the manpower requirements resulting from the new procedures. These requirements may require the hiring of personnel. For example, the procedures for registration in a university may require a demand for extra secretarial or keypunch personnel during the peak period. These personnel must then be selected, hired, and trained.

Training may rely heavily on the Procedures Manual. It specifies the jobs that must be performed, which become the basis for training.

Procedure design is expensive. Estimates in the Federal Government show that it costs between $100–$1000 per page, with an average of $400 per page.[5] This cost has the following breakdown:[6]

Planning	$300
Writing	75
Editing, printing, distributing, and filing	25
Total =	$400

[5] *The Directions Improvement Workshop,* No. 63–3104 (Washington, D.C.: General Services Administration, 1963), pp. 4–5.

[6] For another estimate, see J. G. Hendrick, "Company Manuals," *System & Procedures* (2nd. ed.), ed. V. Lazzaro (Englewood Cliffs, N.J.: Prentice-Hall, Inc., 1968), p. 253. Hendrick estimates that it takes five days of work by an experienced systems analyst to develop an average written procedure.

SUMMARY AND CONCLUSIONS

Procedures are a set of instructions concerning a job and are both descriptive and prescriptive. They are descriptive in that they state what the job is and why it should be done. They are prescriptive in that they state how the job should be performed, when it should be performed, and who should perform it. The procedures should also identify what actions should be taken in all cases including unexpected and emergency situations. They perform the following main functions in a system:

1. They are the memory of the designer and administrator as to how a job should be done.
2. They are a quasi-supervisor over operational personnel.
3. They are a document for training new operational personnel and for orientation of administration and systems personnel.
4. They are used for evaluating manpower needs.

Procedures are heuristic and should be evaluated periodically for effectiveness and efficiency. Provisions for feedback on performance should be provided. Procedures are an important part of the development of a system. It is the procedures that make a system operational. Procedure design may involve value judgments that must be made by the administrator. Procedures must be designed with care, for they can affect system performance, especially response time and accuracy.

General rules for procedure design were discussed. These include the need to assign jobs to personnel in relation to their responsibility, authority, and capability. Procedures must be concerned with human engineering and should specify actions for all alternatives; they must be standardized whenever possible; and finally, procedures must allow for evaluation.

In this chapter, an example of general procedures on input control was discussed. Procedures for input and output were mentioned and their relationship in the developmental process was identified in a network diagram. Procedures for operations were not discussed, assuming that this is the responsibility of the processing center. If, however, the administrator is responsible for equipment, then he will be concerned with operational instructions. Also, programming should be considered carefully as an alternative to procedures only when it has a comparative advantage over human operations. The costs and benefits of each must be carefully weighed before the choice is made between them. Considerations of programming and its role in development of systems will be discussed further in the following chapter.

Guidelines for the preparation of procedures can be formulated as a checklist which facilitates the observance of the guidelines.

KEY TERMS

Procedures
Procedures Manual
Distribution List
Validity Run
Control Loop
Merging
Human Engineering

REVIEW QUESTIONS

1. Distinguish between
   Procedures Manual and User's Manual
   Descriptive and Prescriptive Procedures
2. Why is it important to maintain an accurate distribution list?
3. What are four uses of the Procedures Manual?
4. Why aren't all procedures automated?
5. What are the principal functions of procedures?
6. What are the consequences of not providing adequate procedures?

CHAPTER 15: SELECTED ANNOTATED BIBLIOGRAPHY

BERGSTROM, K. "Procedures and Manuals," *Ideas for Management.* Cleveland, Ohio: Systems and Procedures Assoc., 1962, pp. 90–105. Excellent definitions of procedure and manual are included. The discussion includes the purpose and objective of written procedures, design considerations, and the installation and timing of revised procedures. Steps taken by the procedures analyst for ensuring proper procedure are listed and discussed.

BURCHFIELD, D., "Systems Analysis: Quantified Decision-Making Procedures," *Administrative Management,* XXIX, No. 2 (November 1968), 36–38. This discussion is in general terms and can serve as a base for managers and students; however, it is not specifically aimed at automated systems. Included is a working description of the systems analysis technique and how managers can use it in controlling resources.

CHAPANIS, A., "Words, Words, Words," *Human Factors,* VII (February 1965), 1–17. The words that are used in our man-machine environment must be studied by the human factor engineer. Changes in the words used can produce greater improvements in performance than human engineering changes of the system. Recommended for all who must communicate regardless of content.

FRIEDMAN, L. A., "Design and Production of Systems Procedures," in *Developing a Computer-Based Information System,* ed. P. E. Rosove. New York: John Wiley & Sons Inc., 1967, Chap. VII, pp. 199–234. System procedures are necessary to operate, control, utilize, and prepare an information system, or in other words, they describe and prescribe the operating interconnections of each system component. In addition to giving some good examples of system procedures, ten basic ground rules are listed for use in presenting the procedures and for ensuring that their information content is adequate to enable them to perform their functions. To the credit of the author, he also discusses some human interface requirements and points out that the most useful inputs to procedures design are the human interface requirements.

HAGA, C. I., "Procedure Manuals," *Ideas for Management.* Cleveland, Ohio: Systems and Procedures Assoc., 1968. Questions such as when should written procedures be instituted and how can they be best utilized are answered, the anatomy of a procedure is discussed as well as the use of Hybrid flowcharts in procedures design. Considerations, such as format and indexing, are covered and excellent examples of proper and improper design are given.

HENDRICK, J. G., "Company Manuals," in *Systems and Procedures,* ed. V. Lazzaro. Englewood Cliffs, N.J.: Prentice-Hall, Inc., 1968, pp. 240–62. The author discusses the design and updating procedures and the organization used in the organizational manual and the procedure manual. The techniques discussed can be used as guidelines for the development of other manuals.

KURKE, M. A., "Operational Sequence Diagrams in Systems Design," *Human Factors,* 3 (March 1961), 66–73. The uses of operational sequence diagrams for analysis of alternate actions analysis of communications requirements between groups and coordination of information-decision-action sequences between interfacing subsystems are discussed in specific terms. Included is an introductory description of operational sequence diagrams. Recommended for practicing managers and students.

MATTHIES, L. H., "The Management Role of a Procedures Manual," *Ideas for Management.* Cleveland, Ohio: Systems and Procedures Assoc., 1963, pp. 1–14. Procedure Manuals are discussed as tools of management. The author discusses why some procedure manuals fail to guide the efforts of the people concerned. Included is a breakdown of procedure-manual costs per page. The seven essential types of information and how they should be communicated are discussed. Techniques for distribution, indexing, appearance, and updating are presented.

SONDEL, B., "Systems and Procedures," *Ideas for Management.* Cleveland, Ohio: Systems and Procedures Assoc., 1965, pp. 124–29. This is a discussion from the viewpoint that systems and procedures are separate processes both aimed at achieving a desired goal-state. Included is a section on the operational means-end hypotheses and the cyclic, open-ended feedback loop for procedures.

SULLIVAN, D. C., "Procedures and Manuals," *Ideas for Management.* Cleveland, Ohio:

Systems and Procedures Assoc., 1962, pp. 106–17. Advantages of manuals are listed and the types are each discussed. Included is a discussion of flowcharts used in procedure manuals, and considerations for publication of manuals.

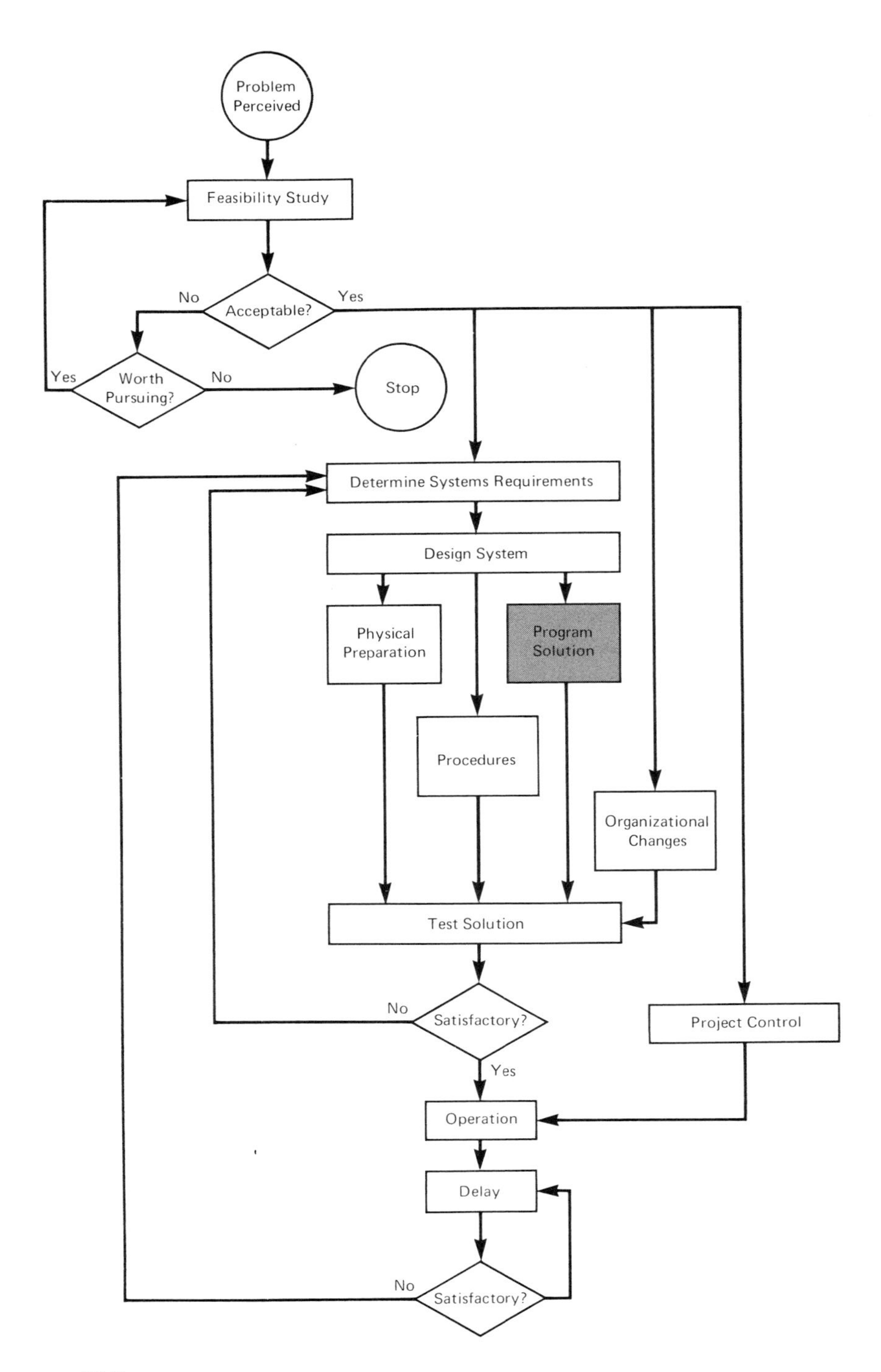
Problem Perceived
Feasibility Study
Acceptable?
No
Yes
Worth Pursuing?
Yes
No
Stop
Determine Systems Requirements
Design System
Physical Preparation
Program Solution
Procedures
Organizational Changes
Test Solution
Satisfactory?
No
Yes
Project Control
Operation
Delay
Satisfactory?
No

16

Determining a Solution

INTRODUCTION

The production of a solution is discussed in this chapter. The activities involved in this phase are primarily programming activities, the details of which do not concern the administration directly. It is important, though, that the administrator appreciate the nature, need, and importance of these activities. The purpose of this chapter is to provide such an appreciation. Also discussed in this chapter is a related set of problems, that of conversion of files —the transformation from the old to the new files.

SOME PROGRAMMING RELATED ACTIVITIES

Selecting Programming Languages

Many systems these days require programming effort. However, before programming starts it is necessary to prepare and plan for the programming effort. This includes the activity of selecting the programming language (activity 400–415 in Figure 16–1).

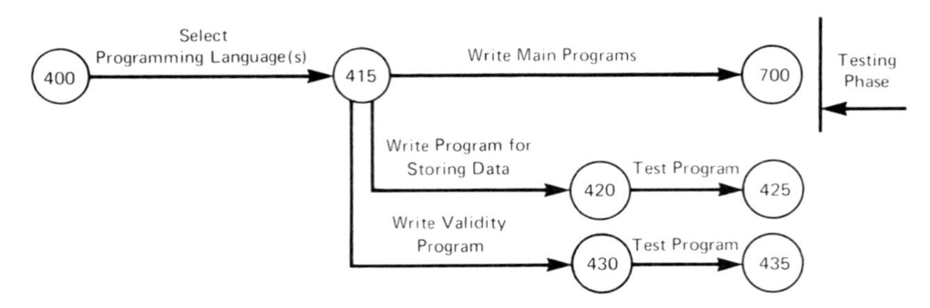

Figure 16–1. Partial Network Diagram Showing Programming Activities

There may be no selection if the programming language to be used is specified as a user requirement (in or before the design phase), or if the choice is constrained due to limitations of equipment and personnel capabilities. However, when there is a choice it must be made with great care because it can affect the flexibility of the system, its efficiency, and its effectiveness.

The consideration of flexibility is important, due to the fact that many languages, especially machine languages, are machine-dependent. With a change in the computer system (and this happens frequently in educational institutions) a machine-dependent programming system becomes useless. A machine-independent language is therefore desirable.[1] Also, it makes the hiring of programming personnel somewhat easier. There are, however, some situations where machine-dependent languages alone can process a file, or can process it much faster. Therefore, the trade-off must be examined carefully before the choice is made.

Too often, the programming language chosen is the one the programming staff knows best. This may or may not be the most efficient and effective language. The programmers may do this because they are under pressure for production work and have no time to investigate other languages. Such a situation should be discouraged. Programmers should be given the time to learn and to keep abreast of their fast-moving field. With the installation of a new computer system it is very important that programmers be freed from production work to study the new languages available to them so that they may use the one best suited for the needs of the institution.

[1]For a comparison between two important machine-independent languages (FORTRAN and COBOL), see *Management Services,* May-June, 1966, p. 47. For a survey evaluation of the most common business oriented language, see A. J. Borenstine, "Over 1000 Systems Men Evaluate COBOL," *Data Processing Magazine,* XVIII, No. 8 (August 1966), 24–30.

The administrator's understanding and encouragement is helpful in this connection. He must consider the time spent in such preparation as an important investment for the future.

Other programming choices concern the use of **packages,** a group of programs designed to perform a specific or general-purpose function.[2] There are many of these available for information retrieval, for management information systems, and for solving operations research problems. For example, for finding a solution to a project network there were 26 selected computer programs available as early as 1964.[3] Many of these have unique capabilities, and their values to the user must be weighed against the cost of acquiring them and their ability to adapt to the local equipment configuration.

Educational institutions are often willing to share their programs at no cost or nominal cost with other educational institutions. Sharing organizations exist and the availability of shared programs could save development costs.[4]

Institutions like to think that they are unique, but many information systems problems are common to most, and administrators should weigh their dislike of borrowing against the savings that are frequently possible. Recently, computer manufacturers and educationally oriented institutions[5] have developed program packages[6] and offered them for functional applications. Some of these are largely machine-independent so that in many institutions they can be quickly adapted with a high benefit-cost ratio. Such packages should be carefully considered before starting one's own programming.

Programming Activities

The actual programming work is identified in Figure 16–1 by activities 415–700, 415–420, and 415–430. The first activity concerns the main program. The latter two activities concern programming for the storing of data and the checking of data respectively. These activities must be tested (activities 420–425 and 430–435 in Figure 16–1) in parallel with the writing of the main program. The latter is tested only after all other related activities are completed.

[2] *IBM System/360 University/College Information System,* No. E20–0192–0, (White Plains, N.Y..: International Business Machines Corporation, 1966), 46 p.

[3] J. J. Moder and C. R. Phillips, *Project Management with CPM and PERT* (New York: Reinhold Publishing Corporation, 1964), pp. 255–60.

[4] *The EIN Software Catalogue* published by EDUCOM has a number of programs available at institutions of higher learning. CAUSE is another institution that facilitates such exchange.

[5] For an example see American College Testing Program, *Financial Aid Services,* 1968–69.

[6] "Applications Packages: Coming Into Their Own," *EDP Analyzer,* V, No. 7 (July 1967), 1–10.

CONVERSION

Conversion in information processing systems is the changing from one type of system to another. The change may be in hardware (discussed in Chapter 14) or in information needs. In the latter case conversion would require changing from an old file (or no file) to a new file. This type of conversion will be discussed below.

The conversion of files requires five distinct steps. These are:

1. Plan conversion
2. Collect data
3. Validate data
4. Store data
5. Test conversion

In this chapter, only the first four steps will be discussed. The fifth step is not discussed in detail in this book, but is referred to later as in Figure 16–2.

Planning Conversion

There are many approaches to conversion. One approach is to collect only the additional data needed. This requires supplementing the existing data available in different files (already in machine-readable form) with additional data needed.

Another approach is to collect all the required data including recollecting what is already available. In some cases, this is better than the method of using the data already available because the latter may be less accurate and hence will contribute to the unreliability of the new information. Also, sometimes the marginal cost of some additional data is small.

The choice of conversion approach may or may not have been specified in the User's Requirement Phase of the Development Process. If not, then the choice must be made before the required data can be collected. This is part of the planning activity shown as activity 400–440 in Figure 16–2.

Another aspect of planning conversion is the need to "freeze" new applications related to the system change being implemented. This moratorium of new applications should apply not only to file conversions where the file is being changed, but also to equipment conversions where the file may or may not change but the existing programs will change because they must be rewritten. If new applications related to conversion are developed during conversion, then they too must be reprogrammed, resulting in considerable wasted effort. There will, of course, always be exceptions. Development of very small programs and very important programs during a long conversion period may be justified. But, in general, new related applications programs should not be developed during a conversion. This decision should preferably be made very early in the development process, immediately after the feasibility study. It was not mentioned in the discussion on feasibility because the term **conversion** was not introduced or defined at that point.

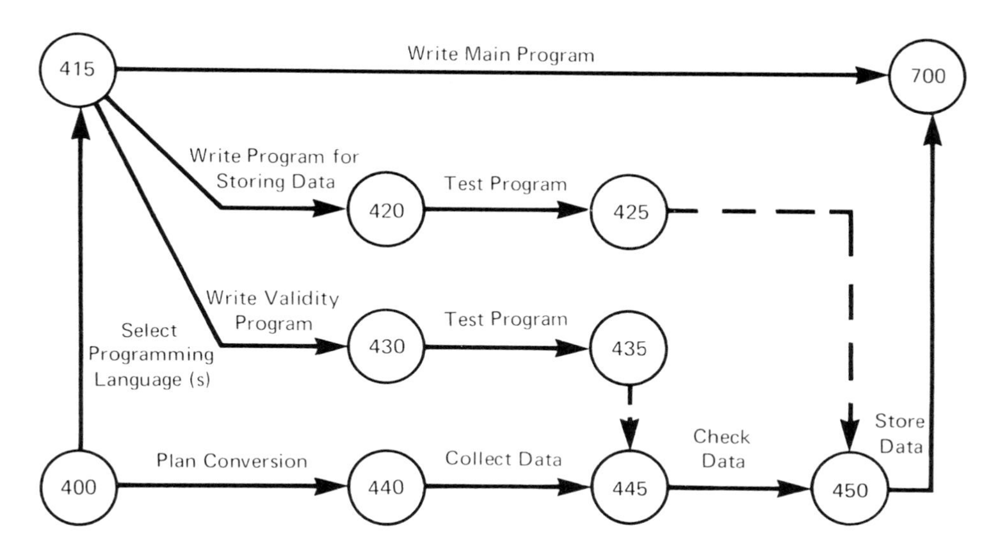

Figure 16–2. Partial Network Diagram Showing Conversion and Related Activities

Collection of Data

If the data is collected from existing machine-readable data, then data-processing operations (perhaps including some programming) are required to collect it. If the data must be collected from the source, such as students or faculty, then various means of input preparation must be considered. Since conversion is a one-shot nonrecurring operation, it is not necessary to be bound by hardware available in the institution. Optical scanning should be considered and such services can be paid for, borrowed from another institution, or traded for other services rendered.

In cases of collecting data from the source, it is often necessary to design special forms and procedures. This is not shown in Figure 16–2 where the entire data collection process (form design, procedure design, equipment acquisition, and data preparation into machine-readable form) is shown as one activity (440–445).

Validating Data

Once the data for the new file has been collected, it has to be checked for validity (activity 445–450). The validity check can be performed by glance verification; machine verification, such as the use of a machine verifier to check the keypunching; or by using computer validity programs[7]; or a combination of the above. The checking should be thorough because the accuracy and usefulness of output is dependent on the accuracy of input.

In Figure 16–2 it is assumed that the data will be checked by a **validity** program (preceded by activities 415–430–435–445). This validity program would identify missing data, data outside expected ranges or specified values, and data format that is meaningless (such as a numeric value for a name data field).

Storing Data

Once the data has been checked satisfactorily, it is ready to store in the file in the prescribed format. This is trivial, in some cases, and depends on the nature of the data and the software available. In other cases, it may require a special program. This possibility is depicted in the partial network in Figure 16–2 where the tested program for storing data in a file (activities 415–420–425–450) is a prerequisite to the storing data activity 450–700.

UPDATING ACTIVITIES

The updating of a file is the recording of changes in the value of the data elements. In other words, it is bringing the file up-to-date with current data.

The need for updating arises because data changes, sometimes regularly, sometimes irregularly. Examples of such changes will be given, followed by a discussion of the specification of an **update** subsystem.

Sources of Changes to a File

In educational institutions many changes in a file are periodic and cyclic. Some occur once a year. For example, the addition of new buildings to a campus and the erasing of old buildings usually occurs at the beginning of an academic year. The space file must accordingly be changed. Other changes

[7]A **validity** program is sometimes confused with an **edit** program. The latter does not check data but adds (such as decimal points or $ signs) or deletes data (such as suppressing leading zeros). For a good discussion of **editing,** see G. Dippel and W. C. House, *Information Systems* (Glenview, Ill.: Scott, Foresman and Company, 1969), p. 260.

occur at the beginning of each semester. For example, new and returning students are admitted and new courses are offered. The student file and the curricula file must be updated. Similarly, at the end of the semester many changes take place. Some students graduate and others drop out. All students get grades and for some students it affects their scholastic standing. In most of the above cases, the majority of the file is affected and hence the entire file is processed, usually, in sequential order.

Other changes can occur irregularly and selectively; for example, when a student changes his address or when a female student gets married and her name and marital status change. Or take the case of the student who discovers that she used her girl friend's social security number to register (this has happened!). Other examples of irregular changes to a file are changes in address, changes in grades, changes in courses being taken, and changes required by a validity program. These changes are not only irregular but selective. They do not affect the entire file. Hence, procedures for updating such information must have a selective capability or else it will be inefficient.

Specification of the Updating Subsystem

The data elements in files that need to be updated must be specified. The activity for establishing the updating specifications is shown in a partial network diagram in Figure 16–3 as activity 400–460. The factors to be considered are:

What to Update?
- Files
  - Data Elements

When?
- Sequence
- Frequency
  - Too Often: Unnecessary Cost
  - Too Seldom: File Becomes Outdated
- Authorization

How?
- Procedures

Designing Forms and Procedures

Once the updating subsystem requirements are specified, the steps must be taken to implement these requirements. One step is to design forms that will collect the data necessary for the updating procedures. The principles of form and procedure design for input and output have already been discussed. They will also apply to the forms and procedures needed for updating. The important objectives of updating procedures are to control unauthorized and unnecessary updating and to ensure that the updating is complete, accurate, and timely.

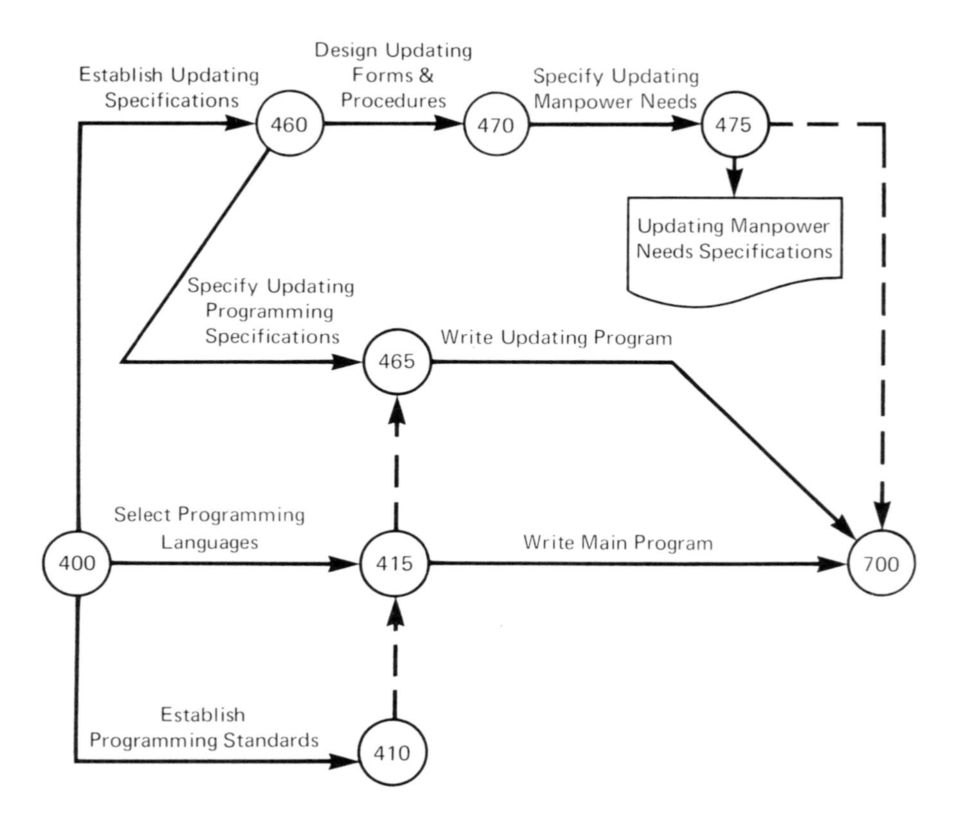

Figure 16–3. Partial Network Diagram Showing Maintenance Programming and Related Activities

Manpower Needs for Updating

The design of forms and procedures needed for updating enables the specification of the manpower requirements for performing this function. This activity is shown as 470–475 in Figure 16–3. The document of manpower specifications generated by this activity should be forwarded to personnel responsible for manpower training so that personnel will be trained to perform this function.

The Updating Program

A set of activities parallel to the designing of forms and procedures is the programming of the update program. The updating specification activity (400–460 in Figure 16–3) is followed by a detailed specification of the programs required (activity 460–465). This is followed by the activity 465–700 in which the actual programming is written. However, this programming activity must be preceded by the activity that establishes programming standards, activity 400–410. The sequence prerequisite is met by the dummy activity 415–465. Another prerequisite is the selection of the programming language shown as activity 400–415.

SUMMARY AND CONCLUSIONS

In this chapter the different programming activities for determining a solution were discussed. For a computer information system there are four sets of programming activities: those for the main program, the data storage program, the validity program, and the update program. The programming of the data storage and validity program can be written along with the main program. Typically, however, they are done independently of the main program because they are needed as prerequisites for the conversion process. The separation thus enables the conversion to proceed parallel to the main program and reduces the overall time span required for project completion. Also parallel is the set of activities for the completion of the update program. These programs are then all ready for the testing stage.

Each of the sets of activities in this stage has been shown in a partial network diagram in Figures 16–1, 16–2, and 16–3. Their interrelationships are shown in Figure 16–4. Some program-related activities are technical and not of interest to a typical administrator. These activities are not shown or discussed.

The practice of separating or combining the design with the programming stages varies with different projects. In some cases, all the designing is done by the systems designer and in other cases the programmer does the design of some subsystems. As Heany puts it, "It is not easy to pinpoint where systems-design work leaves off and programming work begins. One individual may both design and program a system." Heany adds that the programmer's involvement in system development depends on

> the designer's knowledge of programming and the available computer configuration as well as the level of detail reflected in his design specifications. Some designers are content to work out their logic in general terms leaving their programmer free to implement it as he sees fit. Other designers provide so much detail that there is little left for their programmers to do but translate each design

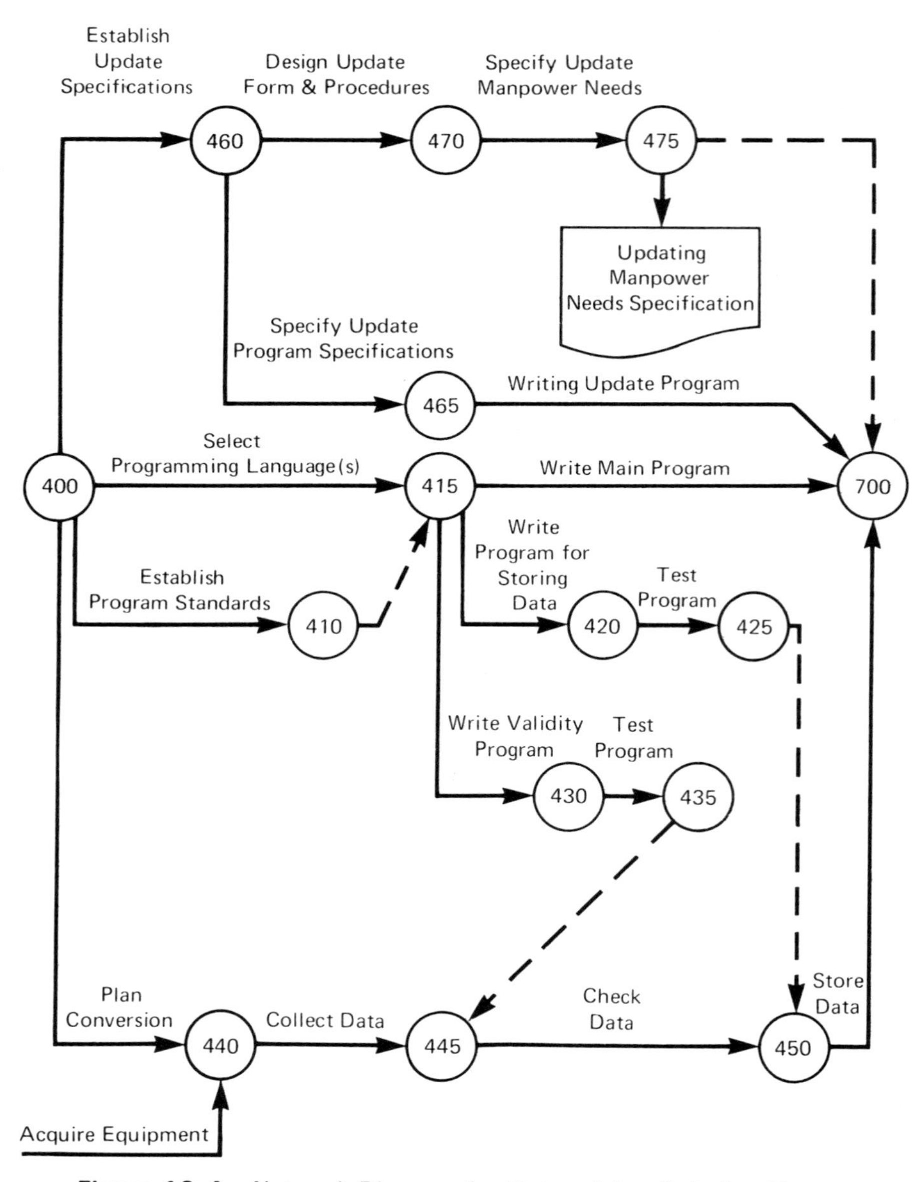

Figure 16–4. Network Diagram for Determining Solution Phase

symbol into a computer instruction. This represents an extravagant use of design talent.[8]

Some of the programs generated in this stage of systems development are not tested. This will be done in a later stage of overall system testing. Meanwhile, one other set of activities being performed in parallel must be discussed: organizational and personnel changes. This is the subject of the next chapter.

KEY TERMS

Conversion	Program Package
Programming Language	Validity Check
Machine-Dependent	Machine-Readable Data
Machine-Independent	Higher-Level Language

REVIEW QUESTIONS

1. Distinguish between
   Update Program and Validity Program
   Edit Program and Validity Program
   Machine-Dependent and Machine-Independent
2. Describe four programming type activities.
3. What are the approaches to conversion? Describe each
4. What methods may be used to validate data?
5. In your functional field, describe five sources of changes to files which would require updating of the files?

CHAPTER 16: SELECTED ANNOTATED BIBLIOGRAPHY

"Application Packages: Coming Into Their Own," *EDP Analyzer,* V, No. 7 (July 1967), 1–10. Application packages are general computer programs written to handle specific problems. Examples of packages already in use are given, and the discussion touches on the trade-off involved when using a package, and some warnings to package subscribers.

BOUTELL, W. S., "Problem-Oriented Languages: FORTRAN vs. COBOL," *Management Services,* May-June 1966, pp. 41–48. A good empirical comparison of the two major languages for business-oriented applications.

[8]D. F. Heany, *Development of Information Systems: What Management Needs to Know* (New York: The Ronald Press, 1968), p. 93.

BRANDON, D. H., "Methods Standards in Programming, Parts 1 and 2," *Management Standards for Data Processing.* New York: D. Van Nostrand Company, Inc., 1963, Chap. IV and V, pp. 69–143. Part One discusses the block method as a standard of analysis, coding standards, and general programming rules. Part Two discusses in some detail program and system-testing procedures, the development of standard techniques and subroutines, and necessary documentation standards and considerations.

CHAPIN, N., "What Choice of Programming Languages," *Computers and Automation,* XIV, No. 2 (1965), 12–14. The author contends that many computer users have their choice of programming language dictated by their hardware or computer manufacturer. Within these limits, Chapin presents eight major considerations that should be contended with when determining the programming language to be used.

CONNELY, J. J., "Design and Production of Computer Programs," in *Developing A Computer-Based Information System,* ed. P. E. Rosove. New York: John Wiley & Sons, Inc., 1967, Chap. V, pp. 138–67. This chapter describes the production process for a set of computer programs in an information system development context. Mr. Connely discusses the specific process actually used in the production of a program system, namely the Strategic Air Command 465L Planning Subsystem. For purposes of discussion the production process is divided into five phases: translation, design, coding, verification, and internal release. In order to produce a good system, managers must themselves utilize a system of production, i.e., a "production process."

KRAUSS, L. I., *Administering and Controlling the Company Data Processing Function.* Englewood Cliffs, N.J.: Prentice-Hall, Inc., 1969, Chap. III, pp. 49–103. Each step in the management effort of producing an applications system is discussed. A discussion of coordination and control for systems programming is presented. Included are work-activity controls, the management of changes, and documentation standards, recommended for practicing and future managers.

RUBEY, R. J., "A Comparative Evaluation of PL/1," *Datamation,* XIV, No. 12 (December 1968), 22–25. This article displays the results of a comparison of PL/1 with the languages COBOL, FORTRAN, and JOVIAL in applications of business, simulations, and data management respectively. Observed variables included are programmer time, total number of source statements required, as well as compilation and execution times. Both business executives and system managers can gain from this article.

SAMMETT, J. E., *Programming Languages: History and Fundamentals.* Englewood Cliffs, N.J.: Prentice-Hall, Inc., 1969, pp. 1–29. This is a general introduction to programming languages. Topics include a classification of languages and a discussion of the factors involved in the choice of a language.

SCHWARTZ, J. E., "Comparing Programming Languages," *Computers and Automation,* XIV, No. 2 (February 1965), 15–16. The author presents a brief discussion of the complexities involved when comparing programming languages, and some specific considerations about several languages such as FORTRAN, ALGOL, JOVIAL, MAD, and LISP. Recommended reading for anyone involved with computers.

SNYDER, R. G., "Programming Documentation," *Datamation,* XI. No. 10 (October 1965), 44–46. This is an excellent guide for anyone interested in programming documentation and suggests answers to two key questions: (1) what should be included in the documentation, and (2) how can maximum use be made of the completed documentation?

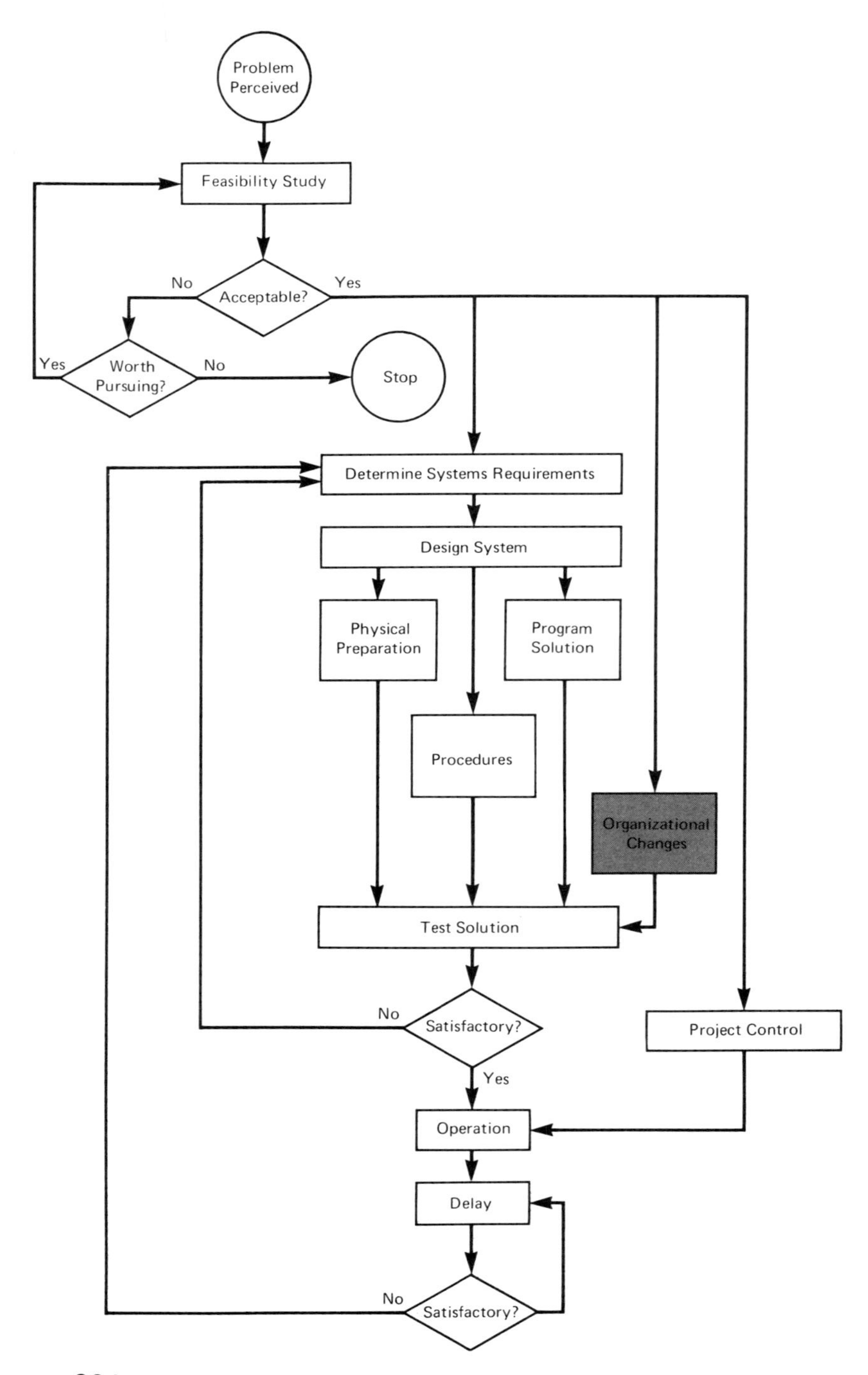
Problem Perceived
Feasibility Study
No
Acceptable?
Yes
Yes
Worth Pursuing?
No
Stop
Determine Systems Requirements
Design System
Physical Preparation
Program Solution
Procedures
Organizational Changes
Test Solution
No
Satisfactory?
Yes
Project Control
Operation
Delay
No
Satisfactory?

17

Organizational and Personnel Considerations

INTRODUCTION

In previous chapters, the roles that equipment, forms, procedures, and programming played in the development of an information system were examined. In this chapter, the design of the last of the important elements in information systems development will be discussed: organizational and personnel changes.

A new information system often affects the manner in which tasks and jobs are performed. Some jobs are eliminated, others are created, and still others are old but have to be performed differently. Personnel have to be selected and trained for jobs to be performed in the new system. Also, supervisors and administrators have to be oriented as to the objectives of the system, its development process, and its operation. These activities require careful planning and execution.

The restructuring of tasks and jobs in the new system affects the span of control[1] of supervisors and administrators, the number of and relationships between staff and line positions, and the style of decision-making and administration. Adjustment to the new environment requires structural changes. Trade-offs between structural changes and personnel changes must be made in order to improve system performance.

The above considerations will be examined in this chapter. The order of topics is as follows:

Training of personnel

Orientation of personnel

Organizational considerations

The discussion in this chapter will exclude the systems department[2] because it does not directly concern the typical administrator in education.

The structure of this chapter will follow that of the previous chapters: discussion of related activities in the context of their partial network diagrams, followed by the overall network diagram of all the activities concerning personnel and organizational changes.

TRAINING AND RELATED ACTIVITIES

All training and orientation starts after the manpower needs for the system are specified. This is identified in Figure 17–1, by the dummy activity 355–615, where event 355 is the generation of the document on manpower specifications discussed in Chapter 13. Another prerequisite is the need for planning and policy-making on personnel and organizational changes. This is identified by activity 610–615 in Figure 17–1.

Planning and policy-making are often required as preparation for a systems change. The magnitude and nature depend, of course, on the nature of the new system. One area that requires planning is job classifications and

[1]This refers to the number of subordinates that report directly to an administrator. For a discussion of this concept, see H. A. Simon, *Administrative Behavior* (2nd ed.) (New York: The Macmillan Company, 1958), pp. 26–28.

[2]For references on this subject, see *DEP Analyzer,* IV, No. 11 (Nobember 1966), pp. 1–11; *IBM Organizing the Data Processing Installation,* No. C20–1622–0, (White Plains, N.Y.: International Business Machines Corporation, n.d.), p. 62; P. H. Thurston, "Who Should Control Information Systems?" *Harvard Business Review,* XL, No. 6 (November-December, 1962), 135–39; L. H. Hattery, Organizing for Data Processing Systems," *Advanced Management,* XXVI (March 1961), 23–25; Dearden, "How to Organize Information System," *Harvard Business Review,* XLIII, No. 2 (March-April 1965), 65–73; and G. J. Brabble and E. B. Hutchins, "Electronic Computers and Management Organization," *California Management Review,* Fall 1963, pp. 33–42.

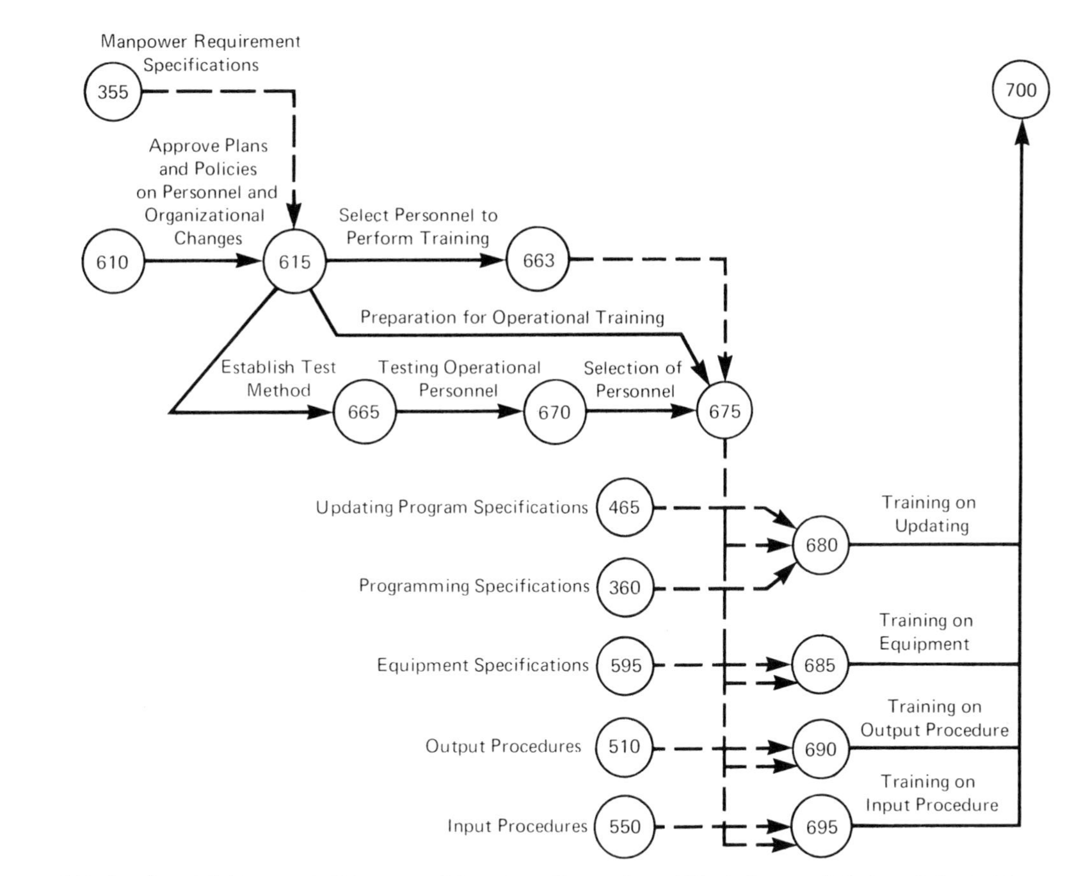

Figure 17–1. Partial Network Diagram Showing Operational Training and Related Activities

job descriptions.[3] In hiring the desired personnel, the colleges and universities are in a relatively favorable position. Even though they cannot always compete with industry in salaries, they can offer educational opportunities and an academic environment attractive to systems personnel. If the institution offers courses in Computer Science, it has a good opportunity for attracting and discovering systems talent. But to retain such personnel, the hiring institution must offer competitive or near competitive salaries in addition to fringe benefits and a desirable working atmosphere.

After planning for changes, a number of parallel activities must be performed. One set consists of three activities in a series: establish test methods (activity 615–665); test personnel (activity 665–670); and finally, select personnel (activity 670–675).

Other sets of activities relate to the preparation of operational training (activity 615–675) and the selection of personnel to perform the training (activity 615–663). The responsibility for training often falls to the systems personnel, who may be the only ones sufficiently acquainted with the new system and who have the ability to train. However, if the supervisors of the new system have the capability to train, then they should do so. This reduces the burden on the systems personnel and increases the involvement of supervisory personnel. Furthermore, supervisory personnel know the organizational process better than the systems personnel. An alternative to such "in-house" training is to send personnel to training schools, either commercial training institutes or schools run by manufacturers. This method reduces the number of personnel required for training but is more costly and does not offer supervisory involvement or organizational knowledge.

Once the operational personnel are selected, training personnel selected, and preparations for operational training completed, the training can then proceed.

Each type of training requires its corresponding specifications. These are shown in Figure 17–1 as 465–680, 360–680, 595–685, 570–690, and 550–695.

The sequence of activities in Figure 17–1 (and other network diagrams) may vary with the project. For example, in a small organization the trainee for updating, equipment, output and input procedures may be one person, and hence the training may best be done in sequence rather than in parallel. This may not pose a serious problem since these activities are typically not on the critical path and hence enough time is available for sequential training. If time is short, then training can be done on overtime.

Another variation in the activity sequence relates to the starting of

[3]For job descriptions in information systems, see *IBM Management Planning Guide for a Manual of Data Processing Standards,* No. C20–1670–1 (White Plains, N.Y.: International Business Machines Corporation, n.d.), pp. 6–10; and D. H. Brandon, *Management Standards for Data Processing* (Princeton, N.J.: D. Van Nostrand Company, Inc., 1963), pp. 345–47.

training activities. Instead of starting after all the trainees are selected (as shown by event 675 in Figure 17–1), each training activity could start after its respective trainees are selected. Thus the trainee selection and training on updating could be done in parallel to the selection and training on input procedures, provided of course other prerequisites are completed. The choice between a parallel set of activities and the sequence shown in Figure 17–1 is a function of the nature of the project and of the resources (time and personnel) available for these activities. It is a project decision that must be made by the project manager.

Training of Systems Analysts and Programmers

Systems analysts and programmers, in some cases, do not report exclusively to the Processing Center but to the administrator needing such personnel. It is then the responsibility of the administrator to select and train his personnel. The relevant activities are shown in Figure 17–2. All are self-explanatory and will not be discussed further.

Selecting[4] and training systems personnel is often a technical matter for which many an administrator relies upon other systems personnel in the institution or on outside consultants. In many cases, all systems personnel are part of a centralized systems department[5] and this problem does not then arise.

ORIENTATION PROGRAM

Nature of Orientation

Orientation must be distinguished from training. As Rosove puts it:

> Objectives of . . . varieties of training were the acquisition of basic skills by personnel, the development of satisfactory personnel, man-machine, and man-computer program interactions, and, in general, over-all improvement in system performance under all varieties of potential real-life situations. Orientation, by

[4]On selection of systems personnel, there are two conflicting viewpoints in W. J. McNamara and J. L. Hughes, "A Review of Research on the Selection of Computer Programmers," *Personnel Psychology,* XIV, No. 1 (Spring 1961), 39–51; and R. C. Vergin, "Staffing of Computer Departments," *Personnel Administration,* XXVIII, No. 4 (July-August 1965), 6–12. See also M. W. Wofsey, *Management of Automatic Data Processing* (Washington, D.C.: The Thompson Book Company, 1968), pp. 43–65.

[5]For the view ". . . *data processing* activity can and should be centralized," see J. Dearden, "How to Organize Information Systems," *Harvard Business Review,* XLIII, No. 2 (March-April 1965), 68.

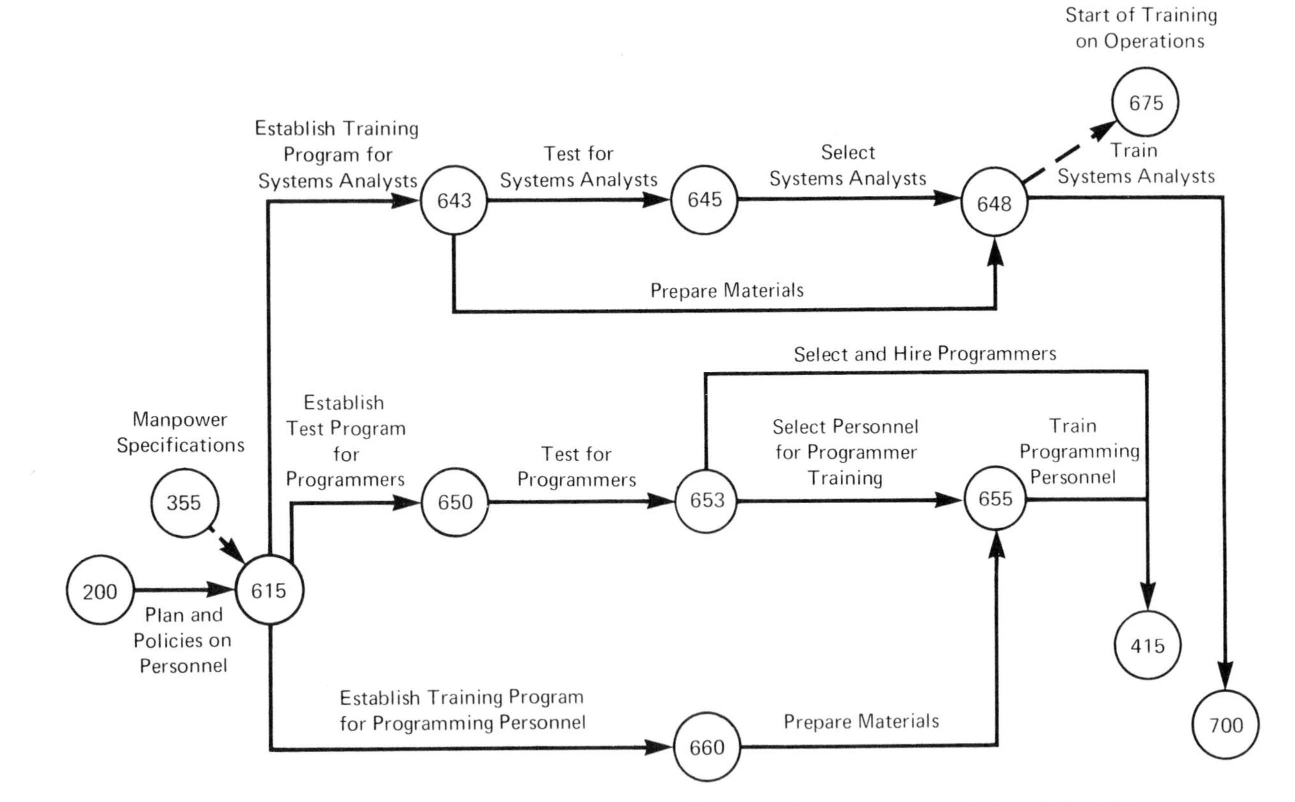

Figure 17–2. Partial Network Diagram for Training of Systems Personnel and Related Activities

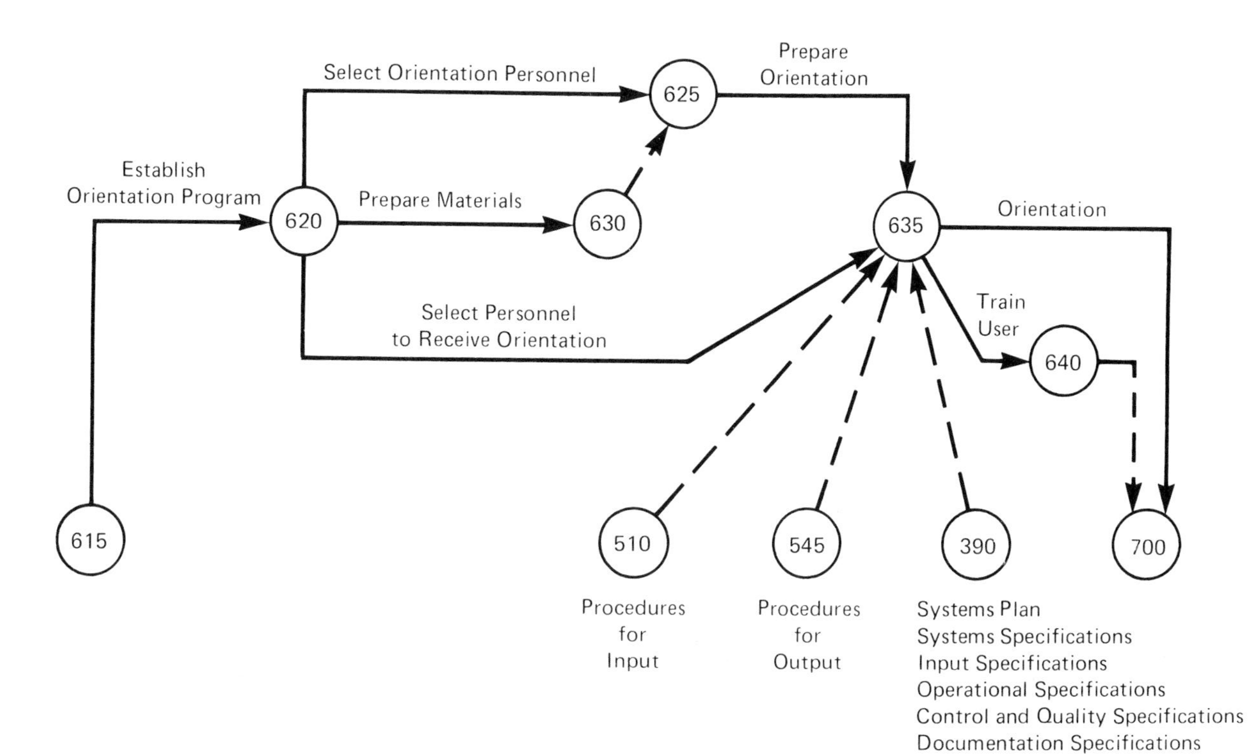

Figure 17–3. Partial Network Diagram Showing Orientation and Related Activities

contrast, is a learning situation in which the users of the system are *introduced* to it. The larger and more complex the information system, the more essential is the requirement for user personnel to be introduced to it at a general level before the installation phase and then again at an intensive, detailed level during this phase. It is the inherent complexity of information systems which compels this distinction between orientation and training. Experience has shown that user personnel must have an opportunity to attempt to comprehend such systems intellectually and as total systems before they undertake more mechanical efforts to make the system work in an operational environment . . . The orientation program is important in that it establishes for user personnel the foundation of knowledge about the system upon which all their future learning will be built. The conduct of the orientation and the substantive knowledge presented to the users also serve to contribute to the establishment of basic attitudes toward the system.[6]

Orientation Activities

To accomplish orientation a set of activities is necessary. This is shown in Figure 17–3. It requires as prerequisites the completion of manpower requirement specifications (event 355 in Figure 17–2), which identify the type, nature, and scope of the orientation program required. It starts with the establishment of an orientation program. This requires a decision on the content of the material to be presented in orientation (activity 615–620 in Figure 17–3). A listing of some of the relevant material follows:

1. Objectives of System
   - Short Term
   - Long Term
   - Relationship to
     - Organizational Goals
     - Overall System's Goals
2. Limitations of System
3. System's Environment
   - Applications
   - Equipment
4. Process of Development
   - Nature
   - Stages
5. Resources Required
   - Time
     - Critical Path

[6]From *Developing a Computer-Based Information System* by Perry E. Rosove. Copyright © 1969 by John Wiley & Sons, Inc. By permission of John Wiley & Sons, Inc.

- Monetary
- Personnel

6. Role of
   - User
   - Systems Personnel

The selection of the personnel to be oriented is important and the decision must be made with care. Traditionally, orientation is directed exclusively towards administrators and supervisors. This practice is shown graphically in Figure 17–4 (a).

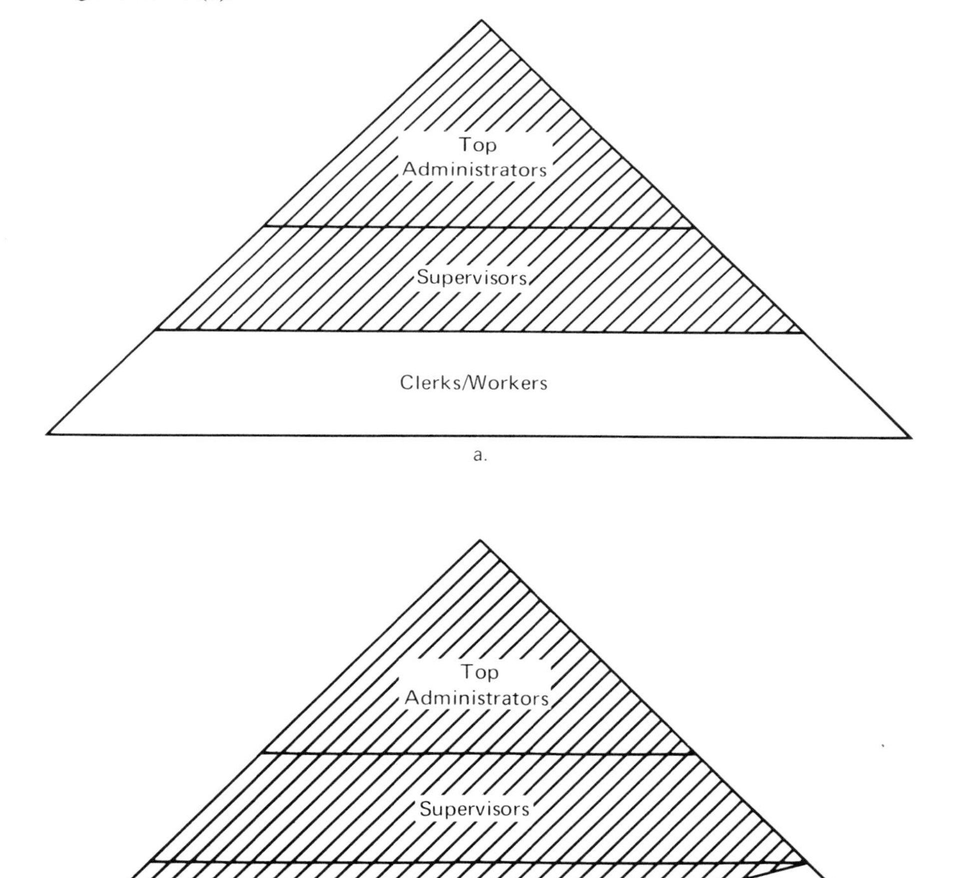

Figure 17–4 (a) (b). Strategies for Systems Orientation

The shaded area shows the level of the users included in the orientation program strategy, and excludes all clerks and workers. This can be harmful to systems effectiveness. System orientation should permeate all through the organization and include the workers and clerks that are affected. This strategy is shown in Figure 17–4 (b). The shaded area would vary with organizational structures and planning strategies, with the depth of material covered depending on the level of personnel being oriented.

Other orientation activities shown in Figure 17–3 are self-explanatory except, perhaps, the training activity (635–640). It is not strictly an orientation activity but it is closely related. It consists of training the administrator and supervisor in using equipment, if any, such as a terminal.

ORGANIZATIONAL CHANGES

An information system can have a profound impact on the organization structure of an institution. This is evidenced in a study done by Wendler, who questioned 75 specialists in the field of systems design and members of the Systems Procedures Association. One question was on the importance of the fact that "management must understand that the impact on organization structure can be far reaching." Three respondents did not consider this a fundamental tenet, 64 considered the tenet of "major" importance, and 8 considered it of intermediate importance. On the proposition that "to achieve the ultimate goal may mean radical reorganization of the company," 49 considered it of major significance, 17 found it of intermediate significance, 1 found it of no significance.[7] Wendler's findings are based on businesses but these seem to be valid for many educational institutions.[8] Wendler concludes:

> The impact of the total systems concept on organizational structure can be far reaching. To achieve the ultimate goal may mean radical reorganization of the company, and its present systems and procedures. It could possibly eliminate whole ranks of supervisors and middle management; some departments may disappear or merge with others; functions will change; and the duties of top management will change. Top management reluctant to make these changes can deter progress. The pertinent point is whether top management is willing to make these changes![9]

In addition to making structural changes in the departments affected by the information system, there is also often the need to develop special organiza-

[7]C. C. Wendler, *Total Systems Characteristics and Implementation* (Cleveland, Ohio: Systems and Procedures Association, 1966), p. 88.

[8]For another view on the importance of structural organizational changes, see C. Argyris, *Integrating the Individual and the Organization* (New York: John Wiley & Sons, Inc., 1964), Chaps. VIII and XIII, pp. 164–91 and 272–78.

[9]Wendler, *Total Systems Characteristics*, p. 45.

tional relationships between the user department and the information processing center. Other organizational effects result from displacement and unemployment of personnel, as well as from resistance to the information system. These considerations will not be developed further, not because they are of little relevance to the administrator, but because they are part of a general problem relating to automation that is well discussed elsewhere.[10]

The organizational activities are shown in a partial network diagram in Figure 17–5.

SUMMARY AND CONCLUSIONS

The partial networks developed in this chapter are aggregated in Figure 17–6. These activities are of three main types: training, orientation, and organizational changes. The first two are educational in nature and unfortunately are often neglected. These activities are crucial to the success of a changed system and hence they must be well planned and carefully implemented. A haphazard exposure can do more harm than good. A little but not enough knowledge can be dangerous. An attempt to provide too much may cause loss of personnel interest or may frighten them away. The right amount presented through appropriate media must be offered at the right time to personnel needing such information.

Organizational changes are sometimes necessary for an information system to be effective. These are:

1. Structural change to user's department
2. Structural change to organization
3. Relationship between user and systems personnel
4. Displacement and unemployment of personnel

These considerations were identified but not discussed because they are part of a general topic discussed elsewhere in the literature.

This concludes the discussion of the development of information systems. The use of such a system is the subject of the remaining part of the book.

[10]On unemployment and displacement, see R. C. Vergin and A. J. Grimes, "Management Myths and EDP," *California Management Review,* VII, No. 1 (Fall 1964), 63–64; E. Weinberg, "Experience with the Introduction of Office Automation," *Monthly Labor Review,* LXXXIII, No. 4 (April 1960), 376–80; and Ida R. Hoos, "When the Computer Takes over the Office," *Harvard Business Review,* XXXVIII, No. 4 (July-August 1960), 103–5. On resistance to computerized information systems, see A. O. Putnam, "The Human Side of Management Systems," *Business Automation,* November, 1968, pp. 42–48; L. P. Smith, "Management Problems in a Changing Technological Environment," *Computers & Automation,* XIV, No. 4 (April 1965), 18–22; L. K. Williams, *Systems & Procedures Journal,* XV, No. 4 (July-August, 1964), 40–43, and A. Zander, "Resistance to Change—Its Analysis and Prevention," *Advanced Management Journal,* January, 1950.

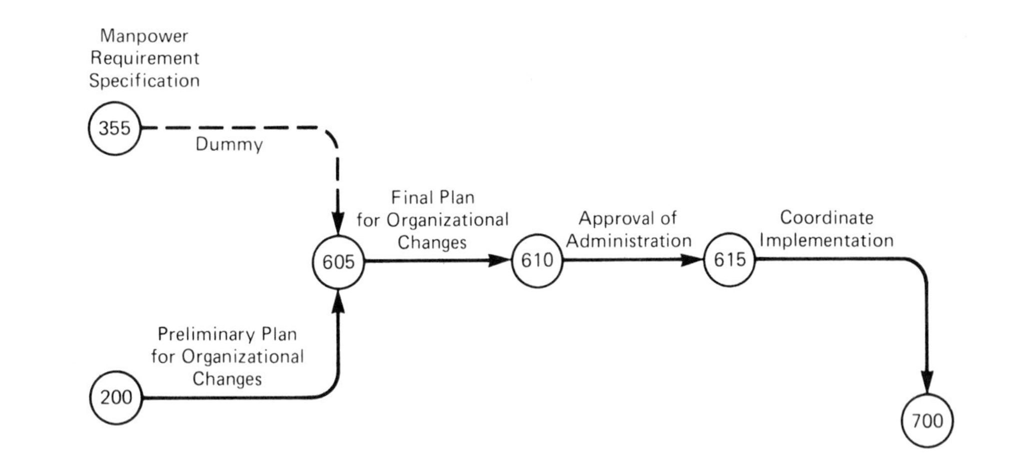

Figure 17–5. Partial Network Diagram for Planning for Organization and Personnel Changes in Activities

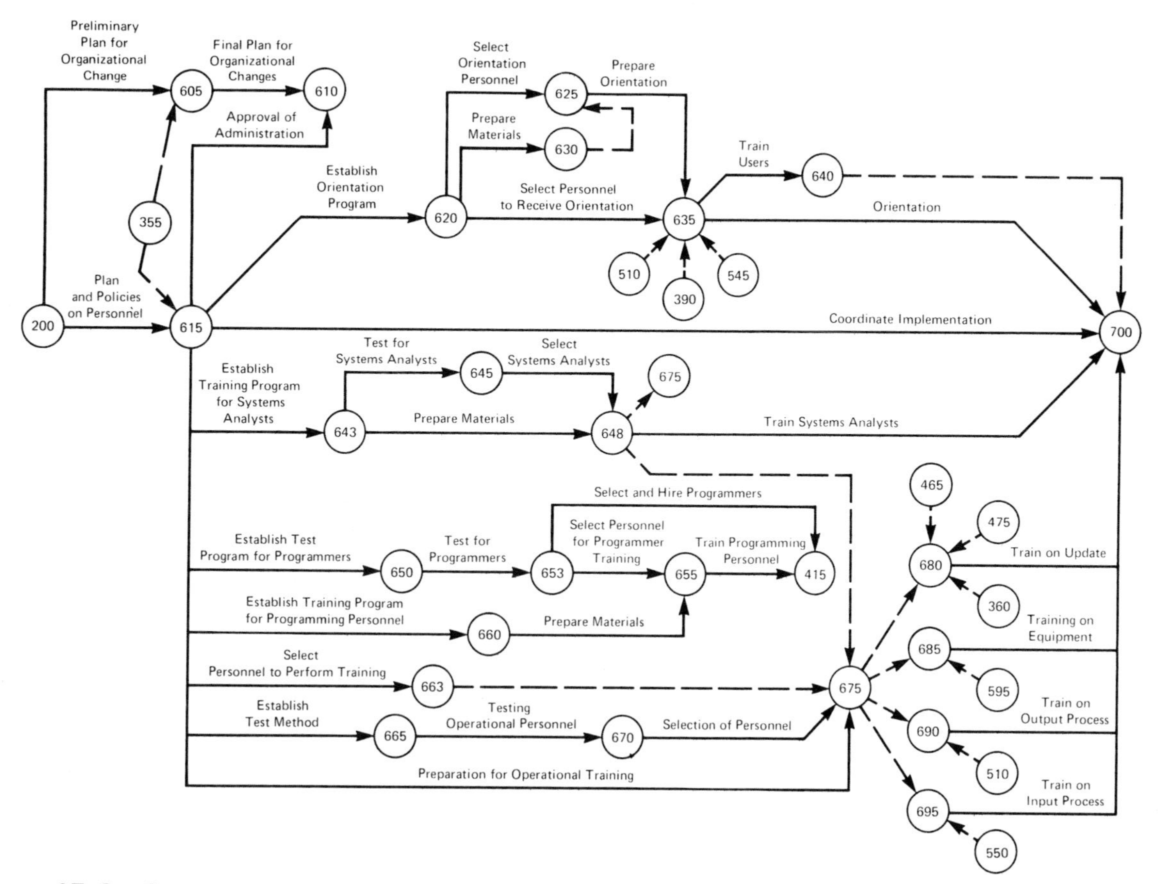

Figure 17–6. Overall Network Diagram for Personnel and Organizational Change Activities

In it the organizational implications of the use of an information system are also discussed. This is distinct from the organizational changes required for the development of an information system—a subject discussed in this chapter.

KEY TERMS

Training
Orientation
Span of Control
Strategies of Orientation

REVIEW QUESTIONS

1. Distinguish between
   Training Systems Analysts and Training Programmers
   Training and Orientation
2. Who in the organization should be oriented?
3. What documents are required to be completed prior to orientation activities?
4. Why should the administrator be trained in system use?
5. Why should system orientation permeate all through the organization?
6. What type of training should be provided to administrators and supervisors?

CHAPTER 17: SELECTED ANNOTATED BIBLIOGRAPHY

BURLINGAME, J. F., "Information Technology and Decentralization," *Harvard Business Review,* XXXIX, No. 6 (November 1961), 121–26. The author believes that with experience in decentralized organizations coupled with a realistic evaluation of the nature and extent of the future impact of information technology in such organizations, a very reasonable basis can be established for concluding that decentralization and the middle manager are much more likely to grow and flourish than to wither and die in the decades ahead. In assessing the future impact of information technology on decentralized business, some attention must be paid to the two important aspects of decision-making: (1) the way decisions are classified and (2) the way responsibility for them is assigned.

DERBY, E. M., "Selecting and Training Systems Man," in *Systems & Procedures* (2nd ed.), ed. V. Lazzaro. Englewood Cliffs, N.J.: Prentice-Hall, Inc., 1968, Chap. XVII, pp. 451–69. In this chapter three main areas are discussed: (1) the qualities of a competent systems man, (2) the methods by which candidates can be selected, and (3) the type of training necessary. Of interest to administrators who may be charged with finding systems men, three fields deserve attention—present employees not engaged in systems work, systems employees of other companies, and recent college graduates.

IBM Management Planning Guide for a Manual of Data Processing Standards (C20–1670–1). White Plains, N.Y.: International Business Machines Corporation, pp. 6–10. The purpose of the manual is to assist in the choice of standards and their implementation. Included here are job descriptions and responsibilities of key management personnel, such as the data-processing manager, staff services manager, senior systems analyst, and several others.

JOHNSON, R. A., F. E. KAST, and J. E. ROSENZWEIG, *The Theory and Management of Systems.* New York: McGraw-Hill Book Company, Inc., 1963, Chap. XIV, pp. 365–400. This is a discussion of the human aspects of the systems concept. Recognition must be given to the needs, motivations, and aspirations of all groups at all levels within the organization. The major problem in terms of systems and people is one of adherence to systems which are already in existence. The crucial problem is ability of the individual and group to change from one type of systematic relationship to another. Resistance develops primarily because of changing sociological relations and because economic well-being is threatened. To lessen resistance to change requires that planning for human components of a system be integrated with planning for machine and technical developments, i.e., man is considered as one of the major components of a total system rather than merely a user.

LOUGHARY, J. W., "Preparation of Educators in the Age of Computers and New Media," in *Man-Machine Systems in Education,* ed. J. W. Loughary. New York: Harper and Row, 1966, pp. 209–22. The following topics are discussed in non-technical terms: the new competencies needed for implementation and operation of man-machine systems in education; the new types of personnel needed; and the changes in professional education programs required to provide the new competencies in educational personnel.

"Management Training in Data Processing," *EDP Analyzer,* VI, No. 5 (May 1968), 1–11. This article provides an excellent guideline for developing a training program for executives. Approaching the project from the position that executive needs are in project selection, systems design, conversion planning, and communication, the article gives the program characteristics, with an hourly breakdown by subject and with the objectives of each seminar. Suggestions on implementation, depth of discussion, and choice of textbooks are included.

MCRAE, T. W., *The Impact of Computers and Accounting.* New York: John Wiley & Sons, Inc., 1964, Chap. VIII and IX, pp. 217–56. Chapter 8 deals with EDP and the structure of management and Chapter 9 deals with the problem of education. The author provides and discusses an organization chart of an EDP department to include a list of duties and responsibilities of each person or each group in the department. The broad solution offered as to the location of the EDP department within the firm is that it should be a part of an "information department," together with the accounting department and, if one exists, the operational research department. EDP education plays a crucial role in the success or failure of every EDP venture and to emphasize this importance, a detailed discussion of a curriculum for information technology is presented in Chapter 9.

MILLER,, R. B., "Task Description and Analysis," in *Psychological Principles in Sys-*

tems Development, ed. R. M. Gagne. New York: Holt, Rinehart and Winston, Inc., 1962, pp. 187–226. This is a comprehensive and readable treatise of task description and analysis. Topics presented are the purposes of task description in conjunction with system development; the general rationale for task description; the nature of task description including categories of operation and vernacular; and finally, the structure of tasks and task analysis.

ROSOVE, P. E., *Developing a Computer Based Information System.* New York: John Wiley & Sons, Inc. 1967, Chap. VI pp. 168–98 and Chap VIII, pp. 235–78. Chapter 6 provides a list and a discussion of the major steps involved in the process of detailed personnel and organizational analysis and design. These steps include: (1) task performance analysis, (2) the identification of special personnel requirements, (3) the grouping of tasks, (4) the definitions of positions, (5) the estimation of personnel manning, (6) the definition of the organization structure, and (7) the creation of the personnel test and evaluation plan. In Chapter 8, the author presents his views on the development of the training program which may be required when an enterprise acquires a "new" large-scale, computer-based information system. The entire orientation of this chapter is derived from experience with training programs developed for military command and control systems. Based on this experience the following basic training principles were developed: (1) exercise as large a part of the system at one time as possible, (2) provide a simulated environment which is as realistic as possible, (3) observe and record selected aspects of system performance, (4) provide system personnel with knowledge of results, (5) exercise the system at a frequency which is consistent with high learning motivation.

SANDERS, D. H., *Computers in Business—An Introduction.* New York: McGraw-Hill Book Company, Inc., 1968, Chap. XIII and XIV, pp. 279–310. These chapters present material concerning the preparation for the changeover from a manual system to an electronic data-processing system. Because resistance to the change to EDP is the rule rather than the exception, personnel preparation should be carried out during and after the feasibility study. The author discusses the following four steps that can be taken to prepare personnel for the computer transition: (1) keep employees informed, (2) seek employee participation, (3) use managerial evaluation, and (4) consider the timing of the change. Chapter 14 is devoted to a discussion of the selection and training of workers for the new jobs connected with EDP and the effects of EDP on existing occupations and on the number of workers employed. Dr. Sanders points out that most businesses have found that it is preferable to select suitable candidates internally; however, when suitable candidates are not available internally, the company must resort to external sources. The selection process may be facilitated by the use of aptitude scores, personal interviews, and background records. From a training standpoint, it is pointed out that the most extensive training must be given to analysts and programmers.

WEINBERG, E., "Experiences with the Introduction of Office Automation," *Monthly Labor Review,* LXXXIII, No. 4 (April 1960), 376–80. Although written in 1960, the summarized findings of a government study of what personnel problems were involved and how they were solved when 20 firms and government agencies installed electronic computers for data processing still have some application. Of particular interest are the findings concerning the extent of displacement and reassignment, and the practices regarding transferring, retraining, and selecting employees for new occupations.

WOFSEY, M. W., *Management of Automatic Data Processing Systems.* Washington, D.C.: Thompson Book Company, 1968, Chap. III, V, and VI pp. 43–66, 97–122. The text results from a doctoral dissertation at the American University. Chapter 3 deals with personnel selection and discusses problems involved in the selection of a data-processing director, systems analysts, and programmers and desirable personal characteristics and selection methods for each. Chapter 5 discusses the relationships between the data-processing department personnel and organizations external to the department. Included are four categories of external relations. Chapter 6 differentiates training and education and discusses the training, both external and internal, of the data-processing department.

part five

USES OF INFORMATION SYSTEMS

18

Uses of an Information System

INTRODUCTION

The previous discussion on the nature and development of an information systems provides the necessary background and knowledge for examining an important set of questions relating to information systems: How can information systems be used for decision-making at the different levels of administration in education? How does the use of information systems alter the data needs of the organization? How does it affect the structure of administrative decision-making and, indeed, the structure of the organization?

These and other related questions are the subject of this chapter. They will be examined in the context of the nature of decision-making in education. To identify the context, we first need a definition of a decision and a classification of decisions in education.

CLASSIFICATION OF DECISIONS

A decision is a choice among alternatives.[1] It may be the choice involved in admitting a student, in hiring personnel, in allocating resources, or in selecting a site for a new campus. A classification of these and other decisions appears in Figure 18–1. The rows therein identify the type of decision, while the columns identify the function of the decision. Each combination of the type of decision and its function is identified by a cell in the table. Each cell will be discussed below.

Function → / Type of Decision ↓	Operations	Operational Control	Management (Administrative) Control	Stategic Planning
Programmed	1	3	5	7
Non-Programmed	2	4	6	8

Figure 18–1. Classification of Decisions

The distinction between programmed and nonprogrammed decisions was first made by Herbert Simon.[2] He identified decisions that can be stated in terms of decision rules (of the type discussed in Chapter 3 on Decision Tables). Computer programs can, then, be written to make such decisions and are called "programmed decisions." These decisions concern situations that are well structured, often conceptually simple, and that occur routinely and repetitively. In contrast, nonprogrammed decisions are those that are ill-structured, typically complex in nature, and that occur once in a while and often involve major consequences.

There are many examples of programmed and nonprogrammed decisions in education. Payroll is typically a programmed decision, while faculty hiring is always an unprogrammed decision. Many classes of problems, how-

[1]For an excellent exposition of decisions and decision-making in higher education, see John Dale Russell "Decision Making in Higher Education," speech at the conference of the Association of Institutional Research, Athens, Georgia, 1967, 23 pp.

[2]H. A. Simon, *The New Science of Management Decisions* (New York: Harper & Row, 1960), pp. 5–8.

ever, involve decisions that are neither completely programmed nor completely nonprogrammed. For example, consider the grading of exams. Some faculty members with large classes prepare an objective exam, assign weights to the questions, and insist on students using mark-sensed sheets for answering the questions; thereafter, grading can be fully programmed and computer programs can do the scoring and assign the grades. In many situations, however, there are borderline and special cases. These can be identified and treated separately as nonprogrammed decisions. In exams of the essay type, all grading decisions are nonprogrammed. Other examples of this continuum between programmed and nonprogrammed decisions are decisions concerning admissions, suspensions, or probations of students. The clear-cut cases are programmed, others are nonprogrammed decisions. Some classes of problems tend to be more programmed than nonprogrammed and this depends on the nature of the functions to be performed. One classification of these functions is shown as columns in Figure 18–1.

Column 1 (from left) of Figure 18–1 is operational decisions. Programmed operational decisions are payroll, sectioning of classes (and in some cases assignment of faculty), student fee computations, accounting of dollars payable, student transcript preparation, and student grade reporting. Nonprogrammed operational decisions include hiring and firing of operational personnel and the assignment of faculty.

Other functional types of decisions are operational control, management or administrative control, and strategic planning. These have been defined by Anthony as follows:[3]

(1) Operational control is the process of assuring that specific tasks are carried out effectively and efficiently.
(2) Management control is the process by which managers assure that resources are obtained and used effectively and efficiently in the accomplishment of the organization's objectives.
(3) Strategic planning is the process of deciding on objectives of the organization, on changes in these objectives, on the resources used to attain these objectives, and on the policies that are to govern the acquisition, use, and disposition of these resources.

Examples of programmed decisions in operational control are inventory control, graduation checks, student status decisions (i.e., probation, suspension, and off-probation), and some decisions in accounting. Examples of non-

[3]Robert N. Anthony, *Planning and Control Systems: A Framework for Analysis* (Cambridge, Mass.: Harvard University, Division of Research, Graduate School of Business Administration, 1965), pp. 16–18. For another set of definitions and in the context of higher education, see R. L. Ackoff, "Toward Strategic Planning of Education," in O.E.C.D., *Efficiency in Resource Utilization in Education* (Paris: O.E.C.D., 1969), pp. 339–57.

programmed decisions in operational control are certain budgetary and financial decisions, including short-term investment decisions and cost control. Examples of programmed administrative control decisions are analysis resulting in such decisions are budget variances, faculty activity (also called faculty load) analysis, student grade analysis, space, utilization analysis, departmental cost analysis, and project control. Examples of unprogrammed administrative control decisions include personnel hiring and firing, and equipment acquisition decisions. Finally, comes the function of strategic planning. There are few, if any, examples of programmed decisions in this category (cell 7). Decisions of strategic planning are typically of the unprogrammed type (cell 8) and include decisions of curricula, selection of sites for campuses, and capital investment decisions.

The above discussion of a classification of decisions now enables us to answer the questions posed earlier: What decisions can be and should be made by information systems? The most logical type of decisions are the programmed operations type decisions (cell 1 in Figure 18–1). Examples have been cited above. The nonprogrammed operational decisions (cell 2 in Figure 18–1) cannot be made by information systems, given the current state of the art, and this is true of all nonprogrammed decisions (cells 4, 6, and 8). These decisions have traditionally been made using judgment, intuition, and creativity. But how this is done cannot yet be stated in terms of operational decision rules. There is no decision theory that fully explains this behavior. Simon predicts that by 1985 "we shall have acquired an extensive and empirically tested theory of human cognitive processes and their interaction with human emotions, attitudes and values."[4] Norbert Wiener predicts that whatever man can do, a computer will also do[5] but does not specify a point in time when this will happen. It seems very probable, though, that it will not happen in the immediate or even near future. Man will still make the decisions that require an ability to recognize and infer patterns from data to allow for nonquantifiable variables—especially the human variable—and to make the value judgments necessary for both programmed and nonprogrammed decisions.

CONTROL DECISIONS

There are two types of control decisions: operational and administrative. The first type is identified by cells 3 and 4 in Figure 18–1. They have been

[4]Quoted by J. M. Bergey and R. C. Slover, "Administration in the 1980's," *S.A.M. Advanced Management Journal,* XXXIV, No. 2 (April 1969), 31.

[5]*Ibid.,* p. 26.

mentioned earlier and need no further discussion. The other type of control —administrative—will be discussed in this section.

Administrative control decisions (cell 5 in Figure 18–1) are not conceptually complex but do require considerable manipulation of data. The most common examples of such decisions are financial. Traditionally, they involved a periodic comparison of budgetary line items with actual expenditures, along with auditing. Advanced information systems also have these features, though the approaches to auditing,[6] and especially the use of an AuditTrail, have changed. Also changed is the derivation of the line item—the source for control. Traditionally, the line items were based on estimates and projections made by the department head and approved or modified by higher levels of administration. In advanced information systems the line items are generated by using PPBS—a Planning, Programming, Budgeting System.[7] In it, planning is the selection of overall long-range objectives translated into programs—a course of action necessary to carry out the plans. These are then translated into budgets necessary to carry out the programs. Furthermore, these budgetary decisions are for one to ten years which is particularly relevant to education where the product (an academic award) has a gestation period of two to ten years.

Another financial control technique is that of costing. Unit costs calculated over a period of time identify trends that must be controlled. Costing should not, however, be used as a measure of performance unless all other conditions, especially the benefits, are the same. This, however, is seldom the case. Differences exist in course requirements, course content, course objectives and philosophy, approaches to teaching, ratios of faculty to students, support facilities, etc. Furthermore, the procedures for allocating indirect and support costs (e.g., library and computational facilities) to academic programs vary greatly. Even the procedures for calculating support costs (e.g., cost of space for a classroom shared by different departments) vary. Finally, there are definitional problems, especially the definition of a program. These problems are important and difficult, but they are not insurmountable. Current research[8] in this area is promising. Meanwhile, institutions can use costing for internal

[6]For a good discussion of this topic see D. H. Li, *Accounting, Computers Management Information Systems* (New York: McGraw-Hill Book Company, 1968); and Gordon B. Davis, *Auditing & EDP* (New York: American Institute of Certified Public Accountants, 1968).

[7]For an excellent discussion of PPBS in higher education, see J. Farmer, *Why Planning, Programming, Budgeting Systems for Higher Education?* (Boulder, Colo.: WICHE, 1970). For a longer discussion see H. J. Hartley, *Educational Planning-Programming-Budgeting—A Systems Approach* (Englewood Cliffs, N.J.: Prentice-Hall, Inc., 1968).

[8]Many national Task Forces are working at the National Center for Higher Education Management Systems on subjects such as Program Classification Structure, Data Element Dictionary, Cost Finding Principles, Cost Exchange, and Faculty Activity Analysis.

purposes. In addition to control, costing can be used for planning and institutional research.

Other techniques of control include statistical analysis; Control Charts used for analyzing variances and deviations; inventory models used for inventory control; and techniques such as GANNT charts, CPM, and PERT[9] used for project control.

Many of the techniques discussed above are referred to as techniques in Operations Research and Management Science. Some are old, such as inventory control, others are relatively new, such as CPM and PERT. All, however, are being increasingly used in computerized information systems. This is sometimes a result of the needs of the data files (e.g., Statistical Control Charts); sometimes because of the needs of both the computational facility and data (e.g., Costing). Such needs of data will be considered after a discussion of planning models, our next subject.

PLANNING DECISIONS

Planning decisions—especially those that allocate resources—are complex and often require mathematical and statistical techniques commonly associated with the discipline of Operations Research and Management Science. They have been used very effectively in many businesses and industries. Unfortunately, they are not all applicable to the educational problem of resource allocation. This is especially true of mathematical programming that calculates the optimal levels of production given resource constraints. The model requires a weighting of each objective. This is not easy in education, in which we cannot even agree on indexes of educational output,[10] let alone be able to measure and weigh them. We cannot, therefore, use mathematical programming or rigorous approaches to cost-benefit analysis. Instead, attempts have been made that are less ambitious and look only at the cost sector. One model used often is a simulation model where the resource consequences of different sets of alternatives are computed and the administrator selects one that is both feasible and, hopefully, has a high-benefit ratio. The choice may not be the best or optimal choice, but it is better than a choice made otherwise.

There are numerous cost simulation models in higher education. CAM-

[9]For the use of these techniques in education, see H. W. Handy and K. M. Hussain, *Network Analysis for Educational Management* (Englewood Cliffs, N.J.: Prentice-Hall, Inc. 1969).

[10]See John Keller, "Higher Education Objectives: Measures of Performance and Effectiveness," in *Management Information Systems: Their Development and Use in the Administration of Higher Education,* eds. John Minter & Ben Lawrence (Boulder, Colo.: WICHE, 1969), pp. 79–84.

PUS (Comprehensive Analytical Models for Planning in University Systems); CAP:SC (Computer Assisted Planning Model for Small Colleges); CSM (Cost Simulation Model), and others.[11]

These models have not been used extensively, largely because they are too complex or make large demands on data and equipment. To make such models more accessible to institutions of higher learning, the U.S. Office of Education subsidized the development and implementation of a model by NCHEMS, the National Center for Higher Education in Management Systems. The model known as RRPM–1, the Resource Requirement Prediction Model 1[12] was released in December 1971. There is a need for this simulation model, or similar models, to be incorporated into information systems for education, because the competition for resources by other welfare needs of the country is demanding a more rational allocation of resources in education, and such a model does offer one viable solution to these problems.

The role of a simulation model in the planning process can be depicted as in Figure 18–2. In it, the model provides information that the decision-maker can use in evaluating the consequences of alternative resource decisions. Faced with the responsibility of decision-making, the administrator is simultaneously concerned with the societal environment and his evaluation of the performance of the institution (box 3 using boxes 1 & 2). Assessment of these and other factors leads to establishment of modification of the goals and objectives as well as priorities and policies for their attainment (boxes 4 and 5). This influences the administrator who then makes a trial decision (exit of box 6) and uses the planning model (box 7) to calculate the resource consequences of that decision. This calculation is based on data (box 9) which consists of the institutional data (box 8) and the environmental data (box 1). The results are displayed in analytical reports (symbol 10).

After reviewing the consequences of his trial decision, the administrator may wish to change the values selected for some of the planning variables and recalculate the resource consequences. The cycle (boxes 6, 7, and 10) continues until the administrator is satisfied. The long-term resource decisions are then translated into budgets and other resource allocations (exit of box 12), result-

[11]For a comparison of thirty such models, see George B. Weathersby and M. C. Weinstein, *A Structural Comparison of Analytical Models for University Planning,* Paper P–12 (Berkeley, Cal.: Office of Analytical Studies, University of California, 1970). For an annotated bibliography of the original sources of some of these models, see K. M. Hussain, *A Resource Requirements Prediction Model (RRPM–1): Guide for the Project Manager,* Technical Report 20 (Boulder, Colo.: NCHEMS at WICHE, 1971), pp. 94–108.

[12]For an introduction to the model, see W. Gulko & K. M. Hussain, *A Resource Requirements Prediction Model (RRPM–1): An Introduction to the Model,* Technical Report 19 (Boulder, Colo.: NCHEMS at WICHE, 1971). For a report on its pilot testing and release, see K. M. Hussain & James S. Martin, *A Resource Requirements Prediction Model (RRPM–1): Report on the Pilot Studies,* Technical Report 21 (Boulder, Colo.: NCHEMS at WICHE, 1971).

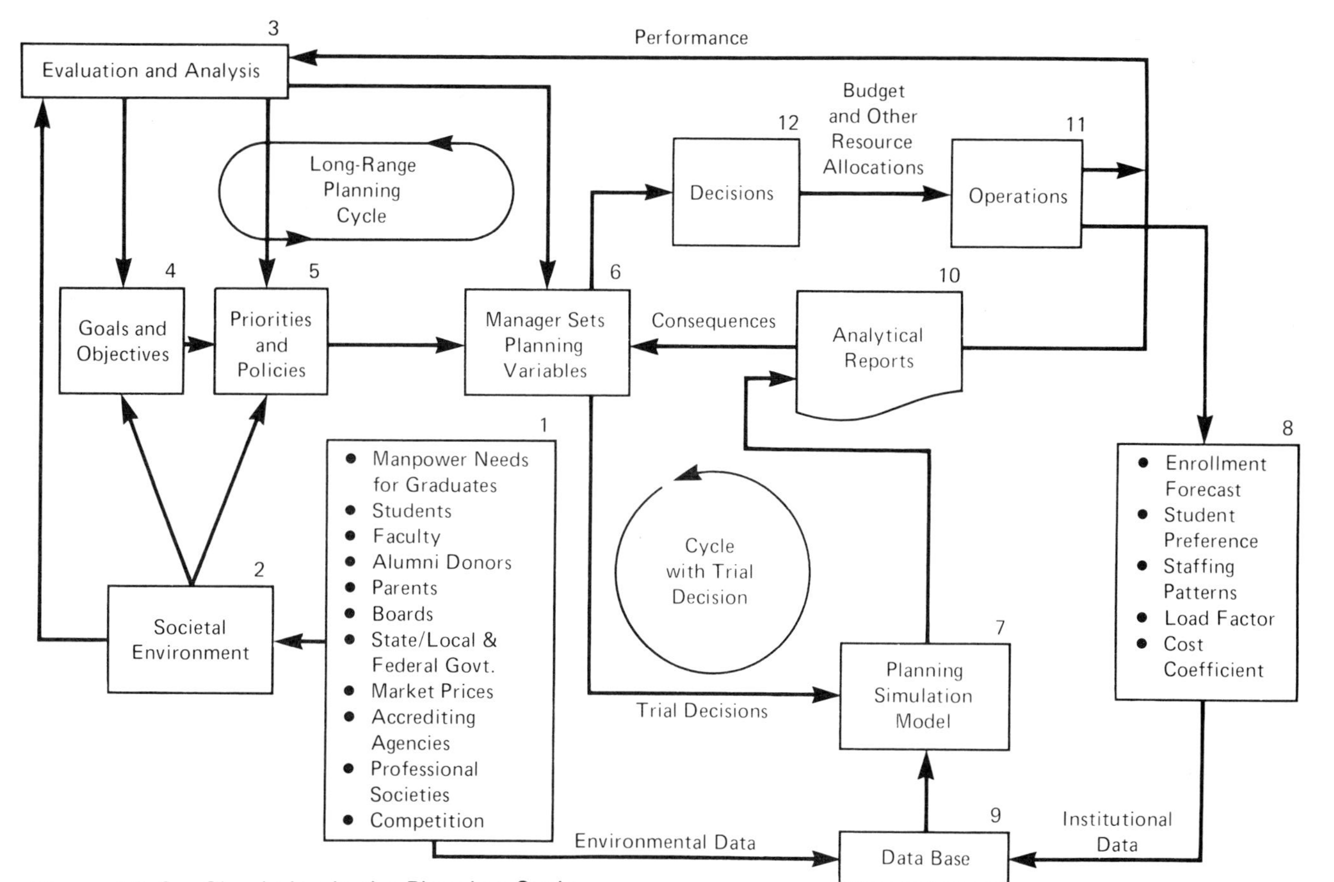

Figure 18–2. Simulation in the Planning Cycle

ing in operations of the institution (box 11). After a period of delay for the operations, say an academic year, the analytical reports from the planning model and reports on the performance of the operations are again evaluated (box 3) and the planning cycle is repeated.

The use of simulation (as shown in Figure 18–2) and other Management Science techniques, when integrated with an information system designed for operations and control will bring the information system close to a true MIS —a Management Information System.[13] The resistance to the acceptance of an MIS in education is partly the result of terminology. Jellema states this problem as follows:

> "Management," ... is an even dirtier word in many circles of academe than "administration." Since it is often difficult to give away, let alone sell, a dog with a bad name, it is unfortunate that a system for supplying information to support wiser decisions has its problem of gaining acceptance made more difficult because of the suspicious sounding name it bears.[14]

The use of models of management science in information systems in education raises two important sets of issues: one, an increased demand on the data base; and two, the need for organizational changes. Both these topics will be discussed in turn below.

DATA FOR PLANNING AND CONTROL

Planning models, especially simulation models of the type mentioned earlier, typically require large amounts of data. Some of this data is unique to the model, but most is also required for operational purposes and consequently is already in the institutional data base.[15] Often the main problem is the fact that such data is not accessible to the planners because the planning department reports to a different administrative unit than the information-processing department. As a result, the planners, and sometimes control personnel, process their data in parallel to the processing of operational data. This parallel effort can be eliminated by organizational restructuring resulting in centralization or coordination of both the planning and control needs with the operational needs of information.

[13]For definitions and a discussion on this subject, see J. D. Aron, "Information Systems in Perspective" *Computing Surveys, I, No. 4 (December 1969), 213–36; G. W. Dickson, "Management Information-Decision Systems,"* *Business Horizons,* XI, No. 6 (December 1968), 17–26 and "What's the Status of MIS?" *EDP Analyzer,* VII, No. 10 (October 1969), 1–14.

[14]See W. W. Jellema, "MIS Adoption and the Educational Environment" in *Focus on MIS,* ed. R. A. Huff (Boulder, Colo.: WICHE, 1969), p. 18.

[15]For empirical evidence of this statement, see Hussain and Martin, *A Resource Requirements Prediction Model,* p. 9.

Through centralization or through coordination, the data files of the institution need to be interrelated in order to meet the control and planning needs of data. One such schema is shown in Figure 18–3. In it, each box is either a data file or an organizational function generating data relevant to an advanced information system. This data must be related by linking elements (such as those discussed in Chapter 9); must be coded in a standardized structure or have crossover tables (discussed in Chapter 8); must have consistent processing procedures (discussed in Chapter 15); and must be designed (the subject of Chapter 13) so that the input and output needs of operations, control, and planning are met.

The input to planning models is often more detailed than that needed for operational information but the marginal cost of this detail is not high if it is anticipated early in the development of the information system. The detailed data is needed not only for calculating endogenous variables, such as faculty load, but also for predicting exogenous variables such as student enrollment.

The output of a planning model, especially a simulation model, can be voluminous because of the many formats, sequences, and levels of aggregation in which information can be presented. But too much information can be just as harmful as too little information. The desired output must therefore be carefully designed and selected. The design should ensure that the output is easily assimilated as well as quickly referenced and accessed. The relevance of the output for each administrator must be established and a schedule made so that each administrator receives only what information is relevant to his needs. Furthermore, such information must be filtered and condensed before reaching the human planner, or else the information can do more harm than good.[16]

The use of models of management science and information systems in administration would result in organizational changes. Some of these will now be discussed.

ORGANIZATIONAL CHANGES

There have been many authors who have predicted organizational changes resulting from the use of computers. One of the early predictions was by Leavitt and Whisler[17] in 1958. They predicted that in the 1980s computers will be king; they will routinize (programmed decisions) many of the traditional middle-management functions, thereby replacing middle management,

[16]For a discussion of this view, see R. L. Ackoff, "Management Misinformation Systems," *Management Science,* XIV, No. 4 (December 1967), B–148.

[17]H. J. Leavitt and T. L. Whisler, "Management in the 1980's," *Harvard Business Review,* XXXVI, No. 6 (November-December 1956), 41–48. For some later comments, see T. L. Whisler and G. P. Shulz, "Automation and the Management Process," in *The Annals of the American Academy of Political & Social Science,* CCCLX (March 1962), 81–89.

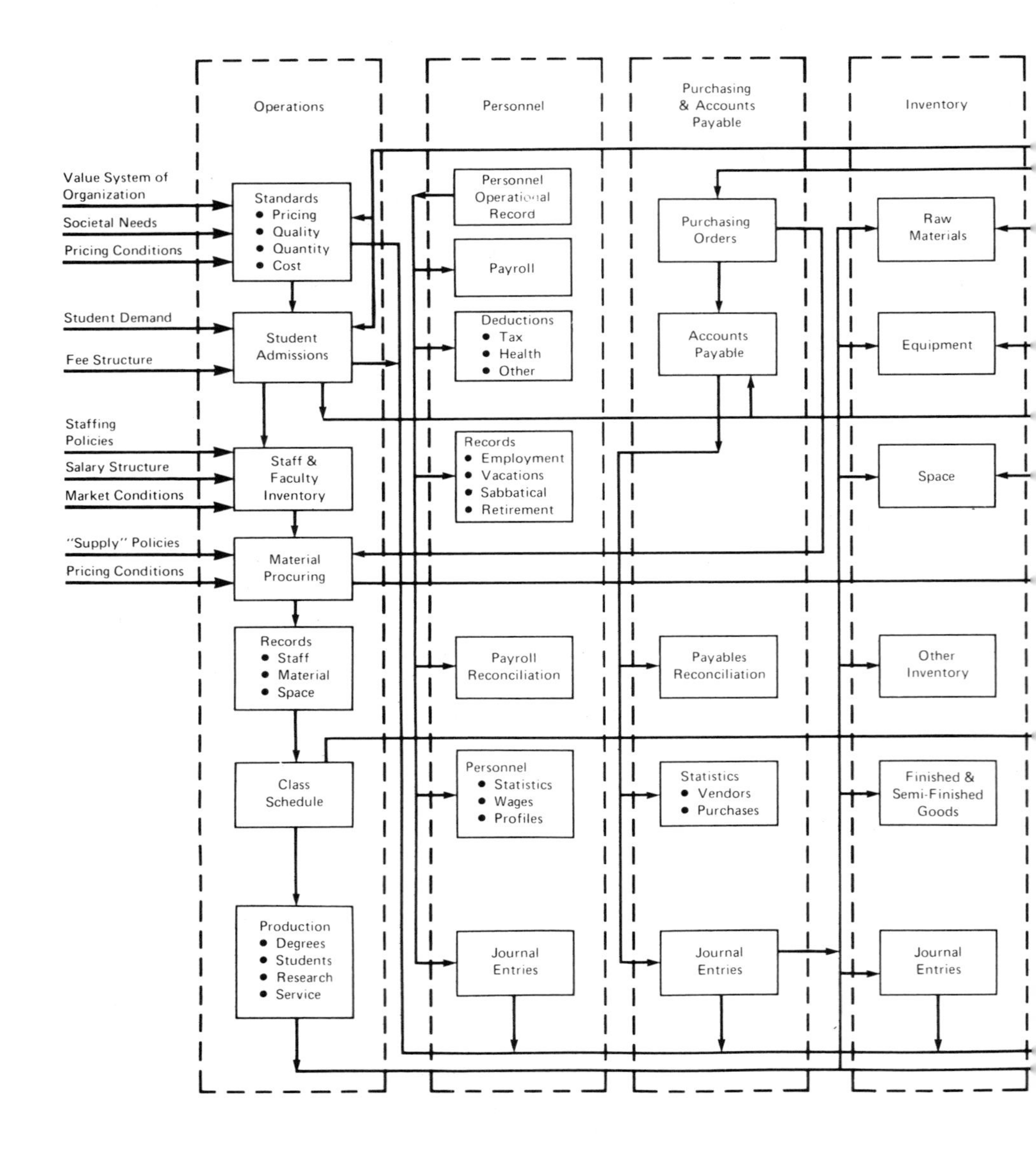
Operations
Personnel
Purchasing & Accounts Payable
Inventory
Value System of Organization
Societal Needs
Pricing Conditions
Standards
• Pricing
• Quality
• Quantity
• Cost
Student Demand
Fee Structure
Student Admissions
Staffing Policies
Salary Structure
Market Conditions
Staff & Faculty Inventory
"Supply" Policies
Pricing Conditions
Material Procuring
Records
• Staff
• Material
• Space
Class Schedule
Production
• Degrees
• Students
• Research
• Service
Personnel Operational Record
Payroll
Deductions
• Tax
• Health
• Other
Records
• Employment
• Vacations
• Sabbatical
• Retirement
Payroll Reconciliation
Personnel
• Statistics
• Wages
• Profiles
Journal Entries
Purchasing Orders
Accounts Payable
Payables Reconciliation
Statistics
• Vendors
• Purchases
Journal Entries
Raw Materials
Equipment
Space
Other Inventory
Finished & Semi-Finished Goods
Journal Entries

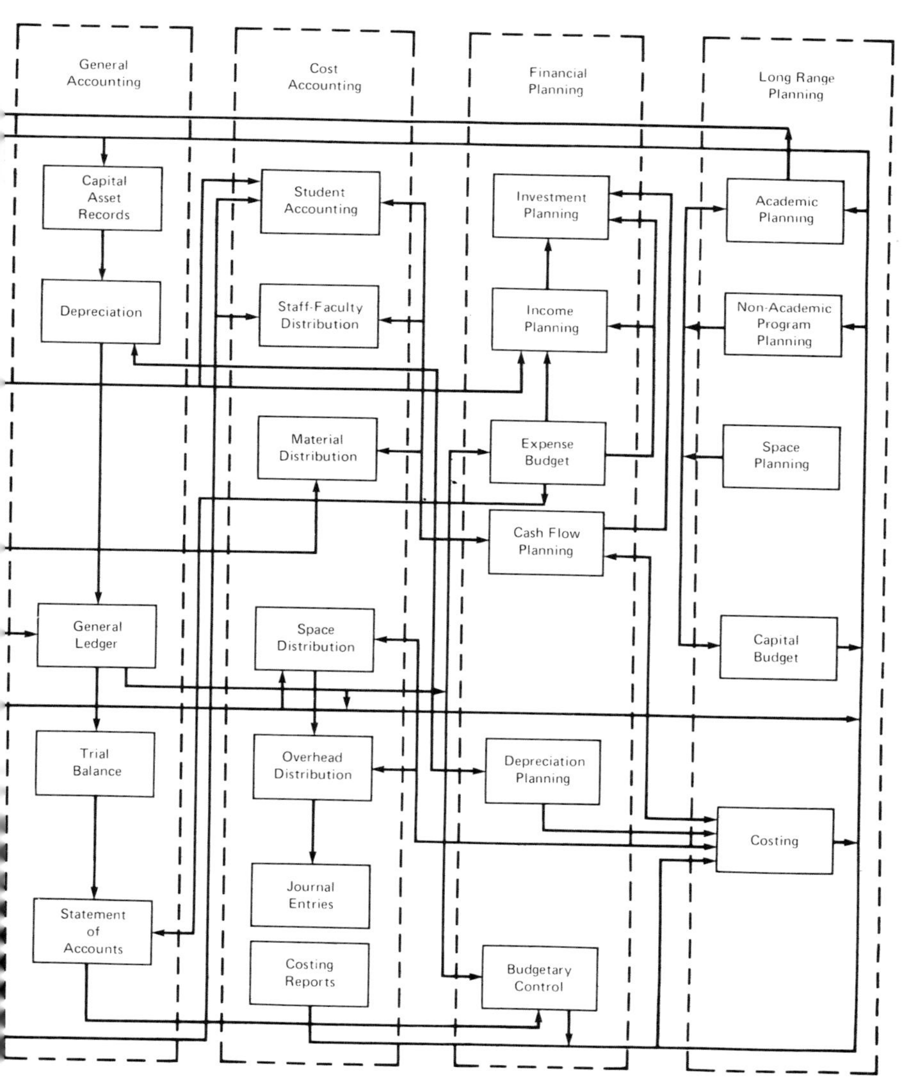

Figure 18–3. Interrelated Files for Operation, Control, and Planning

and will tend to centralize organizations. The information scientists will emerge as an elite, and management science will become a powerful technique in decision-making. These developments will challenge and replace many of the traditional theories of administrative management.

These predictions by Leavitt and Whisler and their supporters have been challenged by many. Koonitz argues that the takeover of administration by computers in the 1980s is unlikely. "Human values, motivation and social responsibility are becoming more important."[18] Dearden believes that computers will have no impact on top administration and limited impact on lower levels of administration.[19] Bergey and Slover predict that the 1980s will not be a computer-dominated technocracy, as implied by Leavitt and Whisler, but one with a humane technology where human values and social awareness will be important.[20]

The assumptions implied by many of the critics of Leavitt and Whisler are outlined by Gallagher:

> In order to give credence to the ideas expressed in these terms [automatic decision making, office revolution], three basic assumptions must be made: (1) that a great deal is known today about the process of decision making at the managerial level; (2) that a great deal is known about how to apply data processing and advanced business-systems techniques to these processes and to the solution of managerial problems; and (3) that the management processes and the rate of introduction of new problems remain static . . . There is little evidence that any one of these conditions is true. Much work, of course, is now in progress in the areas represented by the first two of these assumptions, but nothing will reduce the need for managerial skills. The growth of the demand for these skills is beyond all proportion to the supply and will continue so, even if sophisticated management information systems become more prevalent.[21]

The debate started by Leavitt and Whisler in 1958 has not yet abated. The debators disagree not only on the nature and scope of the organizational changes resulting from computerized information systems but on the timing of such changes. There is, however, general agreement on one proposition: there will be organizational changes and these may be profound. Administration in the 1980s will not be the same. The administrator in education, like the

[18]H. Koonitz, "Management and Challenges of the Future," *Advanced Management Journal,* XXXIII, No. 1 (January 1968), 21–30.

[19]J. Dearden, "Computers: No Impact on Divisional Control," *Harvard Business Review,* XLV, No. 1 (January-February), 104.

[20]See J. M. Bergey and R. C. Slover, "Administration in the 1980's," *S.A.M. Advanced Management Journal,* XXXIV, No. 2 (April 1969), 31–32.

[21]James D. Gallagher, *Management Information Systems and the Computer* (New York: AMA, 1961), p. 56.

manager in business, should look out for such changes and be responsive to making the needed adjustments. He must ask different questions and know how to use the different answers he gets. He must delegate responsibilities to the computer and to techniques of management science in situations where such techniques can be effective. He must recognize the problems and potentials of man-machine interaction. Emery states the potential of such interaction as follows:

> The great advantage of a man-machine partnership is that it permits the allocation of problem-solving tasks according to the comparative advantage enjoyed by each partner. The capabilities of the two are quite complementary; hence the combination of man and computer represents a distinctly more powerful system than one constrained to employ only a single component . . . especially . . . in coping with the enormously complex problems encountered in strategic planning.
>
> To the human component is relegated the responsibility for proposing alternative plans and placing a utility value on the predicted consequences. The machine is assigned the computational task of determining the consequences of each alternative by means of a formal model.
>
> The computer thus serves as an extension to the mind of the planner. The great advantage of such a system is that it does not require the complete formalization of the total decision process. Decisions and utility functions that are well understood and capable of being described formally can be incorporated into the computer model. Decisions and utilities that cannot be so formalized are simply reserved for the human decision maker.[22]

A study on man-machine interaction using graphic display systems (CRTs) was done by M. S. Scott Morton. He examined their use in what he calls an MDS, Management Decision Systems, which included a data-base, a model base, and a careful analysis of key decisions. His findings on the problem follows:

> Nontechnical managers engaged in solving complex problems found the man/machine combination is a highly convenient, powerful adjunct to their decision process. It provided them with flexible access to a large data-base, but more significantly it allowed them to explore the future. They had the ability to look forward and test strategies easily and simply. . . . Problem solving was enhanced by the access to computational power, the ability to specify the required action easily and simply as it was required, and the resulting creation of several viable solutions.[23]

[22]J. C. Emery, "Management Information Systems and Computers," in *Progress in Operations Research,* ed. J. S. Aronotsky (New York: John Wiley & Sons, Inc., 1969), pp. 517–18.

[23]M. S. Scott Morton, *Management Decision Systems* (Boston, Mass.: Harvard University, 1971), p. 17.

Morton, observing the time spent in decision-making, found that "the length of time spent actually working on the problem in order to arrive at a solution was reduced from 6 days to 1 day. . . . The elapsed time also changed significantly—from 22 days to 1 day."[24]

It is interesting to note that the subjects in Morton's study were nontechnical persons "without extensive computer experience; indeed they had never even heard of visual display devices."[25] Morton concludes that

> it is possible for managers to solve certain classes of problem with the MDS even though they have no technical knowledge in the computer field. In other words, a manager with no knowledge, or interest, in computers, or file structure, or similar technical details can find visual display systems and computer-based models and data useful means of problem solving.[26]

This independence of the administrators could be increased by trends in computer technology. Developments in both hardware and softward design tend toward making it easier for the users to program and use the computer. Simon, in *The Shape of Automation for Men & Management,*[27] even predicts a self-programmable computer to which one states what one wants done rather than writes programs on how to do it. This will partly eliminate the current dependence of the typical user on the information analysis and counter the prediction of Leavitt and Whisler that an elite of information scientists will be all-powerful. Some sources of such power will still exist and are inherent in the fact that the information scientist is processing and channeling the information he generates. The power increases when he is allowed to develop the system himself and make the value judgments and set goals for the information system. This has happened in business and industry, as reflected in the survey by the Diebold Research Program. In a "recent" survey reported in 1969, 2500 executives of 140 companies found that technicians, not management, were setting goals for computers.[28] This can be avoided in education by having the administrator participate actively in the development of the information system and recognize his responsibilities for setting its goals and providing the value judgments involved. Such responsibility and the authority for making his decisions should not be allowed to be made by default by the information system, its computers, or its analysts.

[24] *Ibid.,* p. 13.

[25] *Ibid.,* p. 10.

[26] *Ibid.,* p. 11.

[27] H. A. Simon, *The Shape of Automation for Men and Management* (New York: Harper & Row, 1965).

[28] J. Diebold, "Bad Decisions on Computer Use," *Harvard Business Review,* XLVII, No. 1 (January-February 1969), 16.

SUMMARY AND CONCLUSIONS

This chapter discussed the extension of the traditional information system that provides primarily operational information into one that provides information for operations, as well as for control and planning. A summary comparison of such systems, discussed in this and previous chapters, is shown in Table 18–1.

Table 18–1. Summary Comparison of Traditional Advanced Information Systems

	Traditional Information System	Advanced Information Systems
Orientation	Transaction	→ Analytical
	Functional	→ Integrated
	Partial	→ Total
	Data base is operations oriented	→ Data base is planning, research and decision-making oriented
Function	Operations	→ Operations, Control, Planning, and Resource Allocation
Mode	Off-line	→ On-line
	Batch	→ Batch and Terminal
	One-way reporting	→ Interactive Communication
Library Search	Card Files	→ Retrieval Systems Selective Dissemination Systems On-Line Retrieval of Biographical Texts

Techniques of decision-making—traditional and advanced—are compared in Table 18–2.

The use of information systems for control and planning in education will undoubtedly increase. Traditionally, education, being in the public sector, was not subjected to the same hard analysis for performance and accountability as was the private sector. But this is changing. Some state legislatures are demanding a cost analysis of each academic program for comparisons within the state and between states. Other state legislatures are seriously considering

Table 18–2. Comparison of Traditional and Advanced Techniques of Decision-Making

	Traditional Techniques	Advanced Techniques
Control	Line Item and Capital Budgets →	PPBS
	Policies and Procedures →	Control Charts Control Models Faculty Load Analysis Space Utilization Analysis Costing Cost Benefit Analysis
	GANNT →	CPM and PERT
	Inventory Extrapolation →	Inventory Control Optimizing Techniques
Student Enrollment	Extrapolation, hunches, insights, experience, and judgment →	Multiple Regression, Markov Chains, Student Flow Models, and judgment
Resources Allocation	Hunches, extrapolation, experience, and judgment →	Models such as CAMPUS, CSM, HELP, and RRPM, and judgment
Top Administrative Decision	Hunches and judgments →	Some Decision Theory and Heuristic methods of problem solving

Information System and Techniques of Management Science (boxed: PPBS through Models such as CAMPUS, CSM, HELP, and RRPM, and judgment)

the use of PPBS for planning and control of funding of education. Some legislatures have required[29] the use of planning models for resources allocation such as the RRPM–1.

Additional information generated by an information system for control and planning does not automatically lead to better decisions. It is the careful and timely analysis of this information that should aid in decision-making. The quality of the decision is the responsibility of the administrator. It is also his responsibility to participate in the development and implementation of an information system to ensure not only that the true potential of the system is realized but also that it is not misused. As John Caffrey puts it "computers and systems have neither authority not responsibility, nor should we attempt to endow them with such qualities."[30]

The extension of an information system to provide information on control and planning will alter existing and traditional roles of administrators and affect the established administrative and organizational practices. The altered tasks, changing pay and status relationships, as well as changes in organizational levels and control relationships may create considerable organizational strain. There may also be conceptual changes in administrative structure and their functions. Peter Drucker suggests a reassessment of traditional concepts.

> Authority and responsibility may well be the wrong principles of organization. It may well be that we will have to learn to organize not a system of authority and responsibility—a system of command—but an information and decision system—a system of judgement, knowledge, and expectations.[31]

The changed structure of decision-making and organization may result in what Ways calls the "management democracy." It includes "the idea that influence is based on technical competence and knowledge rather than . . . personal whims or perogatives of powers."[32]

KEY TERMS

Administrative Control	Operational Control Decision
Decision	Programmed Decision
Interactive Systems	Resource Allocation Model

[29]California is such an example. See California State Concurrent Resolution No. 73, 1971. Oregon is another example.

[30]J. Caffrey, "The Human Side of MIS Implementation," in *Focus on MIS-A Report on the WICHE–ACE Higher Education Management Information Systems Seminar,* ed. R. A. Huff (Boulder, Colo.: WICHE, 1969), p. 12.

[31]Peter F. Drucker, "Managing the Educated," in *Management's Mission in a New Society,* ed. Dan H. Fenn (New York: McGraw-Hill Book Company, Inc., 1959), p. 174.

[32]Max Ways, "Tomorrow's Management: A More Adventurous Life in a Free-Form Corporation," *Fortune,* LXXIV, No. 1 (July 1966), p. 150.

Management Control Decision
Management Democracy
Management Information System
MDS
Nonprogrammed Decision
Operational Decision
Self-Programmable Computer
Simulation
Strategic Planning
Techniques of Management Science
Techniques of Operations Research

CHAPTER 18: SELECTED ANNOTATED BIBLIOGRAPHY

ANDREW, GARY M., and R. E. MOIR, *Information-Decision Systems in Education.* Itasca, Ill. Peacock Publishers, Inc., 1970. Has an excellent discussion of basic concepts of models, decision-making, and information systems in the context of education.

BERGEY, J. M., and R. C. SLOVER, "Administration in the 1980's," *S.A.M. Advanced Management Journal,* XXXIV, No. 2 (April 1969), 25–32. Excellent survey of the literature predicting the effects of computers on management and administrations. The authors outline the early prognostications starting with Leavitt & Whisler in 1958, discuss the redefined future on the post-1964 writings, and conclude with their own predictions.

EMERY, J. C., "Management Information Systems and Computers," in *Progress in Operations Research,* ed. J. S. Aronofsky. New York: John Wiley & Sons, Inc., 1969, III, pp. 489–524. Much of this article is devoted to the concepts of planning and is a glimpse of the author's excellent book, *Organizational Planning and Control Systems.* Emery also discusses planning and systems in the framework of a management-information system. Recommended for the serious reader.

FARMER, J., *Why Planning, Programming, Budgeting Systems for Higher Education?* Boulder, Colo.: WICHE, 1970, 24 pp. This short booklet has a very high content to space ratio. Using simple numerical examples it explains the basics of PPBS. It is addressed to the administrator in higher education and to him it is highly recommended.

HUFF, R. A., ed., *Focus on MIS.* Boulder, Colo.: WICHE, 1969, 22 pp. This is a collection of brief statements by participants of a national seminar held on MIS in higher education. The authors represent developers and users of MIS and present a wide coverage of concepts and problems of implementation of an MIS. Highly recommended.

JOHNSON, C. B., and W. G. KATZENMEYER, eds., *Management Information Systems in Higher Education: The State of the Art.* Durham, N.C.: Duke University Press, 1969. This volume describes the state of the art as of 1969 and predicts future trends in the development of MIS in higher education. The collection has numerous articles on models, including a good general introduction to modeling by Wallhaus.

WEATHERSBY, GEORGE B., and MILTON C. WEINSTEIN, *A Structural Comparison of Analytical Models for University Planning,* Paper P–12. Berkeley, Cal.: Office of Analytical Studies, University of California, 1970, 45 pp. This document examines thirty models classified into comprehensive university simulation models, university performance optimization models, special-purpose university planning models, and national planning models. The models are compared for function, theory, methods, subjects, data, uses, and status as of 1970. A scholarly document highly recommended to one looking for an overview of planning models in higher education.

Appendix A

A Supplement to Chapter 3: Decision Tables

In this section we will discuss some details of the Else Rule; the concepts of redundancy, contradiction, and completeness; the use of decision tables; and some comments and conclusions on other applications.

THE ELSE RULE

Reviewing the material in the text, the Else Rule identifies a set of actions that should be taken if all other rules in the table are not applicable. It thereby "completes" the table and ensures that all possible sets of conditions have been accounted for.

The Else Rule is very useful in programming since it can be used to identify an unexpected condition or an error. It provides a branch for the unexpected, and thereby encompasses all possibilities. When the Else Rule is used for an expected error condition, the action in the Else Rule column will branch to an error routine.

There is yet another application of the Else Rule. This can best be illustrated by the example in Tables A-1 and A-2.

Table A-1. An Example of a Decision Table

	Rule 1	Rule 2	Rule 3	Rule 4	Rule 5	Rule 6	Rule 7	Rule 8
Condition 1?	Y	N	Y	Y	N	N	Y	N
Condition 2?	Y	N	N	N	Y	Y	Y	N
Condition 3?	Y	N	Y	N	Y	N	N	Y
Action 1	X	—	X	X	X	X	X	X
Action 2	—	X	X	X	X	X	X	X

Note that in Table A-1 all rules other than rules 1 and 2 have the same set of actions. The table can then be simplified by replacing rules 3–8 by an Else Rule, such as shown in Table A-2.

Table A-2. The Else Rule

	Rule 1	Rule 2	Else Rule
Condition 1?	Y	N	
Condition 2?	Y	N	
Condition 3?	Y	N	
Action 1	X	—	X
Action 2	—	X	X

The eight rules in Table A-1 have been reduced to the three rules in Table A-2, a saving of over 60%, resulting in a saving of programming and computer time.

Note that the Else Rule has no condition entries. It is the rule that will be executed only when all other rules have been tested and are not satisfied. It is for this reason that it is in the extreme right-hand column of the table, and, hence, the last rule, since the scanning of rules is conventionally from left to right.

It is not essential for a table to have an Else Rule, except in the DETAB[1] version. If there is no Else Rule and if none of the specified rules are satisfied, then no action is taken.

[1]The DETAB language and other Decision Table languages are discussed in the bibliography at the end of Chapter 3.

REDUNDANCY, CONTRADICTION, AND COMPLETENESS

A decision table has a great advantage over a narrative or a flowchart in that it can be more easily checked for redundancy, contradiction, and completeness. This section includes a discussion of some of the basic theorems related to such a checking process used in the DETAB-X,[2] the most popular form of decision tables. First, however, we need some definitions.

An **AND-FUNCTION** of a decision rule is an ordered set of Y, N, or "dash" where a dash signifies that the condition is immaterial.

A **pure AND-FUNCTION** is one that contains only Y's, and/or N's, i.e., it contains no dashes.

A **mixed AND-FUNCTION** contains one or more dashes as well as Y's and N's.

A **simple decision rule** is one whose AND-FUNCTION is pure.

A **complex decision rule** is one whose AND-FUNCTION is mixed.

Two AND-FUNCTIONS are **dependent** if there exists a set of condition-states such that both AND-FUNCTIONS are satisfied by it. Otherwise, they are **independent.**

Examples of the terms defined above are shown in Table A–3:

Table A–3. Illustrations of Definitions Used

	Rule 1	Rule 2	Rule 3	Rule 4	Rule 5	Rule 6
Condition 1?	Y	Y	Y	Y	Y	Y
Condition 2?	N	Y	–	Y	Y	Y
Condition 3? Age above 30 years?	Y	Y	Y	Y	N	Y
Action 1	X	X	X	X	–	X
Action 2	–	–	–	–	X	–

All rules in Table A–3 are AND-FUNCTIONS. Rules 1, 2, 4, 5, & 6 are **pure AND-FUNCTIONS** and **simple decision rules;** Rule 3 is a **mixed AND-FUNCTION** and a **complex decision rule.** Rules 4 and 5 are **independent** since a person is either less

[2]This discussion relies heavily on a formal development of theorems and their corollaries, in S. L. Pollack, *Analysis of the Decision Rules in Decision Tables,* Memorandum RM–3669–RR (Santa Monica, Ca.: RAND Corporation, May 1963), 69 pp.

than or equal to 30 years (Rule 5) or more than 30 years (Rule 4). Rules 1 and 3 are **dependent.** (Rule 6 will be discussed later).

Before proceeding with this analysis, it is necessary to postulate two requirements for the type of decision table to be considered. These are:

Requirement 1: Every decision rule must specify at least one action.
Requirement 2: Each transaction that tests the decision rules must be able to satisfy one, and only one, of the rules.

REDUNDANCY

Redundancy exists in a decision table when there are more rules than essential. It is important to eliminate redundancy in decision tables in order to reduce programming time and computer time.

A good example of redundancy is a case where the conditions and actions of two decision rules are identical. Such is the case with rules 2, 4, and 6 in Table A–3.

Another example of redundancy is a case where two rules can be replaced by one. The formal theorem that enables us to combine decision rules and eliminate redundancy states:

> if two decision rules have the same action and their AND-FUNCTIONS are alike in every row but one, and in that row they have a Y, N pair, then the two rules can be combined into one.

An example of the use of this theorem appears in Table A–3. Rule 3 is actually a combination of rules 1 and 2; hence both rules 1 and 2 are redundant when rule 3 is present.

Another example of redundancy[3] appears in Table A–4.

Table A–4. Credit Approval Decision Table with Redundancy

	Rule 1	Rule 2	Rule 3
Credit OK?	Y	–	N
Pay experience favorable?	–	Y	N
Approve order	X	X	–
Return order to sales	–	–	X

[3] *Ibid.,* pp. 18–19.

Rules 1 and 2 in Table A-4 can be subdivided into their pure components (containing no dashes) as follows:

		(a)	(b)
Rule 1	$\left\{\begin{bmatrix} Y \\ - \\ \hline\hline X \end{bmatrix}\right.$	$\begin{bmatrix} Y \\ Y \\ \hline\hline X \end{bmatrix}$	$\begin{bmatrix} Y \\ N \\ \hline\hline X \end{bmatrix}$
Rule 2	$\left\{\begin{bmatrix} - \\ Y \\ \hline\hline X \end{bmatrix}\right.$	$\begin{bmatrix} Y \\ Y \\ \hline\hline X \end{bmatrix}$	$\begin{bmatrix} N \\ Y \\ \hline\hline X \end{bmatrix}$

Note that the (a) component of both rules 1 and 2 are identical. This component is "common" to both rules 1 and 2 and, hence, it is redundant. Its elimination from one rule (Rule 2) will give a redundancy-free decision table, as in Table A-5.

Table A-5. Credit Approval Decision Table without Redundancy

	Rule 1	Rule 2	Rule 3
Credit OK?	Y	N	N
Pay experience favorable?	–	Y	N
Approve order	X	X	–
Return order to sales	–	–	X

The following theorem formally identifies redundancy:

The rules contain redundancy if their actions are the same and their AND-FUNCTIONS are dependent.

The reader is invited to check the discussion on redundancy above with the theorem just stated.

CONTRADICTION

A theorem defining contradiction is as follows:

If the actions are different for the two rules that have dependent AND-FUNCTIONS, contradiction exists.

An example is shown in Table A–6.

Table A–6. Example of Contradiction

	Rule 1	Rule 2
Condition 1?	Y	–
Condition 2?	N	N
Action 1	X	–
Action 2	–	X

The dash corresponding to condition 1 in Rule 2 can be considered as a "Y" which makes the conditions in Rules 1 and 2 identical. However, the actions for Rules 1 and 2 are different. Hence, contradiction exists.

COMPLETENESS

One of the most difficult problems in systems design and computer programming is that of completely defining the problem. Failure to do so often leads to incorrect results and situations which are difficult to detect and debug. Fortunately, decision tables provide a framework for checking for the completeness of decision rules. One pertinent theorem is as follows:

> A table based on n conditions contains only one set of 2^n independent pure AND-FUNCTIONS (or 2^n independent simple decision rules).

Applying the above theorem to the example in Table A–1, we have

$$n = \text{number of conditions} = 3$$

Therefore, according to the theorem, the number of independent decision rules = $(2^n) = 2^3 = 8$, which is exactly what we have in Table A–1. Hence, we have no redundancy and the decision table is complete.

The above case involves pure AND-FUNCTIONS. An additional theorem is necessary for tables with mixed AND-FUNCTIONS.

> A complex rule that contains dashes in r positions of its AND-FUNCTIONS is equivalent to 2^r simple decision rules.

The total number of independent simple decision rules in the decision table can now be calculated by the following relationship.

$$N = 2^{r_1} + 2^{r_2} + \ldots\ldots + 2^{r_n}$$

where N = Total number of simple independent decision rules in the table

r_i = number of dashes in the ith decision rule (the condition part only).

n = number of non-redundant decision rules.

Applying this relationship to Table A–5, we have

$$N = 2^1 + 2^0 + 2^0$$
$$= 4$$

Comparing this actual number of independent decision rules with the theoretical value (call it N^1) (as stated in the first theorem discussed in this section) we have $N = N^1 = 4$ where $N' = 2^n$.
Thus, Table A–5 has no redundancy and is complete.

Application of this relationship to Table A–4 yields

$$N = 2^1 + 2^1 + 2^0 = 2 + 2 + 1 = 5$$

which is one more than the theoretical value of N^1 (where $N^1 = 2^n = 4$). There is, therefore, one redundant rule in Table A–4. Both observations on the completeness of Table A–4 and A–5 are consistent with the discussion on redundancy.

In checking for completeness of a decision table, special computations are made for the Else Rule, which is equivalent to (2^n - t) simple independent AND-FUNCTIONS where

n = number of conditions in the table
t = number of specified or implied AND-FUNCTIONS

USE OF DECISION TABLES

Because of some of the advantages discussed above, decision tables are being used widely, as evidenced by a recent survey of 2000 members of the Systems & Procedures Association. Results of this survey,[4] made in 1968, are shown in Table A–7.

Table A–7. Survey of Users of Decision Tables

Size of Staff Analyst Group	Percentage of Users of Decision Tables
1-5	40
6-10	60
$\geq$11	70
Entire sample	50

[4] *EDP Analyzer,* "Managing the System Effort," VI, No. 7 (July 1965), p. 11.

The above table shows that the larger the analyst group, the more they use decision tables. A formal relationship between the choice of decision tables and the structure of the problem has been attempted by Chapin. He suggests that a user ask himself a set of ten questions concerning the potential application and then score the application by Chapin's guide[5] shown in Table A-8.

Table A-8. Usage Guide for Decision Tables

	Scale of Values.		
Characteristic	0	2	5
Total number of mutually exclusive processing actions in the program	Less than 6	6 to 12	More than 12
Number of major parallel alternative processing paths	Less than 3	3 to 5	More than 5
Number of organized data streams or files used as input or output	None	1 to 3	4 or more
Number of levels at which data is to be handled	Less than 3	3 to 5	More than 5
Number of exception cases to be handled	Less than 3	3 to 7	More than 7
Proportion of arithmetic actions that are multiplies or divides	More than 6%	2% to 6%	Less than 2%
Probable proportion of program run time spend in executing iterative loops	More than 60%	25% to 60%	Less than 25%
Number of minor variations to the processing action	None	1 to 4	More than 4
Number of variables that determine the program control sequence	Less than 3	3 to 5	More than 5
Likely need to revise program algorithm within one year to meet changed output or input requirements	Not likely	Likely	Very Likely

[5]From "An Introduction to Decision Tables," by N. Chapin, *DPMA Quarterly,* III, No. 3 (April 1967), 4, published by Data Processing Management Association, Park Ridge, Ill. 60068.

The total score for all the ten questions should then be used in selecting the "best-choice technique" by a table which is shown in a decision-table format in Table A-9.

Table A-9. Decision Table for Using Decision Tables

	Rule 1	Rule 2	Else Rule 3
Score Value ≤ 12?	Y	N	
Score Value ≤ 32?	–	Y	
Use Mathematical Formulas	X	–	–
Use Flow Diagrams	–	X	–
Use Decision Tables	–	–	X

Chapin emphasized that his guide is a preliminary one and that "additional experience will undoubtedly suggest its revisions."

Conclusions and Comments

Currently, most of the checking of decision tables for redundancy, contradiction, and completeness is done manually. When this can always be accomplished by a computer, the value of decision tables will be enhanced.

This discussion of decision tables has been limited largely to their application in the analysis and definition of the logic of the problem. The conversion of decision tables to flowcharts and to computer programs has not been discussed, but references to these subjects are cited in the bibliography to Chapter 3.

Arguments concerning the use of decision tables in compiling, with a "minimum space in computer memory and which require a minimum average number of executions,"[6] have not been discussed and, again, the reader is referred to the bibliography to Chapter 3.

There are a number of decision-table-oriented programming langauges in use. What is needed, however, are languages that are more commonly implemented. Furthermore, these languages should be developed within a framework of industrywide standards; the programs generated by these languages should be optimal or near optimal in terms of storage space used, compile time, and run time; and finally, the languages should have good error diagnostics and program debugging facilities. With such developments, decision tables would become more widely and more commonly used.

[6]M. Montalbano, "Tables, Flow Charts, and Program Logic," *IBM Systems Journal,* I (September 1962), 53.

Appendix B*

Input and Output Equipment

This book assumes some knowledge of input and output equipment. In cases where the assumption is invalid, this appendix may be of some value. It outlines, with the help of illustrations, some of the typical input and output equipment configurations. It is important for the administrator to be knowledgeable of such equipment so that he may participate in the selection of a configuration most appropriate to his needs.

Each equipment configuration will be discussed briefly below and will correspond to the illustrations in Figures B–1, B–2, B–3 (usually from left-to-right and top-to-bottom).

Specifications of speed and cost figures will not be stated since they vary greatly with the manufacturer, the model, and the year of manufacture.

*To be used in conjunction with Chapter 14.

CARD INPUT—FIGURE B–1

1. Keypunch-Verifier

Data cards are punched in a keypunch and then processed through a verifier. Both devices are operated much like a typewriter and use the same document as source data. The physical inputs used in the case of the keypunch are blank cards; in the case of the verifier, they are the previously punched cards produced by the keypunch. In the verifier, the punched holes in the card are compared with the holes that would be generated by the characters keyed from the source document. If a discrepancy is detected, a notch is generated on the top of the card in the column where the discrepancy occurred. If no discrepancies occur, a notch is generated on the right-hand side of the data card identifying a verified card.

In Figure B–1, the keypunch and verifier are two separate pieces of equipment. In small installations, the two functions are combined in one device, not shown in Figure B–1.

The person using the verifier should be different from the person who keyed the document originally. This reduces the chance of a source document being misinterpreted. Also, the verifier should be used for checking all crucial and vital data, such as payroll data, basic student data, and student grades.

The verifier detects errors made by the keypunch operator, but not errors made in the source document since both use the same source document. Some of these errors can be detected by a computer program that checks for the validity of data.

The verified data card (as with other prepared data card input) is read by a card reader and the data is then stored in the computer ready to be processed.

2. Porta-Punch

This equipment has a more limited character set than a keypunch and is used as a portable and inexpensive means of preparing card input. In most cases the data is collected from observation or from memory and not from a document. Hence, it is not verified by a verifier.

The generation of holes by a porta-punch is not always "clean cut" and often leads to card jams in the card-reader.

3. Keypunch

The keypunch can be used without a verifier. This reduces the equipment and labor costs by about half. It is done either for noncrucial data or data that can be carefully checked by validity programs later.

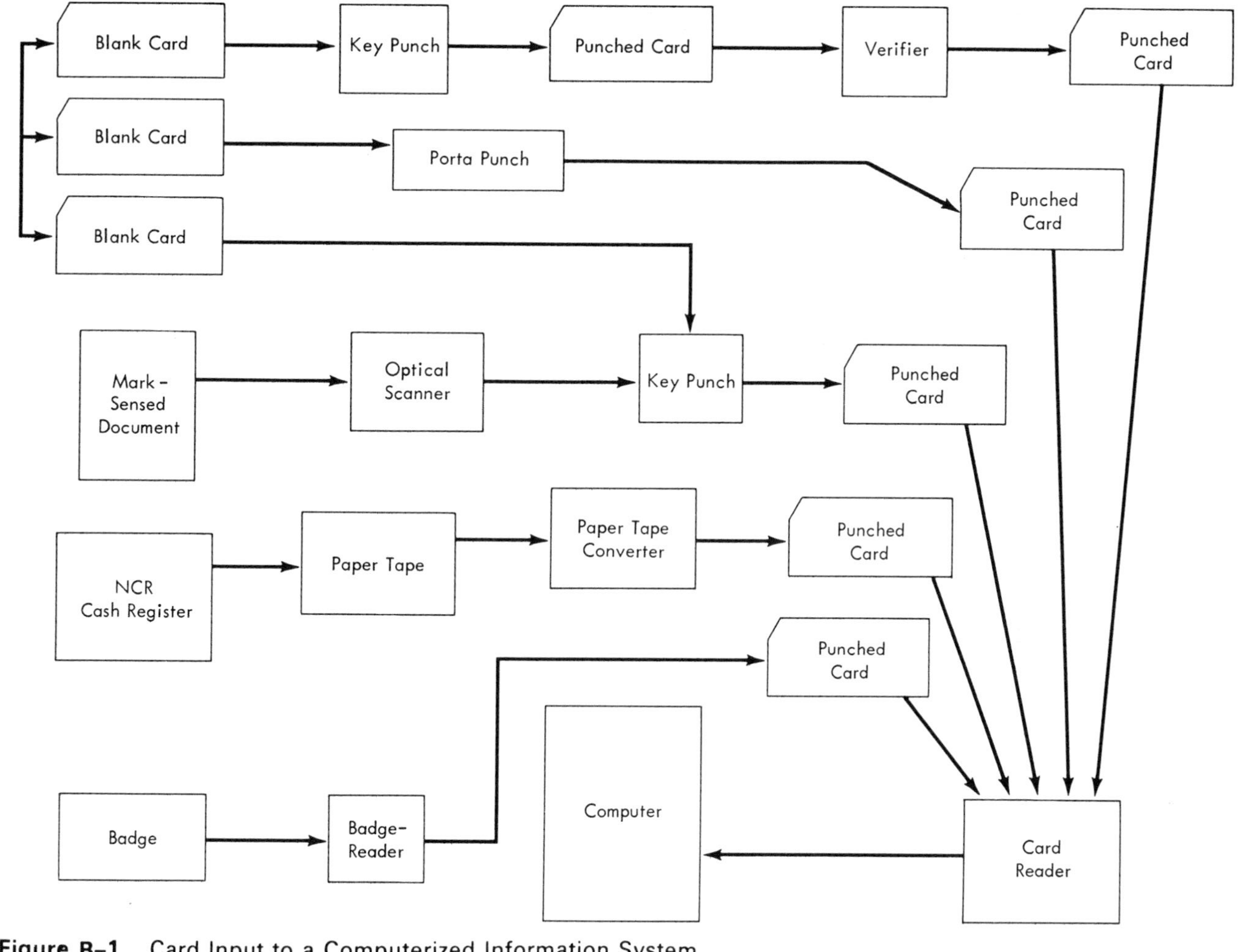

Figure B–1. Card Input to a Computerized Information System

4. Mark-Sensing

This requires a specially designed form (or data cards not shown in Figure B–1) to be marked carefully by a pencil in prescribed spaces that correspond to predetermined responses. Such a document is read by a special optical scanner (shown in Figure B–1) that is connected to a keypunch and generates a punched data card with the corresponding data.

Mark-sensing is used in administrative data processing for applications such as dormitory scheduling, class scheduling, fee payments, exam grading, and numerous applications where most of the data is numeric and needs to be processed rapidly. The mark-sensing source document, however, must be completed with considerable care.

5. Cash Register

Cash transactions are "rung up" on registers much like those found in grocery stores. Such registers are "equipped" with a special device that records the desired transactions on a paper tape which can then be converted to a data card by a paper tape-card converter. Such equipment can be used in the business office, bookstore, and other places where funds are collected.

6. Badge

A badge identifying a person (student, staff, faculty) with the basic information in machine-readable form (holes or machine readable characters) is read from a badge reader that generates a data card with the basic information in it. Such a badge reader can be used with other equipment to capture related data. For example, in a library, a card identifying a book to be checked in or out along with a badge identifying the borrower creates one card document that identifies both the person and the book. This then can be used as input to library book charge-discharge subsystem. The badge in this case is a fast error-free means of machine-recording data on a person using the system.

NON-CARD INPUT—FIGURE B–2

7. Magnetic Tape Encoder

Data from a document is entered (very much like on a keypunch) into a magnetic tape encoder equipment that generates a magnetic tape. Such a tape is read by a magnetic tape unit into a computer.

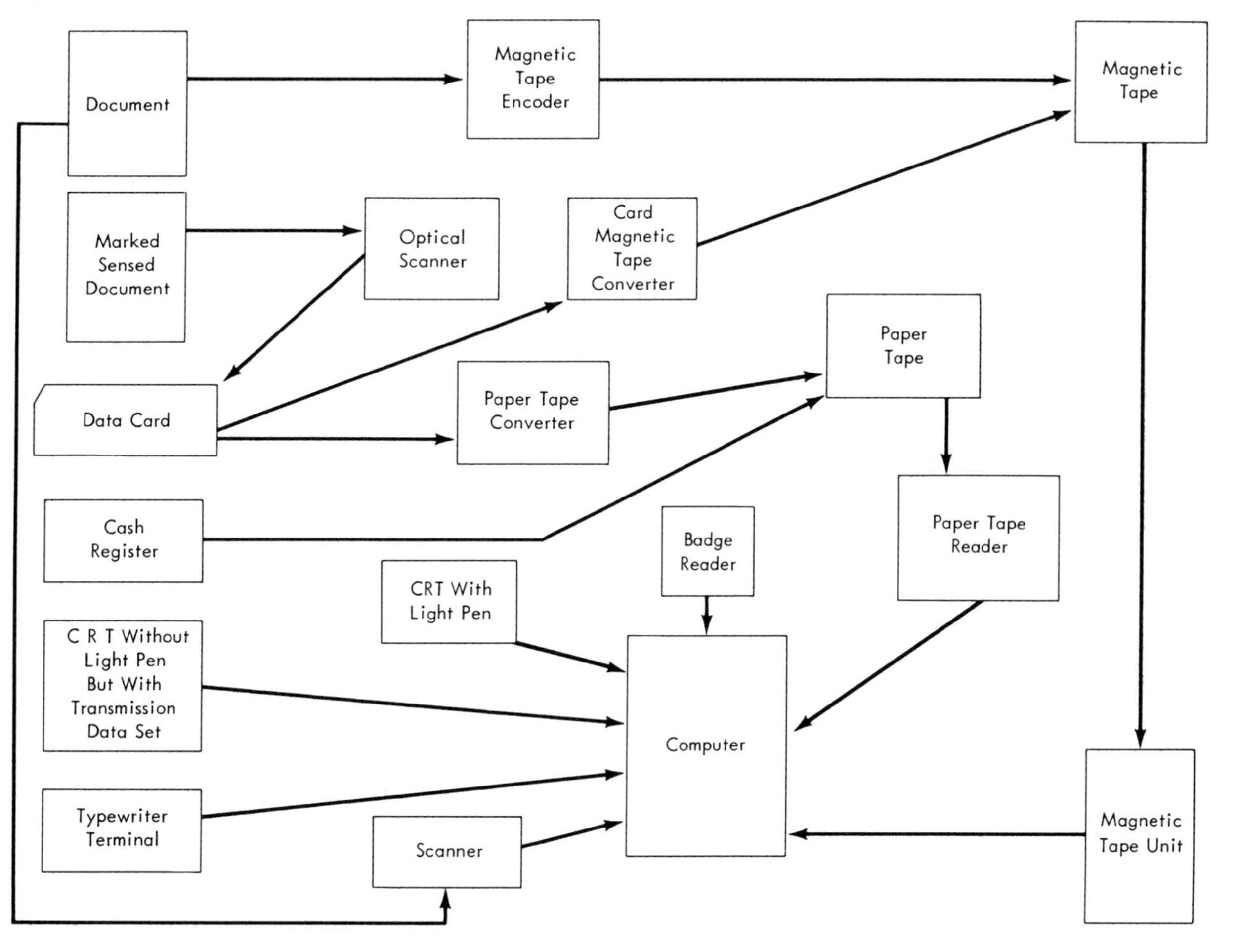

Figure B–2. Non-card Input to a Computerized Information System

8. Mark-Sensing

A mark-sensed document when read by an optical scanner produces a data card (discussed in 4, above). This data card can then be converted to a magnetic tape by a card-magnetic tape converter. The tape is then read by a tape-reader unit and computer.

9. Card-Paper Tape

A data card (generated from mark-sensing equipment or a keypunch) can be converted into paper tape and then processed by a computer through a paper tape reader.

10. Paper Tape Equipment

Data in a paper tape can be generated by equipment such as a cash register (discussed in 5, above). It can be read through a paper tape reader directly to a computer.

11. On-Line Equipment

Some devices enable data to be read directly to the computer. These include a badge reader, a typewriter terminal, an optical scanner, and a cathode ray tube terminal. The latter can be with or without a light pen, which is a device that enables direct communication with the tube screen.

OUTPUT EQUIPMENT—FIGURE B–3

12. Output to Be Used Later as Input

Output is often generated with the intention of using it again as input for further processing. This is done by generating a punched card or by storing data on a disk or a tape.

13. Terminals

Terminals are used as output devices (the same terminals discussed under input devices) and can be of the typewriter or the CRT type.

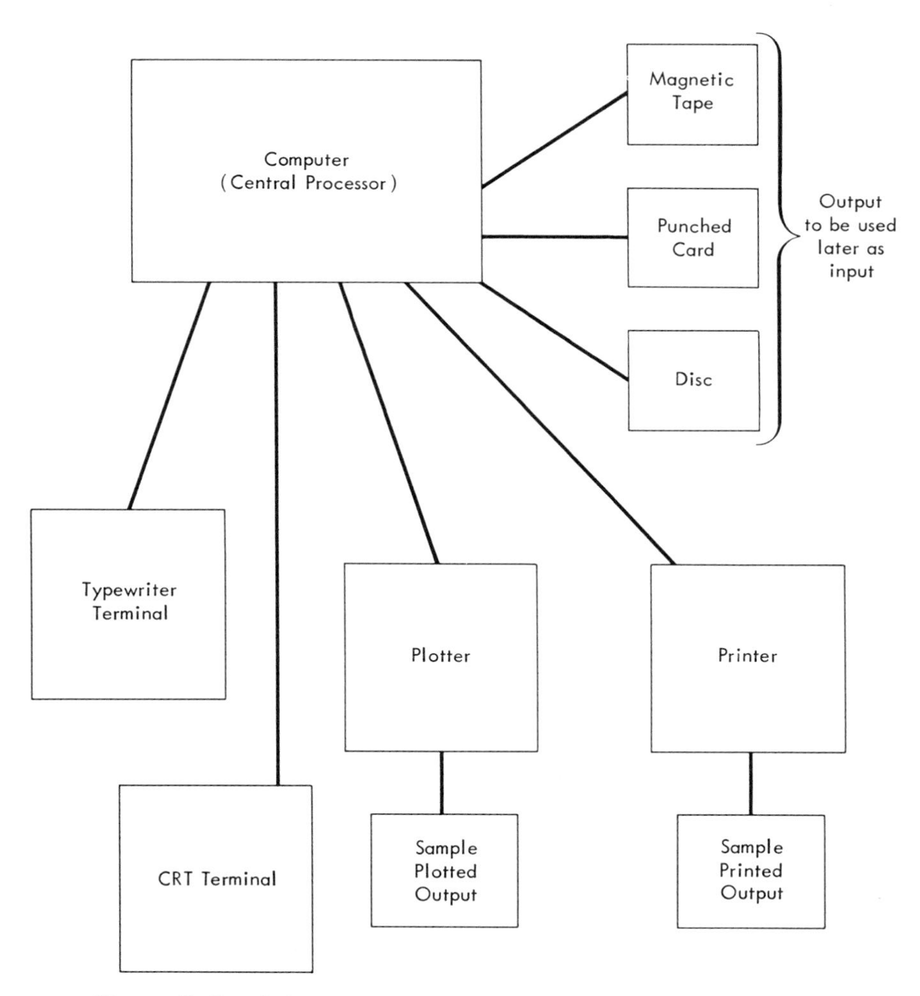

Figure B–3. Schematic Diagram Showing Different Types of Output

14. Plotter

Some information is best displayed graphically as a curve. This can be done by a plotter.

15. Printer

The most common output device from a computer is a printer. If can typically print up to five copies at one time (one original and four carbon copies).

Glossary of Terms Used in Information System Development*

ORGANIZATION OF THE COMMENTARY OF THE GLOSSARY

A commentary consists of one or more items. Each item may be constructed from among the following parts and in the following order: item number, usage label, descriptive phrase, annotation, reference. The definition includes all of these parts except the item number and reference.

Item Number. Each item in a commentary is numbered consecutively starting with item number (1). If the commentary consists of only one item, the item number is omitted.

Usage Label. This label is a word or phrase that indicates the area or

*The following are terms selected from the *American National Standard Vocabulary for Information Processing,* X3.12-1970. They are reproduced with the special permission of their publisher, the American National Standards Institute, 1430 Broadway, New York, New York, 10018.

manner of usage to be associated with the item. For example, the label "programming" indicates an area of usage, and the label "loosely" indicates a manner of usage. The usage label is followed by a comma.

Descriptive Phrase. This states, or provides an initial statement of, the definition of the term, and may be assumed to be preceded by the phrase, "(the term) is defined as." The descriptive phrase completes the initial sentence (which may be preceded by the usage label and unabbreviated term). The part of speech being defined is indicated by the first word in the descriptive phrase, where the word "to" indicates a verb, "pertaining to" indicates a modifier, and "a," "the," "an," "any," "each of," etc. indicate a noun.

Annotation. This part of the definition consists of any number of complete sentences. These sentences follow the descriptive phrase and provide additional descriptive or explanatory information.

Reference. A reference consists of a symbol or phrase to direct the user to another item in the commentary or to another entry or item in the vocabulary. If the term being defined is an acronym or abbreviation, the full, unabbreviated term is referenced. An italicized term indicates that the term is significant in the entry, and it, or a grammatically different form of it, has been defined elsewhere in the vocabulary. Also, the reference symbols (Contrast with, Same as, See, Synonymous with) explain the nature of the reference as follows:

Contrast with. This indicates that the preceding definition is different from that of the referenced term, and this difference should be pointed out to the reader.

Same as. This indicates that the defining phrase is exactly the same as for the referenced term, and the referenced term is the preferred term.

See. This references the multiple-word terms with the same last word.

Synonymous with. This indicates that the referenced term has referred to this term by means of a "Same as" reference symbol.

GLOSSARY

Absolute error. (1) The amount of *error* expressed in the same units as the quantity containing the error. (2) Loosely, the absolute value of the error, i.e., the magnitude of the error without regard to its algebraic sign.

Access Time. (1) The time interval between the instant at which *data* are called for from a *storage device* and the instant delivery begins. (2) The time interval between the instant at which data are requested to be stored and the instant at which storage is started.

Accounting Machine. (1) A keyboard actuated machine that prepares accounting *records.* (2) A machine that *reads data* from external *storage* media, such as cards or tapes, and automatically produces accounting records or tabulations, usually on continuous forms.

Accumulator. A *register* in which the result of an arithmetic or logic *operation* is formed.

Accuracy. The degree of freedom from *error,* that is, the degree of conformity to truth or to a rule. Accuracy is contrasted with *precision.* For example, four-place *numerals* are less precise than six-place numerals, nevertheless a properly computed four-place numeral might be more accurate than an improperly computed six-place numeral.

Address. An identification, as represented by a name, *label,* or number, for a *register,* location in *storage,* or any other *data* source or destination such as the location of a station in a communication network. (2) Loosely, any part of an *instruction* that specifies the location of an *operand* for the instruction. . . .

ADP. *Automatic Data Processing.*

Algorithm. A prescribed set of well-defined rules or *processes* for the solution of a problem in a finite number of steps, e.g., a full statement of an arithmetic procedure for evaluating sin x to a stated *precision.* Contrast with *heuristic.*

Algorithmic Language. A *language* designed for expressing *algorithms.*

Alphabet. (1) An ordered set of all the *letters* and associated marks used in a *language.* (2) An ordered set of *symbols* used in a language, e.g., the Morse code alphabet, the 128 characters of the *ASCII* alphabet.

Alphameric. Same as *alphanumeric.*

Alphanumeric. Pertaining to a *character set* that contains *letters, digits,* and usually other *characters* such as punctuation marks. Synonymous with alphameric.

Analog. (1) (SC1)* Pertaining to representation by means of continuously variable physical quantities. (2) Contrast with *digital.* See *network analog.*

Analog Computer. (1) (SC1) a *computer* in which *analog* representation of *data* is mainly used. (2) A computer that operates on analog data by performing physical processes on these data. Contrast with *digital computer.*

Analysis. (1) The methodical investigation of a problem, and the separation of the problem into smaller related units for further detailed study. (2) See *numerical analysis, operations analysis.*

Argument. An independent variable. For example, in looking up a quantity in a *table,* the *number,* or any of the numbers, that identifies the *location* of the desired value.

Array. An arrangement of elements in one or more dimensions.

Artificial Intelligence. The capability of a device to perform functions that are normally associated with human intelligence, such as reasoning, learning, and self-improvement. Related to *machine learning.*

Automatic. (SC1) Pertaining to a process or device that, under specified conditions, functions without intervention by a human operator.

Automatic Check. A *check* performed by equipment built in specifically for checking purposes. Synonymous with built-in check, hardware check. Contrast with *programmed check.*

Automatic Coding. The machine-assisted preparation of *machine language routi*

*The symbol "(SC1)" at the beginning of a definition is used to identify definitions have been discussed and agreed upon at meetings of the International Organization for Stan zation Technical Committee 97/Subcommittee 1.

Automatic Computer. A *computer* that can perform a sequence of *operations* without intervention by a human *operator.*

Automatic Data Processing. (1) (SC1) *Data processing* largely performed by *automatic* means. (2) (SC1) By extension, the discipline which deals with methods and techniques related to data processing performed by automatic means. (3) pertaining to data processing equipment such as *electrical accounting machines* and *electronic data processing* equipment. Abbreviated ADP.

Automatic Programming. The process of using a *computer* to perform some stages of the work involved in preparing a *computer program.*

Automation. (1) (SC1) The implementation of processes by *automatic* means. (2) The theory, art, or technique of making a process more *automatic.* (3) The investigation, design, development, and application of methods of rendering processes *automatic,* self-moving, or self-controlling. (4) (SC1) The conversion of a procedure, a process, or equipment to *automatic* operation.

Auxiliary Operation. An *offline operation* performed by equipment not under control of the *central processing unit.*

Auxiliary Storage. A *storage* that supplements another storage. Contrast with *main storage.* (2) In *flowcharting,* an *offline operation* performed by equipment not under control of the *central processing unit.*

Backspace. To move back the reading or display *position* according to a prescribed format. Contrast with *space* (4).

Bias. The amount by which the average of a set of values departs from a reference value. (2) See *ordering bias.*

Binary. (1) Pertaining to a characteristic or property involving a selection, choice, or condition in which there are two possibilities. (2) Pertaining to the *number representation* system with a *radix* of two. (3) See *Chinese binary, column binary, row binary.*

Binary Card. A card containing *data* in *column binary* form.

Binary Digit. (1) In binary notation, either of the characters, 0 or 1. (2) See *equivalent binary digits, Abbreviated bit.*

Bit. (1) A *binary digit.* (2) Same as Shannon. (3) See *check bit, information bits, parity bit, sign bit.*

Blank Character. Same as space character.

Block. A set of things, such as *words, characters,* or *digits,* handled as a unit. (2) A collection of contiguous *records* recorded as a unit. Blocks are separated by *block gaps* and each block may contain one or more records. (3) A group of bits, or n-ary digits, *transmitted* as a unit. An encoding procedure is generally applied to the group of bits or n-ary digits for error-control purposes. (4) A group of contiguous characters recorded as a unit. (5) See *input block.*

Block Diagram. A diagram of a *system,* instrument, or computer program in which the principal parts are represented by suitably associated geometrical figures to show both the basic functions and the functional relationships among the parts. Contrast with *flowchart.*

Branch. (1) A set of *instructions* that are executed between two successive *decision* *instructions.* (2) To select a branch as in [1]. (3) A direct path joining two *nodes* of a network or graph. (4) Loosely, a *conditional jump.*

Branchpoint. A place in a *routine* where a *branch* is selected.

Buffer. (1) A *routine* or *storage* used to compensate for a difference in rate of flow of *data,* or time of occurrence of events, when transmitting data from one device to another. (2) An isolating circuit used to prevent a driven circuit from influencing the driving circuit.

Built-In Check. Same as *automatic check.*

Business Data Processing. (1) (SC1) Use of *automatic data processing* in accounting or management. (2) *Data processing* for business purposes, e.g., recording and summarizing the financial transactions of a business. (3) Synonymous with administrative data processing.

Byte. A sequence of adjacent *binary digits* operated upon as a unit and usually shorter than a *computer word.*

Calculator. (1) (SC1) A *data processor* especially suitable for performing arithmetical *operations* which requires frequent intervention by a human *operator.* (2) Generally and historically, a device for carrying out logic and arithmetic digital operations of any kind.

Capacity. See *storage capacity.*

Card. See *binary card, header card, laced card, magnetic card, punched card, tape to card.*

Card Column. A single line of *punch positions* parallel to the short edge of a 3-1/4 by 7-3/8 inch *punched card.*

Card Hopper. The portion of a card processing machine that holds cards to be processed and makes them available to a card feed mechanism. Contrast with *card stacker.*

Card Image. A one-to-one representation of the *hole patterns* of a *punched card,* e.g., a matrix in which a one represents a punch and a zero represents the absence of a punch.

Card Stacker. The portion of a card processing machine that receives processed cards. Contrast with *card hopper.*

Carriage Return. The operation that prepares for the next *character* to be printed or displayed at the specified first position on the same line.

Central Processing Unit. (SC1) A unit of a *computer* that includes the circuits controlling the interpretation and execution of *instructions.* Synonymous with main frame. Abbreviated CPU.

Channel. (1) A path along which *signals* can be sent, e.g., *data* channel, *output* channel. (2) The portion of a *storage medium* that is accessible to a given reading or writing station, e.g., *track, band.* (3) In communication, a means of one-way transmission. Several channels may share common equipment. For example, in frequency multiplexing carrier systems, each channel uses a particular frequency band that is reserved for it. Contrast with *circuit.*

Character. (1) A *letter, digit,* or other *symbol* that is used as part of the organization, control, or representation of *data.* A character is often in the form of a spatial arrangement of connected or adjacent strokes. (2) See . . . *blank character, . . . check character, . . . control character, . . . escape character, . . . special character.*

Character Boundary. In *character recognition,* the largest rectangle, with a side parallel to the *document reference edge,* each of whose sides is tangential to a given *character outline.*

Character Outline. The graphic pattern established by the *stroke edges* of a *character.*

Character Recognition. The identification of graphic, phonic, or other *characters* by *automatic* means. See *magnetic ink, character recognition, optical character recognition.*

Character Set. A set of unique representations called *characters,* e.g., the 26 letters of the English *alphabet,* 0 and 1 of the Boolean alphabet, the set of signals in the Morse code alphabet, the 128 characters of the *ASCII* alphabet.

Check. (1) A *process* for determining *accuracy.* (2) See . . . *automatic check, built-in check, . . . duplication check, echo check, . . . marginal check, . . . modulo n check, odd-even check, parity check, programmed check, residue check, selection check, self-checking code, . . . summation check, transfer check.*

Check Bit. A *binary check digit,* e.g., a *parity bit.*

Check Character. A *character* used for the purpose of performing a *check.*

Check Digit. A *digit* used for the purpose of performing a *check.*

Chinese Binary. Same as *column binary.*

Circuit. In communications, a means of two way communication between two points, comprising associated "go" and "return" *channels.* Contrast with *channel.*

COBOL. (COmmon Business Oriented Language). A *business data processing* language.

Code. (1) (SC1) A set of unambiguous rules specifying the way in which *data* may be represented, e.g., the set of correspondences in the standard code for information interchange. Synonymous with coding scheme. (2) (SC1) In telecommunications, a system of rules and conventions according to which the *signals* representing *data* can be formed, transmitted, received, and processed. (3) (SC1) In *data processing,* to represent data or a *computer program* in a symbolic form that can be accepted by a *data processor.* (4) To write a *routine.* (5) Same as *code set.* (6) Same as *encode.* (7) A *set* of *items,* such as abbreviations, representing the members of another set. (8) Same as *code value.* (9) See . . . *binary code, . . . chain code, computer code, error correcting code, error detecting code, excess three code, gray code, . . . instruction code, . . . machine code, minimum distance code, . . . operation code, . . . reflected binary code, . . . self-checking code, two-out-of-five code.*

Coding. See . . . *automatic coding, . . . relative coding, skeletal coding, . . . straight line coding, symbolic coding.*

Collate. To combine *items* from two or more ordered sets into one set having a specified order not necessarily the same as any of the original sets. Contrast with *merge.*

Collating Sequence. An ordering assigned to a set of *items,* such that any two sets in that assigned order can be *collated.*

Collator. A device to *collate, merge,* or *match* sets of *punched cards* or other *documents.*

Column. (1) A vertical arrangement of *characters* or other expressions. (2) Loosely, a *digit place.*

Column Binary. Pertaining to the *binary* representation of *data* on cards in which the *significances* of *punch positions* are assigned along card columns. For example, each column in a 12-row card may be used to represent 12 consecutive *bits.* Synonymous with Chinese binary. . . .

Command. (1) A control *signal.* (2) Loosely, an *instruction* in *machine language.* (3) Loosely, a mathematical or logic *operator.*

Common Field. A *field* that can be accessed by two or more independent *routines.*

Compile. To prepare a *machine language* program from a *computer program* written in another *programming language* by making use of the overall logic structure of the program, or generating more than one *machine instruction* for each symbolic *statement,* or both, as well as performing the function of an *assembler.*

Compiler. A program that *compiles.*

Computer. (1) (SC1) A *data processor* that can perform substantial computation, including numerous arithmetic or logic operations, without intervention by a human *operator* during the run. (2) See *analog computer, . . . asynchronous computer, automatic computer, . . . digital computer, general purpose computer, . . . incremental computer, . . . special purpose computer, stored program computer, synchronous computer.*

Computer Code. A *machine code* for a specific *computer.*

Computer Instruction. A *machine instruction* for a specific *computer.*

Computer Network. A complex consisting of two or more interconnected *computers.*

Computer Program. A series of *instructions* or *statements,* in a form acceptable to a *computer,* prepared in order to achieve a certain result.

Computer Word. A sequence of *bits* or *characters* treated as a unit and capable of being *stored* in one *computerlocation.* Synonymous with machine word.

Concurrent. Pertaining to the occurrence of two or more *events* or activities within the same specified interval of time. Contrast with *consecutive, sequential, simultaneous.*

Console. That part of a *computer* used for communication between the *operator* or *maintenance* engineer and the computer.

Control Character. A *character* whose occurrence in a particular context initiates, modifies, or stops a *control operation.* e.g., a character that controls *carriage return,* a character that controls transmission of *data* over communication networks. A control character may be recorded for use in a subsequent action. It may in some circumstances have a graphic representation. Contrast with *graphic character. . . .*

Convert. To change the representation of *data* from one form to another, e.g., to change numerical data from *binary* to *decimal* or from cards to tape.

Copy. To reproduce *data* in a new location or other destination, leaving the source data unchanged, although the physical form of the result may differ from that of the source. For example, to copy a deck of cards onto a *magnetic tape.* Contrast with *duplicate.*

Core. See *magnetic core. . . .*

Cybernetics. (SC1) That branch of learning which brings together theories and studies on communication and control in living organisms and machines.

Cycle. (1) An interval of space or time in which one set of events or phenomena is completed. (2) Any set of *operations* that is repeated regularly in the same *sequence.* The operations may be subject to variations on each repetition. (3) See *search cycle.*

Data. (1) (SC1) A representation of facts, concepts, or *instructions* in a formalized manner suitable for communication, interpretation, or processing by humans or automatic means. (2) Any representations such as *characters* or *analog* quantities to which meaning is or might be assigned. (3) See *input data, numeric data, output data.*

Data Flowchart. (SC1) A flowchart representing the path of *data* through a problem solution. It defines the major phases of the *processing* as well as the various *data media* used. Synonymous with data flow diagram.

Data Medium. (1) (SC1) The material in or on which a specific physical variable may represent *data.* (2) (SC1) The physical quantity which may be varied to represent *data.*

Data Processing. (SC1) The execution of a systematic sequence of *operations* performed upon *data.* Synonymous with information processing.

Data Processor. (SC1) A device capable of performing *data processing,* including desk *calculators, punched card* machines, and *computers.* Synonymous with *processor* (1).

Data Reduction. The transformation of raw *data* into a more useful form, e.g., *smoothing* to reduce *noise.*

DDA. *Digital Differential Analyzer.*

Debug. To detect, locate, and remove *mistakes* from a *routine* or *malfunctions* from a *computer.* Synonymous with troubleshoot.

Decimal. (1) Pertaining to a characteristic or property involving a selection, choice, or condition in which there are ten possibilities. (2) Pertaining to the *numeration representation system* with a *radix* of ten. (3) See *binary coded decimal notation.*

Decision. A determination of future action.

Decision Instruction. An *instruction* that effects the selection of a *branch* of a program, e.g., a *conditional jump instruction.*

Decision Table. A *table* of all contingencies that are to be considered in the description of a problem, together with the actions to be taken. Decision tables are sometimes used in place of *flowcharts* for problem description and documentation.

Deck. A collection of *punched cards.* Synonymous with card deck. (2) See *tape deck.*

Decode. To apply a set of unambiguous rules specifying the way in which *data* may be restored to a previous representation, i.e., to reverse some previous *encoding.*

Decoder. (1) A device that *decodes.* (2) A *matrix* of *logic elements* that selects one or more *output channels* according to the combination of input signals present. (3) See *operation decoder.*

Delay. The amount of time by which an *event* is retarded.

Destructive Read. A *read* process that also *erases* the *data* in the source.

Device. See . . . *storage device.*

Diagnostic. Pertaining to the detection and isolation of a *malfunction* or *mistake.*

Diagram. See *block diagram, . . . functional diagram, logic diagram, . . . venn diagram.*

Digit. (1) A *symbol* that represents one of the non-negative integers smaller than the radix. For example, in *decimal notation,* a digit is one of the *characters* from 0 to 9. Synonymous with numeric character. (2) See *binary digit, check digit, . . . equivalent binary digits, sign digit, significant digit.*

Digital. (1) (SC1) Pertaining to *data* in the form of *digits.* (2) Contrast with *analog.*

Digital Computer. (1) (SC1) A *computer* in which *discrete* representation of *data* is mainly used. (2) A *computer* that operates on *discrete data* by performing arithmetic and logic processes on these data. Contrast with *analog computer.*

Digitize. To use *numeric characters* to express or represent *data,* e.g., to obtain from an *analog* representation of a physical quantity, a *digital* representation of the quantity.

Direct Access. (1) Pertaining to the process of obtaining *data* from, or placing data into, *storage* where the time required for such access is independent of the *location* of the data most recently obtained or placed in storage. (2) Pertaining to a *storage* device in which the *access time* is effectively independent of the location of the *data.* (3) Synonymous with random access (1).

Discrete. (SC1) Pertaining to distinct elements or to representation by means of distinct elements such as *characters.*

Display. A visual presentation of *data.* . . .

Display Tube. A tube, usually a cathode ray tube, used to display *data.*

Document. (1) A *medium* and the *data* recorded on it for human use, e.g., a report sheet, a book. (2) By extension, any *record* that has permanence and that can be read by man or machine.

Document Reference Edge. In *character recognition,* a specified *document* edge with respect to which the alignment of *characters* is defined.

Documentation. (1) The creating, collecting, organizing, storing, citing, and disseminating of *documents* or the *information* recorded in documents. (2) A collection of *documents* or *information* on a given subject.

Double Precision. Pertaining to the use of two *computer words* to represent a *number.*

Downtime. The time interval during which a device is *malfunctioning.*

Dummy. Pertaining to the characteristic of having the appearance of a specified thing but not having the capacity to function as such. For example, a dummy *character,* dummy plug, or a dummy *statement.*

Dump. (1) To copy the contents of all or part of a *storage,* usually from an internal storage into an external storage. (2) A process as in (1). (3) The data resulting from the process as in (1). (4) See . . . *dynamic dump, postmortem dump, selective dump, snapshot dump, static dump.*

Duplication Check. A *check* based on the consistency of two independent performances of the same task.

EAM (Electrical Accounting Machine). Pertaining to *data processing* equipment that is predominantly electromechanical such as a keypunch, mechanical *sorter, collator,* and *tabulator.*

Echo Check. A method of checking the *accuracy* of *transmission* of *data* in which the received data are returned to the sending end for comparison with the original data.

Edge. See *document reference edge, stroke edge.*

Edit. To modify the form or *format* of *data,* e.g., to insert or delete *characters* such as page numbers or decimal points.

EDP (Electronic Data Processing). (1) (SC1) *Data processing* largely performed by electronic devices. (2) Pertaining to *data processing* equipment that is predominantly electronic such as an electronic *digital computer.*

Eleven-Punch. A punch in the second *row* from the top, on a *Hollerith punched card.* Synonymous with x-punch.

Emulate. To imitate one *system* with another such that the imitating system accepts the same *data,* executes the same *programs,* and achieves the same results as the imitated system. Contrast with *simulate.*

Encode. To apply a set of unambiguous rules specifying the way in which data may be represented such that a subsequent *decoding* is possible. Synonymous with code (6).

Entry Point. In a *routine,* any place to which control can be passed.

Erase. To obliterate *information* from a *storage medium,* e.g., to clear, to overwrite.

Error. (1) Any discrepancy between a computed, observed, or measured quantity and the true, specified, or theorectically correct value or condition. (2) See *absolute error, inherited error.* . . . (3) Contrast with *fault, malfunction,* and *mistake.*

Error Correcting Code. A *code* in which each acceptable expression conforms to specific rules of construction that also define one or more equivalent nonacceptable expressions, so that if certain *errors* occur in an acceptable expression the result will be one of its equivalents and thus the error can be corrected.

Error Detecting Code. A *code* in which each expression conforms to specific rules of construction, so that if certain *errors* occur in an expression the resulting expression will not conform to the rules of construction and thus, the presence of the errors is detected. Synonymous with self-checking code.

Error Message. An indication that an *error* has been detected.

Error Range. The difference between the highest and lowest *error* values.

Escape Character. A *code extension character* used with one or more succeeding characters to form an escape sequence which indicates by some convention that the succeeding characters are to be interpreted differently. Abbreviated *ESC.*

Event. An occurrence or happening.

Extract. To choose from a *set* of *items* all those that meet some criteria, e.g., to obtain certain specified *digits* from a *machine word* as controlled by an *instruction* or *mask.*

Fault. (1) A physical condition that causes a device, a component, or an element to fail to perform in a required manner, e.g., a short circuit, a broken wire, an intermittent connection. (2) See *pattern sensitive fault, program sensitive fault.* (3) Contrast with *error, malfunction, mistake.*

Ferrite. An iron compound frequently used in the construction of *magnetic cores.*

Field. (1) In a *record,* a specified area used for a particular category of *data,* e.g., a group of card columns used to represent a wage rate, a set of *bit* locations in a *computer word* used to express the *address* of the *operand.* (2) See *common field.*

File. A collection of related *records* treated as a unit. For example, one line of an invoice forms an *item,* a complete invoice forms a *record,* and the complete set of such records forms a file, the collection of inventory control files may form a *library,* and the libraries used by an organization are known as its *data bank.*

File Gap. An area on a *data medium* intended to be used to indicate the end of a *file,* and possibly, the start of another. A file gap is frequently used for other purposes, in particular, as a *flag* to indicate the end or beginning of some other group of data.

File Maintenance. The activity of keeping a *file* up to date by adding, changing, or deleting *data.*

Fixed-Cycle Operation. An *operation* that is completed in a specified number of regularly timed execution cycles.

Fixed Storage. Storage whose contents are not alterable by *computer instructions,* e.g., *magnetic core* storage with a lockout feature, photographic disc. Synonymous with nonerasable storage, permanent storage, read-only storage.

Flag. (1) Any of various types of indicators used for identification, e.g., a wordmark. (2) A *character* that signals the occurrence of some condition, such as the end of a word. (3) Synonymous with mark, sentinel, tag.

Flip-Flop. A *circuit* or device containing active elements, capable of assuming either one of two stable states at a given time. Synonymous with toggle (1).

Flowchart. (1) (SC1) A graphical representation for the definition, analysis, or solution of a problem, in which *symbols* are used to represent *operations, data,* flow, and equipment, etc. Contrast with *block diagram.* (2) See *data flowchart, programming flowchart.*

Flowchart Symbol. (SC1) A symbol used to represent *operations, data,* flow, or equipment on a *flowchart.*

Flow Direction. (SC1) In *flowcharting,* the antecedent-to-successor relation, indicated by arrows or other conventions, between *operations* on a *flowchart.*

Flowline. (SC1) On a *flowchart,* a line representing a connecting path between *flowchart symbols,* e.g., a line to indicate a transfer of *data* or control.

Font. (1) A family or assortment of *characters* of a given size and style, e.g., 9 point Bodina modern. (2) See *type font.*

Formal Logic. The study of the structure and form of valid argument without regard to the meaning of the terms in the argument.

Format. (1) The arrangement of *data.* (2) See *address format.*

FORTRAN (FORmula TRANslating system). A *language* primarily used to express *computer programs* by arithmetic formulas.

Function. (1) A specific purpose of an entity, or its characteristic action. (2) In communications, a machine action such as a *carriage return* or *line feed.*

Functional Design. The specification of the working relations between the parts of a *system* in terms of their characteristic actions.

General Purpose Computer. (SC1) A *computer* that is designed to solve a wide variety of problems.

Graphic. A symbol produced by a process such as handwriting, drawing, or printing.

Graphic Character. A *character* normally represented by a *graphic.* Contrast with *control character.*

Group Mark. A mark that identifies the beginning or end of a set of *data,* which could include *words, blocks,* or other *items.*

Hardware. (SC1) Physical equipment, as opposed to the *computer program* or method of use, e.g., mechanical, magnetic, electrical, or electronic devices. Contrast with *software.*

Head. A device that *reads, writes, or erases data* on a storage *medium,* e.g., a small electromagnet used to read, write, or erase data on a *magnetic drum* or *tape,* or the set of perforating, reading or marking devices used for punching, reading, or printing on paper tape.

Header Card. A card that contains *information* related to the *data* in cards that follow.

Heuristic. Pertaining to exploratory methods of problem solving in which solutions are discovered by evaluation of the progress made toward the final result. Contrast with *algorithm.*

Hit. A successful comparison of two *items* of *data.* Contrast with *match.*

Hole Pattern. A punching configuration within a *card column* that represents a single *character* of a *character set.*

Hollerith. Pertaining to a particular type of *code* or *punched card* utilizing 12 *rows* per *column* and usually 80 columns per card.

Hopper. See *card hopper.*

Identifier. A *symbol* whose purpose is to identify, indicate, or name a body of *data.*

Index. (1) An ordered reference list of the contents of a *file* or *document* together with *keys* or reference notations for identification or location of those contents. (2) To prepare a list as in (1). (3) A *symbol* or a *numeral* used to identify a particular quantity in an array of similar quantities. For example, the terms of an array represented by X_1, X_2, . . . X_{100} have the indexes 1, 2, . . . 100 respectively. (4) To move a machine part to a predetermined position, or by a predetermined amount, on a *quantized* scale. (5) See *index register.*

Industrial Data Processing. *Data processing* for industrial purposes.

Information. (SC1) The meaning that a human assigns to *data* by means of the known conventions used in their representation.

Information Processing. (SC1) Same as *data processing.*

Information Retrieval. The methods and *procedures* for recovering specific *information* from stored *data.*

Information Separator. A *control character* intended to identify a logical boundary of *information.* The name of the separator does not necessarily indicate what it separates. Abbreviated *IS.*

Information Theory. The branch of learning concerned with the likelihood of accurate *transmission* or communication of *messages* subject to transmission failure, distortion, and *noise.*

Inherited error. An *error* carried forward from a previous step in a *sequential* process.

Initialize. To set *counters, switches,* and *addresses* to zero or other starting values at the beginning of, or at prescribed points in, a computer *routine.* Synonymous with prestore.

Input. (1) Pertaining to a device, process, or *channel* involved in the insertion of *data* or states, or to the data or states involved. (2) One, or a sequence of, *input states.* (3) Same as *input device.* (4) Same as *input channel.* (5) Same as *input process.* (6) Same as *input data.* (7) See *manual input, real time input.*

Input Process. (1) The process of receiving *data* by a device. (2) The process of transmitting data from peripheral equipment, or external *storage,* to internal storage. (3) Synonymous with input (5).

Instruction. (1) A *statement* that specifies an *operation* and values or locations of its *operands.* (2) See *computer instruction, decision instruction, extract instruction, logic instruction, machine instruction, macro instruction, repetition instruction.*

Interpreter. (1) A *computer program* that translates and executes each *source language* expression before translating and executing the next one. (2) A device that prints on a *punched card* the *data* already punched in the card.

Interrupt. To stop a *process* in such a way that it can be resumed.

I/O. An abbreviation for *input/output.*

Item. (1) In general, one member of a group, e.g., a *record* may contain a number of items such as *fields* or groups of fields; a *file* may consist of a number of items such as records; a table may consist of a number of items such as entries. (2)A collection of related *characters,* treated as a unit.

Job. A specified group of tasks prescribed as a unit of work for a *computer.* By extension, a job usually includes all necessary *computer programs, linkages, files,* and *instructions* to the *operating system.*

Job Control Statement. A *statement* in a *job* that is used in identifying the job or describing its requirements to the *operating system.*

Jump. (1) A departure from the normal sequence of executing *instructions* in a *computer.* Synonymous with transfer [1]. (2) See *conditional jump.*

Karnaugh Map. In *logic design,* a rectangular diagram of a logic function of *variables* drawn with overlapping subrectangles such that each intersection of overlapping subrectangles represents a unique combination of the logic variables and such that an intersection is shown for all combinations.

Key. (1) One or more *characters* within an *item* of *data* that are used to identify it or control its use. (2) See *actual key, search key.*

Keypunch. A keyboard actuated device that punches holes in a card to represent *data.*

Label. One or more *characters* used to identify a *statement* or an *item* of *data* in a *computer program.*

Laced Card. A *punched card* that has a lace-like appearance, usually without information content.

Lag. The *delay* between two events.

Language. (1) A set of representations, conventions, and rules used to convey *information.* (2) See *algorithmic language, artificial language, . . . machine language, natural language, object language, problem oriented language, procedure oriented language, programming language, source language, target language.*

Length. See . . . *word length.*

Letter. A *graphic,* which, when used alone or combined with others, represents in a written *language* one or more sound elements of the spoken language; diacritical marks used alone and punctuation marks are not letters.

Library. (1) A collection of organized *information* used for study and reference. (2) A collection of related *files.* For example, one line of an invoice may form an *item,* a complete invoice may form a file, the collection of inventory control files may form a library, and the libraries used by an organization are known as its *data bank.* See *program library.*

Library Routine. A proven *routine* that is maintained in a *program library.*

Line Printing. The printing of an entire line of characters as a unit.

Linkage. In *programming, coding* that connects two separately coded *routines.*

Location. (1) Any place in which *data* may be *stored.* (2) See *protected location.*

Logical Record. A collection of *items* independent of their physical environment. Portions of the same logical *record* may be located in different physical records.

Logic Design. The specification of the working relations between the parts of a system in terms of *symbolic logic* and without primary regard for *hardware* implementation.

Logic Diagram. A *diagram* that represents a *logic design* and sometimes the *hardware* implementation.

Logic Element. . . . A device that performs a logic function. . . .

Logic Instruction. An *instruction* that executes an *operation* that is defined in *symbolic logic,* such as *AND, OR, NOR.*

Look-Up. See *table look-up.*

Loop. A *sequence* of *instructions* that is executed repeatedly until a terminal condition prevails. . . .

Machine. See *accounting machine. electrical accounting machine, turing machine, universal turing machine.*

Machine Code. An *operation code* that a machine is designed to recognize.

Machine Instruction. An *instruction* that a machine can recognize and execute.

Machine Language. A *language* that is used directly by a machine.

Machine Learning. (SC1) The ability of a device to improve its performance based on its past performance. Related to *artificial intelligence.*

Machine Word. Same as *computer word.*

Macro Instruction. An *instruction* in a *source language* that is equivalent to a specified *sequence* of *machine instructions.*

Magazine. See *input magazine.*

Magnetic Core. A configuration of magnetic material that is, or is intended to be, placed in a spatial relationship to current-carrying conductors and whose magenetic properties are essential to its use. It may be used to concentrate an induced magnetic field as in a transformer induction coil, or armature, to retain a magnetic polarization for the purpose of *storing* data, or for its nonlinear properties as in a *logic element.* It may be made of such material as iron, iron oxide, or ferrite and in such shapes as wires, tapes, toroids, rods, or thin film.

Magnetic Disc. A flat circular plate with a magnetic surface on which *data* can be *stored* by selective magnetization of portions of the flat surface.

Magnetic Drum. A right circular cylinder with a magnetic surface on which *data* can be *stored* by selective magnetization of portions of the curved surface.

Magnetic Ink. An ink that contains particles of a magnetic substance whose presence can be detected by magnetic sensors.

Magnetic Ink Character Recognition. The machine recognition of *characters* printed with magnetic ink. Contrast with *optical character recognition.* Abbreviated *MICR.*

Magnetic Storage. A *storage device* that utilizes the magnetic properties of materials to *store data,* e.g., *magnetic cores, tapes,* and *films.*

Magnetic Tape. (1) A tape with a magnetic surface on which *data* can be stored by selective polarization of portions of the surface. (2) A tape of magnetic material used as the constituent in some forms of *magnetic cores.*

Magnetic Thin Film. A layer of magnetic material, usually less than one micron thick, often used for logic or storage elements.

Maintenance. (1) Any activity intended to eliminate *faults* or keep *hardware* or *programs* in satisfactory working condition, including tests, measurements, replacements, adjustments, and repairs. (2) See . . . *file maintenance.*

Malfunction. The effect of a *fault.* Contrast with *error, mistake.*

Manual Input. (1) The entry of *data* by hand into a device. (2) The data entered as in (1).

Map. (1) To establish a correspondence between the elements of one set and the elements of another set. (2) See *Karnaugh map.*

Marginal Check. A *preventive maintenance* procedure in which certain operating conditions, such as supply voltage or frequency, are varied about their nominal values in order to detect and locate incipiently defective parts.

Mark. (1) See *group mark.* Same as *flag.*

Mask. (1) A pattern of *characters* that is used to control the retention or elimination of portions of another pattern of characters. (2) A *filter.*

Match. To *check* for identity between two or more *items* of *data.* Contrast with *hit.*

Mathematical Model. A mathematical representation of a process, device, or concept.

Matrix. (1) In mathematics, a two-dimensional rectangular *array* of quantities. Matrices are manipulated in accordance with the rules of matrix algebra. (2) In *computers,* a logic network in the form of an array of *input* leads and *output* leads with *logic elements* connected at some of their intersections. (3) By extension, an array of any number of dimensions.

Medium. . . . The material, or configuration thereof, on which data is recorded, e.g., paper tape, cards, *magnetic tape.* Synonymous with data medium. . . .

Memory. . . . Same as *storage.* . . .

Mercury Storage. A *storage device* that utilizes the acoustic properties of mercury to store data.

Merge. To combine *items* from two or more similarly ordered sets into one set that is arranged in the same order. Contrast with *collate.*

Message. (1) An arbitrary amount of *information* whose beginning and end are defined or implied. (2) See *error message.*

Mistake. A human action that produces an unintended result. Contrast with *error, fault, malfunction.*

Mode. See *access mode.* . . .

Model. See *mathematical model.*

Multiprocessing. (1) Pertaining to the simultaneous execution of two or more *computer programs* or *sequences of instructions* by a *computer* or *computer network* loosely, *parallel processing.*

Multiprocessor. A *computer* capable of employing two or more processing units under integrated control.

Multiprogramming. Pertaining to the *concurrent* execution of two or more *programs* by a *computer.*

Natural Language. A *language* whose rules reflect and describe current usage rather than prescribe usage. Contrast with *artificial language.*

Node. The representation of a state or an *event* by means of a point on a diagram.

Noise. (1) Random variations of one or more characteristics of any entity such as voltage, current, or *data.* (2) A random *signal* of known statistical properties of amplitude, distribution and spectral density. (3) Loosely, any disturbance tending to interfere with the normal operation of a device or *system.*

Nondestructive Read. A *read* process that does not *erase* the *data* in the source. Abbreviated NDR.

Normal Direction Flow. (SC1) A flow in a direction from left to right or top to bottom on a *flowchart.*

Normalize. (1) To multiply a *variable* or one or more quantities occurring in a calculation by a numerical coefficient in order to make an associated quantity assume a nominated value, e.g., to make a definite integral of a variable, or the maximum member of a *set* of quantities, equal to unity. . . . (2) Loosely, to *scale.*

Notation. See . . . *positional notation.* . . .

Number. (1) A mathematical entity that may indicate quantity or amount of units. (2) Loosely, a *numeral.* (3) See *binary number.* . . .

Number Representation System. An agreed set of *symbols* and rules for *number representation.* Synonymous with numeral system, numeration system.

Number System. Loosely, a *number representation system.*

Numeral. (1) A discrete representation of a *number.* For example, twelve, 12, XII, 1100 are four different numerals that represent the same number. (2) A numeric word that represents a *number.* (3) See *binary numeral, decimal numeral.*

Numeral System. Same as *number representation system.*

Numeration System. Same as *number representation system.*

Numerical Analysis. The study of methods of obtaining useful quantitative solutions to problems that have been expressed mathematically, including the study of the errors and bounds on *errors* in obtaining such solutions.

Numerical Control. (SC1) *Automatic* control of a process performed by a device that makes use of all or part of *numerical data* generally introduced as the *operation* is in process.

Numeric Character. Same as *digit.*

Object Language. Same as *target language.*

Object Program. A fully *compiled* or *assembled program* that is ready to be *loaded* into the *computer.* Synonymous with target program. Contrast with *source program.*

OCR (Optical Character Recognition). Machine identification of printed *characters* through use of light-sensitive devices. Contrast with *magnetic ink character recognition.* Abbreviated *OCR.*

Odd-Even Check. Same as *parity check.*

Offline. Pertaining to equipment or devices not under control of the *central processing unit.*

Online. (1) Pertaining to equipment or devices under direct control of the *central processing unit.* (2) Pertaining to a user's ability to interact with a *computer.*

Operand. That which is operated upon. An operand is usually identified by an *address* part of an *instruction.*

Operating System. (SC1) *Software* which controls the execution of *computer programs* and which may provide scheduling, *debugging,* input/output control, accounting, *compilation, storage* assignment, *data* management, and related services.

Operation. (1) A defined action, namely, the act of obtaining a result from one or more *operands* in accordance with a rule that completely specifies the result for any permissible combination of operands. (2) The *set* of such acts specified by such a rule, or the rule itself. (3) The act specified by a single *computer instruction.* (4) A *program* step undertaken or executed by a *computer,* e.g., addition, multiplication, *extraction,* comparison, *shift, transfer.* The operation is usually specified by the *operator* part of an instruction. (5) The event or specific action performed by a *logic element.* (6) See *auxiliary operation, . . . dyadic operation, fixed-cycle operation, monadic operation, . . . sequential operation, serial operation, unary operation.*

Operation Code. A *code* that represents specific operations. Synonymous with instruction code.

Operation Decoder. A device that selects one or more control *channels* according to the *operator* part of a *machine instruction.*

Operator. (1) In the description of a *process,* that which indicates the action to be performed on *operands.* (2) A person who operates a machine. . . .

Optical Character Recognition. See *OCR.*

Optical Scanner. (1) A device that scans optically and usually generates an *analog* or *digital signal.* (2) A device that optically scans printed or written *data* and generates their *digital representations.*

Order. (1) To arrange *items* according to any specified *set* of rules. Synonymous with sort. (2) An arrangement of items according to any specified set of rules.

Ordering Bias. The degree to which the order of a *set* of *data* departs from random distribution. An ordering bias will increase or decrease the effort necessary to order a set of data from the effort anticipated for random distribution.

Organizing. See *self-organizing.*

Output. (1) (SC1) Pertaining to a device, *process,* or *channel* involved in an *output process,* or to the data or states involved. (2) One, or a sequence of, *output states.* (3) Same as *output device.* (4) Same as *output channel.* (5) Same as *output process.* (6) Same as *output data.* (7) See *real time output.*

Output Channel. A *channel* for conveying *data* from a device or *logic element.* Synonymous with output (4).

Output Data. (SC1) *Data* to be delivered from a device or *program,* usually after some processing. Synonymous with output (6).

Output Device. (SC1) The device or collective set of devices used for conveying *data* out of another device. Synonymous with output (3).

Output Process. (SC1) The process of delivering *data* by a system, subsystem, or device. Synonymous with output (5).

Output State. The state occurring on a specified *output channel.*

Overflow. (1) That portion of the result of an *operation* that exceeds the capacity of the intended unit of *storage.* (2) Pertaining to the generation of overflow as in (1). (3) Contrast with *underflow.*

Overlay. The technique of repeatedly using the same blocks of internal *storage* during different stages of a *program.* When one *routine* is no longer needed in storage, another routine can replace all or part of it.

Pack. To compress *data* in a *storage* medium by taking advantage of the known characteristics of the data, in such a way that the original data can be recovered, e.g., to compress data in a storage medium by making use of *bit* or *byte* locations that would otherwise go unused.

Packing Density. The number of useful *storage cells* per unit of dimension, e.g., the number of bits per inch stored on a *magnetic tape* or drum track.

Parallel. (1) Pertaining to the *concurrent* or *simultaneous* occurrence of two or more related activities in multiple devices or *channels.* (2) Pertaining to the simultaneity of two or more *processes.* (3) Pertaining to the simultaneous processing of the individual parts of a whole, such as the *bits* of a *character* and the characters of a *word,* using separate facilities for the various parts. (4) Contrast with *serial.*

Parallel Operation. Pertaining to the *concurrent* or *simultaneous* execution of two or more *operations* in devices such as multiple arithmetic or logic units. Contrast with *serial operation.*

Parallel Processing. Pertaining to the *concurrent* or *simultaneous* execution of two or more *operations* in devices such as multiple arithmetic or logic units. Contrast with *multiprocessing, serial processing.*

Parallel Storage. A *storage device* in which *characters, words,* or *digits* are dealt with *simultaneously* or *concurrently.*

Parameter. A *variable* that is given a constant value for a specific purpose or *process.*

Parity Bit. A *check bit* appended to an *array* of *binary digits* to make the sum of all the binary digits, including the check bit, always odd or always even.

Parity Check. A *check* that tests whether the number of ones (or zeros) in an *array* of *binary digits* is odd or even. Synonymous with odd-even check.

Patch. (1) To modify a *routine* in a rough or expedient way. (2) A temporary electrical connection.

Pattern Recognition. The identification of shapes, forms, or configurations by *automatic* means.

Point. See *branchpoint, breakpoint, checkpoint, . . . entry point, fixed point, floating point, . . . rerun point.*

Position. (1) In a *string* each location that may be occupied by a *character* or *binary digit* and may be identified by a serial number. (2) See *punch position. . . .*

Precision. (1) The degree of discrimination with which a quantity is stated. For example, a three-digit *numeral* discriminates among 1000 possibilities. (2) See *double precision.*

Predefined Process. A process that is identified only by name and that is defined elsewhere.

Prestore. Same as *initialize.*

Preventive Maintenance. *Maintenance* specifically intended to prevent *faults* from occurring during subsequent *operation. . . .*

Problem Description. (1) (SC1) In *information processing,* a statement of a problem. The statement may also include a description of the method of solution, the procedures and *alogrithms,* etc. (2) A statement of a problem. The statement may also include a description of the method of solution, the solution itself, the transformations of *data* and the relationship of procedures, data, constraints, and environment.

Problem Oriented Language. A *programming language* designed for the convenient expression of a given class of problems.

Procedure. (1) (SC1) The course of action taken for the solution of a problem. (2) See *inline procedures.*

Procedure Oriented Language. A *programming language* designed for the convenient expression of procedures used in the solution of a wide class of problems.

Process. A systematic *sequence* of *operations* to produce a specified result. See *input process, output process, predefined process.*

Processing. See . . . *automatic data processing,* . . . *business data processing, data processing, electronic data processing,* . . . *industrial data processing, information processing,* . . . *multiprocessing, parallel processing.* . . .

Processor. (1) In *hardware,* a *data processor.* (2) In *software,* a *computer program* that includes the *compiling, assembling, translating,* and related functions for a specific *programming language,* e.g., *COBOL* processor, *FORTRAN* processor. (3) See *data processor, multiprocessor.*

Program. (1) (SC1) A series of actions proposed in order to achieve a certain result. (2) Loosely, a *routine,* (3) To design, write, and test a program as in (1). (4) Loosely, to write a routine. (5) See *computer program, object program, source program, target program.*

Program Library. A collection of available *computer programs* and *routines.*

Programmed Check. A *check* procedure designed by the *programmer* and implemented specifically as a part of his *program.* Contrast with *automatic check.*

Programmer. (SC1) A person mainly involved in designing, writing, and testing *computer programs.*

Programming. (1) (SC1) The design, the writing, and testing *computer programs.* (2) See *automatic programming,* . . . *linear programming,* . . . *multiprogramming.*

Programming Flowchart. (SC1) A *flowchart* representing the sequence of *operations* in a *program.*

Programming Language. A *language* used to prepare *computer programs.*

Punch. (1) A perforation, as in a *punched card* or paper tape. (2) See . . . *keypunch, eleven-punch,* . . . *twelve-punch, zone punch.*

Punched Card. (1) A card *punched* with a pattern of holes to represent *data.* (2) A card as in (1) before being punched.

Punch Position. A defined *location* on a card or tape where a hole may be *punched.*

Punched Tape. A tape on which a pattern of holes or cuts is used to represent *data.*

Quantize. To subdivide the *range* of values of a *variable* into a finite number of nonoverlapping, but not necessarily equal, subranges or intervals, each of which is represented by an assigned value within the subrange.

Random Access. (1) Same as *direct access.* (2) In COBOL an *access mode* in which specific *logical records* are obtained from or placed into a *mass storage file* in a nonsequential manner.

Range. (1) The *set* of values that a quantity or *function* may assume. (2) The difference between the highest and lowest value that a quantity or function may assume. (3) See *error range.*

Read. (1) To acquire or interpret *data* from a *storage device,* a *data medium,* or any other source. (2) See *destructive read, nondestructive read.*

Real Time. (1) Pertaining to the actual time during which a physical *process* transpires. (2) Pertaining to the performance of a computation during the actual time that the related physical process transpires in order that results of the computation can be used in guiding the physical process.

Real Time Input. *Input data* inserted into a *system* at the time of generation by another system.

Real Time Output. *Output data* removed from a *system* at time of need by another system.

Recognition. See *character recognition, magnetic ink character recognition, optical character recognition, pattern recognition.*

Record. (1) A collection of related *items* of *data,* treated as a unit, for example one line of an invoice may form a record; a complete set of such records may form a *file.* (2) See *logical record, variable-length record.*

Reduction. See *data reduction.*

Register. . . . A device capable of *storing* a specified amount of *data* such as one *word.* . . .

Reliability. The probability that a device will perform without failure over a specified time period or amount of usage.

Reset. (1) To restore a *storage device* to a prescribed initial state, not necessarily that denoting zero. (2) To place a *binary cell* into the state denoting zero.

Restart. To reestablish the execution of a *routine,* using the *data* recorded at a *checkpoint.*

Retrieval. See *information retrieval.*

Reverse Direction Flow. In *flowcharting,* a flow in a direction other than left to right or top to bottom.

Roundoff. To delete the least *significant digit* or digits of a *numeral* and to adjust the part retained in accordance with some rule.

Routine. (SC1) An ordered set of *instructions* that may have some general or frequent use. (2) See *executive routine, library routine, service routine, subroutine, supervisory routine, tracing routine, utility routine.*

Row. A horizontal arrangement of *characters* or other expressions.

Sampling. (1) Obtaining the values of a *function* for regularly or irregularly spaced *discrete* values of the independent *variable.* (2) In statistics, obtaining a sample from a population.

Scale. To adjust the representation a quantity by a factor in order to bring its *range* within prescribed limits.

Scale Factor. A *number* used as a multiplier, so chosen that it will cause a set of quantities to fall within a given *range* of values. To scale the *values* 856, 432, –95, and –182 between –1 and +1, a scale factor of 1/1000 would be suitable.

Scan. To examine *sequentially,* part by part.

Scanner. See *flying spot scanner, optical scanner.*

Search. (1) To examine a set of *items* for those that have a desired property. (2) See *binary search, . . . dichotomizing search. . . .*

Search Cycle. The part of a *search* that is repeated for each *item,* which normally consists of locating the item and carrying out a comparison.

Search Key. *Data* to be compared to specified parts of each *item* for the purpose of conducting a *search.*

Selection Check. A *check* that verifies the choice of devices, such as *registers,* in the execution of an *instruction.*

Self-Adapting. (SC1) Pertaining to the ability of a *system* to change its performance characteristics in response to its environment.

Self-Checking Code. Same as *error detecting code.*

Self-Organizing. (SC1) Pertaining to the ability of a *system* to arrange its internal structure.

Semantics. The relationships between symbols and their meanings.

Sequence. . . . An arrangement of *items,* according to specified set of rules. . . .

Sequential. Pertaining to the occurrence of *events* in time *sequence,* with little or no simultaneity or overlap of events. Contrast with *concurrent, consecutive, simultaneous.*

Serial. (1) Pertaining to the *sequential* or *consecutive* occurrence of two or more related activities in a single device or *channel.* (2) Pertaining to the *sequencing* of two or more *processes.* (3) Pertaining to the *sequential processing* of the individual parts of a whole, such as the *bits* of a character or the characters of a *word,* using the same facilities for successive parts. (4) Contrast with *parallel.*

Serial Access. Pertaining to the *sequential* or *consecutive transmission* of *data* to or from *storage.* (2) Pertaining to the *process* of obtaining *data* from or placing data into *storage,* where the *access time* is dependent upon the *location* of the data most recently obtained or placed in storage. Contrast with *direct access.*

Serial Operation. Pertaining to the *sequential* or *consecutive* execution of two or more *operations* in a single device such as an arithmetic or logic unit. Contrast with *parallel operation.*

Serial Processing. Pertaining to the *sequential* or *consecutive* execution of two or more *processes* in a single device such as a *channel* or processing unit. Contrast with *parallel processing.*

Servomechanism. (1) (SC1) An *automatic* control *system* incorporating feedback that governs the physical *position* of an element by adjusting either the values of the coordinates or the values of their time derivatives. (2) A feedback control *system* in which at least one of the system *signals* represents mechanical motion. (3) Any feedback control system.

Set. (1) A collection. (2) To place a *storage device* into a specified state, usually other than that denoting zero or *space character.* Contrast with *clear.* (3) To place a binary cell into the state denoting one. (4) See . . . *preset, reset.*

Shift. . . . A movement of *data* to the right or left.

Signal. (1) (SC1) A time-dependent value attached to a physical phenomenon and conveying *data.* (2) The event or phenomenon that conveys data from one point to another. (3) See *inhibiting signal.*

Significant Digit. A *digit* that is needed for a certain purpose, particularly one that must be kept to preserve a specific *accuracy* or *precision.*

Simulate. (1) (SC1) To represent certain features of the behavior of a physical or abstract *system* by the behavior of another system. (2) To represent the functioning of a device, *system,* or *computer program* by another, e.g., to represent the functioning of one *computer* by another, to represent the behavior of a physical system by the execution of a computer program, to represent a biological system by a *mathematical model.* (3) Contrast with *emulate.*

Simulator. (SC1) A device, *system,* or *computer program* that represents certain features of the behavior of a physical or abstract system.

Simultaneous. Pertaining to the occurrence of two or more *events* at the same instant of time. Contrast with *concurrent, consecutive, sequential.*

Skip. To ignore one or more *instructions* in a *sequence* of instructions.

Software. (SC1) A set of *computer programs, procedures,* and possibly associated *documentation* concerned with the *operation* of a *data processing system,* e.g., *compilers, library routines,* manuals, circuit diagrams. Contrast with *hardware.*

Solid State Component. A component whose *operation* depends on the control of electric or magnetic phenomena in solids, e.g., a transistor, crystal diode, *ferrite* core.

Sort. (1) To segregate *items* into groups according to some definite rules. (2) Same as *order.*

Sorter. A person, device, or *computer routine* that *sorts.*

Source Language. The *language* from which a statement is translated.

Source Program. A *computer program* written in a *source language.* Contrast with *object program.*

Space. (1) A site intended for the *storage* of *data,* e.g., a site on a printed page or a *location* in a *storage medium.* (2) A basic *unit* of area, usually the size of a single *character.* (3) One or more *space characters.* (4) To advance the *reading* or *display position* according to a prescribed *format,* e.g., to advance the printing or display position horizontally to the right or vertically down. Contrast with *backspace.*

Space Character. A normally nonprinting *graphic character* used to separate *words.* The space character is also a format effector which controls the movement of the printing or display position, one position forward. The space character may also be considered in the hierarchy of *information separators.* Synonymous with blank character. Abbreviated *SP.* . . .

Special Character. A graphic *character* that is neither a letter, nor a *digit,* nor a *space character.*

Special Purpose Computer. (SC1) A computer that is designed to handle a restricted class of problems.

Statement. (1) In *computer programming,* a meaningful expression or generalized *instruction* in a *source language.* (2) See *job control statement.*

Step. (1) One *operation* in a *computer routine.* (2) To cause a *computer* to execute one *operation.* (3) See . . . *single step.*

Storage. (1) Pertaining to a device into which *data* can be entered, in which it can be held, and from which it can be retrieved at a later time. (2) Loosely, any device that can store *data.* (3) Synonymous with memory. (4) See . . . *associative storage, auxiliary storage,* . . . *content addressed storage,* . . . *electostatic storage, fixed storage,* . . . *magnetic storage,* . . . *mercury storage,* . . . *nonerasable storage, parallel search storage, parallel storage, permanent storage, read-only storage,* . . . *temporary storage, volatile storage, working storage.*

Storage Allocation. The assignment of *blocks* of *data* to specified blocks of *storage.* . . .

Storage Capacity. The amount of *data* that can be contained in a *storage device.*

Storage Device. A device into which *data* can be inserted, in which it can be retained, and from which it can be retrieved.

Store. (1) To enter *data* into a *storage device.* (2) To retain data in a *storage device.* (3) A *storage device.* . . .

Stored Program Computer. (SC1) A *computer* controlled by internally stored *instructions* that can synthesize, *store* and in some cases alter instructions as though they were *data* and that can subsequently execute these instructions.

String. . . . A linear *sequence* of entities such as *characters* or physical elements. . . .

Stroke. . . . In *character recognition.* A straight line or arc used as a segment of a *graphic character.* . . .

Stroke Edge. In *character recognition,* the line of discontinuity between a side of a *stroke* and the background, obtained by averaging, over the length of the stroke, the irregularities resulting from the *printing* and detecting *processes.*

Subroutine. (1) A *routine* that can be part of another routine. (2) See *closed subroutine, direct insert subroutine,* . . . *open subroutine.*

Summation Check. A *check* based on the formation of the sum of the *digits* of a *numeral.* The sum of the individual digits is usually compared with a previously computed value.

Symbol. (1) A representation of something by reason of relationship, association, or convention. (2) See . . . *flowchart symbol,* . . . *logic symbol.* . . .

Symbolic Coding. *Coding* that uses *machine instructions* with *symbolic addresses.*

Symbolic Logic. The discipline that treats *formal logic* by means of a formalized *artificial language* or symbolic calculus whose purpose is to avoid the ambiguities and logical inadequacies of *natural languages.*

Syntax. (1) The structure of expressions in a *language.* (2) The rules governing the structure of a language.

System. (1) (SC1) An assembly of methods, *procedures,* or techniques united by regulated interaction to form an organized whole. (2) (SC1) An organized collection of men, *machines,* and methods required to accomplish a set of specific *functions.* (3) See . . . *number system, numeral system, numeration system, operating system.*

Table. (1) A collection of *data* in which each *item* is uniquely identified by a label, by its relative position to other items, or by some other means. (2) See *decision table, truth table.*

Table Look-Up. A *procedure* for obtaining the *function* value corresponding to an *argument* from a *table* of function values.

Tabulate. (1) To form *data* into a *table.* (2) To print totals.

Tag. (1) One or more *characters* attached to an *item* or *record* for the purpose of identification. (2) Same as *flag.*

Tape. See . . . *magnetic tape, punched tape.*

Tape Deck. Same as *tape unit.*

Tape Drive. A device that moves tape past a *head.* Synonymous with tape transport.

Tape to Card. Pertaining to equipment or methods that *transmit data* from either *magnetic tape* or *punched tape* to *punched cards.*

Tape Transport. Same as *tape drive.*

Tape Unit. A device containing a *tape drive,* together with *reading* and *writing heads* and associated controls. Synonymous with . . . tape station.

Target Language. The *language* to which a *statement* is *translated.* Synonymous with object language.

Target Program. Same as *object program.*

Telecommunications. Pertaining to the *transmission* of *signals* over long distances, such as by telegraph, radio, or television.

Temporary Storage. In *programming,* storage locations reserved for intermediate results. Synonymous with working storage.

Terminal. A point in a *system* or communication network at which *data* can either enter or leave.

Time Share. To use a device for two or more *interleaved* purposes.

Time Sharing. Pertaining to the *interleaved* use of the time of a device.

Track. . . . The portion of a moving *storage medium,* such as a drum, tape, or *disc,* that is accessible to a given *reading head position.* . . .

Transfer. (1) Same as *jump.* (2) Same as *transmit.* . . .

Transfer Check. A *check* on the *accuracy* of a *data transfer.*

Transform. To change the form of *data* according to specific rules.

Translate. To *transform statements* from one *language* to another without significantly changing the meaning.

Transmission. (1) The sending of *data* from one *location* and the receiving of data in another location, usually leaving the source data unchanged. (2) The sending of *data.* (3) In *ASCII* and communications, a series of *characters* including headings and texts. . . .

Transmit. To send *data* from one *location* and to receive data at another location. Synonymous with transfer, (2) move.

Troubleshoot. Same as *debug.*

Truncate. To terminate a computational *process* in accordance with some rule, e.g., to end the evaluation of a power series at a specified term.

Twelve-Punch. A *punch* in the top row of a *Hollerith punch card.* Synonymous with y-punch.

Type Font. Type face of a given size and style, e.g., 10-point Bodoni Modern.

Underflow. Pertaining to the condition that arises when a machine computation yields a nonzero result smaller than the smallest nonzero quantity that the intended *unit* of *storage* is capable of storing. Contrast with *overflow.*

Unit. (1) A device having a special *function.* (2) A basic element. (3) See *arithmetic unit, central processing unit, control unit, . . . tape unit.*

Variable. A quantity that can assume any of a given *set* of values.

Variable-Length Record. Pertaining to a *file* in which the records are not uniform in length.

Verify. (1) To determine whether a transcription of *data* or other *operation* has been accomplished accurately. (2) To *check* the results of *keypunching.*

Void. In *character recognition,* the inadvertent absence of ink within a *character outline.*

Word. (1) A *character string* or a *bit string* considered as an entity. (2) See . . . *computer word, . . . machine word. . . .*

Word Length. A measure of the size of a *word,* usually specified in *units* such as *characters* or *binary digits.*

Write. To record *data* in a *storage device* or a data *medium.* The recording need not be permanent, such as the writing on a *cathode ray tube display* device.

X-Punch. Same as *eleven-punch.*

Y-Punch. Same as *twelve-punch.*

Zero Suppression. The elimination of nonsignificant zeros in a *numeral.*

Zone Punch. A *punch* in the eleven, twelve, or zero row of a *punched card.*

Index

TOPIC INDEX

AUTHOR INDEX